MW00811575

Exploring Language Structure

Designed for those beginning to study linguistics, this is a lively introduction to two key aspects of the structure of language: syntax (the structure of sentences) and morphology (the structure of words). It shows students in a step-by-step fashion how to analyze the syntax and morphology of any language, by clearly describing the basic methods and techniques, and providing almost 100 practical exercises based on data from a rich variety of the world's languages. Written in an engaging style and complete with a comprehensive glossary, *Exploring language structure* explains linguistic concepts by using clear analogies from everyday life. It introduces a range of essential topics in syntax and morphology such as rules, categories, word classes, grammatical relations, multi-clause constructions, and typology. Providing a solid foundation in morphology and syntax, this is the perfect introductory text for beginning students, and will fully prepare them for more advanced courses in linguistic analysis.

THOMAS E. PAYNE is Research Associate in the Department of Linguistics, University of Oregon, and International Linguistics Consultant at SIL International. He specializes in the grammatical description of undocumented languages, and has traveled extensively in Asia, Africa, and the Americas lecturing and conducting his research. He is author of *Describing morphosyntax: A guide for field linguists* (Cambridge University Press, 1997).

Exploring Language Structure
A Student's Guide

THOMAS E. PAYNE

CAMBRIDGE
UNIVERSITY PRESS

CAMBRIDGE
UNIVERSITY PRESS

University Printing House, Cambridge CB2 8BS, United Kingdom

Cambridge University Press is part of the University of Cambridge.

It furthers the University's mission by disseminating knowledge in the pursuit of education, learning and research at the highest international levels of excellence.

www.cambridge.org
Information on this title: www.cambridge.org/9780521671507

© Thomas E. Payne 2006

First published 2006
8th printing 2015

Printed in the United States of America by Sheridan Books, Inc.

A catalogue record for this publication is available from the British Library

ISBN 978-0-521-85542-6 Hardback
ISBN 978-0-521-67150-7 Paperback

To all beginning students of linguistics who have ever felt they were drowning in a sea of strange terminology and mysterious concepts.

Contents

Figures

Tables

Preface

> Alice thought to herself, "There's no use in speaking." The voices didn't join in this time, as she hadn't spoken, but, to her great surprise, they all thought in chorus (I hope you understand what thinking in chorus means – for I must confess that I don't), "Better say nothing at all. Language is worth a thousand pounds a word!"   Lewis Carroll, *Through the Looking Glass* (1872)

If we could "think in chorus," we would not need language. Language is one very important tool whereby individuals share and negotiate representations of situations, ideas, and feelings. Through language, individual minds are constantly influencing one another in sometimes subtle, and sometimes obvious, ways. The result is a culture, a society, a "common mind" that has many characteristics of a single organism. For example, it may "change," "grow," "stagnate," "thrive," "become sick," "heal," or "die." Language is a physical, outward representation of individual mind-internal states. Communication, via language and other similar tools, is an essential component of all human collective activity. Perhaps this is why "Language is worth a thousand pounds a word!"

At present (2005), there is a body of terms and concepts that is an implicit part of the "common mind" that constitutes the culture of linguistic science. This book is, in part, an attempt to explicate a portion of that implicit common mind for beginning students. In other words, the book attempts to reify an array of ideas that exist tacitly in the minds of many autonomous individuals, as though there were one, unitary whole. Of course, such a task is inherently impossible on several counts. First, linguists are notorious for generating new terminology and co-opting familiar terminology in new and intriguing ways. Thus the common mind that this book attempts to explicate resembles Wittgenstein's "enclosure with holes" (1958:45) more than a bounded container with fixed and invariant content. Second, linguists are legendary "hair splitters" – linguistic texts and theoretical works are filled with endless modification and qualification of terms and concepts. What seems to be very clear and unambiguous to one linguist encompasses a whole range of possibilities to the next. Finally, language itself is constantly breaking free of the terminological cubby holes that linguists are so fond of making for it. Even as the range of ideas people care to communicate is infinite, so the means languages provide to express those ideas vary in vast and often mysterious ways.

In spite of this inherent elusiveness of the subject matter, this introductory text is respectfully submitted as a first attempt to spell out in simple terms the common mind of one small corner of early twenty-first century linguistic science. Just as any communicative act is an approximation, a partial representation of internal mental states of communicators, so this book is a partial representation of its subject matter, namely analytical methods in morphology and syntax. While no particular linguistic theory is promoted, terms, methods, and formalisms that have stood the test of time, and have become part of the implicit common mind of most linguists, are employed and explained. I am thinking in particular of such diagnostic displays as position-class diagrams and process rules (chapter 2), "classic" generative phonological rule notation (chapter 3), phrase structure rules and tree diagrams (chapter 6). These are methods that many linguists use in the ordinary work of describing and understanding linguistic structures, even if they do not use them very much in their published work. Understanding these methods is essential for basic linguistic analysis and as background for more advanced courses in linguistic theory.

This book has been written for, and in consultation with, undergraduate linguistics students, primarily in the system of higher education in the United States of America. A previous or concurrent course in phonetics would be helpful, but even this is not necessary, if the instructor will take one or more class hours to explain the phonetic transcription used, beginning in chapter 3. Charts of the International Phonetic Alphabet for pulmonic consonants and vowels are found immediately before the text proper. These may be used for reference, as needed.

Another reference that students have requested is a comprehensive glossary. In this book, specialized linguistic terms are highlighted when they are first introduced and/or when they are discussed. All of these terms are given concise definitions in the glossary at the end of the book.

As this preface is being written, many universities in North America are changing calendars from a "quarter system" (three major 12-week sessions per year, plus a summer session), to a "semester system" (two major 18-week sessions per year, plus a summer session). The ideal use of this book would be for a 16- to 18-week semester course in morphology and syntax. Since there is more material than can be assimilated comfortably in a 12-week quarter course, I would recommend treating one or more of chapters 3, 6, 7, 9, and 10 lightly (or eliminating some altogether) if the course must be taught in 12 weeks or fewer.

If anyone finds a piece of data that needs correction, or an inaccurate acknowledgment of a source, please notify me at tpayne@uoregon.edu.

Finally, I am still actively seeking additional data and problem sets that illustrate points made in the text. If you have such material, and would like to submit it for the internet collection of data sets (http://www.uoregon.edu/~tpayne/problem_sets/), please send it to me. In this way, I hope this work will become an ongoing resource for those who study and teach introductory and advanced-level linguistics courses.

Acknowledgments

I would like to acknowledge and thank all of the students, linguists, and others who have submitted problem sets, data, and interesting observations that have been incorporated into this work. I have tried to acknowledge all sources and be true to the original data as much as possible, but there are undoubtedly still corrections to be made.

For guidance and many suggestions on earlier drafts of portions of this work, I wish to thank the many students of Analytical Methods in Morphology and Syntax courses at the University of Oregon, Northwest Christian College, Indian Institute for Cross-Cultural Communication, Novosibirsk State University, and Universidad Ricardo Palma, Lima, Perú. In addition, I would like to personally acknowledge the following colleagues: Colleen Ahland, Andy Black, Beth Bryson, Bob Carlson, Joyce Carlson, Wally Chafe, Bernard Comrie, Scott DeLancey, Bob Dixon, Matthew Dryer, Sylvia Earnest, Bob Eaton, Rhonda Fraser, Danielle Gordon, Nelleke Goudswaard, Colette Grinevald, John Haiman, Bernd Heine, Kendall Isaac, Eric Jackson, Christian Lehmann, Steve Marlett, Marianne Mithun, Arlyne Moi, Johanna Nichols, Ken Olson, Doris Payne, Stephanie Payne, Eric Pedersen, Maggie Romani, Omana Sounderaraj, Naoaki Tai, Masahiro Takata, Prang Thiengburanathum, Sandy Thompson, Cynthia Vakareliyska, and David Weber.

A note on transcriptions

This book contains examples and exercises from dozens of languages around the world. Whenever possible, examples are presented in the official writing systems of the languages represented. In these cases, standard capitalization and punctuation are used for the language data. Sometimes, however, it is necessary or advisable to use a romanized transcription, instead of or in addition to the official writing system. In such cases, no capitalization or punctuation is used.

For Russian examples, I use standard roman transliteration as recommended by the American Library Association and the Library of Congress (Barry 1997:138–55).

For Korean examples, I use the "Yale system" (Martin 1992) for transliterating Hangul characters.

For other languages, I use the International Phonetic Alphabet (see end of preliminary matter).

Abbreviations

1	First person (I, me, we, us, etc.)
2	Second person (you, y'all, etc.)
3	Third person (he, him, she, her, they, them, it, etc.)
ABL	Ablative case
ABS	Absolutive case
ACC	Accusative case
ACT	Actor
AN	Animate
ANT	Anterior
APL	Applicative
ARR	On arrival (directional marker)
ART	Article
ASP	Aspect
ASSOC	Associative
AUG	Augmentative
AUX	Auxiliary
BEN	Benefactive
CAUSE	Causative
CL	Classifier
COM	Comitative
COMP	Complementizer
COMPL	Completive aspect
CONJ	Conjunction
CONT	Continuative aspect
COP	Copula
DAT, D	Dative
DEF	Definite
DEM	Demonstrative
DEP	Dependent
DIM	Diminutive
DIR	Directional
DISJUNCT	Disjunctive mode
DIST	Distal deixis

DISTR	Distributive
DL	Dual (two things)
DR	Downriver
DS	Different subject
DTRNS	Detransitive
E	Epenthetic form
ERG	Ergative case
EXCL	Exclusive
F, FEM	Feminine
FOC	Focus
FUT	Future tense
GEN	Genitive case
GNO	Gnomic aspect
I, INTRNS	Intransitive
IMP	Imperative mode
IMPERF	Imperfective aspect
INAN	Inanimate
INC	Inclusive
INCEP	Inceptive
INCHO	Inchoative
INCLD	Included
INCOMPL	Incompletive aspect
IND	Indicative
INF	Infinitive
INST	Instrumental
INTS	Intensive
IRR	Irrealis mode
LOC	Locative
M	Masculine
MALF	Malefactive mode
MAN	Manner
MID	Middle voice
NEG	Negative
NEU	Neutral
NF	Non-future
NOM	Nominative
NOMLZ	Nominalization
NONSPEC	Nonspecific aspect
NPAST	Non-past
NS	Non-subject
OBJ	Object
OBL	Oblique
PART	Participle

PASS	Passive voice
PAST, PT	Past tense
PAT	Patient
PERF	Perfective aspect
PL	Plural (several things)
PN	Pronoun
POS	Possessed
POT	Potential mode
PPART	Past Participle
PR	Present tense
PROG	Progressive aspect
PROX	Proximal deixis
PURP	Purpose
REAS	Reason
RECIP	Reciprocal
REFL	Reflexive
REL	Relativizer
REX	Response to expectation
SEQ	Sequential
SG	Singular (1 thing)
SIM	Simultaneous
SS	Same subject
STAT	Stative
SUBJ	Subject
TOP	Topic
TRNS	Transitive

Abbreviations used in syntactic structure diagrams

ADJ	Adjective
ADV	Adverb
AUX	Auxiliary
COMP	Complementizer
CONJ	Conjunction
D	Determiner
DP	Determiner Phrase (or "determined noun phrase")
I	Inflection (or "inflectional particle")
IP	Inflectional Phrase (or "inflected verb phrase")
N	Noun
NP	Noun Phrase
P	Preposition or Postposition
PP	Prepositional or Postpositional Phrase

S	Clause (or "Sentence")
V	Verb
VP	Verb Phrase

Other abbreviations

A	Most AGENT-like argument of a multi-argument clause
C	Any consonant
Chô	Chômeur
D	Dative or indirect object of a multi-argument clause
N	Any nasal consonant
O	"Other," less AGENT-like argument of a multi-argument clause
OBL	Oblique clausal element (non-argument)
S	Single argument of a one-argument clause
V	Any vowel

Table A *The International Phonetic Alphabet (revised to 1993): Consonants (pulmonic) Used with permission of the IPA (see http://www.arts.gla.ac.uk/ipa/pulmonic.html)*

	Bilabial	Labiodental	Dental	Alveolar	Postalveolar	Retroflex	Palatal	Velar	Uvular	Pharyngeal	Glottal
Plosive	p b			t d		ʈ ɖ	c ɟ	k g	q ɢ		ʔ
Nasal	m	ɱ		n		ɳ	ɲ	ŋ	ɴ		
Trill	ʙ			r					ʀ		
Tap or flap				ɾ		ɽ					
Fricative	ɸ β	f v	θ ð	s z	ʃ ʒ	ʂ ʐ	ç ʝ	x ɣ	χ ʁ	ħ ʕ	h ɦ
Lateral fricative				ɬ ɮ							
Approximant		ʋ		ɹ		ɻ	j	ɰ			
Lateral approximant				l		ɭ	ʎ	ʟ			

Where symbols appear in pairs, the one to the right represents a voiced consonant. Shaded areas denote articulations judged impossible.

Table B *International Phonetic Alphabet: Vowels*
(Used with permission of the IPA [see
http://www.arts.gla.ac.uk/ipa/pulmonic.html])

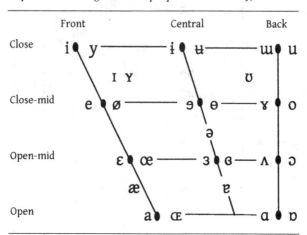

Where symbols appear in pairs, the one to the right
represents a rounded vowel.

1 Introduction to morphology and syntax

If you were to ask anyone the question "What is language?" you would probably receive an answer that includes the word "communication." Most of us, if we think about our language at all, have the common-sense notion that language exists for the purpose of communication. This way of thinking views language as a "tool" that people use to accomplish the "job" of communication. It may not be the only tool that people use for this job, and it may help accomplish other jobs as well. However, many people, both linguists and non-linguists, have the idea that the *main* purpose of human language is communication.

Viewing language as a tool has profound consequences for all kinds of applications. Whether you are planning to contribute to linguistic theory, document one of the many unwritten languages of the world, prepare educational materials, or simply learn to speak a second language, you will profit greatly from a perspective that considers language as a tool for communication. In this introductory section, we will explore this perspective in some detail, after which we will discuss some fundamental concepts of linguistic analysis.

 Every tool has two components: a **FUNCTION** and a **FORM**. The function is the job the tool is designed to accomplish, and the form is the tangible structure that accomplishes that job. For example, the main function of the kind of hammer pictured here is to pound nails into wood and to remove them. The form is the shape of the iron head attached to a handle, as in this picture. Though individual hammers may differ from one another in many ways, they also have a lot in common. This particular form is specially adapted to the function of pounding nails. If it had a form that was very different from this, it would not serve this purpose. Imagine a hammer with a paper head, or one lacking a handle. Such poor excuses for hammers would not be very useful for pounding nails (though they might serve some other purpose). So the function "motivates" (provides a reason for) the form of this very useful device. Without a function, the form would be simply an odd-shaped lump of iron and wood.

Of course, you don't *have* to use a hammer to pound nails – a hard rock or the heel of your shoe might do. Furthermore, because the hammer has its particular form, it also may be used to accomplish other functions, perhaps straightening metal, or breaking up concrete. But its main function has the greatest influence on its basic form.

Language also consists of a function and a form. Common sense tells us that the main function of language is to help people communicate. The form consists of sounds, gestures, or other physical variations in the environment capable of being perceived by other people. Furthermore, as in the case of the hammer, the form of language makes sense in terms of its basic function, as we will see throughout this book. Without the function of communication, language would be no more than random noises or other physical variations in the environment.

While the hammer analogy may be helpful in understanding the relation between function and form, in fact language is a much more complex tool than a hammer in a number of ways. First of all, the function of language is more complex. While there are many kinds of nails, and several ways you may want to pound them in or pull them out, the ways of using a hammer are rather limited. On the other hand, there is an infinite number of ideas that people want to communicate every day, and many subtle kinds and shades of meaning that people feel a need to express. Second, the form of language is more complex than that of a hammer. The form of most languages consists of a small number of sounds, organized into **WORDS, PHRASES, CLAUSES, SENTENCES**, and **DISCOURSES**, including conversations, sermons, speeches, arguments, and other highly complex communicative structures.

As with any tool, the forms of a language "make sense" in terms of their functions, though they are not precisely determined (or mathematically "predicted") by those functions. Indeed, what we first notice about a new language is how different it is from our own. If all languages are tools to accomplish the job of communication, why are they so different from one another? To begin to answer this question, let's consider another cultural tool that varies greatly around the world – the structure of houses. The vast differences among houses from one part of the world to another reflect different solutions to similar problems – the needs for shelter, warmth, space for food preparation, rest, etc. The different solutions are motivated by many factors, including the local ecology, but the structure of a particular house is not *inevitable* given the various motivating factors. Even in my own town, some houses have flat roofs, and others have sloping roofs. The different forms of roofs all fulfill the same function of providing shelter. In a similar way, different languages may use very different forms to express the same concept.

Linguists have found that, in spite of the many superficial differences among languages, there is a core of basic similarities. Can you imagine a language without words?[1] Without sentences? Such ways of communicating do exist, e.g., facial expressions, and styles of dress. These systems do help people understand one another to a certain extent, but we would hardly want to call them languages. They compare to languages as rocks and shoes may compare to hammers – capable of being used to pound nails, but not uniquely adapted or designed for that purpose. A language, however, is a highly complex system of interrelated parts uniquely adapted for the purpose of human communication. Though individual languages

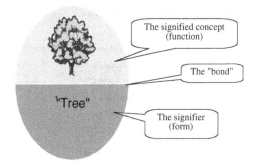

Figure 1.1 *The form–function composite*

do differ greatly in many respects, the functions of language provide a motivation for the many basic similarities in form.

In the following sections we will discuss some of the terms and concepts that linguists use to explore the structure of languages.

The form–function composite

Linguists usually assume that language consists of elements of form that people employ to "mean," "express," "represent," or "refer to" other things. Although linguists often imply that the linguistic forms themselves express concepts, this must be taken as a shorthand way of saying that speakers *use* linguistic forms (among other tools) to accomplish acts of expressing, referring, meaning, etc. (Brown and Yule 1983:27ff.). For example, a word is a linguistic form. In and of itself it is just a noise made by someone's vocal apparatus. What makes it a *word* rather than just a random noise is that it is produced intentionally in order to express some idea. When used by a skilled speaker, words can combine into larger structures to express very complex ideas. While linguistic forms help people formulate ideas, and may constrain the concepts that can be entertained, the linguistic forms themselves are logically distinct from the ideas that might be expressed, in the same way that the form of a hammer is distinct from the job of pounding nails.

Langacker (1987), building on Saussure (1915), describes linguistic units as consisting of **FORM–FUNCTION COMPOSITES**, as illustrated in figure 1.1.

The upper half of the diagram in figure 1.1 represents the meanings, concepts, or ideas expressed in language, while the bottom half represents the linguistic units themselves. The line across the center represents the relationship, or the "bond" between the two. Various terms have been used to refer to the parts of this composite. Terms associated with the top half include "signified," "meaning," "semantics," "function," "conceptual domain," and "content." Terms associated with the bottom half include "sign," "signifier," "symbol," "structure," and "form."

In ancient times, philosophers who thought about language often considered words to be inherently connected to their meanings. Invariably, the language the philosopher spoke (Sanskrit, Greek, or Latin) was considered to be the language that expressed the "true" meanings of words. In more recent times, linguists have tended to emphasize the **ARBITRARINESS** of linguistic signs. That is to say, there is not necessarily an inherent connection between the form of a sign and its meaning. The noise spelled *tree* in English certainly has no inherent connection to the range of concepts that it can express. Indeed, even in related languages, such as German and French, very different noises (spelled *baum* and *arbre* respectively) express roughly the same idea. Even more recently, linguists are beginning to notice that linguistic signs are arbitrary to a certain extent, but that they are also **MOTIVATED** by factors such as understandability, **ICONICITY** (including **SOUND SYMBOLISM**), and economy.[2]

Why is the bond between sign and signified concept, form and function, motivated? Linguists assume that the bond between symbol and signified concept is intentional. That is, language users *intend* to establish a link between form and meaning – they consciously *want* their utterances to be understood. From this it follows that the forms used to represent concepts will be structured so as to make the link obvious, within limits of cognitive ability, memory, etc. This is not to deny the possibility that certain aspects of language may actually have no relation to the concepts expressed or may even serve to *conceal* concepts. However, we make it a working assumption that in general language users want and expect linguistic forms to represent concepts to be communicated.

In any symbolic system, there must be consistency in the relationship between the symbols and categories or dimensions in the symbolized realm. We do not live in a "Humpty Dumpty world" where words mean anything we want them to mean (Carroll 1872). In order to communicate with others, we rely on the probability that words in our language mean approximately the same thing to other people as they do to us. Ideal symbolic systems (e.g., computer "languages") maximize this principle by establishing a direct, invariant coding relationship between every form and its meaning or meanings. However, real languages are not ideal symbolic systems in this sense. They exist in an environment where variation and change are normal rather than exceptional. New functions appear every day as new situations, concepts, and perspectives speakers wish to express. Vocal and auditory limitations cause inexact pronunciation and incomplete perception of messages. These and many other factors lead to variation in the form of language, even in the speech of a single speaker. The bond between form and meaning in real language, then, is neither rigid nor random; it is direct enough to allow communication, but flexible enough to allow for creativity, variation, and change.

Creativity and recursion

As discussed above, any language is a highly structured symbolic system consisting of many interrelated parts. It is also a very human phenomenon, used by people every day in new and creative ways to accomplish an infinite number of communicative tasks. Let's discuss some examples of how people can creatively mold and shape their language in response to specific needs.

Lewis Carroll's famous poem *Jabberwocky* (1872) starts out with the following verse:

> 'Twas brillig, and the slithy toves
> Did gyre and gimble in the wabe;
> All mimsy were the borogoves,
> And the mome raths outgrabe.

Even though many of the words in this verse are nonsense, in context we can infer a lot about the linguistic structure, and even develop a rough image of the scene being described. For example, we know that *brillig* probably refers to a time, because it is preceded by *'twas*. We also know that *toves* refers to something that can perform actions (probably persons or animals of some sort), because they *did gyre and gimble*, and these words obviously refer to actions. We also know that *wabe* must describe a place where *gyring* and *gimbling* may occur. *Slithy* and *mimsy* must be modifiers (ADJECTIVES) that describe properties of the *toves* and *borogoves* respectively.

The overall impression one gets from this verse is probably something like a forest setting involving strange, mythical creatures in some kind of special state or condition. We wait expectantly for the second verse to help fill in the gaps in our mental scene.

This example is from a famous author, but we don't even have to study great literature to see how language is used creatively to accomplish communicative work. Everyday conversation will easily suffice. For example, I recently heard the following sentence in an actual conversation:

(1)   My dog just snerdled under the fence.

I don't find the word *snerdle* in any of my dictionaries. Yet, this sentence is immediately understandable, in the right context, to anyone who is a fluent speaker of English. We know *snerdle* must be a VERB, because it has a SUBJECT (*my dog*) and takes the PAST TENSE ending *-ed*. These are structural facts about this sentence. Because the sentence has these structural features, we can make a very good guess about what the function, i.e., the *meaning*, of the sentence might be. Because we know something about dogs and fences, and we know about verbs that start with *sn-* (*snort, sniff, sneeze, snore*, etc.), and verbs that end in a PLOSIVE CONSONANT plus *-le* (*wiggle, waddle, fiddle, jiggle, sidle, giggle*, etc.), we can develop a very specific mental image based on this sentence. You may even say that the speaker provides a meaning for the verb *snerdle* by using it in exactly this context. It would be quite difficult to guess what this word "means" apart from its use in a specific communicative context. If this new verb fills a gap in the vocabulary of English, it may catch on to the point where it may even begin to appear in dictionaries. This kind of inventiveness characterizes every language on earth and is one way that new words are added to the vocabulary of any language.

Throughout this book we will see examples of how the forms of language arise in response to communicative needs. Here is one more important example. As mentioned above, there is an infinite number of ideas and **NUANCES** that people may care to express using language. However, the human mind is finite. It is not possible for one person to store or to learn an infinite amount of information. How is it, then, that a speaker of a human language can potentially express an infinite number of ideas, using a finite mind? Any system that is charged with this task must exhibit what linguists call **RECURSION**. In other words, any system that takes a limited input and produces an unlimited output must be able to combine elements in the input recursively – over and over again – with enough complexity that the appropriate infinite range of outputs is possible. Here is a simple example. Take a phrase like:

(2)   The cat

We all know that there are many cats in the world. If I need to distinguish among them, I can "modify" this phrase:

(3)   The cat in the hat

There are also many hats in the world. If I need to distinguish which hat I am talking about, I can modify the **NOUN** *hat* in the same way that I modified the noun *cat* earlier:

(4)   The cat in the hat with a yellow ribbon

There are also many yellow ribbons in the world . . .

I think you can see where this is going. Since I can use a noun to modify another noun, I can potentially express an infinite number of ideas, starting with just a few basic words. The above examples illustrate **EMBEDDING**, which is just one of many respects in which all languages are recursive. Words, such as nouns, can be embedded within larger structures which can in turn be embedded within others, up to infinity. Any system that did not provide for such recursion would not qualify as a language. Why? Because it wouldn't be able to do the job of a language. So the forms of the language, in this case the way speakers construct noun phrases, are determined by the function, in this case, the need to express a potentially infinite number of ideas. Recursion is another respect in which every language is creative. It allows everyone who is a fluent speaker to formulate and express an infinite number of ideas. The only limitations are the communicative needs and imagination of the speaker.

Grammar

What image comes to mind when you hear the word **GRAMMAR**? For many people this word brings back painful childhood memories involving lists of "do's" and "don'ts" in speech and writing: "never say 'ain't'," "never split an infinitive," "never say 'him and me'," etc.

To a linguist, the word "grammar" has a very different meaning. Grammar in the broadest linguistic sense is simply everything a person needs to know in order to be a fluent speaker of a language. For example, the way of forming a noun phrase discussed above is part of the grammar of English – it is something that all English speakers unconsciously "know." Sometimes the word **TACIT** is used to describe a person's linguistic knowledge (as well as other culturally conditioned behavioral patterns). What this means is that people are not normally aware of their internalized grammar. They can become aware of it, for example by taking a linguistics class. However, most people simply use their grammar without thinking about it, just as they use their tacit knowledge of other aspects of social behavior, like facial expressions, ways of eating, walking, expressing emotions, and many others. Grammar, to a linguist, is something to be discovered, described, and explained, rather than something to be invented and enforced. It includes a good portion (some would say all) of the mental habit patterns and categories that allow people in a community to communicate with one another. Grammar is internal to the human mind, but allows the mind to "connect" to other minds that have similar grammatical patterns.

Under the heading of "Grammar" there are traditionally several subheadings, including **PHONETICS**, **PHONOLOGY**, **MORPHOLOGY**, **SYNTAX**, and **SEMANTICS**. In the rest of this chapter we will discuss some of these subheadings.

Morphology and syntax

In this section we will briefly discuss how the subject matter of this book, sometimes referred to as **MORPHOSYNTAX**, relates to the other subheadings within the domain of Grammar.

Phonetics and phonology have to do with how the sounds of language are produced in the human vocal organs (lungs, larynx, mouth, nasal cavity), and how sounds are systematically organized in particular languages. Morphosyntax has to do with how these sounds combine to form words and sentences. Semantics has to do with the meanings of individual elements of linguistic structure and their combinations. **DISCOURSE ANALYSIS** is a term that describes the study of how sentences combine to form conversations, stories, lectures, and other extended forms of speech.

Actually, the term "morphosyntax" is a hybrid word that comes from two other words – morphology and syntax. Since "morphosyntax" sounds better than "syntophology," the former is the word that linguists prefer to use.

Morphology is simply the study of shapes. For example, zoologists may study the morphology of camels – how their bodies are shaped. Different species of camels have different body shapes. Some have one hump and others have two. Morphology in linguistics has to do with how words are shaped, and how the shapes of words may be systematically adjusted in order to accomplish communicative tasks. You can also think of morphology as the study of how meaningful units combine to shape words.

Syntax, on the other hand, is how words combine to form sentences. One reason many linguists like to talk about morphology and syntax together is that sometimes a communicative job that is performed by word shapes (morphology) in one language is performed by combinations of words (syntax) in another. So if linguists want to compare different languages, it helps to be able to refer to "morphosyntax." For example, look carefully at the following sentences from Naga, a Tibeto-Burman language of Northern India, with their English equivalents:

(5) a.   ngama ate hethoang   'I will teach him.'
            I   him will.teach

    b.   ate hethoang ngama   'I will teach him.'
    c.   atema nganang hethohang   'He will teach me.'
    d.   nganang hethohang atema   'He will teach me.'

In example 5a, meanings are given in English directly under the Naga words. In Naga, the main way in which a speaker communicates who is teaching and who is being taught is by the shapes of the words. In all of these sentences, the word that mentions the person who is teaching ends with *-ma*, no matter where this word appears in the sentence. It can appear at the beginning (examples 5a and 5c) or at the end (examples 5b and 5d). In all these sentences, the word that mentions the primary *actor* (in this case the person who teaches) ends in *-ma*. Therefore we say that the job of expressing who the actor is in a sentence is accomplished morphologically, i.e., by the shapes of words, in Naga.

In English the situation is quite different. In English, the way a speaker communicates who is acting and who is being acted upon is mostly word order. Consider these examples:

(6) a.   Zarina taught Aileron.
    b.   Aileron taught Zarina.

These sentences do not mean the same thing, even though the shapes of all the words are identical. The difference in meaning is expressed only by the order of the words. Therefore we say that the job of identifying the actor in English is accomplished *syntactically*.

The first part of this book (chapters 1 through 5) deals mostly with morphology. The second part (chapters 6 through 10) deals mostly with syntax. However, it should be kept in mind that these are not necessarily two completely distinct domains. Syntactic structure certainly affects morphology, and morphology is one very important way that syntactic structure is revealed. The main ideas to keep in mind to this point are:

- Language is a tool for communication; therefore structural similarities among unrelated languages can, in most cases, be attributed to common communicational functions.
- Languages can accomplish the same or similar communicative tasks by changing the shapes of words (morphologically) or by changing how words are arranged (syntactically).

Lexicon

So far we have described two subheadings within the general domain of Grammar in any language – the morphology and the syntax. We have seen that communicational jobs that are accomplished morphologically in one language can be accomplished syntactically in another. There is one other subheading that perhaps should be considered alongside these two. This is the LEXICON. Different linguistic theories have vastly different ideas of what constitutes the lexicon of a language. The characterization presented here is flexible enough to encompass most of the theoretical variation, while remaining true to a common understanding of what linguists mean when they talk about the lexicon of a language.

In the broadest sense, the lexicon of a language consists of a list of all the UNITS in that language. Units in the lexicon are IDEALIZED mental constructs, or images. They are not actual words, phrases, or sentences, but rather mental "pictures" that can be called up from memory when needed for the purpose of producing actual words, phrases, and sentences. Sometimes these pictures are referred to as "representations" or "templates." Such units are called LEXICAL ENTRIES. For example, *cat* is an entry in my internal mental lexicon of English. As such, it is no more than an idealized representation – a memory, so to speak, of a noise that has served a certain range of functions in previous conversations I have been involved in. Because I can depend on the probability that other English speakers share a similar memory, that representation is available in English conversations as the need arises. In the lexicon, however, it is no more than a potentiality, an abstract representation of the possibility of some specific linguistic behavior.

The lexical entry for a linguistic unit consists of a cluster (conceived sometimes as a list and sometimes as an image) of all its characteristics. The term "entry" is based on the metaphor of the lexicon as a dictionary. We talk about the "dictionary entry" of a word as consisting of information about its spelling, pronunciation, meanings, and usages. Lexical entries are something like that, except they are conceived of as unconscious mental pictures stored in individual speakers' minds, rather than in published books or computer disks.

In addition to whole words, like *cat*, parts of words can also be units in the lexicon. For example, the *-ed* part of a word like *walked* means PAST TENSE. This is part of what one has to know in order to know English, therefore *-ed* is in the lexicon of English. It may be more accurate to say that the *pattern* of a verb followed by *-ed* is in the lexicon of English. This may be represented in a formula as:

(7)   VERB + -ed = [VERB]$_{\text{past tense}}$

In other words, it is not just any *-ed* that means "past tense," but only those instances of *-ed* that are attached to verbs. The formula in 7 is one way of representing on paper the unconscious pattern in the minds of all English speakers that allows them to express the past tense of many verbs.

In this broad notion of the lexicon, SYNTACTIC STRUCTURES may also be located there. Actual phrases and sentences are not part of the lexicon, but abstract, idealized patterns are. For example, 8 is a syntactic pattern of English:

(8)   PREPOSITION + NOUN PHRASE

This pattern specifies that any member of a class of things called PREPO- SITIONS and any member of a class of things called NOUN PHRASES can combine to form a unit. This idealized pattern gives rise to a whole range of possible linguistic structures in use, for example:

(9) a.   in the house
    b.   under the bed
    c.   with a hammer
    d.   on the mat
    e.   down the rabbit hole
    f.   through the mystical forest inhabited by strange beings and fraught with
             unfathomable dangers, none of which were apparent to Alice when she
             first began following the White Rabbit

The phrases in 9 are not in the lexicon. Rather, they are composed of other elements that are in the lexicon. The pattern in 8 is one of those elements, under a broad view of the lexicon.

> The difference between lexicon and (morpho-) syntax is the difference between what speakers need to know outright, vs. what they can construct based on what they already know.
>
> *— Charles Fillmore*

There are, however, several narrower views of the lexicon. Often syntactic patterns, such as 8, are not considered part of the lexicon. Rather, they are part of a separate component of the grammar of a language. Under this view, the lexicon can be thought of as a mental dictionary of all the **WORDS** and **MORPHEMES** (meaningful pieces of words). Syntactic patterns, such as 8, are mental images, but they are not part of the lexicon, in the narrower view.

The feature common to all conceptualizations of the lexicon, however, is that it contains lists of units. This is usually thought of as distinct from morphosyntax, which describes rules for constructing new ideas. The key concept here is "list" rather than "rule." Lists involve itemized pieces of information, each of which must be memorized on its own. Rules, on the other hand, involve regular patterns for creating new information. Rules themselves may be items in the list that constitutes the lexicon, but the outputs of rules are not. The difference between lexicon and morphosyntax, then, is the difference between what speakers need to know outright, vs. what they can construct based on what they already know.

Three expression types compared

Now that we have discussed the three major subheadings under Grammar that we will be most concerned with in this book, we can compare different **EXPRESSION TYPES** that languages provide to allow speakers to express variations in meaning. These expression types are **LEXICAL EXPRESSION, MORPHOLOGICAL PROCESSES**, and **SYNTACTIC** (or **ANALYTIC**) **PATTERNS**.

A lexical expression is one which requires the speaker to turn to the lexicon in order to express a particular nuance of meaning. Often this involves substituting one lexical item for another. Morphological processes are those which express variations in meaning by altering the shapes of words in some predictable way. Finally, syntactic patterns express regular variations in meaning by combining or rearranging lexical items in relation to each other. Let me explain by using some further examples.

The difference between the noises represented by the spellings *call* and *called* follows a regular pattern. We may say that speakers **DERIVE** the form *called* from *call* by adding an *-ed* to the end. This pattern applies to many verbs in English, and its function is to allow English speakers to express the past tense. There is no need to memorize both *call* and *called* (as well as *stall* and *stalled*, *walk* and *walked*, etc.) as members of one long list of words that are not necessarily related to one another in any way. Instead, all you need is a rather shorter list of individual verbs, plus one morphological pattern (or "rule") that says "add -*ed* to form the past tense." The pattern itself may be in the lexicon (under the broad view discussed above), but its existence makes the lexicon as a whole considerably shorter. This is because, with the pattern, words such as *called*, *walked*, etc., do not need to be listed – they can be derived (or "generated") from *call* and *walk* respectively.

On the other hand, the noises spelled *go* and *went* in English are not derivable, one from the other by any regular pattern. Speakers *do* have to memorize these two forms, as well as forms like *eat* and *ate*, *buy* and *bought*, *think* and *thought*, and many others. The meanings of the forms *go* and *went* are related to each other, but the forms are not. *Went* includes the idea of "past-tense" in its basic meaning. You cannot separate out the part that means "past" from the part that means "go." So we say that the lexical entry for *went* includes the notion of past tense.

Therefore, in order to express the past tense of the verb *go* in English, we don't use the regular past-tense pattern. If we did, we would come up with the form *goed*.[3] Rather, we turn to our mental list – our lexicon – in order to retrieve the correct past-tense form of this verb. People learning English could not possibly guess that the past tense of *go* was *went* if they had never heard it before. On the other hand, learners can quickly guess what the past tense of a nonsense verb like *blick* might be, even though they had never heard it before. The relationship between *go* and *went* is based on their related meanings, not their forms. Therefore we say that this difference is a lexical difference, rather than a morphological or a syntactic one. You might hear a linguist say something like "the past tense of the verb *go* is expressed lexically."

Finally, a syntactic pattern involves the arrangement of lexical items in a phrase or sentence (see the examples in 6 above), or the combination of separate lexical items. For example, the common future tenses of English are expressed syntactically. If I want to express the idea of "calling" in the future I can say:

(10)   I will call.

The shape of the verb *call* does not change, rather a separate word, *will*, is added in order to express the idea of future tense. Therefore you may hear linguists say things like "future tense is a syntactic pattern in English," or "future tense is expressed syntactically in English." Other terms that are used for this kind of expression are "analytic" or "periphrastic" patterns.

Subtypes of lexical expression

Substituting one lexical item for another in order to express a regular meaning variation (as with the *go/went* pair discussed above) is one kind of

lexical expression. This particular kind of lexical expression is sometimes called
STEM SUPPLETION, or, as we will see below, **STRONG STEM SUPPLETION**.
There are at least two other kinds of expression that make crucial reference to
memorized properties, rather than predictable patterns. The three subtypes of
lexical expression are:

- (Strong) stem suppletion – use a completely different stem (*go* → *went*)
- Weak stem suppletion – use a somewhat different stem (*buy* → *bought*)
- Isomorphism – use the same stem (*hit* → *hit*)

WEAK STEM SUPPLETION can be thought of as falling "in between" the
other two types of lexical expression. This is substitution of one stem for another
that is vaguely similar to the first, but which cannot be derived by any rule. For
example, the forms of the English words *buy* and *bought* "feel" like they are
related – they both start with *b*. However, there is no regular pattern (or *rule* of
grammar) that derives one of these from the other, in the way that the past-tense
rule described earlier derives *called* from *call*. How do we know there is no rule
that relates these forms? There are two ways: first, there are no other pairs that
can be related in exactly the same way. Yes, there are past-tense verb forms that
sound like *bought* (*brought*, *thought*, and others), but the present tenses of these
verbs are *bring* and *think*, not *bruy and *thuy,[4] which is what they would have
to be if they were subject to the same (nonexistent) rule that derived *bought* from
buy. The second way we know there is no rule that relates *buy* and *bought* is that
other verbs that sound like *buy* cannot logically undergo the (nonexistent) rule.
So, not only is it **UNGRAMMATICAL**, but also not even logical to think of the
past tense of *cry* as *crought, or *die* as *dought, etc.[5]

Notice that "irregular" grammatical patterns (such as *buy/bought*) are not
always examples of lexical expression. Sometimes they *can* be related to rules.
For example, the alternation between *sing* and *sang* follows a rule, and is therefore not, strictly speaking, an example of lexical expression. Why? Because
(1) there are at least a few analogous pairs – *sink/sank*, *ring/rang*, *drink/drank*, and
perhaps a few others. (2) There is a logic even to ungrammatical applications of
this rule. Most of us have heard children say things like *I brang my new toy*. This
kind of example proves that the child has a mental pattern that says "change *-ing*
to *-ang* to form the past tense." Therefore, this is a morphological process. However, there is no such logic to a rule that would say "change *-uy* to *-ought*."

In summary, the **IDIOSYNCRATIC** (apparently random) formal variation used
to express the past tense must be listed in the lexical entry of the verb *buy*. It
cannot be guessed from the form of the verb itself. Therefore it involves lexical
expression.

Finally, the last subtype of lexical expression is sometimes termed **ISOMOR-
PHISM**. This is where a regular, expected adjustment in meaning is accomplished
by not changing anything. For example, what is the past tense of the verb *hit* in
English? It is *hit*. The same stem is used, and there is no *-ed* added. This is a fact
of the verb *hit* that just has to be memorized. It cannot be guessed (or "predicted")

by applying a rule, therefore it involves lexical expression. The lexical entry for the verb *hit* has to specify, among many other things, that the past tense is simply *hit*.

Why would we say that the past tense of the verb *hit* is "expressed" at all when there is no part of the word that "means" past tense? Why don't we just say that past tense is not expressed for this verb? Aren't there a lot of other meaning components that have no overt (obvious) expression? For example, a sentence like *Nicolino is working* leaves a lot of information out, some of which may be expressed grammatically in some languages. He may be working upriver or downriver, during the day or at night, with an axe or with his hands, etc. If we say that *hit* expresses past tense lexically, would we want to say that all of these other notions (and many more) are also expressed lexically in English?

What expresses the past tense of the verb *hit* in English is our expectation that all English verbs must have a past-tense form. The fact that *hit* doesn't change the way many other verbs do is meaningful. You may say that there is a "conspicuous absence" of something that means past tense for the class of verbs to which *hit* belongs. There is no analogous expectation that English verbs should express whether the action takes place upriver or downriver, at night or during the day, with hands or with an axe.

In summary, the three subtypes of lexical expression we will be considering in this book are (1) (strong) stem suppletion (replacing one stem with a completely different one), (2) weak stem suppletion (replacing one stem with a randomly similar one), and (3) isomorphism (expression of a regular, expected meaning adjustment with no overt structural change).

The triad of lexical expression, morphological processes, and syntactic patterns is relevant to many different functional tasks in language. Some tasks that are typically accomplished by one expression type in one language may be accomplished by one of the others in the next language. For example, as we have seen, past tense is often expressed morphologically in English by a rule that adds a verb ending. In other languages the time of a situation is expressed syntactically by phrases such as *two days ago*, etc. Furthermore, as we have also seen, languages often allow certain tasks to be accomplished in more than one way. Finally, languages often combine expression types. *She did go* is an example of a combination of expression types. It involves a syntactic pattern in that two distinct items are used to combine the notions of *go* and *past*, but it is also lexical in that the past-tense part employs the word *did*, which is a weakly suppletive form of the verb *do*.

Classes in the lexicon

In this section we will briefly discuss the internal structure of the lexicon of any language, as understood by linguists. Within the lexicon, there are

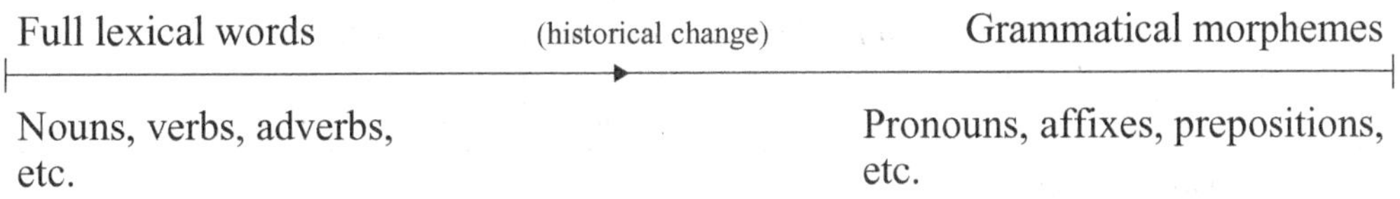

Full lexical words	(historical change)	Grammatical morphemes
Nouns, verbs, adverbs, etc.		Pronouns, affixes, prepositions, etc.

Figure 1.2 *Continuum between full lexical words and grammatical morphemes*

always several different "classes" of entries. A class of lexical entries is simply a group of entries that act the same in some way. In chapter 4 we will discuss how to identify **WORD CLASSES**, such as nouns, verbs, prepositions, etc. Here we need to discuss another, more basic, division in the lexicon. This is the distinction between **FULL LEXICAL WORDS** and **GRAMMATICAL MORPHEMES**.

As you will soon see as you progress in your study of linguistics, most distinctions that linguists make are not absolute but describe the ends of a **CONTINUUM**, with many intermediate possibilities. This is the case with the distinction between full lexical words and grammatical morphemes. There are very good examples of full lexical words, and very good examples of grammatical morphemes, but there are also many examples of items that have some properties of full lexical words and some properties of grammatical morphemes. This is because every language is in the process of change. As items in the lexicon of a language undergo normal change over time, they often start out as full lexical words and become grammatical morphemes (rarely the reverse). Since at any given stage of a language, there are units at various points along this path, these units may not be easily classified as belonging to one class or the other.

Nevertheless, it is useful to try to classify the lexical entries in a language between full lexical words on the one hand and grammatical morphemes on the other. Doing so will help tremendously in the analysis of individual languages, and in the conceptualization of how grammatical structure functions and changes over time. First I will present a few examples of full lexical words and grammatical morphemes, and then give lists of characteristics of both groups.

Grammatical morphemes include elements that occur in relatively small sets (or **PARADIGMS**), such as pronouns (*I, me, you, we, us, she*, etc.), prepositions (*in, on, of, under*, etc.) and affixes, such as the past-tense *-ed*, and the **PLURAL** *-s* in English. They also tend to be smaller than full lexical words, both in number of phonetic segments, and in the number of meaning components that they express. Full lexical words, on the other hand, tend to be much larger in every way. First, they belong to larger classes; e.g., there are many more nouns in any language than there are pronouns. Second, it is much easier to add a full lexical word to the vocabulary of a language than it is to add a grammatical morpheme. Some examples of full lexical words in English are *rabbit, Alice, fall*, and *ramification*. Sometimes it is said that full lexical words have a high degree of **SEMANTIC CONTENT**, or **LEXICAL CONTENT**, in comparison to grammatical morphemes. For example, a word like *rabbit* evokes a rather complex image with many semantic features:

Table 1.1 *A comparison between full lexical words and grammatical morphemes*

Full lexical words	Grammatical morphemes
Tend to be larger in form.	Tend to be smaller in form.
Occur in relatively open classes. It is fairly easy to add new members to a class of lexical words, via borrowing from other languages, innovation of new terms, etc.	Occur in relatively closed classes. It is difficult to add new members to classes of grammatical morphemes.
Occur in relatively large classes.	Occur in relatively small classes. There are only a few items in each class of grammatical morphemes.
Tend to have rich meanings, such as "Alice," "frumious," or "evaluate." Lexical words express many semantic features.	Tend to have narrow meanings, such as "feminine, singular," or "past tense."
Tend to stand on their own as free morphemes.	Tend to bind to other items, i.e., they tend to be clitics or affixes (see below).

mammalian, long ears, soft fur, wrinkly nose, moves by hopping, and many more. A pronoun like *she*, on the other hand, evokes exactly three semantic features, namely third person, singular, and feminine.

Some characteristics of these two general classes of items are listed in table 1.1.

As you are working on the exercises at the end of this chapter, it will be helpful to be aware of the difference between full lexical words and grammatical morphemes. When it comes to analyzing a real language, it will be essential.

Some basic concepts in morphology

Morphemes

A **MORPHEME** is a minimal shape. In linguistics, the classic definition of a morpheme is a minimal structural shape or piece that expresses meaning. For example the English word *dogs* contains two morphemes: *dog* which expresses the main meaning of the word, and *-s* which expresses the meaning of plurality (more than one). The form *dog* cannot be divided into smaller meaningful pieces (e.g., the *d-* at the beginning does not itself express a meaning). Therefore *dog* is a morpheme – a minimal shape. In most situations this definition works fine. However, recent linguistic theories acknowledge the fact that particular meanings are not necessarily directly linked to particular pieces of form. We will have more to say about this later.

Other problems with the traditional definition of a morpheme include such facts as (1) the meaning contributed by a morpheme may vary depending on other morphemes in the word, and (2) the whole message may be more, less than, or simply different from the sum of the "meanings" of all the morphemes in the message. For these reasons, it is appropriate to think of morphology as an established system of variations in the shapes of words, rather than simply strings of meaningful pieces.

Types of morphemes

A **BOUND MORPHEME** is a morpheme that must be attached to some other morpheme in order to be used naturally in discourse. Bound morphemes can be **AFFIXES**, **ROOTS**, or **CLITICS**. The *-s* in *dogs* is an example of a bound morpheme, since it has no plural meaning when uttered by itself. The root, *dog*, on the other hand, is a **FREE MORPHEME** since it does not have to attach to some other form. In many languages roots are bound morphemes because they cannot be used in discourse without having something attached to them, e.g., the Spanish root *habl-* 'speak' must have an ending added to it before it can be used in conversation.

Often, a grammatical morpheme will be associated with more than one meaning at the same time. Consider the following partial paradigm for the Spanish verb *hablar* 'to speak':

(11)   a. hablo   'I speak'   d. habla   'he/she speaks'
       b. hablé   'I spoke'   e. habló   'he/she spoke'
       c. hablaré 'I will speak' f. hablará   'he/she will speak'

The only part of these Spanish words that does not change is *habl-*, therefore we hypothesize that this is the root (see below). So the difference in meaning, as expressed in the English free translations, must be expressed via the verb suffixes. In example 11a, what does the *-o* ending mean? Does it mean "I" (first person)? Well, examples 11b and c have first person as part of their meaning, and they don't have this *-o* suffix. So *-o* means more than just first person. It means first person, present tense. If you change the tense, you have to change the suffix. Also, if you change the actor from first person to third person (*he* or *she*), again you have to change the suffix. So these suffixes in Spanish express *both* person of the subject *and* tense (present, past or future). The common linguistic term for grammatical morphemes that express more than one meaning is **PORTMANTEAU** morphemes. The English word *portmanteau* refers to a kind of suitcase.[6] I think its application to morphemes that express more than one meaning is an extension of the idea that you keep lots of different things in a suitcase – it "carries" lots of stuff. Portmanteau morphemes "carry" lots of meanings.

The term **AFFIX** is a cover term for **PREFIX**, **SUFFIX**, and **INFIX**. Prefixes are bound morphemes that occur at the beginning of a root. For example, the form *un-* in *unable* is a prefix. Suffixes are bound morphemes that occur at the end of a root. For example, the *-s* in *walks* is a suffix. Infixes do not occur in Standard Englishes,[7] but they are bound morphemes that occur *inside* a root. Infixes and other kinds of affixes are exemplified and discussed in more detail in chapter 2. In addition, words can have multiple "layers" of affixes. This is also discussed in chapter 2.

The terms **ROOT** and **STEM** are sometimes used interchangeably. However, there is a subtle difference between them: a **ROOT** is a morpheme that expresses the basic meaning of a word and *cannot be further divided* into smaller morphemes. Yet a root does not necessarily constitute a fully understandable word in and of itself. Another morpheme may be required. For example, the form *struct* in English is a root because it cannot be divided into smaller meaningful parts, yet neither can it be used in discourse without a prefix or a suffix being added to it (*construct, structural, destruction*, etc.).

A **STEM** may consist of just a root. However, it may also be analyzed into a root plus **DERIVATIONAL MORPHEMES** (discussed in chapter 2). Like a root, a stem may or may not be a fully understandable word. For example, in English, the forms *reduce* and *deduce* are stems because they act like any other regular verb – they can take the past-tense suffix. However, they are not roots, because they can be analyzed into two parts, *-duce*, plus a derivational prefix *re-* or *de-*.

The form *habl-* 'speak' in Spanish is a root and a stem. It is a root because it expresses the main meaning of whatever word it is a part of, yet it is not divisible into smaller parts. It is a stem because it can be integrated into discourse like any other verb. The only morphemes that need to be added in order to make *habl-* into a pronounceable word are **INFLECTIONAL MORPHEMES**.

So some roots are stems and some stems are roots (*dog, habl-*), but roots and stems are not the same thing. There are roots that are not stems (*-duce*) and there are stems that are not roots (*reduce*). In fact, this rather subtle distinction is not extremely important conceptually, and some theories do away with it entirely. They may talk only of simple stems ("roots" as defined here) and derived or complex stems ("stems"). Furthermore, the distinction is complicated by layers of historical change, including roots, stems, and whole word forms borrowed from other languages. This is particularly apparent in regard to the layers of Greek, Latin, and French influence that English has passed through on the way to its current state. However, the terms *root* and *stem* are traditional, and are still common in the literature, so linguistics students should be aware of them. Figure 1.3 is a "Venn diagram" that may or may not help conceptualize this overlapping relationship.

A **CLITIC** is a bound morpheme that accomplishes a task in a structural unit that is larger than just a word, but still must attach phonologically to some other word. The word a clitic attaches to is known as the **HOST**. Clitics often attach to either the first or the last word of a syntactic phrase, whether the word is a noun, a verb, an adverb, an **AUXILIARY**, or any other word class (see chapter 4 on word classes).

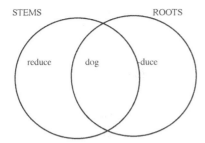

Figure 1.3 *Venn diagram showing the interrelated meanings of terms "stem" and "root," with examples from English*

The words *a* and *the* in English are clitics, because (a) they cannot be used in standard discourse without being attached to some other form, and (b) their host can be any of several noun phrase parts:

(12)   the dog   *the* cliticized to a noun
             the big dog   *the* cliticized to a modifier
             the two big dogs   *the* cliticized to a numeral

We should not be confused by the fact that the English writing system treats *a* and *the* as separate words. There is very good linguistic evidence that these forms are bound to the word that follows. This evidence includes the fact that, in most spoken varieties of English, sound rules affect the boundary. These same rules do not affect separate words that happen to come together in discourse. These rules are:

1.   The vowel of *the* is fully pronounced when it appears before a word that starts with a vowel and **REDUCED** when appearing before a word that starts with a **CONSONANT**:[8]

         (13)   [ðiǽpl] 'the apple'
                  [ðədɔ́g] 'the dog'

2.   The article *a* is followed by [n] when it appears before a vowel, but not when it appears before a consonant. It also reduces to ə (the "uh" sound, like the last vowel sound in the word *sofa* or the first vowel sound in the word *terrain*) before a consonant:

         (14)   [ænǽpl] 'an apple'
                  [ədɔ́g]   'a dog'

These rules do not apply between separate words, as illustrated in the following examples:

(15)   [géilə ǽpl] 'Gala apple'   Not: *[géilanǽpl] 'galan apple'
             [síli dɔg]   'silly dog'   Not: *[sílədɔg]   'silla dog'

Since *a* and *the* change their forms depending on the word that follows, while full words (such as "Gala" and "silly") don't, *a* and *the* must not be full words. Therefore they must be bound morphemes. Because they are bound morphemes that bind (attach) to a range of possible hosts (see example 12 above), they must be clitics.

Types of words, prototypes, and penguins

A **WORD** is a difficult concept to define. Our working definition is "the smallest structural unit that can occur between pauses." However, empirical studies are inconclusive as to whether this definition really corresponds to any universal linguistic category. Words may contain one or more morphemes. Free morphemes can be words (*dog*), but not all words are free morphemes – they may be morphologically complex (*dogs*).

A **PROTOTYPE** is the best example of a category (see, e.g., Coleman and Kay 1981). For instance, for most English speakers a sparrow is probably close to the prototype for the category of "bird." Penguins, turkeys and chickens are also birds, but they are not the best examples of the category. They are not normally the first thing that comes to an English speaker's mind when someone mentions the word *bird*. In linguistics, most definitions are based on prototypes. For example, the definitions given below of "noun" and "verb" are prototype

A penguin is not your prototypical bird.

definitions. The *best* examples of nouns are words that refer to things that don't change over time. However, there are many nouns that refer to things that do change significantly over time, such as *sincerity, fist,* or *explosion*. We know these are nouns because they have many of the **GRAMMATICAL PROPERTIES** of **PROTOTYPICAL** nouns, and few of the grammatical properties of prototypical verbs. The concept of **PROTOTYPICALITY** is important at many levels of linguistic analysis, and will be discussed in more detail in chapter 4.

Introduction to the exercises

The following exercises will give you some practice in looking at a number of different languages in terms of their morphosyntax. All of the exercises in this book deal with real languages. Some of the languages are very well known, and some are not. But all of them are tools used by real people to help them communicate with one another on a daily basis. It can be challenging and fascinating to try to "get inside" the minds of speakers of these languages to figure out the logic of how ideas are expressed.

Another respect in which these exercises may be useful is that they provide an opportunity to begin to comprehend the vast complexity and diversity of the world's languages. Many of the exercises include questions of the form "Where is this language spoken?" or "How many speakers does this language have?" In most cases, these questions will require you to do some library or internet research. The best source of information for these questions is probably the *Ethnologue* (Grimes 2004, http://www.ethnologue.com), though there may be other relevant sources as well. Be careful, however, because sometimes two quite distinct languages may have the same name, or very similar names.

Finally, some of the exercises that follow (such as Yaqui and O'odham) are "logic puzzles" that require you to use your own creative problem-solving skills, in addition to the analytical methods you will be learning in class. Although the processes involved in solving these puzzles may not all be directly applicable to real-world linguistic analysis, they do illustrate the fact that linguistic analysis of any type cannot be absolutely programmed. No matter how many courses in linguistics you take, or how many academic degrees you receive, you will still need to use your own imagination and creativity to infer your own solutions to many of the problems you will face in the analysis of a language. Linguistic analysis is sometimes more an art than a science.

How to gloss linguistic data

Many of the exercises in this book ask you to "gloss" linguistic units. A GLOSS is simply a brief characterization of the meaning of a linguistic form, usually in another language. For example, a good English gloss for the Spanish word *comer* would be 'eat.' Since *comer* is a full lexical word (it belongs to the class of verbs), the gloss is given in English, in small letters. When you gloss a grammatical morpheme, however, there is a tradition in linguistics of using all capital letters, and a kind of abbreviation of the meaning. For example, a gloss for the suffix -*ed* in English might be PAST, or PT (for Past Tense), or something like that. Here is a fully glossed linguistic example that will give you an idea of how linguists tend to gloss examples:

(16)   Y-apooñe-n   këj   i'yaka-e   y-uw-ëj-pu'ma-sa'.
        3-arrive-NONSPEC.I   AN.PROX   3.family-POS   3-I-DTRNS-hit-PPART
        'Some family members of the fallen one arrive.'

This happens to be an example from Panare, a Cariban language spoken in Central Venezuela. Don't worry about what all the glosses and morphemes mean at this point. I just want to illustrate what it means to gloss an example, and alert you to some of the conventions used by linguists. The most important principle to remember about glossing is to *be consistent*.

The first line of data in example 16 is the Panare language as it is officially written. In this line words are divided into morphemes by dashes. The second line of data consists of the glosses of all the morphemes in the first line. Notice that there are just as many dashes in the gloss line as there are in the language line. This is because each morpheme has a gloss. Individual words are aligned with their glosses, but morphemes are not necessarily aligned with their glosses. The way you know which morpheme is associated with which gloss is by counting the dashes. Though there is only one gloss per morpheme, some glosses are complex. For example, the third morpheme in this example is glossed as NONSPEC.I. This is an abbreviation for the two components of meaning that are expressed in this one morpheme. In this case the two components happen to be "non-specific aspect" and "intransitive." The two components are separated by a dot. There are many variations on this method of glossing linguistic examples, but all variations need to be able to explicitly associate glosses with elements of form. Also, all abbreviations need to be explicitly listed somewhere in the article or book that employs them.

The last line of data in example 16 is the "free translation." Free translations are very different from glosses. The free translation should be a natural-sounding expression that is a reasonable equivalent of the translated language example. If it is not possible to provide a reasonable, natural-sounding free translation, then sometimes a "literal" translation is given. Literal translations do not have to sound natural, but they should provide insight into what the expression means in the language being described. For example, a literal translation of example 16 might be: "They arrive the family of the hit one." I would use this translation in addition to the free translation if I felt that the free translation did not capture something significant about the form or meaning of the translated example.

If you were asked to "list and gloss" the morphemes in example 16, this is what you would come up with:

y-	3
apooñe	'arrive'
-n	NONSPEC.I
këj	AN.PROX
i'yaka	'3:family'
-e	POS
uw-	I
ëj-	DTRNS
pu'ma	'hit'
-sa'	PPART

Notice that *prefixes* (bound morphemes that occur at the beginning of a root) are written with a following dash. *Suffixes* (bound morphemes that occur after a root) are written with a preceding dash. Roots are normally written without dashes. However, sometimes roots are written with dashes to indicate that another morpheme is needed in order to transform them into full, pronounceable words, e.g., the Spanish root *habl-* meaning 'speak,' or the English root *-duce*, as in *reduce* or *introduce*.

Notice also that glosses of grammatical morphemes are given in small capital letters, with no quotation marks. Glosses of full lexical words are given in lower case, surrounded by single quote marks, when appearing in a list of this sort.

Glossing is not meant to exhaustively express the meanings of morphemes – a list of glosses is not a substitute for a dictionary. Rather, glosses simply aid readers in understanding brief samples of languages they are not very familiar with. All linguistic examples used in linguistic articles and books must be carefully and thoroughly glossed, otherwise readers who do not understand the language being described will not be able to follow the reasoning in the article. Part of the job of descriptive linguists is to make information about little-known languages available to the outside world. In order to do this, linguistic examples must be presented clearly and accurately. See chapter 2 for a more detailed discussion of some of the problems and principles involved in glossing linguistic examples.

Rules

I have great respect for English teachers and even aspired to be one at one point in my life. However, we must make it clear that linguists use the notion "rule of grammar" in a very different way than English teachers do. To a linguist, a rule of grammar is simply a regular pattern of behavior – part of what you unconsciously know when you know a language. When we write morphological or syntactic rules, we are not trying to tell people what they should or shouldn't say. That is called **PRESCRIPTIVE GRAMMAR**. Rather, linguists simply *describe* the way people actually do speak. This is called **DESCRIPTIVE GRAMMAR**. Rules of grammar to linguists are somewhat analogous to "laws of nature" to naturalists. A law of nature, such as gravity, is not a prescriptive command that instructs natural bodies on how they should act. Rather it is simply a regular pattern of behavior that all bodies follow naturally, and which is *discovered* and *explained* (not invented or enforced) by physicists.

In some of the exercises in this book, you will be asked to "write a rule" for accomplishing some function, e.g., expressing plurality or past tense, in some language. What you will do is look carefully at the data presented in the exercise, noting any regular patterns. When you discover a pattern, you try to express it in a simple yet accurate form. For example, here are some data on **PLURALS** in Michoacán Nahuatl nouns (based on Merrifield *et al.*, 1987):

(17) Michoacán Nahuatl word: English gloss:
  a. kali   'house'
  b. kalimes   'houses'
  c. pelo   'dog'
  d. pelomes   'dogs'
  e. kwahmili   'cornfield'
  f. kwahmilimes   'cornfields'

As you inspect these data, you notice that all the plural words (those that refer to several things) end in *-mes*. You also notice that none of the **SINGULAR** words end in *-mes*. Finally, you note that the plural form of every noun looks just like the singular form of that noun, except the plural has this *-mes* added. Therefore, you have discovered a regular pattern. The job of writing a rule consists simply of describing this pattern in a precise way. For example, you could simply describe the pattern in prose:

(18) Add *-mes* to a noun to form the plural of that noun.

Of course this is a very easy exercise. I can guarantee that not all the exercises in this book will be this straightforward. However, the analytical process is always the same – look for variations in meaning (singular vs. plural) that correlate with variations in form (absence vs. presence of -*mes*).

Such prose descriptions as 18 are often perfectly adequate ways of representing a rule. However, there are many different notational systems that linguists are inclined to use. For example, someone might express the Michoacán Nahuatl pattern described above as:

(19)   NOUN + -*mes* = Plural noun

Or they may express it as

(20) $$\frac{\text{NOUN}}{\text{NOUN} + \textit{-mes}} = \frac{\text{Singular noun}}{\text{Plural noun}}$$

The last two formulations are given as mathematical equations. The statement in 19 is an example of a "process rule" (see chapter 2), and is conceptually equivalent to the prose statement in 18. Example 20 is in the form of a proportion, and might be read as "a plain noun is to a noun plus the suffix -*mes* as a singular noun is to a plural noun." This formulation is a little more explicit than the other two, simply because it specifies the condition of the noun (singular) when there is no affix applied, as well as when the affix -*mes* is added. Linguists often like to use mathematical notations because it is possible to be very explicit and precise using notational systems developed by mathematicians. However, I would caution students about the dangers of getting too excited about notational systems. Often regularities can be easily expressed in ordinary prose, and I encourage students to use ordinary English prose to describe patterns whenever possible. Notational systems can be helpful at times, but we must not forget that we are dealing with languages and not mathematical systems.

Conceptual outline of chapter 1

I.   Language is a complex tool uniquely designed to aid human communication. For this reason, the forms of language make sense in terms of their functions in communication.

II.   Grammar is the internalized, unconscious knowledge that every speaker of a language must know in order to speak that language.

III.   Grammar is traditionally divided into several subheadings by linguists. The ones we will be most concerned about in this book are: Lexicon, Morphology, and Syntax.
  • The lexicon is a "list" of all the cognitive units that must be part of a speaker's unconscious knowledge of his or her language. Lexical expression consists of ways that languages express meaning that crucially require the language user to employ lexical knowledge.

- (Strong) stem suppletion. Lexical expression that involves exchanging one lexical stem for another completely distinct stem.
- Weak stem suppletion. Lexical expression that involves exchanging one stem for a similar one that cannot be predicted by a regular pattern (or rule).
- Isomorphism. Lexical expression that involves no change whatsoever in the stem form of a lexical item.
- Morphology is the study of the "shapes" of words and the different meaning adjustments that are expressed by patterned adjustments in the shapes of words. Morphological processes are ways that languages express meaning by adjusting the shapes of words in systematic ways. These include prefixation, suffixation, and others.
- Syntax is the study of how words combine to form larger structures, such as phrases and clauses. Syntactic (also "analytic") patterns are systematic ways that languages express meaning by combining words or arranging words in phrases and clauses.

IV.   Introduction to the exercises.
- How to "gloss" linguistic data.
- How to describe a "rule of grammar."

Exercise 1.1: English morpheme boundaries

Tom Payne

Divide the following English words into morphemes. Label each morpheme as a root, prefix or suffix (do not worry about the distinction between root and stem at this point). There may be some interesting, controversial and tricky examples here, but they will provide some good points to ponder and discuss:

example:	finger|s	
	root-suf	
thickness	acceptance	underfed
nasty	enlighten	different
linguistic	nationalistically	unrealistically
universal	walked	enlargement
dirty	overemphasized	hopefully
neighborhood	inequality	unattainable
untitled	capable	incomprehensibilificationalism

Exercise 1.2: Telugu

Adapted from Merrifield et al. 1987, problem #1

1. pilla	'child'	3. puwu	'flower'
2. pillalu	'children'	4. puwulu	'flowers'

5. čiima 'ant'	8. godugu 'elephant'
6. čiimalu 'ants'	9. čiire 'sari'
7. turailu 'sponge gourds'	10. annagaaru 'elder brother'

A. Where is Telugu spoken?

B. Describe the rule that allows speakers to express the plural of a noun in Telugu.

C. What are the Telugu translations for the following English words likely to be?
sponge gourd:
elephants:
saris:
elder brothers:

Exercise 1.3: Czech

Tom Payne (based on data in Cowan and Rakušan 1998)

1. novi:	'new'	5. nevini:	'innocent'
2. nevinʲejʃi:	'more innocent'	6. novʲejʃi:	'more new'/'newer'
3. mora:lnʲejʃi:	'more moral'	7. nadani:	'gifted'
4. u:plni:	'complete'	8. u:plnʲejʃi:	'more complete'

A. Describe the grammatical rule that allows speakers to express the comparative degree ("more X") of an adjective in Czech.

B. What are the Czech translations for the English words "more gifted" and "moral" likely to be?

Exercise 1.4: Yaqui

Adapted from Farmer and Demers (1996:135)
The following are eight emphatic clauses in the Yaqui language. The English translations of these clauses are given below in random order:

1. Inepo siika.	_____	English translations (in random order):
2. Empo nee aniak.	_____	a. you helped me.
3. Inepo apo'ik aniak.	_____	b. You danced.
4. Inepo apo'ik vichak.	_____	c. I saw you.
5. Inepo enchi vichak.	_____	d. I saw him.
6. Inepo enchi aniak.	_____	e. I helped you.
7. Empo ye'ek.	_____	f. I helped him.
8. Aapo enchi vichak.	_____	g. He saw you.
		h. I left.

A. Where is Yaqui spoken?

B. Match the correct English translation to each Yaqui sentence.

C.   Does this exercise illustrate lexical, morphological, and/or syntactic expression type or types? Please explain:

Exercise 1.5: Standard Swahili

Adapted from Merrifield et al. 1987, problem #4

Swahili belongs to a large language sub-family, called Bantu, of the Niger-Kordofanian group of languages. Bantu languages are spoken by more than 100 million people in southern and eastern Africa. Swahili is the mother tongue of about 5 million people and is the common language of trade along much of the east coast of Africa.

1.	mtoto	'child'	5.	watoto	'children'
2.	mtu	'person'	6.	watu	'people'
3.	mpiʃi	'cook'	7.	wapiʃi	'cooks'
4.	mgeni	'stranger'	8.	wageni	'strangers'

A.   List and gloss all the morphemes in these data.
B.   What type of expression is evident in these data?

Exercise 1.6: Kurmanji Kurdish

Nick Bailey

The following are six clauses in the Kurmanji Kurdish language. The English translations of these clauses are given below in random order:

1. Ez hꞌirçꞌê dibînim _____
2. Tu dirꞌevî _____
3. Tu min dibînî _____
4. Hꞌirçꞌ dirꞌeve _____
5. Ez dirꞌevim _____
6. Tu hꞌirçꞌê dibînî _____

English translations in random order:
A.   You see bear.
B.   You see me.
C.   Bear runs.
D.   You run.
E.   I see Bear.
F.   I run.

A.   Where is Kurmanji Kurdish spoken? How many speakers are there?
B.   Match the Kurmanji Kurdish sentences with the correct English sentence translations.
C.   What would the following English sentence be in Kurmanji Kurdish?: Bear sees me. _____

Exercise 1.7: O'odham

John Damon and Tom Payne

A.   What language family does O'odham belong to?
B.   About how many fluent speakers are there?

C.   Match the O'odham words with the correct English meanings given on the right:

English meanings in random order:

1. pa:n   _____   a. to buy
2. golont   _____   b. a thing for counting, ruler, calculator, etc.
3. pa:ntakud   _____   c. to rake
4. kuintakud   _____   d. to make bread
5. nolawtakud   _____   e. a place or thing for buying; money, store, etc.
6. pa:nt   _____   f. a thing used for making bread; oven, pan, etc.
7. nolawt   _____   g. bread
8. wakontakud   _____   h. a thing used for washing
9. wakon   _____   i. clean clothes

D.   How would you say the following in O'odham?

10. a rake (thing for raking):   _____
11. to count: _____
12. to wash: _____

E.   Explain how you arrived at this solution:

Exercise 1.8: Kaqchikel

Adapted from Cutzal (1990)

Kaqchikel:	English translation:
1. nimajay	'hall'
2. n̠unimajay	'my hall' `nu' = 'my'`
3. raxkej	'cramp'
4. k'ixawuch'	'porcupine'
5. samaj	'work'
6. animajay	'your hall' `a' = 'your'`
7. ruraxkej	'his cramp' `ru' = 'his'`
8. ruk'ixawuch'	'his porcupine'
9. kisamaj	'their work' `ki' = 'their'`
10. kinimajay	'their hall'
11. araxkej	*your cramp*
12. nuk'ixawuch'	*my porcupine*
13. *ru nimajay*	'his hall'
14. *kik'ixawuch*	'their porcupine'
15. *nuraxkej*	'my cramp'

A.   Where is Kaqchikel spoken?
B.   Fill in all the blanks in the above data.
C.   List and gloss all the morphemes in these data (be sure to include free and bound morphemes):

Exercise 1.9: plurals in four languages

Tom Payne

"Plural" is a very common meaning element that is expressed on nouns in many languages. Like many meaning elements, plurality can be expressed lexically, syntactically, or morphologically. Your task is to determine which type of expression is used to form plurals in each language illustrated. As is the case with most distinctions in language, these three expression types really represent a continuous scale. For this reason, it may not be absolutely obvious which expression type is involved in every case. Just give the best answer you can. Also, some examples may involve a combination of expression types:

Language	Meaning	Singular	Plural	Lexical, syntactic, morphological, or . . .?
English	'dog'	dog	dogs	_____
—	'deer'	deer	deer	_____
—	'person'	person	people	_____
—	'goose'	goose	geese	_____
—	'ox'	ox	oxen	_____
—	'child'	child	children	___✓___
Archaic Eng.	'cow'	cow	kine	_____
Tagalog	'child'	bata	manga bata	_____
—	'woman'	babae	manga babae	_____
—	'man'	lalaki	manga lalaki	_____
Indonesian	'child'	anak	anakanak	_____
—	'person'	orang	orangorang	_____
Maa	'tree'	ɔlčaní	ɪlkeék	_____
—	'ox' (male)	ɔlkítéŋ	ɪlmóɲí	_____
—	'cow'	ɛŋkítéŋ	iŋkíšú	_____
—	'wild beast'	olowuarú	ilówúárâk	_____
—	'leopard'	olkerî	ilówúárâk kerîn	_____

Exercise 1.10: comparative adjectives in six languages

Tom Payne

"Comparison" is a very common meaning element that is expressed on adjectives in many languages. Like many meaning elements, comparison can be expressed lexically, syntactically, or morphologically. Your task is to determine which expression type is used to form comparative adjectives in each set of examples illustrated:

Language	Meaning	Non-comparative	Comparative	Lexical, syntactic, morphological, or . . . ?
Russian	'good'	xoróʃij	lúʃʃe	_____
	'bad'	ploxój	xúʒe	_____
English	'small'	smɔl	smɔlɚ	_____
	'big'	bɪg	bɪgɚ	_____
Spanish	'small'	pekéɲo	más pekéɲo	_____
	'big'	gránde	más gránde	_____
Portuguese	'small'	pekéno ·	menór	_____
	'big'	gránde	majór	_____
Fijian	'good'	vina'a	vina'a ca'e	_____
	'bad'	caa	caa ca'e	_____
Dyirbal	'good'	ɖigal	ɖigalbaɽa	_____
	'big'	bulgan	bulganbaɽa	_____
	'small'	midi	midibaɽa	_____

Notes

1. There are languages that exist without sounds, e.g., sign languages used by the deaf. However, it is arguably the case that nothing that qualifies as a "language" exists without words or sentences.

2. There is a very large literature on the pervasiveness of sound symbolism and iconicity in language. Iconicity is the more general term referring to any respect in which the form of language is a "picture" (an icon) of its meaning. Sound symbolism refers to iconicity that specifically relates to how certain sounds seem to inherently, and often universally (i.e., in all languages), evoke particular images in the minds of speakers. For example, Köhler (1929) showed people two arbitrary figures, one very angular and sharp, and one having a more curved and rounded shape. He invented the nonsense words *takete* and *maluma* and asked his subjects to guess which word applied to which figure. The subjects almost unanimously assigned *takete* to the angular figure and *maluma* to the more rounded one. Since then, many researchers have elaborated Köhler's experiment to include speakers of many different languages, controlling for various complicating factors such as the written forms of words, the cultural context, etc. The accumulated results of all these experiments have been taken as demonstrating a universal parallelism between visual and auditory images (see, e.g., Allot 1995 for an excellent synopsis and bibliography).

3. Though children often do apply rules where adults would not. This is one major source of language change. No language is totally regular in its patterns. The reasons for this are manifold, and form the subject matter for the subfield known as historical linguistics. In this book, we want to be aware of the effects of time and history on language structures, but we will primarily be concerned with patterns and regularities that exist at one given time in the history of a language.

4. Because of the effects of language change over time, writing systems seldom directly reflect the sounds of a language. This is particularly true with respect to modern English writing systems. Descriptive linguists are primarily concerned with *spoken* language, i.e., how language sounds rather than how it is spelled. In spite of the

spelling differences, the words *buy*, *cry*, and *die* all end in the same sound in modern English.

5. A tradition often used by linguists is to place an asterisk (*) before a form if it is not attested in the language. These are hypothetical forms that a speaker's internal grammar does not recognize or produce. Sometimes linguists will say that such forms are *ungrammatical*.

6. Of course, this word comes from the French word *portemanteau*, which means something slightly different, namely a kind of coat rack or coat hanger. *Porte* 'to carry,' plus *manteau* 'mantle,' or 'cloak,' hence 'cloak carrier.'

7. There is no one "Standard English," therefore it is more appropriate to speak of "standard Englishes." By this, I mean the established, written varieties of English used in various countries around the world, e.g., the UK, Ireland, India, the Philippines, Zimbabwe, Canada, Australia, New Zealand, and others. These can be quite different from one another, as well as from the multitude of "non-standard," or spoken, Englishes that exist as sociologically or geographically determined varieties throughout the world.

8. It is standard in descriptive linguistics to use square brackets, [ ], to indicate phonetic representation, and slashes, //, to indicate phonemic representation. Any good introduction to phonetics or phonology will define these terms and other notation that appears in this chapter. For example, see Burquest (2001).

2 Morphological processes and conceptual categories

Having discussed the differences among lexical, syntactic, and morphological expression types, we will now concentrate more specifically on kinds of morphological processes, and the CONCEPTUAL CATEGORIES they express. For example, "past tense," "plural," "masculine," and many other elements of meaning are all conceptual categories that are often expressed morphologically in the world's languages. In this chapter we will discuss the notion of conceptual categories in some depth, and then describe three analytical methods that linguists often use to represent and analyze morphological patterns.

Conceptual categories and the problem of labeling

Each language categorizes the universe in its own unique way. This truism is obvious to anyone who has tried to learn a second language. In fact, one could go a step further and say that each individual person categorizes the universe in a unique way. A good part of the art of human communication involves figuring out how our individual categorization scheme compares with the schemes of people we are trying to communicate with, whether we are speaking the "same language" or not. For example, native English speakers who learn Spanish are often perplexed by the fact that Spanish has two "past tenses." It seems at first that there are two ways to translate a sentence like the following into Spanish:

(1)   English sentence: I knew Aileron when she was a child.
        Spanish translation #1: Yo conocía a Aileron cuando ella era niña.
        Spanish translation #2: Yo conocí a Aileron cuando ella era niña.

Notice that the Spanish verb *conocer* occurs in two different forms, both of which refer to a past situation. However, bilingual speakers know that Spanish sentence #2 really does not mean 'I knew Aileron when she was a child.' In fact it means something more like 'I met Aileron when she was a child.' The different endings on the Spanish verb categorize the world differently than the tenses in English do, therefore English speakers must "reconceptualize," or reorganize, their native categorization scheme in order to become fluent speakers of Spanish. This is just one simple example of how categorization varies from language to language. If you have ever studied a second language, you can come up with many similar examples, in lexicon, grammar, and patterns of conversation.

The word "category" is a very useful and common word in linguistics. In this section we are going to define the term "conceptual category" in a very specific way to describe some specific element of meaning that speakers of a language pay special attention to grammatically.

In order to be a conceptual category a particular element of meaning must determine some pattern of grammatical (lexical, morphological, or syntactic) expression. It does not need to be a perfectly consistent or regular pattern, but there needs to be a pattern. For example, as mentioned in chapter 1, "past tense" is an element of meaning that speakers may express when they use any English verb. There is an expectation that verbs in English can be "tweaked" morphologically (often with the ending -ed) if the event described happened prior to the time the verb is uttered. The particular rule for expressing past tense varies considerably from verb to verb, but every verb has a past-tense form. New verbs that come into the English language also must be assigned a past-tense form. This is evidence that a recurring pattern exists, and therefore past tense is a conceptual category in English.

In order to clarify the notion of conceptual category, it may help to contrast conceptual categories with other possible meaning elements that are never categories in any language, and some that are categories in some languages, but not others. For example, I do not believe there is any language in the world that includes, in its list of grammatical patterns, an expectation that verbs express the altitude above sea level of the speech event or the event described by the verb. Such a language is conceivable, because this meaning element can probably be expressed in any language:

(2) a.   We slept at 2,000 meters.
    b.   They ordered rice and dal at sea level.

However, I doubt whether any language has a recurring grammatical pattern (prefixes, suffixes, a set of **AUXILIARIES**, etc.) that regularly shapes clauses for this precise parameter of meaning.

In addition to elements of meaning that are not conceptual categories in any language, there are also elements of meaning that are categories in some languages but not in others. For example, "location downriver" is not a conceptual category that is relevant to the grammar of English, though in Yagua (and many other languages in the riverene areas of South America), it is. The reason that location downriver is not a category that is relevant to English grammar is that there is no regular expectation that clauses involve *grammatical* indication that an action happens "downriver" of the place of speaking. Certainly English speakers *may* specify that an action occurs "downriver" by enriching the clause with additional material, e.g.:

(3)   He went fishing downriver.

However, without the adverb "downriver" in this example, no assertion is made as to where the event occurred:

(4)   He went fishing.

The event described by this clause could have happened anywhere, including downriver from the place of utterance or any other conceivable reference point. In Yagua, however, there is a set of verb suffixes that do orient the location of the event to the location of the other events in the discourse. Consider the following set of examples:

(5) a.   Naada-rąą-yąą-*mu*-nada.
              3DL-dance-DISTR-DR-PAST3
              'They two danced around downriver.'

    b.   Naada-rąą-yąą-*nuvee*-nada.
              3DL-dance-DISTR-ARRI-PAST3
              'They two danced around on arrival (here).'

    c.   Naada-rąą-yąą-*nuvaa*-nada.
              3DL-dance-DISTR-ARR2-PAST3
              'They two danced around on arrival (there).'

    d.   Naada-rąą-yąą-nada.
              3DL-dance-DISTR-PAST3
              'They two danced around (continuing scene).'

The suffixes glossed DR, ARR1, and ARR2 are members of a set of about ten suffixes that specify the location of the event described by the clause. If none of the suffixes in this set are used (example 5d) the implication is that the event happened in a neutral location, normally at the same place as the other events in the particular episode, and NOT downriver, on arrival, etc. Therefore, we want to say that *location* describes a set (or paradigm) of conceptual categories in Yagua, similar to the way *tense* describes a set of conceptual categories in English.

Here is another way of understanding what a conceptual category is and is not. Every language has sets of roots that differ according to some definable element of meaning. For example, the verbs *watch* and *see* describe very similar concepts – they both describe scenes[1] in which someone or something perceives some visual stimulus. However, they differ in that *watch* is intentional, while *see* is experiential; the person who sees something does so without necessarily intending to, whereas the person who watches something does so on purpose. Nevertheless, one wouldn't want to say that *watch* is the "intentional mood" form of the verb *see*, or something like that. Why not? Don't we say that *went* is the "past tense" form of the verb *go*? These forms are as different from one another as *watch* and *see* are. Why can't *watch* be the suppletive intentional mood form of the verb *see*? The reason is that there is no *pattern* for intentional mood formation for English verbs. It is not the case that for every English verb there is a specific intentional mood form. There is, on the other hand, a very well-established conceptual category of past tense in English. English speakers are well aware of the past-tense forms of verbs in their language, and new verbs that come into the language are automatically assigned a past-tense form that is consistent with the pattern. None of this is true for "intentional mood" in English (though it may be in other languages).

There are thousands of potential conceptual categories that are relevant to the grammars of the world's languages, and a similar number of ways in which they may be expressed. In this book we can discuss and present examples of only a subset of this total range of variation; the rest is up to you. The hope is that the book will give you the tools (the "analytical methods") for making reasonably insightful hypotheses about the conceptual categories in any language. It will illustrate a large selection of the important conceptual categories known to exist in the world's languages, as well as the ways in which they are characteristically expressed. However, in many cases, in real life and in the exercises in this book, you will have to infer (make a reasonable guess) what the conceptual categories are, based on limited evidence. This is yet another respect in which grammatical description is an art.

The notion of conceptual categories is closely tied to the problem of how to provide meaningful glosses, or labels, for grammatical units (words, morphemes, etc.). In order to discuss this problem, we will consider the following data from Central Yup'ik (Reed *et al.*, 1977:99):

(6)   a. cali   'work'   f. calivik   'workshop'
       b. nere   'eat'   g. nervik   'restaurant'
       c. eke   'get in'   h. ekvik   'bank of river'
       d. kumarte   'ignite'   i. kumarrvik   'fireplace'
       e. mi'te   'alight'   j. misvik   'landing strip'

The first question to ask about these data is "Is there a pattern?" Is there any variation in form that seems to correlate, even partially, with a particular variation in meaning? Clearly there is a formal relationship between the words in the left-hand column and those in the right-hand column. The words on the right all end in -*vik*, and seem to be based on the corresponding words on the left, though there is some variation. Now the question is, "is there any conceptual pattern that corresponds to the observed formal pattern?" The idea is to come up with an insightful, but brief, description of the common *meaning* expressed by the particular formal pattern displayed by these examples. Just going by the English translations, you may guess that the words in the left column are verbs and the ones in the right column are probably nouns. Furthermore, you notice that 6f through 6j all describe places. In particular, most of them seem to describe a place that is the characteristic location of the activity described by the related verb in the left-hand column – a workshop is a place for work, a restaurant is a place for eating, a fireplace is a place for igniting, etc.

At first glance, the relationship between "get in" and "bank of river" may not seem comparable to the other pairs in this list. It may be the case that this suffix -*vik* expresses two (or more) conceptual categories (as the ending spelled -*er* in the

English words *worker* and *smarter* means two very different things). Or it may be that we just need to get creative and try to discern a connection that isn't obvious given the English translations. How could a river bank be understood as a "place for getting in"? Well, the bank of a river is where Yup'ik speakers get in their boats. So the use of this *-vik* suffix on the word that means "bank of river" makes sense, in terms of the other uses of this form.

This is how linguists make hypotheses regarding conceptual categories – they stand back and make an educated guess about the general function of any grammatical pattern based on evidence from the clear examples, and observation of native speakers in conversation. For most of the exercises in this book, the only evidence you have to go on will be the English free translations and/or glosses. Translation equivalence in another language is often not the best evidence for linguistic analyses. However, within the constraints of a textbook of this sort, it is pretty much all that we have. In a real field situation, the linguist would want to collect many forms, from several speakers, and observe how the forms are used in natural discourse. Eventually, the linguist will begin to internalize the grammatical system her- or himself, and perhaps be able to come up with a deeper analysis of the conceptual categories that are truly relevant to native speakers. The better you know a language, the more insightful your linguistic analyses will be.

In the case of the Yup'ik examples 6f through 6j, we've hypothesized that the conceptual category expressed by this particular morphological pattern can be described as "a place where someone performs the activity described by the stem." This is too long a description to put in glosses of linguistic examples, so we want to come up with a short, concise label that helps readers of our description understand and remember how this *-vik* suffix functions. For some reason, linguists like to label conceptual categories with words ending in *-ative*, *-ization*, or some other Latinate suffix. Since the category in question forms a noun, we may want to call this "nominalization" (the word "nominal" comes from the Latin word for "name" or "noun," so to "nominalize" something means to make it into a noun). But there are many kinds of nominalization (as discussed in chapter 4). Since these Yup'ik nominalizations refer to places, we may want to call the category "place nominalization." An even more "linguisticky" label may be "locative nominalization" or something like that. Then abbreviations such as LOC.NOMLZ can be used in glossing linguistic examples (in conjunction with a list of abbreviations at the beginning or the end of the description).

The actual term one chooses to label a category is important, but choosing a term isn't necessarily an analytical decision in and of itself. Rather, it is a *pedagogical* or *communicative* decision. What makes one term better than another is how well it communicates to the reader of your description (or the grader of your homework assignment!). You want to use terms that insightfully capture the essence of the conceptual category involved, without confusing your readers with terms that may have other, unrelated, meanings associated with them. Occasionally, a conceptual category may be so unusual that it needs an entirely new term. In these cases, be sure to justify your decision fully and provide very good definitions.

Of course, there is a complete continuum between conceptual categories that are very common and easy to label and those that are so unusual that new labels need to be invented for them. For example, plural and past tense are often clearly distinguished conceptual categories in languages – though even these can be problematic. On the other end of the continuum, every language has grammaticalized patterns that defy a straightforward functional label. Occasionally such patterns can simply be glossed formally, for example, "the prefix *di-*." Then their functions should be explained in rich (detailed) prose in the body of the description, or even left for future investigation, if time and other resources do not permit a full analysis.

Whenever you attach a familiar label (such as "past tense") to a form, you are claiming that its meaning is "the same" in some crucial respect to the meanings of other forms in other languages that also have received that label. Since forms in different languages seldom serve *exactly* the same range of functions, the practice of using familiar terms in glossing is always, at some level, misleading. However, since it is impossible to exhaustively and precisely characterize the conceptual categories in any language, it has become commonplace to use familiar terms whenever possible, and to explain the unique features of the conceptual category in question to the extent that time and resources permit. Because a grammatical description is a communicative act (Payne forthcoming), there will always be a trade-off between inclusiveness and usefulness – a totally inclusive description will not be very useful, first because it will never be published, and second because the unique characteristics of the described language will be buried in reams of detail that will be impossible for a reader to sort through. So linguists must always strive for a balance between inclusivity and communicativity in the way they gloss and represent language data. Labels for conceptual categories should be insightfully familiar, but not overly particular. This is another respect in which linguistic analysis is an art (in addition to being a science).

The important ideas to keep in mind at this point are:

> A conceptual category exists when there is an *expectation of patterned behavior* – a recurring relationship between variation in form and variation in meaning. Conceptual category labels (or "glosses") are interpretations designed to help readers of a grammatical description understand and remember the functions of particular structures.

Derivational vs. inflectional categories

Languages often exhibit an important contrast between INFLECTION and DERIVATION. In most of the linguistics literature, this distinction is understood as a difference between types of morphological or lexical expression. It is not often applied to syntactic constructions, though I suppose it could be. Sometimes you will hear or read about inflectional and derivational *categories* (as subsets of conceptual categories), inflectional and derivational *morphology*, or inflectional and derivational *processes*. These terms are all roughly analogous. However, this use of the term *derivation* is distinct from **MORPHO-PHONEMIC DERIVATION**, which is quite a different notion, to be discussed in chapter 3.

As with the distinction between grammatical morphemes and full lexical words, and many other important distinctions in linguistics, there is often a continuum between inflection and derivation. Nevertheless, it is usually helpful to make this distinction when analyzing a little-studied language, and it is necessary to understand the distinction in order to read and appreciate descriptive and theoretical literature in linguistics.

The difference between derivation and inflection is best characterized in terms of prototypes, and clusters of features that tend to go together. Prototypical derivational categories *create new stems* (recall the definitions of *root* and *stem* from chapter 1). Often the new stems created by a derivational category belong to a different word class than the stem that is the basis of the derivation (example 7 below), and sometimes the derivational category just significantly changes the meaning of the base stem (example 8):

(7)   NOMINALIZATION:

VERB → NOUN:	grow	growth	(*growtion)
	destroy	destruction	(*destroyth)
ADJ → NOUN:	wide	width	(*widity, ?wideness)
	happy	happiness	(*happity, *happyth)
	sincere	sincerity	(*sincereness, *sincereth)

(8)   COMPARISON:

ADJ → COMPARATIVE ADJ:	wide	wider
	happy	happier
	weird	weirder
	good	better

Inflectional categories, on the other hand, don't change word classes, and don't adjust the meanings of roots in major ways. They simply add some important information that may be required by the syntactic or situational context. Here are some examples of quite prototypical inflectional categories in English:

(9)   NUMBER:

SINGULAR → PLURAL:	dog	dogs
	cat	cats
	man	men
	ox	oxen

(10)   TENSE:

PRESENT → PAST:	walk	walked
	sing	sang
	go	went
	bring	brought

Table 2.1 *A comparison between derivational and inflectional categories*

Derivational categories	Inflectional categories
often change the word class of a root (i.e., change a noun into a verb, a verb into a noun, etc.)	seldom "change" the word class. If they do, it is a secondary effect, e.g., "Verbing weirds language."
are seldom "required" in order to incorporate the form into discourse	are often required by the syntactic environment (e.g., "tense," "case," "agreement")
significantly affect the meaning of a root	contribute relatively "small" meaning adjustments, such as number, tense, aspect, etc. Do not change the basic lexical meaning of a root
are relatively "non-productive" in that: • they tend to not apply to all stems of a class • they tend to not have precisely the same effect every time they apply • they tend to be idiosyncratically related to other derivational categories	are relatively "productive" in that: • they tend to apply to all stems of a class or subclass • they tend to have the same effect every time they apply • they tend to occur in well-defined sets, or **PARADIGMS**

Table 2.1 lists the general characteristics normally associated with derivational vs. inflectional categories. The prototypical examples will have all the properties associated with its type.

In English the distinction between derivation and inflection is fairly clear, but this is not the case in every language. Even in English there are some categories that are more prototypical than others. For example, nominalization, as illustrated in 7 above, has all the characteristics of a prototypical derivational category – it usually changes the word class, it has various forms, it is very "irregular," etc. The examples of comparison in 8, on the other hand, are not prototypical for a derivational category. The comparative *-er* suffix in English is very regular, it applies to just about every adjective, and it has the same effect every time it is applied. However, it is nevertheless clearly derivational in that it creates a subclass of adjectives that have different syntactic properties from other adjectives – you can put comparative adjectives into a comparative construction, which you cannot do with other adjectives:

(11)   The grass here is greener than it is on the other side of the fence.
        *The grass here is green than it is on the other side of the fence.
        *The grass here is greenest than it is on the other side of the fence.

Similarly, the examples in 9 and 10 are quite prototypical inflectional categories, though tense 10 is less regular than plurality in English. There are more different past-tense forms and more irregularity in the system of tense inflection of verbs than there is for number inflection on nouns. This makes tense less proto-typically inflectional than number. Nevertheless, tense is still clearly inflectional since it does not change the meaning of a verb significantly. It simply **GROUNDS** the meaning of the scene described by the verb in terms of time.

The "big ten" morphological processes

Chapter 1 distinguished three general expression types that languages use to accomplish communicative work. These were lexical expression, syntactic patterns, and morphological processes. In this chapter we are concentrating on morphological processes. First we will describe and exemplify ten morphological processes that will be important in the rest of this book. We will refer to these as the "big ten." These are listed below, with brief explanations and examples:

• Morphological process #1, Prefixation: (English) selfish → unselfish
PREFIXATION involves the addition of a morpheme (a prefix) to the beginning of a root. In English the morpheme *un-* is a prefix. Often languages allow several prefixes to be attached to one root. An example of this in English would be a word like: *antidisestablishment*. This word has at least two prefixes, *anti-* and *dis-*.

• Morphological process #2, Suffixation: (Spanish) hablar → hablaré
SUFFIXATION involves the addition of a morpheme (a suffix) to the end of a root. In English, the past tense is often expressed with a suffix spelled *-ed* as in *called*. As with prefixes, there can be more than one suffix on a word. A word like *establishments* in English has a suffix *-ment* and another suffix *-s*.

• Morphological process #3, Infixation:
   (Bontoc) fikas 'strong' → fumikas 'strength'
INFIXATION involves the addition of a morpheme (an **INFIX**) in the middle of a root. Standard Englishes do not employ infixation, but many other languages do. The example above is from Bontoc, an Austronesian language spoken in the Philippines. Various spoken varieties of English do employ infixes, usually for emotive, humorous, or social solidarity reasons. The following naturally occur-ring examples are from "Rapper" English, an oral variety of African American Vernacular English (Mufwene *et al.* 1998).[2] In this variety of English, the infix *-izz-* is inserted, normally after the first consonant or consonant sequence of a word. It may have originated as a way to increase the number of syllables in a word in order to make it fit the rhythm of a line of rap music. However, it is now clearly used to express a range of emphatic, emotive, and/or humorous effects:

(12)   From an internet chat room:
     a.   i mean, that movie sizzucked.   'That was a terrible movie.'
     b.   i knizzow.   'I wholeheartedly agree.'

In these examples, the infix *-izz-* intensifies the intended effect of the verbs *sucked* and *know*. If the word starts with a vowel, *-izz-* is the first syllable of the word: .

(13) a.   izzengland   'England, for heaven's sake.'
     b.   dat's izzall   'That's absolutely all.'
     c.   cuz' he be who he izzis. 'Because he is none other than who he is.'

This is a completely regular and common process that (as of 2005) is becoming more widespread in spoken varieties of English, chiefly in the USA.

It is important to distinguish infixation from multiple prefixation or suffixation. If we look at a very long English word like *antidisestablishmentarianism*, we will not find infixation – only multiple layers of prefixes and suffixes. This word can be broken up into morphemes as follows:

(14)   anti-dis-e-stabl-ish-ment-ari-an-ism

The root of this word is *-stabl-*.[3] There are no morphemes inserted inside of this root, so there are no infixes. There are, however, two or three "layers" of prefixation and five layers of suffixation. These "layers" can be considered to apply in order:

Root: -stabl-	
Prefixation, layer 1:	e-stabl
Suffixation, layer 1:	e-stabl-ish
Prefixation, layer 2:	dis-e-stabl-ish
Suffixation, layer 2:	dis-e-stabl-ish-ment
Prefixation, layer 3:	anti-dis-e-stabl-ish-ment
Suffixation, layer 3:	anti-dis-e-stabl-ish-ment-ary
Suffixation, layer 4:	anti-dis-e-stabl-ish-ment-ari-an
Suffixation, layer 5:	anti-dis-e-stabl-ish-ment-ari-an-ism

As you can see, layers of prefixation and suffixation proceed outwards from the root. There are no affixes that appear inside the root, so there are no infixes.

In Bontoc, on the other hand, the "f" in *fumikas* is not a morpheme distinct from the *-ikas* part. The affix *-um-* can appear after the first consonant of a number of roots in order to express a certain kind of meaning. The first consonant must be considered part of the root, so *-um-* must be an infix.

• Morphological process #4, Circumfixation
CIRCUMFIXATION is a rare morphological process in which one morpheme has two parts – one that appears before the root and another after the root. The only non-controversial examples of circumfixation that have been documented to date involve the expression of negation, as in the following examples from Chukchee, a Chukotko-Kamchatkan language spoken in northeastern Siberia, Russia (Skorik 1961, as cited in Marusic 2002):

(15)   a. jatjol   'fox'   b. *a*-jatjol-*ka*   'without a fox'
        c. cakett   'sister'   d. *a*-cakettə-*ke*   'without a sister'

In examples 15b and 15d the two parts, *a*- ... -*kV* (where V indicates a vowel that changes its form depending on the context) jointly express the negative **INFLEC-TION**. Neither one occurs independently. Therefore, this must be considered one morpheme with two separate parts.

Often, examples which may appear to be circumfixation can be analyzed as two separate morphemes – a prefix and a suffix – that just happen to appear frequently together to express a particular meaning. For example, Panare, a Cariban language spoken in Venezuela, expresses negation in a manner that is surprisingly similar to Chukchee. However, this inflection in Panare does not represent true circumfixation:

(16)   a. Yu-suru'-sa'   b. A-suruku-'ka.
           3-worry-PPART   NEU-worry-NEG
           'He/she's worried.'   'He/she doesn't worry.'

        c. Wĕ-runkami-n   yu.   d. A-runkami-'ka   yu.
           1-have.fever-PAST1 1SG   NEU-have.fever-NEG 1SG
           'I have a fever.'   'I don't have a fever.'

This kind of negation in Panare is expressed via an inflection that consists of two parts, *a*- ... -'*ka*, as illustrated in examples 16b and 16d. However, this is not true circumfixation, since the *a*- part is in fact a distinct prefix that occurs in a number of other inflections in the language:

(17) a.   A-suru'-nëpëj   këj.   'He/she's worrying.'
           NEU-worry-IMPERF   3SG

     b.   A-runkami-nya.   'while having a fever . . .'
           NEU-have.fever-SIM

If the negative inflection in Panare were considered circumfixation, then all the other inflections that occur with the form *a*- would also need to be considered circumfixation, that just happen to share the same initial portion. There is good evidence, however, that this *a*- is in fact a distinct morpheme.[4] This is quite different from the Chukchee situation, in which both parts of the *a*- ... -*kV* inflection only occur in the negative. Therefore, the Chukchee examples do illustrate true circumfixation.

• Morphological process #5, Stem modification: (English) sing → sang
STEM MODIFICATION is a change in shape that does not involve the addition of any affix. The difference in form between *sing* and *sang* in English cannot be called infixation because there is no specific form that has been added to the root. Rather, the root vowel has just changed into something else. One might ask how this is different from "weak stem suppletion" described in chapter 1. The difference is that *sing* and *sang* can be related by a rule ("change -*ing* to -*ang* to

form the past tense"). See chapter 1 for a discussion of how to determine whether a particular alternation is predictable by a rule or not.

- Morphological process #6, Autosegmental variation:

    (English) convért → cónvert

AUTOSEGMENTAL VARIATION is a change in shape that does not involve consonants and vowels. Rather, it consists of adjustments in features such as **STRESS**, **TONE**, and **NASALIZATION**. The best example of autosegmental variation as a morphological process in English is the difference between some nouns and verbs that is signaled by nothing but a change in stress, as in the above example. This difference is not indicated in the regular English spelling system, so I have placed a stress mark in these words to highlight the difference between *convért* (a verb) and *cónvert* (a related noun).

Here is an example of autosegmental variation marking plurality in Dungra Bhil, an Indo-Aryan language spoken in Gujarat state in India (Matthew and Susan 2000). In this case the autosegmental feature is nasalization:

(18) a. t̪ijaʔa 'his' t̪ĩjaʔa 'their (masc)'
     b. t̪ijʌʔʌ 'hers' t̪ĩjʌʔʌ 'their (fem)'

Note that the only difference between the singular and plural possessive pronouns is that the plurals have a nasalized vowel (indicated by a tilde "~") in the first syllable.

- Morphological process #7, Reduplication:

    (Ilokano) pingan 'dish' → pingpingan 'dishes'

REDUPLICATION involves the repetition of part or all of a root. Plurality in Ilokano (another Austronesian language spoken in the Philippines) is expressed by reduplicating the first syllable of the root, as in the above example. Here are some further examples:

(19) a. ulo   'head'   ululo   'heads'
     b. talon 'field' taltalon 'field'
     c. biag   'life'   bibiag   'lives'
     d. mula   'plant' mulmula 'plants'

This is called **PARTIAL REDUPLICATION**, because only part of the root is repeated. In the case of Ilokano, the only part that is reduplicated is the first syllable of the word. Some languages, like Indonesian, repeat the whole root. So in Indonesian "child" is *anak* and "children" is *anakanak*. This is called **COMPLETE REDUPLICATION**. Plural is not the only conceptual category that is expressed by reduplication, but it is quite common.

- Morphological process #8, Non-concatenative morphology:

    (Hebrew) sefer 'book' → sfarim 'books'

NON-CONCATENATIVE MORPHOLOGY is common in Semitic languages, such as Hebrew and Arabic, but rare elsewhere. It involves superimposing a pattern of vowels, and possibly other morphological pieces, on a root that consists only of consonants. For example, 20 illustrates a few of the verb forms for the root *ktb* in Biblical Hebrew. This root can never be pronounced on its own, but must appear in an inflected form (examples courtesy of David Andersen, as cited in van der Merwe, Naudé, and Kroeze 1999):

(20)	a.	ktb	root	(no meaning on its own)
	b.	kətob	imperative	'write!'
	c.	katob	infinitive	'to write'
	d.	kotɛb	present participle	'writing'
	e.	katub	past participle	'written'
	f.	katab	perfective	'wrote'

- Morphological process #9, Subtractive morphology:
  (Murle) nyoon 'lamb' → nyoo 'lambs,' wawoc 'white heron' →
  wawo 'white herons'

SUBTRACTIVE MORPHOLOGY is another quite rare process, whereby one or more segments are omitted from a word in order to express a particular conceptual category. Murle (along with several other Nilo-Saharan languages of East Africa) is one of the few languages of the world that illustrate true subtractive morphology. In each of the Murle examples above, the stem-final consonant is omitted in order to form the plural.

One has to be careful to distinguish subtractive morphology from simple zero realization of certain categories, especially when those categories have overt marking in another language the linguist is familiar with. For example, in Arbore (a Cushitic language of Ethiopia) for some nouns the singular ends in *-in* while the plural is unmarked (Hayward 1984:159–83, cited in Corbett 2000:17):

(21)		Singular		Plural	
	a.	tiisin	'a maize cob'	tiise	'maize cobs'
	b.	nebelin	'a cock ostrich'	nebel	'ostriches'

One may be tempted to analyze this as an instance of subtractive morphology, because the plural nouns are formally simpler than the singular. However, this would be a mistake. In many languages, including English, the plural is marked and the singular is unmarked. However, in this class of Arbore nouns (items that normally occur in groups), the plural is the unmarked number, while the suffix *-in* is a marker of singular. Sometimes this is called a **SINGULATIVE**. Notice that this is quite different from Murle. In Murle, there is no one suffix that indicates singular. Rather, the last consonant of the stem, no matter what it is, is eliminated in order to form the plural. Here are some more nouns that illustrate this feature of Murle (Arensen 1982:40–41):

(22)		Singular		Plural	
	a.	onyiit	'rib'	onyii	'ribs'
	b.	rottin	'warrior'	rotti	'warriors'

Notice that the last consonant of any stem, whether it is *-t, -n, -c*, or any number of others, is simply left out to mark the plural. These cannot all be different forms of one "singulative" morpheme, so they must be considered part of the stem, and the morphological process that expresses plurality involves *removing* that last consonant.

- Morphological process #10, Compounding:
  (English) black+bird → bláckbird

COMPOUNDING involves combining roots to form new stems. In the English example above, it is impossible to identify one part as the root and the other as an affix. *Black* and *bird* are both roots that clump together morphologically to form a stem. The new stem, *blackbird*, expresses an idea that is more than simply the combination of the meanings of the two roots – this word does not refer to any bird that happens to be black, but rather to a specific species of bird. Even though this word is formed out of two roots, it functions just like other noun stems in the language.

Having introduced ten major morphological processes, we now turn to a discussion of various methods linguists use to "model" or represent morphological processes and the conceptual categories they express.

Methods for representing morphological processes

Prose

As mentioned in chapter 1, many of the grammatical patterns in language may be expressed in ordinary prose. When doing morphosyntactic analysis, it is very important to be explicit, and sometimes grammatical patterns are so complex that explicit prose statements become difficult to follow. In these cases linguists have found it useful to employ various notational systems. In the following sections we will discuss two mathematically explicit methods for representing patterns of linguistic behavior. These are particularly useful for representing morphological processes, though they could, in principle, be used to express syntactic patterns as well. It should be kept in mind, however, that prose statements are often the most communicative way of expressing facts about grammatical structure.

Position-class diagrams

The second method of representing linguistic knowledge we will discuss is called POSITION-CLASS DIAGRAMMING. This method is a variation on a general approach to morphological structure that is called the ITEM AND ARRANGEMENT model (Hockett 1958). It can be very useful for describing languages that tend to have lots of morphemes per word, especially if the morphemes tend to fall into well-defined sets, or PARADIGMS. While there are several inadequacies to position-class diagramming, some of which will be discussed at the end of this section, every field linguist needs to be familiar with this method, at least as a beginning point for a full morphosyntactic analysis of a language.

In languages that express many of their conceptual categories morphologically, there are typically several "layers" of prefixes and suffixes, as described above. For example, here are some data from Sierra Nahuatl (from Merrifield *et al.*, 1987). Four of the free translations have been omitted from these data, just to make it a little more interesting:

(23) a. nimicita   'I see you.'
     b. nikita   'I see him.'
     c. tikmaka   'You give it to him.'
     d. tinečita   'You see me.'
     e. nannečmaka   'You (pl) give it to me.'
     f. tikonmaka   'You give it to him, sir.'
     g. tikonitatihcinoh   'You see him, most honored sir.'
     h. tikonmakatihcinohtikah 'You give it to him, most very honored sir.'
     i. tinečonita   'You see me'
     j. tinečonmakatihcinoh   'You give it to me, most honored sir.'
     k. nannečonmakatikah   'You (pl) give it to me, honored sirs.'
     l. nannečonitatihcinohtikah
     m. tinečonitatikah
     n. nannečonmakatihcinoh

The process of constructing a position-class diagram for data such as these will be given below in step-by-step fashion, though the steps are more a descriptive tool than a "program" for analyzing morphology. As you will discover if you ever have the privilege of doing fieldwork on a real language, morphosyntactic analysis is an art that is trying to be a science. As linguists, we want to be as rigorous and scientific as possible in our research and presentation of findings. However, since our subject matter involves human behavior, there will always be indeterminate cases, educated guesses, and subjective interpretations. So there is no absolute "procedure" that will lead to one correct analysis of a range of linguistic facts. There are only better and worse analyses, and better and worse arguments for them.

Step 1: Isolate the roots. As we look over the free translations of the Sierra Nahuatl data, we see that there seem to be two basic verbs involved: one meaning 'see' and another meaning 'give.' Since we expect similarity of meaning to correlate with similarity in form (see chapter 1, p. 3), we look down the left column to see what elements of form correlate with the meanings 'see' and 'give.' What do you notice? You should see that in the Nahuatl sentences the form *ita* consistently matches 'see' in the translation, while *maka* consistently matches 'give.' Therefore we hypothesize that *ita* and *maka* are the roots meaning 'see' and 'give' respectively. We list and gloss these roots in a position-class diagram as follows:

ROOT	
ita	'see'
maka	'give'

I must emphasize that this is a hypothesis. Your initial impressions need to be held lightly, until they are confirmed by further data. I suggest that everyone use pencil when approaching these kinds of problems.

Step 2: Estimate the affix positions. Since in the Nahuatl examples there is material to the left and the right of these roots, we suspect there are prefixes and suffixes. So we want to leave room for these elements:

P3	P2	P1	ROOT		S1	S2	S3
			ita	'see'			
			maka	'give'			

Notice that the affix positions are numbered outward from the root. This diagram leaves room for three prefix positions (P1, P2, P3) and three suffix positions (S1, S2, S3). Again, this is only an estimate. At this stage you want to allow for what you consider to be the maximum number of affixes, within reason. In this case we have guessed the same number of prefixes as suffixes, but this need not be the case. Furthermore, in step 1 you may have noticed that the roots come at the beginning or the end of the structure you are analyzing. You would need no positions for affixes that obviously don't occur.

Step 3: Begin to analyze prefixes. Since in this problem the first examples seem to contain just prefixes, we will start by trying to analyze the prefixes. Remember the basic principle that similarity in form usually expresses similarity in meaning. In examples 23a and b, we see that the formal variation between *nimic-* and *nik-* correlates with a meaning variation between 'I > you' ('I' acting on 'you') and 'I > him' ('I' acting on 'him'). Within these two possibilities, we see a common element, *ni-*, and variation between *mic-* and *k-*. Since the common element of meaning is 'I,' and the variation is between 'you (object)' and 'him,' we suspect that there are two prefix positions, with *ni-* coming earlier, and *mic-* and *k-* following. Since these kinds of prefixes are likely to be grammatical morphemes, we will gloss them according to reasonable guesses as to their conceptual categories:

P3	P2	P1	ROOT		S1	S2	S3
	ni- 1SG.SUBJ	mic- 2SG.OBJ	ita	'see'			
		k- 3SG.OBJ	maka	'give'			

The next three examples help us fill out this chart a little more, as follows:

P3	P2	P1	ROOT	S1	S2	S3
ni- 1SG.SUBJ ti- 2SG.SUBJ nan- 2PL.SUBJ	mic- 2SG.OBJ k- 3SG.OBJ nеč- 1SG.OBJ		ita 'see' maka 'give'			

When we get to example 23f, however, we encounter a difficulty. We notice that there is a form *on-* which seems to come in between the root and the prefixes we have posited. We notice that this *on-* correlates with the meaning 'sir.' Therefore, we need to move our two prefix positions to the left, and add *on-* in the P1 position (this is why I suggest you use pencil). We guess that a good grammatical gloss for this *on-* might be 'the speaker expressing respect for the hearer.' Therefore we gloss it with the abbreviation 'RESP':

[handwritten margin note: Is there a way that this should all be ordered?]

P3	P2	P1	ROOT	S1	S2	S3
ni- 1SG.SUBJ ti- 2SG.SUBJ nan- 2PL.SUBJ	mic- 2SG.OBJ k- 3SG.OBJ nеč- 1SG.OBJ	on- RESP	ita 'see' maka 'give'			

This analysis seems to take care of all of the prefix combinations in the data set. At this point, we can calculate the probable free translation for example 23i. I will let you figure out what that should be.

Step 4: Analyze the suffixes. This step will be very similar to the previous one. Comparing 23g and h, we see that the difference in the forms of the suffixes is related to the difference between 'most honored sir,' and 'most very honored sir.' Since there is some commonality in form (*tihcinoh*) to both of these examples, we suspect that there are two suffix positions. The two suffixes in question may be particularly difficult to gloss, but we can make a stab at it, as follows:

P3	P2	P1	ROOT	S1	S2	S3
ni- 1SG.SUBJ ti- 2SG.SUBJ nan- 2PL.SUBJ	mic- 2SG.OBJ k- 3SG.OBJ nеč- 1SG.OBJ	on- RESP	ita 'see' maka 'give'	-tihcinoh HONOR1	-tikah HONOR2	

The glosses 'HONOR1' and 'HONOR2' are impressionistic guesses as to the meanings of these suffixes. The idea is that *-tihcinoh* probably expresses a first degree of honorific status, while *-tikah* expresses the second, higher, degree. At this point these are just educated guesses, so the actual glosses chosen are not terribly significant. The point is to notice what the affixes are, and how they are related to one another in the verb word.

Inspection of the rest of the data reveals that the hypothesis that there are two suffix positions, instantiated by *-tihcinoh* in position S1 and *-tikah* in position S2, holds true. At this point, you can fill in probable free translations for examples 231 through n.

Step 5: Label the columns. Positions in complex morphological structures tend to be associated with particular sets of conceptual categories. For example, verbs in a highly morphological language might have one position for tense, another position for **ASPECT**, another for **PERSON** and **NUMBER** of the **SUBJECT**, etc. As we inspect the diagram given above, we notice that all the forms in the P3 position express the person and number of the subject. All the forms in the P2 position express the person of the object. In this example, there is only one form in each of the other affix positions, so it is difficult to infer a meaning category for the whole column. Nevertheless, it does not hurt, at this point, to hazard a guess. Here is one possible way of completing our sample position class diagram:

Subject	Object	Respect	ROOT		Honor1	Honor2
ni- 1SG	mic- 2SG	on-	ita	'see'	-tihcinoh	-tikah
ti- 2SG	k- 3SG		maka	'give'		
nan- 2PL	neč- 1SG					

Further data may cause us to revise this hypothesis, but just based on the data given in the problem set this seems to be a reasonable analysis. There are many aspects of the morphology of a language that this kind of diagram simply does not capture. For instance, even in this small data set, it seems to be the case that the honorific suffixes always co-occur with the 'respect' prefix. More data would be needed to see if this is always the case, or just an incidental property of the examples chosen. There often are these kinds of long-range "dependencies" between elements (the presence of one element "depends" on the presence of another one somewhere else in the structure). There are ways of annotating position-class diagrams to show this, but it can get rather messy.

Other problems for position-class diagrams are situations where morphemes can occur in more than one place in a structure, or, as we will see in the following chapter, morphemes that are pronounced differently depending on the context. Position-class diagrams are not very useful for describing non-concatenative morphology, autosegmental phonology, stem modification, reduplication, or compounding. In spite of these problems, a position-class diagram is a good start on the road to building a solid and insightful morphosyntactic description of a language, especially if the language uses lots of prefixes and suffixes, which are, after all, the most common kinds of morphological processes found in the world's languages.

Process rules

While position-class diagrams are the mainstay of basic morphological analysis, their shortcomings have led many linguists to devise a number of alternative schemes for representing morphological structures. Most of these additional schemes can be described as **PROCESS RULES**. A process rule is a representation that describes relationships among the various shapes of words as though they were *changes* that the words undergo. This general approach to morphological structure has been described as the **ITEM AND PROCESS MODEL** (Hockett 1958). Process rules were hinted at in chapter 1. For example, the structure of regular nouns in English can easily be represented in a simple position-class diagram as follows:

Root	Number
cat	∅ SG
dog	-s PL
mat	
tree	
. . .	

In a process rule, the formation of the plural (and perhaps the singular as well) would be treated as a "process" that changes a root into the appropriate **INFLECTED** form. For example, one could say:

(24)   Singular noun + -s = Plural noun

The insight behind this particular type of rule is that, since some forms are "simpler" than others, it makes sense to think of the more complex forms as being based on the simpler ones. Forms "start out" simple, and "end up" complex.

Though there are many different ways to formulate process rules, the ways we will discuss in this text all involve three parts: the conceptual category that is expressed, a structural description of the form *before* the process occurs, and a description of what the form changes into *after* the process occurs. These can be abbreviated as:

CC = Conceptual Category
SD = **STRUCTURAL DESCRIPTION** (starting form)
SC = **STRUCTURAL CHANGE** (ending form)

The rules themselves will always have the following pattern:

(25)   CC: SD → SC

For example, the regular pattern for plural formation of English nouns may be expressed as:

(26)   Plural: N → N + -*s*

One way this formula may be read would be: "To express plurality, start with a noun, and end with that same noun plus an -*s* suffix."

How would one employ process rules to describe complex data such as the Sierra Nahuatl verbs given above? Well, each conceptual category would require its own rule. Here is a possible subset of process rules for the Sierra Nahuatl data:

(27)	CC:		SD:	SC:
a.	Respect:		Verb	→ on- + Verb
b.	2sg object marking:		Verb	→ mic- + Verb
c.	3sg object marking:		Verb	→ ke- + Verb
d.	1sg object marking:		Verb	→ neč- + Verb
e.	1sg subject marking:		Verb	→ ni- + Verb
	etc.			

There are many ways of representing morphological process rules. For example, Haspelmath (2002:47–51) provides a very nice system which he terms the "word-based model." The formulas in Haspelmath's system contain all the elements of process rules and can be very helpful in describing and understanding the morphological patterns of a language that has only a few morphemes per word. However, when analyzing complex data, like Sierra Nahuatl above, that involve affix "positions" in word structure, some form of a position-class diagram (or "morpheme-based model") may be more useful.

Process rules, of the sort illustrated above, can be very useful for describing non-concatenative morphology. For example; here are some data from Arabic (these data have been slightly regularized but are true to the general facts of most varieties of Arabic):

(28)		Root:	slm		Root:	ktb
	a.	muslim	'person of peace'	g.	muktib	'literate person/scribe'
	b.	salima	'he was safe'	h.	katiba	'he was reading'
	c.	ʔislaamun	'Islam'	i.	ʔiktaabun	'literature'
	d.	salaamun	'peace'	j.	kataabun	'book'
	e.	saalimun	'safe'	k.	kaatibun	'writing'
	f.	salama	'he was calm'	l.	kataba	'he wrote'

The first step in analyzing these data is to determine the conceptual category, as discussed earlier in this chapter. What conceptual category do you think is expressed by examples 28a and g? Can you come up with a good description of the meaning expressed by the particular morphological pattern displayed by these two examples? Looking at the English translations, you may guess that the Arabic words are probably nouns, and you know that they both describe people. If the root *slm* means something like 'peace,' and *ktb* means something like 'read,' then perhaps the pattern can be thought of as expressing the idea of 'someone who is/does the concept described by the root.' What is a good name for such a function? As with the Yup'ik examples discussed earlier, we may want to call this "nominalization," and since this nominalization refers to people, we may want to call it "person nominalization." This is only one possible label for this particular conceptual category.

These data illustrate six conceptual categories as expressed in two distinct roots. Since Arabic is a typical Semitic language, it exhibits non-concatenative morphology. The problem we will now address is how to represent such interesting morphological patterns in terms of a process rule. So far we have a name for the first conceptual category. Now we need a Structural Description and a Structural Change:

(29)   CC   SD   SC
              Person nominalization: ?   →   ?

If we think of this process as "starting out" with the roots *slm* and *ktb*, and ending up with the inflected forms, we can describe the data in two separate statements as follows:

(30)   CC   SD   SC
    a.   Person nominalization: slm   →   muslim
    b.   Person nominalization: ktb   →   muktib

These provisional statements are the first step in formulating rules; however, we cannot really call them "rules" yet. They simply restate the data in terms of a process, but they don't capture the fact that there is really only one process involved – one pattern that applies consistently to both roots (and many more that are not in this data set). Since part of what an Arabic speaker must unconsciously "know" is that this pattern affects different roots in the same way, we want to generalize our representation of this knowledge so that one statement covers all relevant forms. If we can do this, our linguistic description will be consistent with the unconscious knowledge of Arabic speakers.

We can see that both 28a and g begin with a prefix *mu-*, followed by the first consonant of the root, then the second consonant of the root, then an *i* vowel, and finally the last consonant of the root. We can use the symbol C to represent any consonant, and number them C_1, C_2, and C_3 in order to represent the order in which they occur in the root. Then we can simply substitute these symbols for the consonants that enter into the pattern:

(31)   CC   SD   SC
              Person nominalization: $C_1C_2C_3$ → $muC_1C_2iC_3$

Since C represents any consonant, this rule applies to both *slm* and *ktb*. The subscripted numbers link the consonants in the output (the SC) with the consonants in the input (the SD), no matter what the actual consonant is. If C_1 is an *s* in the SD, C_1 will be an *s* in the SC, etc. If there were no subscripts, there would be no way to distinguish the consonants from one another (since C is an abstract symbol, and not a particular sound).

How would the other patterns illustrated in 28 be formulated using this system? I'm sure you can figure that out by now! Here is one more, just for fun. Examples 28b and h express a conceptual category that may be interpreted as "past continuous." Why would it not be sufficient to call this conceptual category simply "past tense"? The reason is that there is another category, represented in 28f and l, that also expresses events in the past. So we know there are at least two past "tenses." In order to distinguish these two, the term "past continuous" for the category illustrated in 28b and h, and perhaps "simple past" for the category represented in 28f and l, seem like reasonable labels. So if we use the term "past continuous" for the conceptual category illustrated in 28b and h, and apply the same reasoning as we did above to describe the morphological manifestation of this category, we would come up with the following process rule:

(32)   CC   SD   SC
          Past continuous: $C_1C_2C_3$ $\rightarrow$ $C_1aC_2iC_3a$

This rule describes both of the following actual changes:

(33)   s l m $\rightarrow$ s a l i m a
            k t b $\rightarrow$ k a t i b a

In addition to non-concatenative morphology, such as found in Semitic languages, process rules of this sort are particularly useful for expressing other kinds of morphological patterns, in particular, morphological patterns that involve reordering, or **METATHESIS**, of sounds in a word, and reduplication (see above).

As far as we know, no language uses metathesis alone to express conceptual categories. This is why it is not one of the "big ten." However, metathesis does occasionally accompany one of the other processes, such as prefixation or suffixation. For example, consider the following data from Yagua:

(34) a.   rakyáraay   'I go astray.'
     b.   hikyáraay   'You go astray.'
     c.   sakáray   'He/she goes astray.'
     d.   naakyáraay   'We go astray.'
     e.   naadakáraay   'They 2 go astray.'
     f.   rikyáraay   'They go astray.'

As you inspect these data, you notice that in examples 34a, b, d, and f, there is a *y* sound that appears *after* the first consonant of the root. The fact that this *y* does not appear in all the **INFLECTIONS** suggests that it is not part of the root, but part of the prefix. In fact, this is completely regular in the language, and it is quite easy to show that the prefixes are the following:

(35) ·   a. ray-   1SG   d. naay-   1PL
           b. hiy-   2SG   e. naada-   2DL
           c. sa-   3SG   f. riy-   3PL

So in order for Yagua speakers to inflect their verbs, they must "know," subconsciously of course, that if the prefix ends in a *y*, you have to switch the order of this *y* with the first consonant of the root. It turns out that this is a perfectly regular pattern in the language, so we don't need to restrict it to any particular conceptual category (see chapter 3 on the difference between phonological rules and morphophonemic rules). We can simply state it as a rule with no restrictions:

(36) $yC \rightarrow Cy$

This rule simply says that whenever a *y* occurs before any consonant, the *y* and the consonant switch places. In this case, we do not need to use a subscripted number after the C, since there is no other unspecified consonant (C) in the rule that may cause confusion.

Finally, process rules can be very useful for representing stem modification and reduplication. For example, consider the following data from Sierra Nahuatl (Elson and Pickett 1988:51):

(37)   a. se   'one'   f. sehse   'ones/one by one'
        b. ome   'two'   g. ohome   'twos/two by two'
        c. eyi   'three'   h. eheyi   'threes/three by three'
        d. makwil   'five'   i. mahmakwil   'fives/five by five'
        e. čikasen   'six'   j. _____ 'sixes/six by six'

For the conceptual category (call it "multiplicative") represented by the words in the right-hand column, the initial **SYLLABLE** (consonant plus vowel, or just a vowel) of the root is reduplicated and followed by an *h* sound. This can be nicely represented with the following process rule:

(38)   CC   SD   SC
       Multiplicative: $(C_1)V_1X$ $\rightarrow$ $(C_1)V_1h(C_1)V_1X$

In this formula, the Consonant is placed in parentheses to indicate that it may or may not be present. This notation allows this rule to apply both to consonant-initial stems (examples 37a, d, and e), and vowel-initial stems (examples 37b and c). The V is a cover symbol that stands for any Vowel. The X is a cover symbol that stands for anything, including silence at the end of a word. This notation allows the rule to apply to stems of any length – it essentially says that whatever comes after the first syllable of the root (including silence, as in 37a) does not affect the rule at all.

While this formula may appear quite complex, it is absolutely explicit, and accurately captures something that Sierra Nahuatl speakers must unconsciously "know" about their language. Using this rule, I'm sure you can infer the form of the word meaning 'sixes/six by six' (37j). If you can, then you have assimilated and applied part of the knowledge that every Sierra Nahuatl child has concerning the expression of numbers in this language.

Conceptual outline of chapter 2

I.   Conceptual categories:

      • A conceptual category exists when there is an expectation of pat-
        terned behavior – a consistent relationship between variation in form
        and variation in function.
      • Conceptual category labels (or "glosses") are interpretations
        designed to help readers of a grammatical description understand

and remember the functions of particular grammatical constructions or units such as words, roots, and affixes.

II.   Morphological processes. There are ten major morphological processes:
- Prefixation
- Suffixation
- Infixation
- Circumfixation
- Stem modification
- Autosegmental variation
- Reduplication
- Non-concatenative morphology
- Subtractive morphology
- Compounding

III. Three methods for representing morphological processes and conceptual categories include:
- Prose
- Position-class diagrams
- Process rules

Exercise 2.1: Swahili of Eastern Congo

Ronnie Sim

There are many varieties of Swahili spoken throughout Eastern and Southern Africa. The variety represented in this problem is spoken hundreds of miles inland, and is quite different from that which is spoken near the coast (as represented in exercise 1.5):

1.	ninasema	'I speak'
2.	wunasema	'you speak'
3.	anasema	'he speaks'
4.	wanasema	'they speak'
5.	ninaona	'I see'
6.	niliona	'I saw'
7.	ninawaona	'I see them'
8.	niliwuona	'I saw you'
9.	ananiona	'he sees me'
10.	wutakaniona	'you will see me'
11.	—	'he saw them'
12.	—	'I will see you'
13.	—	'He saw me.'

A.   Fill in the probable Swahili for examples 11–13.

B.   Provide a position-class diagram of the Swahili verb as represented in these data.

Exercise 2.2: Chickasaw

Tom Payne, with thanks to Pam Munro and Catherine Willmond

Chickasaw is a Native American language of the Muskogean language family. Currently, there are about 3,000 fluent speakers of Chickasaw, most of whom live in Oklahoma. However, the homeland of the Chickasaw people at the time of the arrival of Europeans in North America was in what is now Alabama and Mississippi (a tilde over a vowel, like this, ã, indicates nasalization of the vowel).

1. Ofi'at kowi'ã lhiyohli.   'The dog chases the cat.'
2. Kowi'at ofi'ã lhiyohli.   'The cat chases the dog.'
3. Ofi'at shoha.   'The dog stinks.'
4. Ihooat hattakã shooli.   'The woman hugs the man.'
5. Lhiyohlili.   'I chase her/him.'
6. Salhiyohli.   'She/he chases me.'
7. Hilhali.   'I dance.'

A.   Translate the following into Chickasaw:

8. The man hugs the woman.
9. The cat stinks.
10. I hug her/him.
11. The woman dances.

B.   Translate the following into English:

12. Ihooat sashooli.
13. Ofi'at hilha.
14. Kowi'ã lhiyohlili.

C.   Provide a position-class diagram of nouns in Chickasaw as represented in these data.

D.   Provide a position-class diagram of verbs in Chickasaw as represented in these data.

Exercise 2.3: Katu

Adapted from Merrifield et al. 1987, problem #19

A.   Where is Katu spoken?

1. gap	'to cut'	5. ganap	'scissors'
2. juut	'to rub'	6. januut	'cloth'
3. panh	'to shoot'	7. pananh	'crossbow'
4. piih	'to sweep'	8. paniih	'broom'

B.   What morphological process is illustrated in these data?

C.   Describe the conceptual category that distinguishes the words in the second column from the corresponding words in the first column.

Exercise 2.4: English

Tom Payne

The English words in the first column are stressed (or accented) on the second syllable, while those in the second column are stressed on the first. Since these pairs of words are spelled the same, we have added accent marks to indicate stress:

1. permít   pérmit
2. recórd   récord
3. convért   cónvert
4. rejéct   réject
5. prodúce   próduce

A.   Describe the difference in meaning that is expressed by this stress shift.

B.   How regular is this rule? Can you think of any additional pairs that follow the same pattern?

Exercise 2.5: Terêna

Adapted from Merrifield et al. 1987, problem #16

A.   Where is Terêna spoken?

B.   How many speakers are there?
     Note: The tilde over certain vowels indicates nasalization.

1. ēmõ?ū   'my word'   6. yowoku   'your house'
2. ãyõ   'my brother'   7. emo?u   'his word'
3. õwōkū   'my house'   8. ayo   'his brother'
4. yemo?u   'your word'   9. owoku   'his house'
5. yayo   'your brother'

(handwritten margin notes: emo?u 'word' / ayo 'brother' / owoku 'house' / y 'his' / ~ ~~ my / root 'his')

C.   Assuming the pattern illustrated in these data is regular, fill in the Terêna forms for 'your house' and 'his house.'

D.   List and gloss all the morphemes in these data. Which morphological process is represented by the morpheme meaning 'my'?

Exercise 2.6: Agta

Adapted from Healey (1960)

The following list of words is from the Agta language of the Central Cagayan Valley in the Northern island of Luzon, in the Philippines. There are now only about 600 speakers of this variety of Agta, although there are perhaps 10,000 people in the Philippines who speak other varieties also known as Agta. All the Agta languages are now seriously endangered.

1. wer	'creek'	7. bag	'loincloth'
2. balabahuy	'little pig'	8. walawer	'little creek'
3. talobag	'beetle'	9. balabag	'little loincloth'
4. bakbakat	'granny'	10. takki	'leg'
5. palapirak	'little money'	11. labang	'patch'
6. bahuy	'pig'		

A.   Now, assuming the pattern illustrated above is regular, translate the following words into Agta:

12. 'little leg'
13. 'money'
14. 'little beetle' (this is the word for 'lady bug')
15. 'little patch'

B.   What is the morphological process and the conceptual category that is evident in these data?

Exercise 2.7: Samoan

O'Grady et al. 2001

Note: In this exercise the symbol ? represents a glottal plosive, which is an important consonant in Samoan.

1. mate	'he dies'	8. mamate	'they die'
2. nofo	'he stays'	9. nonofo	'they stay'
3. galue	'he works'	10. galulue	'they work'
4. tanu	'he buries'	11. tatanu	'they bury'
5. alofa	'he loves'	12. alolofa	'they love'
6. ta?oto	'he lies'	13. ta?o?oto	'they lie'
7. atama?i	'he is intelligent'	14. atamama?i	'they are intelligent'

A.   What morphological process is illustrated in these data?
B.   Describe the rule as explicitly as you can.
C.   If 'he is strong' is *malosi*, how would you say 'they are strong' in Samoan?   *mamalosi*

Exercise 2.8: Modern Hebrew

Adapted from Merrifield et al. 1987, problem #20

1. nahal	'inherit'	6. hinhil	'bequeath'
2. qara?	'read'	7. hiqri?	'make read'
3. taraf	'hire'	8. hitrif	'feed' ?
4. raqad	'dance'	9. —	
5. ʃa?al	'borrow'	10. hiʃ?il	'lend'

A.   Write an explicit rule that will derive the words in the right-hand column from the words in the left-hand column.

B.   What kind of morphological process is this?
C.   Apply your rule to the form in 4, to fill in 9. What do you think this
means?

Exercise 2.9: Arabic

Adapted from Merrifield et al. 1987, problem #21

1. laqima	'gobble'	7. ʔalqama	'make gobble'
2. ʃariba	'drink'	8. ʔaʃraba	'make drink'
3. laʕiqa	'lick'	9. ʔalʕaqa	'make lick'
4. labisa	'wear'	10. ʔalbasa	'dress (someone)'
5. xasira	'lose'	11. ʔaxsara	'make lose'
6. samiʕa	'hear'	12. —	—

A.   Write an explicit rule that will derive the words in the right-hand
column from the words in the left-hand column.
B.   Which morphological process is this?
C.   Apply your rule to the form in 6, to fill in 12. What do you think
12 means?

Exercise 2.10: English compounds

Adapted from Finnegan (1994:110)
Find a passage of at least 500 consecutive words in an English language
newsweekly, such as *Time* or *Newsweek*. Make a list of all the compound nouns
and verbs (if any) in the passage.

A.   Identify the word class of each part of each compound.
Example: 'pickpocket' pick = verb, + pocket = noun.
B.   Choose five of the compounds, and explain the relationship between
the meaning of the elements and the meaning of the compound.

Example: Pick+pocket. A pickpocket is a person who picks pockets. The noun
'pocket' is the direct object of the verb 'pick' when used in this sense.

Exercise 2.11: 'Ebembe

Myra Adamson and Tom Payne

1. namona   'I see.'
2. 'umona   'You see.'

3.	'utoca	'You ask.'
4.	'untoca	'You ask me.'
5.	'umtoca	'You ask him/her.'
6.	na'waca	'I believe.'
7.	na'u'waca	'I believe you.'
8.	namtoca	'I ask him/her.'
9.	namtocile	'I asked him/her.'
10.	na'umona	— I see you
11.	na'umonile	'I saw you.'
12.	na'u'wacile	'I believed you.'
13.	twamtoca	'We ask him/her.'
14.	twamtocile	'We asked him/her.'
15.	na'utoca	'I ask you.'
16.	na'utocila	'I ask for you.'
17.	na'utocilile	'I asked for you.'
18.	twamonana	'We see each other.'
19.	'umonanile	'You saw each other.'
20.	twamonanile	'We saw each other.'
21.	twatocanile	'We asked each other.'
22.	na'u'wacilile	'I believed for you.'
23.	'ukyum'waca	'You always believe him/her.'
24.	akyuntoca	'He/she always asks me.'
25.	'ukyummona	'You always see him/her.'
26.	nakyu'umonile	'I always saw you.'
27.	twakyu'umonile	'We always saw you.'
28.	twakyumonana	'We always see each other.'
29.	twakyumonanile	'We always saw each other.'

A.   Fill in all of the missing translations, either English or 'Ebembe.

B.   Make a position-class diagram of the 'Ebembe verb. Include every morpheme represented in these data, along with its gloss.

Exercise 2.12: Palantla Chinantec

Adapted from Merrifield et al. 1987, problem #44

A.   Where is Palantla Chinantec spoken?

B.   How many speakers are there?

The Chinantecan languages are among the most highly 'tonal' languages on earth. In fact, there are so many distinct tones, that the writing system employs small raised numbers to indicate the tones on most syllables. This makes the writing system look very difficult, but hundreds of Chinantec children and adults have learned to read very well using this system.

1. ʔlia ʔ^{12}hni	'I speak.'		7. ʔlia ʔ^{12}za	'He/she speaks.'
2. ʔo^{12}hni	'I cry.'		8. ʔo^{12}za	'He/she cries.'
3. hú ʔ^{2}hni	'I cough.'		9. hú ʔ^{2}za	'He/she coughs.'
4. ney^{12}hni	'I go.'		10. zaw^{12}za	'He/she goes.'
5. gi ʔ^{12}hni	'I drink.'		11. ʔɨ ʔ^{2}za	'He/she drinks.'
6. hma ʔ^{12}hni	'I grab.'		12. cą ʔ^{12}za	'He/she grabs.'

C.   List and gloss all the morphemes in these data.

D.   Which process or processes are evident in examples 10, 11, and 12?

Exercise 2.13 Orkhono-Yeniseyan

Svetlana Burlak

The following sentences are from the Orkhono-Yeniseyan language, an ancient language of Western Asia. Scrolls containing passages in this language were found near the confluence of the Orkhon and Yenisey rivers.

1. Oghuling baliqigh alti.   'Your son conquered the city.'
2. Baz oghuligh yangilti.   'The vassal betrayed the son.'
3. Siz baliqimizin buzdingiz.   'You (pl) destroyed our city.'
4. Qaghanimiz oghulingin yangilti.   'Our king betrayed your (sg) son.'
5. Oghulim barqingin buzdi.   'My son destroyed your (sg) house.'
6. Siz qaghanigh yangiltingiz.   'You (pl) betrayed the king.'
7. Biz baliqigh altimiz.   'We conquered the city.'
8. Bazim qaghanimizin yangilti.   'My vassal betrayed our king.'

A.   List all the morphemes in these data, along with their English glosses. There may be more than one adequate way of dividing morphemes. Whichever way you choose, be sure it is consistent.

B.   Translate the following into English (Yes, you can figure out what *men* means!):

9. Qaghan baliqigh alti
10. Men barqigh buzdim.

C.   Translate into the Orkhono-Yeniseyan language:

11. The son conquered your city.
12. The king betrayed the vassal.
13. Your vassal destroyed my house.

Notes

1. Recent work in Cognitive Linguistics (e.g., Lakoff 1987) has shown that much of human categorization, thought, and communication involves images, or "scenes." See chapter 9, p. 241 for a brief discussion of this perspective.
2. Thanks to Mike Matloff for drawing my attention to this infix.

3. It is questionable whether the root of this word is -*stabl* or *establ*-. The fact that there are forms in English without the *e*- (*stable, stabilize*, etc.) is one piece of evidence that the *e*- is some kind of prefix, even if it has no discernible meaning in modern English. The fact is that words based on this root have come into English at different points in its history, from different historical sources, so whether one treats the *e*- as a prefix or not is at some level an historical decision. For our purposes (illustrating the differences among prefixing, suffixing, and infixing), it will suffice to treat *e*- as a prefix in this discussion.

4. We gloss the *a*- prefix as 'person neutral' (NEU) because it replaces prefixes that express the person of the subject and/or object in most verb forms. This prefix occurs in a variety of dependent and **IRREALIS MODE** clauses (see chapter 10).

3 Morphophonemics

Sometimes a morpheme has more than one shape, depending on the **ENVIRON-MENT** in which it occurs. The shape of a morpheme may be affected by nearby sounds, by the kind of stem it is attached to, or by other conditioning factors. The systematically distinct shapes of a morpheme are called its **ALLOMORPHS**. When a morpheme changes its shape in response to the sounds that surround it in a particular context, linguists often call the variation **MORPHOPHONEMICS** (or **MORPHOPHONOLOGY**), and the patterns that describe the appearance of the allomorphs **MORPHOPHONEMIC RULES** (or **MORPHOPHONOLOGICAL RULES**). Morphophonemic rules are very different from the morphological rules described in chapters 1 and 2, and should always be kept quite distinct conceptually. Morphophonemic rules do not express conceptual categories. Rather, they simply specify the pronunciations (the "shapes") of morphemes in context, once a morphological rule has already applied.

Things are not always as they appear . . .

Morphophonemics can also be thought of as the interface between **PHONOLOGY** and morphology. **PHONOLOGICAL PATTERNS** (or "rules") specify the pronunciation of *sounds* in particular environments. They only make reference to sequences of sounds, and not to whether those sequences involve particular morphemes or not. Morphophonemic patterns in most cases are just phonological patterns that come into play when morphemes come together in words. Occasionally, however, there are morphophonemic patterns that *only* apply when certain morphemes come together. These are morphophonemic patterns that are not, strictly speaking, phonological patterns. We will see examples of morphophonemic patterns that are phonological, and some that are strictly morphophonemic in the following pages. Our aim in this chapter is to present enough background in morphophonemics for you to understand and solve morphology problems that involve allomorphs. You will learn much more about phonological and morphophonemic patterns in phonology courses.

One metaphor that linguists sometimes use to describe the process of communication is that utterances "start out" in the mind as concepts – ideas to be communicated. These concepts (including conceptual categories, as described in chapter 2) are represented by "underlying"

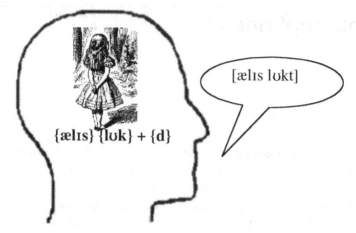

{ælɪs} {lʊk} + {d}

[ælɪs lʊkt]

Figure 3.1 *"Alice looked"*

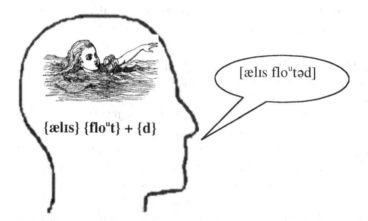

{ælɪs} {floᵘt} + {d}

[ælɪs floᵘtəd]

Figure 3.2 *"Alice floated"*

symbolic units, usually consisting of idealized sequences of sounds. In the process of speaking, these idealized sequences may change their shapes due to factors not at all related to meaning.[1]

Figures 3.1 through 3.3 illustrate this metaphor. The idea to be communicated is conceptualized (pictured) in the speaker's mind. Then a message is formulated using the morphemes and grammatical rules of a language that the speaker and hearer share. Underlying forms of morphemes are sometimes represented in {curly brackets} when it is important to distinguish them from actual pronunciations. In figure 3.1, the morphemes that are needed to express the speaker's thought mean 'Alice,' 'look,' and PAST TENSE. These symbols exist as idealized forms in the mind of the speaker. But something happens to them on the way to the mouth. Can you see what happens?

In figure 3.2, a different verb is illustrated. In this example, we see that the idealized form of the morpheme meaning PAST TENSE is the same as in

Figure 3.3 *"Alice played"*

figure 3.1 – namely {d}. However, the way it is pronounced in the context of the verb *float* is different. In this case a schwa vowel, [ə], appears between the root and the suffix.

Finally, figure 3.3 illustrates one more possible pronunciation of the PAST-TENSE morpheme. After the verb *play*, the surface form seems to be the same as the "underlying" form.

Now, it could be the case that this variation in the pronunciation of the PAST-TENSE morpheme is random. Certainly if we just listen to one person say three things, we cannot make very grand generalizations about the pronunciation patterns of the speaker's language. Random variation clearly does exist in every language. Therefore, before we make any claims about how this language works, we would want to listen to several speakers pronouncing these expressions, as well as many others. However, the pattern illustrated here does turn out to be very regular in English, and so will suffice for our illustration.

Normally, of course, the way a linguist analyzes morphophonemics is in the opposite direction from what is illustrated in figures 3.1 through 3.3. All we have available to us are the words as they are pronounced and a general sense of their meanings. Our analytic task is to "work backwards" to infer the underlying forms and rules that give rise to the actual pronunciations. This is the job of morphophonemics.

There are several reasons why a morpheme may vary in shape depending on its context. First of all, it may **ASSIMILATE**, i.e., become more similar to surrounding sounds. This is illustrated in figure 3.1 above. The past-tense morpheme {-d} becomes voiceless, [t], after the voiceless sound [k] in the root. In other words, the past-tense morpheme assimilates to the [k] in voicing. Second, it may preserve the language's general word or **SYLLABLE STRUCTURE**. This is illustrated in figure 3.2. English word structure does not permit a sequence of [td] at the end of a word. Another way of saying this is that it would be "hard

to pronounce" a word that ended in [td], for example *floatd* [floᵘtd]. Therefore, when the morphology of English brings a [t] and a [d] together at the end
of a word, a schwa vowel is automatically inserted in order to make the word
pronounceable.

Finally, the underlying form of a morpheme may **DISSIMILATE**, i.e., become
more different from surrounding sounds. Dissimilation is less common than
assimilation and structure preservation but does exist in many languages. We
will see examples of all these types of morphophonemic variation, and more,
in the following pages. The English examples presented in this section illustrate
assimilation and structure preservation.

By the way, the writing system of a language, if there is one, may or may not
be helpful in dealing with morphophonemics. For the moment, we are ignoring
traditional English spellings, basing our analysis only on pronunciation, as would
be the case if we were analyzing a language for the first time.

Now that we've described the concept of underlying forms, and how they may
be related to actual pronunciations by morphophonemic patterns, we'll take a
closer look at the example of regular plural nouns in English. This time we will
walk through the steps of morphophonemic analysis, starting with the surface
pronunciations and meanings.

Many nouns in English have plural forms that end in either [-s], [-z], or [-ɨz]
(see 1 below). Since these sounds are all very similar, and they express the same
conceptual category (PLURAL), we suspect we are dealing with allomorphs of one
morpheme. One notation for representing allomorphs, or suspected allomorphs, is
to place them between vertical bars, like this: |-s|, |-z|, and |-ɨz|. Sometimes double
vertical bars are used, like this: ||-s||, ||-z||, and ||-ɨz||. This double-bar notation
may be particularly useful if you are completing your analysis (or homework
assignment) by hand. This is because handwritten single vertical bars can easily
be confused with slashes indicating phonemic transcription.

As we begin to collect examples of English plural nouns, we notice that the
plural morpheme has different forms in different contexts. Consider the following
English words:

(1)
'cats'	kæt -s	'dogs'	dɔg -z	'bushes'	bʊʃ -ɨz
'socks'	sɔk -s	'tabs'	tæb -z	'boxes'	bɔks -ɨz
'tops'	tɔp -s	'lads'	læd -z	'cheeses'	ʧiz -ɨz
'laughs'	læf -s	'hives'	haⁱv -z	'watches'	waʧ -ɨz
'fifths'	fɪfθ -s	'beans'	bin -z	'wedges'	wɛʤ -ɨz
'bows'	boᵘ -z	'lashes'	læʃ -ɨz		
'sofas'	soᵘfə -z	'kisses'	kɪs -ɨz		
'walls'	wal -z	'colleges'	kaləʤ -ɨz		
'lathes'	leⁱð -z	'wishes'	wɪʃ -ɨz		

The problems for morphophonemics are twofold:

- What are the conditions under which the various allomorphs appear?
- What is the "basic" or "underlying" form of each morpheme?

The first problem involves identifying the environments in which each allomorph occurs. This is where morphophonemic rules come in. These will be discussed in detail in the following section.

The second problem involves abstracting one common form that "underlies" or "gives rise to" the observed allomorphs. It is important from a theoretical, and sometimes a practical, point of view to determine what the basic form of a morpheme would be if there were no extraneous conditioning factors. This is because the basic (or "neutral" or "underlying") form of a morpheme is likely to be how speakers store the morpheme in memory. Therefore for purposes of writing-system development, as well as linguistic analysis, it is often better to represent morphemes in their basic forms, rather than in all the variations that may occur in actual speech.

In the following sections we will discuss analytical methods used by linguists to address these two major problems in morphophonemics.

Specifying the environments for morphophonemic rules

As mentioned above, morphophonemic rules are very different from the grammatical (including lexical, morphological, and syntactic) rules described in chapters 1 and 2. Those were patterns that express conceptual categories, e.g., "add -ed to form the past tense of a verb." Morphophonemic rules in some sense "come after" such grammatical rules. They specify the various pronunciations of morphemes as they are used in different contexts, or environments. In the example of the English plural morpheme, we are only talking about one grammatical rule, namely "add something to a noun in order to make the noun plural." The "something" is the idealized underlying form of the plural morpheme. Morphophonemic rules then specify the actual pronunciation of morphemes in various contexts.

Now that we have seen that the English plural morpheme has at least three allomorphs, we will try to specify the environments. After that we will discuss the process of identifying the best underlying form.

Specifying the environments of allomorphs involves two steps: (1) listing the environments, and (2) generalizing the environments. The first step can involve simply making prose observations, such as the following:

(2)   The PLURAL morpheme is pronounced -s after p, t, k, f, or θ.

However, there are good reasons (discussed below) for wanting to express patterns such as this in explicit formulas, rather than simple prose statements. Linguists often present morphophonemic rules in mathematically precise formulas using a process metaphor (again, please keep these distinct from the "process rules" described in chapter 2). According to this metaphor, a default, idealized "underlying" form appears (or "is realized") as the various allomorphs under explicitly defined conditions. Such formalizations have three main parts – the Underlying Form (UF), the Surface Form (SF), and the Environment (E), connected by an arrow and a forward slash, as follows:

(3)   UF → SF / E

This rule says that the UF appears as the SF in the Environment. Since the underlying form of a morpheme isn't always obvious, we will often use a question mark to represent it, at least until we have some reason for suggesting a particular underlying form. So a provisional rule for the appearance of the |-s| allomorph of the English PLURAL morpheme can be expressed as:

(4)   UF   SF   E
          PLURAL: {?} → |-s| /   p, t, k, f, θ —

This rule says exactly the same thing as 2 above – the underlying form of the PLURAL morpheme (whatever it is) appears as |-s| following /p, t, k, f/ or /θ/. The environment in this type of rule is a kind of generalized "template" that represents all the situations under which the SF occurs. The blank line (__) in the E represents the place where the change occurs. Since the |-s| allomorph follows these sounds in words, the blank follows the sounds in the formula.

The second step in specifying the environments for a group of allomorphs is to **GENERALIZE** the class of sounds that occur in the environment. The idea is to identify exactly the **NATURAL CLASS** that includes all the sounds that comprise the environment while excluding all the sounds that do not. The sounds *p, t, k, f*, and *θ* are all **VOICELESS** consonants, but not all voiceless consonants are in this set. Some voiceless consonants, namely *s, ʃ*, and *ʧ*, condition the |-ɨz| allomorph (see the examples in 1 above). Therefore we cannot simply say the environment for this rule consists of voiceless consonants. Only *certain* voiceless consonants qualify. Which ones?

If we limit ourselves to the **PLACE** and **MANNER OF ARTICULATION** features suggested by the International Phonetic Association (see end of preliminary matter), we can classify the sounds *p, t, k, f,* and *θ* as voiceless **PLOSIVES**, voiceless **DENTAL FRICATIVES**, and voiceless **LABIODENTAL FRICATIVES**.[2] This is a pretty complicated and diverse set of features, and linguists usually prefer to use another feature that does not appear on the IPA chart to distinguish this group of sounds. The feature is called **SIBILANT** and refers to the presence of a large amount of high-frequency friction that accompanies the pronunciation of certain fricative consonants. In English the sibilant consonants are *s, z, ʃ, ʒ, ʧ,* and *ʤ*. These are fricatives or **AFFRICATES** that are pronounced with air flowing in a small stream over the center of the tongue, causing a high-frequency fricative noise. These are distinct from the non-sibilant fricatives *θ, ð, f,* and *v*, which are pronounced with air flowing over a wider area, thus producing lower-frequency fricative noise.

All of this is just to say that the natural class of sounds that occur before the |-s| allomorph of the plural morpheme in English consists of all voiceless consonants that are *not* sibilants. This group can be formalized as follows:

(5)   C
          [voiceless]
          [non-sibilant]

This characterization identifies all and only consonants (signified by the capital C) that have the features of voiceless, and non-sibilant – in other words, exactly the set consisting of *p, t, k, f*, and *θ*.

With this generalization, we can revise our provisional statement as follows:

(6)   UF   SF   E
          {?} → |-s| /   C ___
                             [voiceless]
                             [non-sibilant]

Don't forget the blank line that indicates where the change takes place. The blank does not always come after the sounds that condition the change. In the pages that follow, and in the exercises at the end of this chapter, you will encounter rules in which the blank occurs in other places.

The rule in 6 describes the environment for the allomorph |-s| of the plural morpheme. What is the rule for the voiced allomorph, |-z|? Again, the first step is to just make a provisional statement, listing all of the sounds that may comprise the environment:

(7)   UF   SF   E
          {?} → |-z| /   g, b, d, v, n, o, ə, ɹ, l, ð —

The next step is to try to generalize the set of sounds in the environment in terms of a natural class. Here is my first pass at trying to generalize this set of sounds:

(8)   UF   SF   E
          {?} → |-z| /   ⎧   V   ⎫
                              ⎪   C   ⎪ ___
                              ⎨ [voiced] ⎬
                              ⎩[non-sibilant]⎭

The curly brackets in this formula enclose a list of choices, one and only one of which must be selected. What this provisional statement says is that the allomorph |-z| occurs after any Vowel (capital V), or after a consonant that is voiced and non-sibilant.

Now let us try to formulate the rule for the |-iz| allomorph. The straight observational statement would be the following:

(9)   UF   SF   E
          {?} → |-iz| / s, z, ʃ, ʒ, ʧ, ʤ —

How would you generalize this pattern? Is there any natural commonality to the sounds that appear in the environment? Of course – they are all and only sibilants. Therefore it is fairly easy to write a rule that uniquely describes this pattern:

(10)   UF   SF   E
            {?} → |-ɨz| /   C __
                        [sibilant]

This rule just says that the PLURAL morpheme is realized as |-ɨz| after sibilant sounds.[3]

Rules such as 6, 8, and 10 may seem like complicated ways of expressing some very simple facts, but it is important to be comfortable with this notation for several reasons. First, it is helpful to be absolutely explicit about all the structural patterns in a language. After all, something like these rules must be a part of the unconscious knowledge that all English speakers have about their language. Since part of the job of a linguist is to make these unconscious patterns explicit, it helps to have a mathematically precise way of expressing them. Second, the notion of *natural class* can be very helpful in understanding *why* particular pronunciations occur. In most cases (not all) morphophonemic rules can be explained by common-sense principles (e.g., sounds tend to become like the sounds that surround them). Such explanations are possible only if an attempt is made to identify the environments very explicitly. Third, although these particular English rules may be easy to express in plain prose, others are much more complex. The formalisms are particularly helpful in dealing with complex morphophonemic variation, especially in languages that the linguist does not speak natively. Finally, these are the kinds of formalisms that are used extensively in the linguistics literature. Anyone who is planning to read and contribute to this literature must be able to understand and manipulate the formalisms.

How to pick an underlying form

We have just taken the first two steps in morphophonemic analysis: (1) List the environments, and (2) Generalize the environments to account for any natural classes of sounds. Before we go on to the final step – determining the underlying form – we will make a slight detour to explain the theoretical notion of underlying form a little more. Then we will see how this notion is applicable to morphophonemic analysis.

There are two basic considerations in choosing an underlying form for a particular morpheme:

•   The underlying form should be the allomorph that occurs in the largest number of environments.
•   The underlying form should be the allomorph that is most difficult to derive by a rule.

Let's discuss the first consideration. If you think of the underlying form as the "default case," it makes sense that it should occur in the largest number of environments. The "special cases" are probably the ones that would need to be specified by rules. This is *not* the same as saying that the underlying form is the one that occurs in the largest number of examples. The number of *environments* is the key. Let me explain. Let's say you were trying to determine what the normal (underlying?) color for books in a bookstore is. You look at 1,000 individual books and find that 900 of them are red, while the remaining 100 are ten different colors. Would you automatically say that red is the normal color? Not necessarily. What if you find that all 900 of those red books are copies of the same title? Of course they are the same color – they are all the same book! Among the 100 remaining books, let's say there are 50 different titles represented, and 30 *different titles* have brown covers. The other titles have a variety of other colors. Then you would say that the color brown occurs in 30 environments, whereas the color red only occurs in one, even though you have more actual examples of red books than you do of brown ones. This is one argument that brown is the logical "underlying" color.

[margin: DEFAULT CASE]

[margin: MOST ENVIRONMENTS]

As for the second consideration in choosing an underlying form, linguists are always interested in reducing the number and complexity of the grammatical rules they posit for a language. The assumption is that if two rules will both work, the simpler one is more likely to accurately represent the mental processes involved (since people are basically lazy). Returning to the example of books in a bookstore for a moment, you can see that it would be simpler to write a rule for which books are red than for which ones are brown. In order to know whether a book is red or not, all you would need would be one title. However, in order to know (or to "predict" in a mathematical sense) whether a book is brown or not, you would need to specify thirty titles. Therefore it makes sense to say that books are *basically* brown, and that they "become" red under one well-defined condition. If that condition is not met, they don't change at all – they just keep their underlying color.

[margin: OCCAM'S RAZOR]

Here is how the rules for which books are red and which are brown might be written:

Hypothesis 1: Red is the underlying color:

(11)   UF   SF   E
         {red} → |brown| /   { title 1
                                 title 2
                                 title 3
                                 ...
                                 title 30 }

         {red} → |red| /   elsewhere

Hypothesis 2: Brown is the underlying color:

(12)   UF   SF   E
         {brown} → |red| /   title 31
         {brown} → |brown| /   elsewhere

Table 3.1 *Basic data on English plurals*

|-s|		|-z|		|-ɨz|	
'cats'	kæts	'dogs'	dɔgz	'bushes'	bʊʃɨz
'socks'	sɔks	'tabs'	tæbz	'boxes'	bɔksɨz
'tops'	tɔps	'lads'	lædz	'cheeses'	čizɨz
'laughs'	læfs	'hives'	haɪvz	'watches'	watʃɨz
'fifths'	fɪfθs	'beans'	binz	'wedges'	wɛdʒɨz
		'bows'	bouz	'lashes'	læʃɨz
		'sofas'	sofəz	'kisses'	kɪsɨz
		'tears'	tiɹz	'buzzes'	bʌzɨz
		'walls'	walz	'garages'	gəɹaʒɨz
		'lathes'	leiðz	'colleges'	kalədʒɨz
				'wishes'	wɪʃɨz

As you can see, positing brown as the underlying color results in simpler rules. This is another argument that brown is the "normal," or default, color of our books.

Now, let us return to the morphophonemic rules for English plural formation to see if we can determine which of the three allomorphs, |-s|, |-z|, or |-ɨz|, is the most likely underlying form. Table 3.1 shows the data presented in example 1 organized according to the three allomorphs of the plural morpheme.

In this data set, there are more examples of the |-ɨz| allomorph than any other. However, as mentioned above, this in itself is not evidence that |-ɨz| is the underlying form. The best underlying form is the one that occurs in the largest number of environments, and/or that results in the simplest rules. Let's look at the three observational statements we made in the previous section to see which one is the most complex. Which one do you think it is? Number 6, 8, or 10? Obviously it is number 8. The allomorph |-z| appears after vowels and fricative, plosive, lateral, and approximant consonants. There are more different kinds of situations in which the |-z| allomorph appears than any of the others. It's like the color brown appearing on a wide variety of book covers. So, in order to simplify our analysis, what if we hypothesize that |-z| is the underlying form of this morpheme? That way we can get rid of rule 8 altogether, and just consider the other two allomorphs to be variations on the basic {-z} form.

Thus the final form of the morphophonemic rules for the regular PLURAL morpheme in English would be:

(13)   {-z} → |-s| /   C —
                               [voiceless]
                               [non-sibilant]
          {-z} → |-ɨz| /   C —
                               [sibilant]
          {-z} → |-z| /   elsewhere

It is that simple. Notice that these patterns represent both assimilation and structure preservation. The voiceless allomorph (|-s|) only appears after voiceless

Table 3.2 *More data on English plurals*

meaning	singular	plural		meaning	singular	plural	
'pint'	paɪnt	paɪn	-s	'pine'	paɪn	paɪn	-z
'pant'	pænt	pæn	-s	'pan'	pæn	pæn	-z
'tent'	tɛnt	tɛn	-s	'ten'	tɛn	tɛn	-z
'tint'	tɪnt	tɪn	-s	'tin'	tɪn	tɪn	-z

sounds. In this respect the underlying form has *assimilated* to its environment. The |-ɨz| allomorph can be thought of as the result of an *insertion*, or **EPENTHESIS**, rule that inserts an *ɨ* vowel in order to preserve normal English word structure. If there were no *ɨ* in these examples, the words would end in sequences of consonants that never appear at the ends of words in English (ʤz, ʧz, ʃz, and ʒz). English speakers would say these sequences are "hard to pronounce" (though they may be totally natural in other languages).

By the way, this may be a good point to remember again that spelling is not evidence for or against morphophonemic analyses. The fact that the plural morpheme is *spelled* with an *s* letter in English writing has nothing to do with what the underlying form should be. Sometimes spelling can suggest hypotheses, since spelling often represents pronunciations at earlier stages of the language, and underlying forms are generally historically older than the allomorphs. However, spelling itself does not constitute evidence for morphophonemic analyses.

Rule ordering

Sometimes several morphophonemic rules may apply to the same form. When this happens, it may be necessary to specify that the rules apply in a particular order. To illustrate morphophonemic rule ordering, let's consider the additional data in table 3.2.[4]

In these data there are several rules that interact. One set of rules are the morphophonemic rules presented in 13 that specify which allomorph of the plural morpheme should be used, and the other is a rule that affects the stems of nouns that end in *nt*.

In order to talk about the various rules, it sometimes helps to *name* them. For example, the two rules that specify the allomorphs of the PLURAL morpheme can be called "devoicing" ({-z} → |-s|) and "ɨ-insertion" ({-z} → |-ɨz|). The new rule that is evident in the data in table 3.2 is a phonological rule that gets rid of a *t* when the plural morpheme is added to a stem that ends in *nt*. For convenience, let us call that rule "t-deletion." It can be formulated as follows:

(14)   t-deletion: t → Ø / n — s

This rule says that *t* turns into nothing (it deletes) when it finds itself between an *n* and an *s*. Why didn't I say between an *n* and a *z*? Didn't we just conclude that

Table 3.3 *Complete derivations for some English plurals*

input:	'laughs' $\{læf\} + \{z\}$	'tabs' $\{tæb\} + \{z\}$	'cheeses' $\{ʧiz\} + \{z\}$	'pints' $\{pa^int\} + \{z\}$	'pines' $\{pa^in\} + \{z\}$
devoicing	læfs	N/A	N/A	pa^ints	N/A
i-insertion	N/A	N/A	ʧizɨz	N/A	N/A
t-deletion	N/A	N/A	N/A	pa^ins	N/A
output:	læfs	tæbz	ʧizɨz	pa^ins	pa^inz

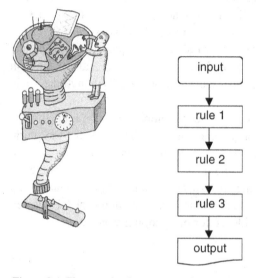

Figure 3.4 *The morphophonemic machine*

input

↓

rule 1

↓

rule 2

↓

rule 3

↓

output

the underlying form of the plural morpheme is $\{-z\}$? Well, let's actually write out a derivation and see what happens. Sometimes that's the only way to test a rule.

You might think of **MORPHOPHONEMIC DERIVATION** as a machine that takes underlying forms as input and produces surface forms as output. This machine operates "blindly" on the input. Underlying forms enter at the top, and if the environment for a rule is met, the rule applies, and sends the form on for further processing. If the environment for a rule is not met, the rule does not apply (N/A), and the output of that rule is identical to the input (figure 3.4).

Let's do the actual derivation for some of the English nouns discussed earlier (see table 3.3).

As you can see, the input to this "machine" is the underlying forms. This includes each underlying word stem and the underlying form of the plural morpheme, which is always going to be $\{-z\}$. Remember, we would need more complicated rules if we used |-s| or |-ɨz| as the underlying form. The outputs are the words as they are normally pronounced.

Consider the derivation for the form spelled *pints*. The underlying forms are given at the top. The devoicing rule applies, changing the underlying form of the

Table 3.4 *Faulty derivations for English plurals*

input:	'laughs' {læf} + {z}	'tabs' {tæb} + {z}	'cheeses' {tʃiz} + {z}	'pints' {paɪnt} + {z}	'pines' {paɪn} + {z}
t-deletion	NA	NA	NA	NA	NA
devoicing	læfs	NA	NA	paɪnts	NA
i-insertion	NA	NA	tʃizɪz	NA	NA
output:	læfs	tæbz	tʃizɪz	*paɪnts	paɪnz

plural morpheme, {-z}, to |-s| following the [t] in the root. Then the i-insertion rule does not apply, because [t] is not a sibilant, so it is not an environment that triggers this rule. Then the new t-deletion rule applies, eliminating the [t] between an [n] and an [s]. Thus, the correct actual pronunciation, [paɪns], is produced as the output.

The next thing to notice is that the rules must apply in order. What would happen if, for example, we put the t-deletion rule first? We would get the faulty derivations illustrated in table 3.4.

By reordering the rules, we end up with the incorrect output for the plural of *pint* (the asterisk indicates an incorrect form). If we change the t-deletion rule to apply between an *n* and a *z* (instead of *n* and *s*, the way it is written above), then it would apply to the form [paɪntz] to produce [paɪnz]. However, then devoicing would not apply, since the [z] would follow an [n] and [n] is not one of the environments for our devoicing rule. Therefore the plural of *pint* would end up sounding the same as the plural of *pine*. This is clearly wrong. Therefore we conclude that t-deletion must follow devoicing. This fact confirms that the environment for t-deletion must contain an [s] and not a [z].

Again, though this derivational apparatus may appear overly complex, it does capture an intuitively reasonable fact of English articulation, namely that the voiceless sound at the end of words like *pint* conditions (or causes) the plural suffix that follows to be voiceless. After that, another rule gets rid of the voiceless sound that conditioned the voiceless allomorph. This rule makes sense because English word structure does not easily tolerate the sequence *nts* at the end of a word.

Nasal assimilation in English

In this section we will discuss one more example of allomorphic variation in English. In the process, we will introduce an important notion in morphophonemic analysis: the **ALPHA NOTATION**.

One of the most common pronunciation patterns in the world's languages is **NASAL ASSIMILATION**. This is a pattern whereby a nasal consonant takes on the place of articulation of the sound that follows. For example, consider the following English data:

(15)
a.	ækjəɹət	'accurate'	ɪnækjəɹət	'inaccurate'
b.	kɔŋgɹuəs	'congruous'	ɪŋkɔŋgɹuəs	'incongruous'
c.	pɔsəbl̩	'possible'	ɪmpɔsəbl̩	'impossible'
d.	dəskɹaɪʲbəbl̩	'describable'	ɪndəskɹaɪʲbəbl̩	'indescribable'
e.	tɔləɹənt	'tolerant'	ɪntɔləɹənt	'intolerant'
f.	sɛnsɪtɪv	'sensitive'	ɪnsɛnsɪtɪv	'insensitive'
g.	vɛɹiəbl̩	'variable'	ɪnvɛɹiəbl̩	'invariable'
h.	gloɹiəs	'glorious'	ɪŋgloɹiəs	'inglorious'
i.	mɛʒəɹəbl̩	'measurable'	ɪmmɛʒəɹəbl̩	'immeasurable'
j.	bæləns	'balance'	ɪmbæləns	'imbalance'

Applying our steps of morphological analysis to these data, we notice that the forms on the right consist of the forms on the left plus a prefix. The prefixes have various forms, either *ɪn-*, *ɪŋ-*, or *ɪm-*.

The first question for morphophonemics is whether these are different prefixes, or allomorphs of one prefix. What do you think? Of course – they represent one underlying prefix. Why? Because they all seem to express the same conceptual category (something like NEGATION), and they are all very similar in shape. Therefore we hypothesize that they are allomorphs of one morpheme. Whenever we think we have allomorphs, we try to identify the environments in which each allomorph occurs and suggest an underlying form for the morpheme, if possible.

What are the environments for each allomorph of the negative prefix in these data? Here are some provisional statements:

(16) a.   {?} → |ɪn-| / — æ, d, t, s, v
     b.   {?} → |ɪŋ-| / — k, g
     c.   {?} → |ɪm-| / — p, m, b

The next step is to try to generalize the environments. Is there a natural class of sounds that conditions the |ɪn-| allomorph? Not really. The environment for 16a includes vowels, plosive consonants, fricative consonants, alveolar consonants, and a labio-dental fricative. This would be a pretty complicated environment to state in terms of features, so we won't even try for now. How about 16b and c? The environment for the |ɪŋ-| allomorph consists of velar plosive consonants, and the environment for the |ɪm-| allomorph is all bilabial consonants. So which of the three allomorphs do you think should be the underlying form? Sure! The form |ɪn-| satisfies both criteria for underlying forms: (1) it occurs in the largest number of environments, and (2) positing it as the underlying form results in the simplest rules. With {ɪn-} as the underlying form, we can restate the rules in 16 as follows:

(17) a.   {ɪn-} → |ɪŋ-| / __ C
                              [velar]

      b.   {ɪn-} → |ɪm-| / __ C
                              [bilabial]

      c.   {ɪn-} → |ɪn-| / elsewhere

Note that the blank line in the environment occurs before the conditioning sounds this time. This is because we are dealing with a change that occurs in a prefix, and the conditioning sounds follow the place where the change happens. By making {ɪn-} the underlying form of the prefix, we avoid having to write a rule that changes something else to |ɪn-| in a very complicated set of environments that includes vowels and several quite different kinds of consonants. It also makes sense that {ɪn-} should be the underlying form because there is a natural motivation for the other two forms – the n becomes velar before a velar consonant and bilabial before a bilabial consonant. This is a very understandable assimilation process. On the other hand, why would some other nasal consonant, say *m*, become alveolar before a vowel? There is nothing particularly alveolar about the vowel æ or the consonant *v* that would plausibly cause such a change.

However, there is still a way to make the rules as stated in 17 even more accurate. These rules treat the changes from {ɪn-} to |ɪŋ-| and {ɪn-} to |ɪm-| as two distinct patterns, when in fact they seem to be saying something quite similar – namely that the *n* of the prefix takes on the place of articulation of the consonant that follows, whatever that may be. Since there is really only one process involved, it would be a Good Thing if there were a way to "collapse" the two separate rules into one. A method that linguists often use to collapse rules of this sort is called the **ALPHA NOTATION**.

The alpha notation is useful whenever an underlying form takes on one of several possible features of sounds in the environment. Nasal assimilation is an excellent situation for the use of the alpha notation. The idea is that instead of writing a separate rule for each individual variant of the negative prefix, you write one rule and simply link the feature that changes to the feature in the environment that causes the change. In this case, the Greek letter alpha (α) stands for any place of articulation. The change in place of articulation of the nasal consonant in the prefix is represented as a change to "alpha place" ([α place]) in the environment of a plosive consonant which is also "alpha place." Thus the first two rules in 17 could be collapsed as follows:

(18)   Nasal assimilation: / n / → [α place] / __ C
                                                    [plosive]
                                                    [α place]

Notice that now we are talking only about the *n* of the prefix, rather than the whole prefix. This makes rule 18 a phonological rule, rather than a morphophonemic rule. Nevertheless, it does seem to help us state the generalization in a more "elegant" manner. The way this rule may be read is "an /n/ takes on the same place of articulation as the consonant that follows it." The alpha notation simply links the place of articulation feature for the consonant in the environment to the place feature that changes. This phonological rule is preferable to listing two separate morphophonemic rules because it "captures" the intuition that this is really just one pattern.

Now let us look at some further allomorphs of the {ɪn-} negative prefix:

(19) a.   ɹæʃənl̩   'rational'   ɪɹɹæʃənl̩   'irrational'
     b.   ɹɛgjəlɹ̩   'regular'   ɪɹɹɛgjəlɹ̩   'irregular'
     c.   ɹəspɔnsɪbl̩ 'responsible'   ɪɹɹəspɔnsɪbl̩ 'irresponsible'
     d.   ligl̩   'legal'   ɪlligl̩   'illegal'
     e.   laʤɪkl̩   'logical'   ɪllaʤɪkl̩   'illogical'
     f.   lɪtəɹət   'literate'   ɪllɪtəɹət   'illiterate'
          etc.

In these examples we see that the same negative prefix has additional allomorphs when appearing on roots that begin with *r* or *l*. These rules can be informally stated as phonological rules as follows:

(20) a   n → ɹ / __ ɹ
     b.   n → l / __ l

In prose, these would be stated as "n becomes ɹ before ɹ" and "n becomes l before l." However, we have a problem. These rules don't apply everywhere. In particular, the prefixes spelled *un-* and *non-* do not exhibit this pattern:

(21)   unresponsive   (*urresponsive)
          unreliable   (*urreliable)
          unreached   (*urreached)
          unlimited   (*ullimited)
          unleash   (*ulleash)
          non-lethal   (*nol-lethal)
          etc.

Therefore these rules are *not* strictly speaking phonological rules – they don't occur in every situation where the environment is met. They must be specified as occurring only with the prefix {ɪn-}. In these cases it is necessary to specify that only a particular morpheme undergoes the rule. Sometimes a simple prose qualifier is also used to further specify when the rule applies and when it doesn't, as follows:

(22) a.   {in-} → |iɹ-| / __ ɹ   Where {in-} is the negative prefix.
     b.   {in-} → |il-| / __ l

Types of morphophonemic rules

There are six basic types of morphophonemic rules that we will be concerned with in this book. The first five are listed below roughly in order of likelihood of occurrence. Insofar as possible, analyses that propose more likely rules are preferred over those that propose less likely rules. For example, if a particular range of data can be explained equally well using a deletion or an insertion rule, the one involving the deletion rule would be preferred, because deletion rules are more likely (more "normal," or more "natural") than insertion rules. Insertion rules do occur, but they are quite a bit less common than deletion rules. The final type, affix suppletion, is a type of morphophonemic pattern in which the allomorphs are simply different from one another, without being obviously related by any of the patterns represented by the first five types.

1. **Assimilation rules**: These are rules that change a morpheme in such a way that it becomes more like its environment. They are very common in the world's languages. For example:

(23)		Example 1	Example 2
a.	Voicing assimilation:	$s \rightarrow z$ / C__# [voiced]	$z \rightarrow s$ / C__# [voiceless]
b.	Place of articulation assimilation:	$s \rightarrow č$ / __ V [close]	$n \rightarrow ŋ$ / __ C [velar]
c.	Manner of articulation assimilation:	$t \rightarrow s$ / __ C [fricative]	$d \rightarrow n$ / # __ C [nasal]
d.	Vowel harmony:	$V \rightarrow V$ / V (C) __ [front] [front]	$V \rightarrow V$ / __ C V [open] [open]
e.	Autosegmental feature spreading:	$V \rightarrow V$ / __ V [nasal] [nasal]	$σ \rightarrow σ́$ / σ́ __

2. **Deletion rules**: These are also very common. They are often motivated by the need to simplify overly complex word structures that result when morphemes come together:

(24)		Example 1	Example 2
a.	Cluster simplification:	$C \rightarrow Ø$ / C C __ #	$V \rightarrow Ø$ / V __ V
b.	Word-final deletion (also called truncation, or apocape)	$C \rightarrow Ø$ / __ #	$V \rightarrow Ø$ / __ #

3. **Insertion rules**: Insertion (or EPENTHESIS) rules are not as common as deletion rules. Sometimes you may be torn between two analyses – one that proposes an underlying form that has a segment that deletes in certain environments, and another that proposes an underlying form that lacks the segment, and therefore the segment has to be inserted in certain environments. All other things being equal, the analysis that proposes deletion is preferred over the one that proposes insertion (see the Asheninka exercise below).

(25)		Example 1	Example 2
a.	Consonant insertion:	$Ø \rightarrow t$ / o __ V	$Ø \rightarrow n$ / V __ C [nasal] [alveolar]
b.	Vowel insertion:	$Ø \rightarrow a$ / # __ CC	$Ø \rightarrow i$ / C __ C [plosive]

4. Dissimilation rules: Very occasionally morphophonemic rules will adjust the shapes of sounds in order to make them more distinct from their environments. Such rules may be functionally motivated when, for example, an important morpheme would otherwise be inaudible (indistinguishable from its environment). Such rules are quite rare, and should be proposed only when there is no alternative explanation for a particular range of facts:

(26)   Example 1   Example 2
        Voicing dissimilation: $s \rightarrow z$ / $C\_\#$ $z \rightarrow s$ / $C\_\#$
                                    [voiceless]   [voiced]

5. Metathesis: Very occasionally a morphophonemic rule will reverse the order of segments. This is called METATHESIS. Often, metathesis rules can be most insightfully written without an environment. In other words, the presence of two segments together is all that is needed to trigger the application of a metathesis rule:

(27)   Example 1   Example 2
    a.   Consonant metathesis: $C_i y \rightarrow y C_i$ $C_i C_{ii} \rightarrow C_{ii} C_i$
    b.   Vowel metathesis: $V_i V_{ii} \rightarrow V_{ii} V_i$ $ai \rightarrow ia$
    c.   Vowel/consonant metathesis: $C_i V_i \rightarrow V_i C_i$ $it \rightarrow ti$

6. Affix suppletion (also called "suppletive allomorphs"): Affix suppletion occurs when a conceptual category is expressed by two (or more) different allomorphs which cannot be related by any of the first five processes discussed above. For example, English *-en* PL, as in *oxen*, is a suppletive allomorph of the regular plural *-z*. There is no natural rule or set of rules of English which turns *-en* into *-z*, or vice-versa, whether by assimilation, deletion, insertion, etc. Such suppletive allomorphy is not necessarily more or less common than any of the other morphophonemic patterns. It arises because of complex historical processes that descriptive linguists may have no direct access to when analyzing a language for the first time. For example, here is a partial paradigm of two verbs in Ixil, a Mayan language spoken in Guatemala (examples courtesy of Paul Townsend):

(28)   Consonant-intial stem: Vowel-initial stem:
        un-ʧok 'I look.'   v-iq'o 'I take.'
        a-ʧok 'You look.'   i-iq'o 'You take.'
        i-ʧok 'He looks.'   t-iq'o 'He takes.'

These examples illustrate two allomorphs of the second person category, *a-* and *i-*, which are not affix suppletion. These can be related by a straightforward assimilation rule – the underlying form is *a-*, and it completely assimilates to the following vowel of any vowel-initial stem. The allomorphs of the first and third person forms, however, are not obviously related by any of the usual types of rule. For example, it would be quite difficult to derive *v-* from *un-* (or vice-versa) by phonological processes of deletion and assimilation. The same is true of the relation between the allomorphs of the third person prefix, *i-* and *t-*. Therefore we can say that these allomorphs are suppletive. Affix suppletion will be discussed in more detail in chapter 5.

There are other types of rules that have been proposed in the literature, but these are the main types that occur in the world's languages and are all that will be relevant for the exercises at the end of this chapter.

Possession in Asheninka

Earlier in this chapter we illustrated the concept of morphophonemics using examples from English. Before leaving this topic, we will go over one more example, this time from Asheninka, a Pre-Andine Arawakan language spoken in central Peru (data courtesy of Maggie Romani).

Table 3.5 displays the possessive paradigm for five nouns in Asheninka. The noun stems are given in the first column, and possessive forms are given in the other columns. There are a few suffixes illustrated in these data, but for the purpose of this exercise we will only be concerned with the prefixes.

Table 3.5 *Asheninka possessed nouns (consider prefixes only)*

	stem	gloss	"my ..."	"Your ..."	"His ..."	"Our ..."
1.	okitsi	'eye'	noki	poki	oki	oki
2.	mat^hantsi	'clothes'	nomat^ha	pimat^ha	imat^ha	amat^ha
3.	iŋki	'peanut'	niŋkine	piŋkine	iŋkine	iŋkine
4.	čekopi	'arrow'	nočekopite	pičekopite	ičekopite	ačekopite
5.	akotsi	'hand'	–	–	–	–

We notice that the prefixes on the nouns vary depending on who the possessor is. There are various prefixes involved, so we want to determine whether all the different prefixes express different conceptual categories, or whether some of them are allomorphs of others. Applying our usual techniques of correlating variations in form with variations in meaning, we come up with the following list of possessive prefixes:

(29) 'my' n- (exs. 1 and 3), no- (exs. 2 and 4)
  'your' p- (exs. 1 and 3), pi- (exs. 2 and 4)
  'his' Ø (exs. 1 and 3), i- (exs. 2 and 4)
  'our' Ø (exs. 1 and 3), a- (exs. 2 and 4)

Why didn't we say that the form for 'my' is *no-* for 1, and *ni-* for 3? After all, these forms are *noki* and *niŋkine* respectively. The answer is that the stems in 1 and 3 begin with the vowels *o* and *i*. In order to consistently correlate changes in form with changes in meaning, we have to consider the *o* and *i* in the first person forms of 1 and 3 as part of the stem. The first vowel *o* in examples 2 and 4, on the other hand, does not occur in the stem, therefore it must be part of the prefix. Similar observations can be made with respect to the prefixes meaning 'your.'

In comparing the forms for 'his' and 'our' we notice an interesting problem. In examples 1 and 3, the forms are the same, whereas in 2 and 4 there is a difference. In all of these examples, we see that there is a difference in patterning between examples 1 and 3 on the one hand and 2 and 4 on the other. What could be determining this difference?

When we look at the stems, we notice that 1 and 3 both start with vowels, while 2 and 4 both start with consonants. Perhaps this is what conditions the various forms of the possessive prefixes. We can formulate this hypothesis in a preliminary way as follows:

(30)

		UF	SF	E
'my'	?	→	n- /	___ V
	?	→	no- /	___ C
'your'	?	→	p- /	___ V
	?	→	pi- /	___ C
'his'	?	→	Ø /	___ V
	?	→	i- /	___ C
'our'	?	→	Ø /	___ V
	?	→	a- /	___ C

In 29 we have listed the environments and generalized them in one step. Now we want to try to determine what the underlying forms are. In each case, we see that one of the allomorphs has a vowel, and the other doesn't. Thus we conclude that the morphophonemic pattern will either involve the *deletion* of a vowel or the *insertion* of a vowel. In other words, if the underlying form for the prefix meaning 'my' is *n-*, then there must be a morphophonemic rule that inserts an *o* vowel after the prefix when the stem begins with a consonant. Call this the insertion analysis. On the other hand, if *no-* is the underlying form, then the *o* must delete before stems that begin with a vowel. Call this the deletion analysis. What do you think is the most reasonable approach?

Well, if we vote for the insertion analysis, we have several big problems. First, we have to have three different rules. An *o* gets inserted in the first example, an *i* in the second and third examples, and an *a* in the fourth example. With the deletion analysis, we can have just one rule that says any vowel deletes.

Second, the rule that inserts an *a* when the possessor is 'our' has to be specified as only occurring in the context of this particular morpheme, and not the identical one that means 'his.' In other words, there would have to be two distinct morphemes whose underlying forms are zero (Ø), only one of which, for some totally arbitrary reason, causes an *a* to be inserted before roots that begin with consonants, whereas the other one doesn't. Rules like this do occur occasionally in languages, but if there is a simpler analysis, it is much to be preferred over such a random (or **AD HOC**) solution.

Finally, as we have just discussed, deletion rules are much more common than insertion rules in the world's languages. Even if the deletion analysis were just as complicated and apparently random as the insertion analysis, still the deletion analysis would be preferred, simply because it is more natural. Linguists only posit insertion rules when a deletion analysis would clearly result in more complex rules.

Therefore, we can infer that the allomorphs that contain vowels are the underlying forms, and that these vowels are deleted in a very well-defined environment: before another vowel:

(31) $V \rightarrow \emptyset / \underline{\quad} V$

This is a very natural rule that basically says "whenever two vowels come together in a word, the first one deletes." Since it appears that there are no two-vowel sequences in the data, we can hypothesize that this is a general characteristic of word structure in Asheninka. This rule then can be understood as a structure-preserving phonological rule. Of course, this hypothesis would have to be checked against further data, but it looks good as far as the data we have available are concerned.

Now we can make hypotheses about the forms in 5. Since the stem *akotsi*, 'hand,' begins with a vowel, the vowel-deletion rule in 30 would apply. Here are the derivations for the four prefixed forms:

(32)

	'my hand'	'your hand'	'his hand'	'our hand'
UF:	{no+ako}	{pi+ako}	{i+ako}	{a+ako}
V-deletion:	n+ako	p+ako	$\emptyset$+ako	$\emptyset$+ako
SF:	nako	pako	ako	ako

Summary of notational conventions

The following is a summary of the notational conventions described in this chapter, along with a few others that may be useful for insightfully solving the exercises that follow:

Variables: Certain symbols are used as "cover terms" or "wildcards" to abbreviate natural classes of sounds that commonly enter into morphophonemic patterns. These are:

C = any consonant
V = any vowel
N = any nasal consonant

Boundary symbols: You may see the following special symbols to indicate various "boundaries" that affect morphophonemic rules:

= word boundary (_ # = end of a word, # _ = beginning of a word)
$ = syllable boundary
+ = morpheme boundary

Parentheses ( ): Segments or variables (C, V, N, etc.) in parentheses are "optional." For example, a rule such as $C \rightarrow \emptyset / \#(C) \underline{\quad}$ means that a consonant is deleted in either of two environments, # __ (at the beginning of a word) and # C __ (after another consonant at the beginning of a word).

Curly brackets { }: There are two conventions that linguists are prone to use regarding so-called "curly brackets." First, segments, variables, or features listed between curly brackets indicate a choice: "Pick one and only one of these." For example, the following rule says that a consonant is deleted before another consonant that is either alveolar OR bilabial:

(33) $C \rightarrow \emptyset$ / __   C
                                   $\begin{Bmatrix} \text{[alveolar]} \\ \text{[bilabial]} \end{Bmatrix}$

Thus this rule can be considered a way of "collapsing" the following rules (and more):

(34) $C \rightarrow \emptyset$ / __ t
            $C \rightarrow \emptyset$ / __ m
            $C \rightarrow \emptyset$ / __ n
            $C \rightarrow \emptyset$ / __ b, etc.

Second, curly brackets are sometimes used to enclose underlying forms of morphemes. For example:

(35)   {-z} $\rightarrow$ |-s| /   C __
                                   [voiceless]

It should be obvious when curly brackets are used in this sense, since there will be only one form between the brackets. If the brackets are used to indicate a choice among possibilities, there will be a list consisting of at least two items, as in example 32 above.

Vertical bars | |, or || ||: Forms between vertical bars (or double vertical bars) represent allomorphs of some morpheme (see 34 above).

Square brackets [ ]: Square brackets enclose phonetic transcription or phonetic "features." This is just one way of characterizing the properties of sounds that enter into morphophonemic patterns.

Slashes / /: Forms between slashes are phonemic representations. These are the sounds as they are relevant within the *sound system* of a particular language, rather than necessarily actual pronunciations (see, e.g., Burquest 2001).

The important thing to remember when using these conventions is that the rules you propose should apply EVERYWHERE and ONLY in the situations you intend them to apply. For example, the environment:

(36)   __ C
            [alveolar]

refers to all positions before any alveolar consonant. If you have a rule that applies before [t] and [d], but not [n], it is true that all the consonants in the environment are alveolar, but it is not true that all alveolar consonants are in the environment. Therefore the environment as stated would not be specific enough.

Conceptual outline of chapter 3

I. Morphophonemics concerns how the shapes of morphemes vary depending on the phonological context, or environment, in which the morphemes occur.

II. According to a well-established metaphor often used by linguists, utterances "start out" in the mind as concepts represented by strings of idealized, or "underlying," forms of morphemes. These idealized forms may change their actual shape "on the way" to the mouth, under the influence of the other sounds that surround them. The changes they undergo are called morphophonemic rules, and the process of undergoing a series of such changes is called "morphophonemic derivation."

III. There are three major questions for morphophonemic analysis:
   • Do you have allomorphs of one morpheme or separate morphemes?
   • What are the environments in which the various allomorphs occur?
   • What is the underlying, or "basic," form of the morpheme?

IV. How to specify the environments for morphophonemic rules.
   • Environments should be stated in terms of "natural classes" whenever possible.
   • Environments should be as simple as possible, while still accounting for all of the data.

V. The underlying form is likely to be:
   • The allomorph that occurs in the largest number of environments.
   • The allomorph that is the most difficult to derive from any of the others.

VI. Rule ordering. Sometimes an environment for one morphophonemic rule is eliminated by another one. Therefore, in order for both rules to work, the one whose environment is eliminated must occur "first" in an ordered set of rules in a morphophonemic derivation.

VII. Naturalness of morphophonemic rules. Certain kinds of morphophonemic rules are more common, or "natural," than others. For example, deletion rules are more common than insertion rules. All other things being equal, analyses that involve more natural rules are preferred over those that involve less natural rules.

Exercise 3.1: English

Tom Payne

Consider the following English verbs in the present and past tenses, and answer the questions below:

Meaning	Present	Past	Meaning	Present	Past
1. 'look'	lʊk	lʊkt	10. 'belong'	bəlɔŋ	bəlɔŋd
2. 'float'	floᵘt	floᵘtəd	11. 'sip'	sɪp	sɪpt
3. 'play'	pleⁱ	pleⁱd	12. 'create'	kɹieⁱt	kɹieⁱtəd
4. 'wash'	waʃ	waʃt	13. 'bomb'	bɔm	bɔmd
5. 'plod'	plɔd	plɔdəd	14. 'watch'	watʃ	watʃt
6. 'peer'	piɹ	piɹd	15. 'want'	want	wantəd
7. 'laugh'	læf	læft	16. 'breathe'	bɹið	bɹiðd
8. 'draft'	dɹæft	dɹæftəd	17. 'grease'	gɹis	gɹist
9. 'drag'	dɹæg	dɹægd	18. 'call'	kal	kald

A. How many morphemes are represented in these data?

B. If there are allomorphs, identify them, and write distribution statements that describe the environments in which each one occurs.

C. Generalize your statements to account for natural classes of sounds in the environments.

D. What is the best hypothesized underlying form for the English past-tense morpheme? Give the evidence for your claim.

E. Write final morphophonemic rule(s) to describe the appearance of the allomorphs.

Exercise 3.2: Amharic

Adapted from Hudson (1999)

The following are eight verbs in Amharic. All of these are in the past tense, and each is given in the forms used for four different subjects:

'he'	'she'	'we'	'they'	Gloss
1. kəffələ	kəffələtʃ	kəffəlin	kəffəlu	'paid'
2. fələgə	fələgətʃ	fələgin	fələgu	'wanted'
3. bəllə	bəllətʃ	bəllən	bəllu	'ate'
4. ləkkə	ləkkətʃ	ləkkən	ləkku	'measured'
5. k'omə	k'omətʃ	k'omin	k'omu	'stood'
6. hedə	hedətʃ	hedin	hedu	'went'
7. səmə	səmətʃ	səmin	səmu	'kissed'
8. fənəddə	fənəddətʃ	fənəddən	fənəddu	'burst'

A. Give the best underlying form for each root and suffix in these data. Write rules to describe any morphophonemic variation that you see.

B. Give complete morphophonemic derivations for the following words: 'he paid,' 'we wanted,' 'she ate,' 'they wanted,' 'we ate,' and 'they ate.'

Exercise 3.3: Bilaala

Data from Olson and Schultz (2002)

The following words are from Bilaala. The digraphs *tʃ* and *dʒ* represent single, alveopalatal consonants:

1.	bobdʒə	'his/her father'	13.	kuzdʒə	'his/her hut'
2.	bobmə	'my father'	14.	kuzmə	'my hut'
3.	gagdʒə	'his/her plant'	15.	monɲə	'his/her child'
4.	gagmə	'my plant'	16.	nanɲə	'his/her children'
5.	gotmə	'my place'	17.	osʃə	'pour (water) on it'
6.	gotʃə	'his/her place'	18.	tʃeɲə	'his/her mother'
7.	gurusʃə	'his/her money'	19.	uguɲə	'he/she hit him/her'
8.	gurusmə	'my money'	20.	waʃɲə	'his spear'
9.	gɔrddʒə	'his/her knife'	21.	bɛrɲə	'his/her slave'
10.	gɔrdmə	'my knife'	22.	ɗokmə	'my wife'
11.	kawɲə	'its length'	23.	ɗokʃə	'his/her wife'
12.	kuhulɲə	'his/her hip'			

A. Where is Bilaala spoken?

B. Determine the best underlying forms for the roots and suffixes in these data, and give rules that derive the various allomorphs from your proposed underlying forms.

Exercise 3.4: Hanunoo

McManus et al. (1987:146).

A. Where is Hanunoo spoken?

B. What language family does it belong to?

1. ʔusa	'one'	kasʔa	'once'	ʔusahi	'make it one'
2. duwa	'two'	kadwa	'twice'	duwahi	'make it two'
3. tulu	'three'	katlu	'three times'	tuluhi	'make it three'
4. ʔupat	'four'	kapʔat	'four times'	ʔupati	'make it four'
5. lima	'five'	kalima	'five times'	limahi	'make it five'
6. ʔunum	'six'	kanʔum	'six times'	ʔunumi	'make it six'
7. pitu	'seven'	kapitu	'seven times'	pituhi	'make it seven'

C. What morphological processes do you see operating in these data? Cite an example of each one.

D. Write rules to describe the morphophonemic changes in these data.

E. Give complete morphophonemic derivations for the words for 'three times,' 'four times,' 'five times,' and 'make it six.'

Exercise 3.5: Agbala verbs

Ronnie Sim

	Gloss	3SG	1SG
1.	'laugh'	mada	nada
2.	'bless'	mulay	nulay
3.	'cry'	nano	mənano
4.	'curse'	noway	mənoway
5.	'drink'	gugbay	ŋgugbay
6.	'eat'	ʧilay	nʧilay
7.	'fall'	dumbe	ndumbe
8.	'fly'	huiva	nəhuiva
9.	'greet'	sehay	nsehay
10.	'hiccup'	nabi	mənabi
11.	'hit'	hagbay	nəhagbay
12.	'jump'	hipu	nəhipu
13.	'whistle'	siba	nsiba

A. What is the best underlying form of the 1SG prefix? *Explain your answer.*

B. Write a rule or rules that will derive the allomorphs of the 1SG verbs.

Exercise 3.6: Mongolian

Adapted from Cipollone, Keiser, and Vasishth (1994:162)

	gloss	stem	future imperative
1.	enter	or	oro:roy
2.	go	yav	yava:ray
3.	sit	su:	su:ga:ray
4.	come	ir	ire:rey
5.	do	xi:	xi:ge:rey
6.	come out	gar	gara:ray
7.	take	av	ava:ray
8.	study	sur	sura:ray
9.	finish	byte:	byte:ge:rey
10.	drink	y:	y:ga:ray
11.	find out	ol	olo:roy
12.	conquer	yal	yala:ray
13.	beat	dev	deve:rey
14.	give	øg	øgø:røy
15.	say	xel	xele:rey
16.	meet	u:lz	u:lza:ray
17.	become	bol	___
18.	write	bič	___
19.	develop	xøgž	___
20.	ask	asu:	___

A.   What are the allomorphs of the future imperative suffix in Mongolian?
B.   Fill in the probable future imperative form of examples 17 through 20.
C.   What is the most reasonable underlying form for the future imperative suffix? Explain why.
D.   Write a morphophonemic rule or rules that describe the distribution of the allomorphs.

Exercise 3.7: Hungarian

Adapted from Cowan and Rakušan (1998:128)
The following Hungarian words are represented in the International Phonetic Alphabet.

A.   Isolate and gloss each morpheme in these data.
B.   Write a rule or rules to describe any morphophonemic variation.

1. e:rtek	'I understand.'	18. seret	'She/he loves.'
2. yl	'She/he sits.'	19. repylnek	'They fly.'
3. seretnek	'They love.'	20. mond	'She/he says.'
4. tudok	'I know.'	21. ert	'She/he understands.'
5. repyløk	'I fly.'	22. serets	'You love.'
6. serettek	'Y'all love.'	23. mondunk	'We say.'
7. tuds	'You know.'	24. repyls	'You fly.'
8. mondotok	'Y'all say.'	25. ylynk	'We sit.'
9. seretynk	'We love.'	26. tudunk	'We know.'
10. yløk	'I sit.'	27. e:rtenek	'They understand.'
11. repyltøk	'Y'all fly.'	28. mondanak	'They say.'
12. e:rtynk	'We understand.'	29. tudtok	'Y'all know.'
13. e:rtes	'You understand.'	30. tud	'She/he knows.'
14. tudnak	'They know.'	31. mondas	'You say.'
15. yls	'You sit.'	32. e:rtetek	'You understand.'
16. yltøk	'Y'all sit.'	33. mondok	'I say.'
17. repyl	'She/he flies.'	34. seretek	'I love.'

Exercise 3.8: Ngiti

Data courtesy of Connie Kutsch-Lojenga. Problem and transcription conventions by Tom Payne
(Nilo-Saharan, Central Sudanic, Republic of Congo)

1. mbi	'rope/ropes'
2. ádzì mbi	'a long rope'
3. ádzàdzì mbi	'long ropes'
4. ídò dy	'a short hoe'

5.	ídìdò dy	'short hoes'
6.	odu	'stone/stones'
7.	odú odu	'a heavy stone'
8.	odódú odu	'heavy stones'
9.	ízò	'reed/reeds'
10.	iví ízò	'a young reed'
11.	ivíví ízò	'young reeds'
12.	isɔ́ tsu	'a light piece of wood'
13.	isɔ́sɔ́ tsu	'light pieces of wood'
14.	ìtù ànɔ̀	'heavy luggage'
15.	tùtútú ànɔ̀	'very heavy luggage'
16.	ìmvù rɔ́ʔɔ sìtà	'a sweet potato'
17.	mvùmvúmvú rɔ́ʔɔ sìtà	'very sweet potato'
18.	isɔ́ ànɔ̀	'light luggage'
19.	sɔ́sɔ́sɔ́ ànɔ̀	'very light luggage'
20.	indú rɔngy ìzà	'bad-smelling meat'
21.	ndúndúndú rɔngy ìzà	'very bad-smelling meat'

A. What morphological processes does Ngiti employ to distinguish singular from plural in nouns? In noun phrases? In adjectives?

B. Write an explicit rule for plural formation in Ngiti adjectives.

C. What means does Ngiti employ to express intensification in adjectives?

D. Write an explicit rule for intensification in Ngiti adjectives.

E. How do you think Ngiti speakers say 'very young reeds'? 'Very heavy stones'?

Exercise 3.9: Indonesian

Juliana Wijaya and Doris Payne

	Column 1		Column 2	
1.	peɲaɲi	'singer'	meɲaɲi	'to sing'
2.	adʒakan	'invitation'	meŋadʒak	'to invite'
3.	peŋadʒar	'teacher'	meŋadʒar	'to teach'
4.	peŋadʒaran	'tuition, teaching'	—	—
5.	peladʒar	'student'	—	—
6.	pembantu	'assistant'	membantu	'to help'
7.	bantuan	'assistance, aid'	—	—
8.	pendaftaran	'registration'	mendaftar	'to enroll'
9.	daftar	'(a) list'	—	—
10.	pendoroŋ or doroŋan	'stimulant'	mendoroŋ	'to push, stimulate'
11.	peŋgali	'(a) spade'	meŋgali	'to dig'
12.	baraŋ galian	'mineral'	—	—
13.	hina	'ignoble, mean'	meŋhina	'to humiliate'

14. kehinaan	'humiliation'	—	—
15. kenalan	'acquaintance'	meŋenal	'to know, be acquainted'
16. peṟkenalan	'specimen, sample'	—	—
17. keṟitik	'criticism'	meŋeritik	'to criticize'
18. leŋas	'moist'	meleŋas	'to become moist'
19. masakan	'dish, cooking'	memasak	'to cook'
20. peṟnikahan	'marriage'	menikah	'to marry'
21. beṟpakaian	'to dress (someone)'	memakai	'to wear'
22. pakaian	'clothes'	—	—
23. pukulan	'(a) stroke, (a) beat'	memukul	'to hit'
24. pemukul	'hammer'	—	—
25. beṟpukul …	'to beat each other'	—	—
26. ṟusak	'damaged, defective'	meṟusak	'to ruin'
27. peŋrusak	'destroyer'	—	—
28. taṟi	'(a) dance'	menari	'to dance'
29. penaṟi	'dancer'	—	—
30. taṟik gaja	'attractive power'	menarik	'to pull'
31. kapal penaṟik	'tugboat'	—	—
32. peŋurus	'manager, director, organizer'	meŋurus	'to look after'
33. uṟusan	'arrangement'	—	—
34. waṟnai	'(a) color'	mewarnai	'to color'
35. jakin	'serious'	mejakini	'to believe'
36. kejakinan	'conviction'	—	—
37. mesin dʒahit	'sewing machine'	meɲdʒahit	'to sew'
38. tabuṟan	'seed (that has been sown)'	menabur	'to sow, scatter'

A.   List all the roots in these data. For any root that has more than one allomorph, list the allomorphs.

B.   All the words in column 2 contain a prefix. List all allomorphs of this prefix, and assign a meaning to it.

C.   What is the best underlying form of the prefix that occurs in column 2? Justify your answer by demonstrating why each of the other allomorphs is a less good choice.

D.   Write and give a name to each of the morphophonemic rules needed to derive the surface forms of all words in Column 2 from your proposed underlying forms.

E.   Identify all the rest of the affixes. (a) For any that has more than one allomorph, list all the allomorphs. (b) Insofar as possible, identify the function of each affix; also indicate whether it is inflectional or derivational, and explain why.

F.   Give complete morphophonemic derivations for the words meaning 'to dig,' 'to run after,' 'to look after,' 'to wear,' 'to believe,' and 'to sing.'

Notes

1. In this chapter, English forms will usually be cited in a phonemic representation. Following earlier traditions, basic forms of morphemes will be represented between {curly brackets}. Allomorphs will be represented between vertical bars: |a|. The plus sign (+) means a boundary between morphemes within a word. Phonetic forms will be cited between [square brackets].
2. Refer to the chart of the International Phonetic Alphabet at the end of the front matter for reference to the manner and place of articulation features for consonants.
3. Another way of formulating this rule is to posit the insertion of an [ɨ] vowel between the root and the plural suffix. This solution requires the application of morphophonemic and phonological rules in a specified order. Rule ordering is described in a later section of this chapter. For now we would just like to illustrate the process of identifying the environments for morphophonemic changes.
4. The phonetic forms given in table 3.2 are characteristic of relaxed speech in most varieties of English. Some English speakers may disagree with some of these pronunciations. However, they will serve as introductory examples of how morphophonemic rule ordering is sometimes necessary. If you think there is a "t sound" between the *n* and *s* in the word spelled *tents*, compare it to the word spelled *tense*. Is there really a difference in pronunciation between these words?

4   Word classes

We have already been using word-class terms, such as "noun," "verb," "adjective," and "adverb" in our descriptions of the morphosyntactic tools that people use to express conceptual categories. In this chapter we will discuss word classes in a little more detail, giving prototype definitions of the major classes and suggesting methods for determining word classes in an unfamiliar language.

In traditional grammar, **WORD CLASSES** are called "parts of speech." Every language has at least two major word classes – nouns and verbs.[1] Two other major classes, adjective and adverb, may or may not occur in any given language, though they usually do to some extent. Most languages also have smaller, or "minor," word classes such as **CONJUNCTIONS**, **PARTICLES**, and **ADPOSITIONS**. As with most classification schemes in linguistics, word classes tend to be interestingly untidy. Nevertheless, core notions, or **PROTOTYPES**, can usually be identified.

One important property of word classes is that the class of any given word often varies according to how it is used in discourse (see Hopper and Thompson 1984). Sometimes subtle morphosyntactic "tests" are needed to determine the class of a given word, and other times the class can only be inferred from the context. For example, it is impossible to say whether English words like *rock* or *run* are nouns or verbs apart from a context:

(1) a.   Fezzik threw a *rock* at Wesley.   (*rock* used as a noun)
    b.   We'll *rock* tonight!   (*rock* used as a verb)
    c.   They *run* the department like a circus. (*run* used as a verb)
    d.   She's going for a *run* right now.   (*run* used as a noun)

Many English stems can be used either as nouns or verbs, though others tend strongly to favor one class or the other:

(2) a.   Let's watch *television*.   (*television* used as a noun)
    b.   ?She *televisioned* her children into submission. (*television* used as a verb)
    c.   Harold *lingered* on the veranda.   (*linger* used as a verb)
    d.   ?He went for his *linger* at noon.   (*linger* used as a noun)

The important point is that the word class of any form is not necessarily given once and for all in the lexical entry of the root.

Word classes are distinct from grammatical relations such as subject and object, or functional roles such as AGENT, **TOPIC**, or **DEFINITE** noun (these terms will be discussed in later sections of this book). Word classes are the building blocks of clause structure. In the following sections we will discuss various characteristics of the major word classes (nouns, verbs, adjectives and adverbs), and give some suggestions for how to identify them and classify them in any language.

Nouns

For nouns and verbs, prototypes can be identified in terms of meaning. The class of **NOUNS** in any language includes words that refer to highly **BOUNDED** or **INDIVIDUATED** entities, e.g., 'tree,' 'mountain,' 'mausoleum,' etc. These are concepts that tend not to change very much over time, and which can be referred to repeatedly in discourse as the *same thing*. For example, a storyteller may refer to one of the characters in a story as *a king*. From then on the same character may be freely mentioned, sometimes as *the king*, other times as *he, her husband, the princess' father, the tyrant*, etc. In context, each of these expressions could be understood as making mention of the king. Hopper and Thompson (1984) describe this property of prototypical nouns as **DISCOURSE MANIPULABILITY**.

To decide whether any given word is a noun or not, you must first determine the morphosyntactic properties of prototypical nouns. Then the properties of a questionable word can be compared to those of prototypical nouns. So, for example, you wouldn't want to start identifying nouns in an unfamiliar language using words that mean 'fist,' or 'explosion.' These are concepts that do not have clear boundaries and/or do not persist over a long period of time. Therefore you don't want to use the grammatical properties of these words to define nouns in general, just in case they belong to some other word class. However, we can be fairly confident that words referring to bounded and individuated items that are stable over time, like 'house' and 'tree,' will be nouns in most contexts in any language.

Grammatical properties of word classes generally involve the ways they may be adjusted to express conceptual categories, and their syntactic **DISTRIBUTION** within larger structures such as phrases, clauses, and texts. In this section we will describe some grammatical properties that tend to be associated with nouns. There is probably no language in which nouns exhibit all of these properties, but the more "noun like" a word is, the more of these properties it is likely to have.

Distributional properties of nouns

Nouns function as heads of Noun Phrases (sometimes abbreviated as NPs). We will have a lot more to say about phrases in chapter 6. For now you can think of a phrase as simply a group of one or more words that "clump together" syntactically.

There are at least two senses in which linguists use the term **HEAD** of a phrase. It seems to be the case that, in all syntactic clumps, there is one word that determines the distributional, or syntactic, properties of the whole clump, and one word that expresses the main meaning of the clump. The word that determines the syntactic properties of the clump is sometimes referred to as the **SYNTACTIC HEAD**, whereas the word that expresses the main meaning of the clump is referred to as the **SEMANTIC HEAD**.

Often the same word is both the syntactic and semantic head of a phrase. This is almost always true of noun phrases. For example, in a noun phrase like *old man* there is no question that *man* is both the syntactic and the semantic head. It is the syntactic head because, for example, if you remove *old*, the part that is left still has the same syntactic properties as the original clump. In examples 3b and e we see that *man* can occur in the same syntactic slot as *old man*. However, if you remove *man*, *old* alone cannot be used in the same way as the original clump (examples 3c and f):

(3)   a. The old man of the sea   d. He told a story about this old man.
       b. The man of the sea   e. He told a story about this man.
       c. *The old of the sea   f. *He told a story about this old.

So it appears that the phrase *old man* and the noun *man* have the same distributional properties, but *old* by itself has different properties, therefore *man* is the syntactic head of this phrase. Another way of saying this is that a noun phrase is a **PROJECTION** of its syntactic head. That is, the syntactic head noun "projects" its nouniness onto the whole phrase.

The word *man* is also the semantic head of the phrase *old man* because the whole phrase refers to a man, and not to "oldness." This property is perhaps easier to illustrate in English using an example in which either of the words in the phrase could refer to something concrete. For example, an English phrase like *computer man* refers to a bounded, individuated concept, so we suspect it is a noun phrase. However, it contains two words that also refer to bounded, individuated concepts, *computer* and *man*. So the question arises as to which of the two nouns is the semantic head of the NP. The answer in this case is easy: the whole phrase probably refers to a man, not a computer, therefore the noun *man* is the semantic head of the NP.

In languages for which there is no word class of adjectives, or in which adjectives and nouns are very similar grammatically, the identification of the syntactic and/or semantic head of a noun phrase can be more difficult. In a clump like *red hen*, in such a language, the words meaning *red* and *hen* could equally refer to the entity that the whole phrase refers to. That is, the color terms and other descriptive words can function just like nouns. For these languages, NPs such as *red hen* are often considered to be examples of **APPOSITION**, i.e., *the red one, the hen*. For example, the Spanish equivalents of all the examples in 3 above are grammatical:

(4) a.   El hombre viejo del mar . . .   'The old man of the sea . . .'
    b.   El hombre del mar . . .   'The man of the sea . . .'
    c.   El viejo del mar . . .   'The old (one) of the sea . . .'
    d.   Contó un cuento sobre este hombre viejo.
           'He told a story about this old man.'
    e.   Contó un cuento sobre este hombre.
           'He told a story about this man.'
    f.   Contó un cuento sobre este viejo.
           'He told a story about this old (one).'

Examples 4c and f show that the adjective *viejo*, 'old,' may function as the syntactic head of a noun phrase. There are other syntactic tests that show that Spanish does, in fact, have a distinct class of adjectives, but they are much more subtle than the comparable tests in English.

While it is almost always the case that for noun phrases the syntactic head and the semantic head are the same word, this is not always true for other kinds of phrases. We will see examples of a "mismatch" between types of heads in the following paragraphs, and in chapter 6.

At this point it may be helpful to say something about syntactic "tests," such as those used above to show that *man* is the syntactic and semantic head of the phrase *old man*. Like all sciences, linguistics has its ways of "probing and poking" its subject matter in order to understand it better. Even as chemists use various techniques for analyzing chemical compounds, so linguists use various techniques for analyzing linguistic structures. Usually the techniques employed by linguists involve changing the order of pieces, adding pieces and/or taking pieces out of a linguistic structure, and then seeing how native speakers react to the resulting structures. Some techniques are better for analyzing certain kinds of structures, or for elucidating certain kinds of properties, than others. For example, the tests for syntactic headship illustrated in the examples in 3 will not necessarily work in all situations. In other situations, other tests may be more appropriate. This is similar to the problem a chemist faces when analyzing, for example, a piece of rock, versus an unknown liquid – the goal may be the same (come up with a chemical analysis), and there will probably be a good deal of methodological overlap, however the exact techniques and procedures will not be identical.

The important point to remember about syntactic headship is that the syntactic head of a phrase is that element of the phrase that determines the syntactic properties of the whole phrase. Another way of saying this is that a phrase is a *projection* of its syntactic head. The main point about semantic heads is that the semantic head of a phrase is the element of the phrase that expresses the main semantic content of the whole phrase (see chapter 1 for a discussion of the notion of semantic content). For different kinds of phrases, and different languages, there may be different tests that are appropriate for determining syntactic and/or semantic headship. We will have more to say about syntactic tests in chapters 6 and 7.

Conceptual categories likely to be associated with nouns or noun phrases

The grammatical properties of nouns or Noun Phrases include ways they can be altered in order to express conceptual categories. Here is a list of conceptual categories likely to be expressed in nouns or NPs. Many of these categories will be elaborated in the following sections and chapters. For now we will just give a list:

- number (singular, **PAUCAL**, **DUAL**, **TRIAL**, plural, **COLLECTIVE**)
- gender (any essentially semantically based noun-classification system)
- **DIMINUTIVE/AUGMENTATIVE**
- **CASE** (**NOMINATIVE**, **ACCUSATIVE**, **GENITIVE**, etc.) (see chapter 8)
- **DESCRIPTIVE MODIFIERS**
- pragmatic status markers (e.g., **ARTICLES**)
- **DEMONSTRATIVES**
- possessive pronouns, or **AGREEMENT** affixes (expressing person, number and/or gender of a possessor of the head noun)
- **DENOMINALIZATION**

Prototypical nouns will probably exhibit all of the grammatical properties of nouns relevant in a given language. Less than prototypical nouns may exhibit some of these properties, but not all. Verbs probably won't exhibit any of the grammatical properties of nouns. However, every language has forms that are "somewhat nouny," and "somewhat verby." Dealing with such intermediate cases can be a real headache for a descriptive linguist.

In this section we will consider English words suffixed with -*ing* in order to illustrate how to determine the word class of a form that is sort of "nouny" and sort of "verby." It is very difficult to think of a word such as *dancing* as expressing a bounded, individuated concept – *dancing* inherently involves motion and change, therefore this form is probably not going to be a prototypical noun. So, let's look at the grammatical properties of this form to determine just how "nouny" it is.

In English, grammatical properties of prototypical nouns include, first of all, the ability to function as heads of noun phrases. Noun phrases, in turn, can be subjects or objects of clauses. Can *dancing* be the subject or object of a clause? The following examples show that *dancing* passes this distributional test for nounhood:

(5) a.   subject: *Dancing* is good for you.
    b.   object: I like *dancing*.

Other properties of prototypical nouns in English are: (1) the possibility of taking descriptive modifiers (*red* car), and (2) the use of **GENITIVE** case pronouns (*my* car). Again, the word *dancing* passes both of these tests:

(6) a.   descriptive modifiers: 'I like *slow dancing*.'
    b.   genitive case pronouns: '*His dancing* is annoying.'

Even though *dancing* passes the first three tests for nounhood, other tests reveal that it is not the best example of a noun. For example, ability to pluralize and take articles, quantifiers and numerals are also properties of prototypical nouns in English. It is rare or odd-sounding for verbs with the *-ing* suffix to possess these properties:

(7) a.   pluralization: '?*Dancings* are hard on the feet.'
    b.   articles: '?*The dancing* in the streets is annoying.'
    c.   quantifiers: '?*Every dancing* is different.'
    d.   numerals: '?I met her *one dancing* ago.'

In addition to these properties of nouns that are *not* possessed by the form *dancing*, there are also some properties of verbs that *are* possessed by this word. For example, verbs can be modified with adverbs while nouns cannot. The following examples show that an adverb like *slowly* can more comfortably modify the word *dancing* (8a and b) than a prototypical noun like *cars* (8c and d), even though the notion of slowness is a semantically reasonable property to apply to cars:

(8)   a. ?I like *slowly dancing*.   c. *I like *slowly cars*.
        b. I like *dancing slowly*.   d. *I like *cars slowly*.

Second, verbs can take direct objects, while nouns cannot. Even when functioning as the subject or object of another verb, the form *dancing* can have a direct object:

(9) a.   *Dancing the tango* is good for you.
    b.   I enjoyed *dancing the night* away.

These morphosyntactic properties make the form *dancing* seem a little bit like a verb, though there are several properties of prototypical verbs that *dancing* does not possess (like ability to be marked for tense or aspect).

Solutions to the problem of which word class *dancing* belongs to vary. Such solutions include:

1.   Taking some property as criterial. For instance, we could simply define *noun* for English as a word that can be modified with a genitive pronoun. In this case *dancing* is a noun. However, if we decide that ability to pluralize were the criterion for nounhood, then *dancing* would not be a noun.

2.   Making up a different word class for each cluster of noun properties possessed by some form or forms in the language. In this case only those words that have all noun properties would be considered nouns. Forms such as *dancing* would be considered something else, such as participles (see below for a definition of the term "participle").

3.   Acknowledging that the difference between nouns and verbs is a con-
          tinuum, and that verbs with the *-ing* suffix fall somewhere in between
          the two extremes.

Solution #1 above is problematic because (a) it cannot be applied in all languages because there is no one property of nouns that is consistent among all
languages, and (b) it ignores the obvious, though inexact, semantic basis for the
word class.

For example, to define nouns as all words that can be modified with a genitive
pronoun is like defining the class of human beings as all "featherless bi-peds."
Though this "definition" may succeed in distinguishing to a large extent the
class of human beings from all other animals, it focuses on incidental rather
than definitional (or necessary) properties. In other words, it begs the question of
why one would even consider featherless bi-peds as a class apart from all other
potentially arbitrary classes of items in the natural world, say red socks, or broken
sticks. Certainly, if we were to take a feathered bi-ped and remove all of its
feathers (poor thing), it would not become a human being. Furthermore, while
we can conceive of a world in which human beings were not featherless bi-peds,
it is much harder to conceive of a world in which some category lacks one of
its necessary properties. For example, try to imagine a world in which red socks
were green – by definition, if a sock is red, it is not green! This shows that
the class "human" consists of more than merely the conjunction of the features
"featherless" and "bi-ped." Another way of saying this is that "featherless bi-peds"
is a sufficient but not a necessary definition of the class "human being."

The best criterial definitions are those which include both necessary and sufficient conditions. Unfortunately such definitions are extremely uncommon in
linguistics. If a criterial definition such as ability to take genitive case pronouns is
suggested for the class of nouns, one should also ask: what is it about items that
take genitive case pronouns that makes them adhere as a class? Why should *that*
property be necessary, and not some other (say, high tone on the first syllable)?

Solution #2 is the approach traditionally taken by linguists. It has the advan-
tage of providing pigeonholes within which to place the various word types in the
language. The basic problem with this approach is that, like solution #1, it is not
universally applicable. The classes derived from various clusters of morphosyntactic properties are (a) not necessarily related to one another in any systematic
way, and (b) not comparable from one language to the next. This situation makes
for a grammatical description that is less readable to someone with no previous
experience with the language. For example, the term **PARTICIPLE** is found in
many grammar descriptions. Nevertheless, what constitutes a participle in language A may or may not have any commonality with what is called a participle
in language B. Therefore someone who knows language B may be misled when
reading the description of language A.

Solution #3 reflects most accurately the nature of linguistic categorization. This
in itself is a point in favor of this approach. However, it also has its disadvantages

to the field linguist attempting to present information about a language clearly and precisely in a grammatical description. These disadvantages include:

1. There is no explicit way of determining exactly *where* on the continuum between noun and verb a particular class falls. One could conceivably count nominal properties and verbal properties, and assign items with more verbal properties to a position closer to the verb extreme, and vice versa for nouns. However, this approach assumes that all properties are weighted equally in terms of their effect on the class membership of the form. There is no a priori reason to accept this assumption. In fact, solution #1 above is based on precisely the opposite assumption, namely that there exists one and only one property that is important enough to distinguish the class, all the other properties being incidental. In any case, it is futile to try to rank morphosyntactic properties according to their importance.

2. It is often the case that a linguist just doesn't know what all of the relevant properties are for a given form. For example, some verbs with *-ing* may take plurals more easily than others: *his many failings* vs. *?his many eatings*. This fact puts *failing* closer to the noun end of the continuum than *eating*. These subtle differences among the behaviors of various forms are probably not available to the fieldworker faced with thousands of words, each potentially exhibiting a cluster of from zero to about ten nominal properties.

3. A description of a grammar is essentially a communicative act. The point is to help readers understand how particular constructions function within the grammatical system of a language. It is clear that a detailed ranking of structures according to their relative nounhood would be of limited use in accomplishing this task. Given the observation above that such a task would also potentially be of unlimited complexity, it is not likely that many linguists would attempt such a ranking.

The recommended approach is to combine solutions 2 and 3 in something like the following manner: forms that are unclear as to their word-class membership (such as verbs with *-ing* suffixes in English) can be given strictly formal labels (e.g. "*-ing* participles"), with an explanation given of their characteristic functions and key morphosyntactic properties. In most cases it is just not worth the effort to be more explicit than this. The payoff in terms of clarity of description is too minuscule. "Participle" is a relatively widely understood term for verb forms that have reduced verbal properties, but which are not full nominalizations. Clauses in which the main verb is a participle are often referred to as PARTICIPIAL PHRASES. However, languages normally have more than one such form and, as mentioned above, the term participle has no more specific universal definition. Therefore, it is important to clarify that the label is simply a shorthand way of referring to the formal class as a whole, and that it should not imply that the form is directly comparable to forms that have been called participles in other languages.

Types of nouns

Every language has certain grammatically defined, but semantically motivated, subclasses of nouns. The following sections describe some common subclasses, including **PROPER NAMES**, and the distinctions between **POSSESS-ABLE** vs. **NON-POSSESSABLE** and **COUNT** vs. **MASS** nouns. Many languages also have a **NOUN CLASS SYSTEM** that consists of many finer distinctions.

Proper names are nouns that are used to address and identify particular persons or culturally significant personages or places. Since proper names are normally used to refer to specific entities both speaker and hearer can identify, they do not usually appear with **ARTICLES**, modifiers, possessors, **RELATIVE CLAUSES** or other elements that make nouns more specific. For example, in English, proper names are distinguished in that they do not (easily) take articles, quantifiers, or other modifiers:

(10)   Proper names   Common nouns
        Mt. Rushmore   house
        ?the Mt. Rushmore   the house
        ?several Mt. Rushmores   several houses
        ?an outlandish Mt. Rushmore   an outlandish house
        ?a Mt. Rushmore that has four   a house that has four
        Presidents' faces carved in it Presidents' faces carved in it

All of the expressions preceded by "?" above can be used in English, but the context must be such that the **REFERENTS** are understood as not being unique (i.e., in a strange situation in which there were more than one Mt. Rushmore). This is not the normal circumstance for the use of proper names.[2]

Proper names sometimes differ from common nouns in other grammatical respects. For example, in many Austronesian languages special case markers are used with proper names. The following examples are from Cebuano, the major language of the Southern Philippines. This language employs the **PRENOMINAL CASE MARKERS** *ni* 'actor' and *si* 'patient' for proper names only. For common names the markers are *sa* and *ang* respectively:

(11) a.   Gibalhin *sa*   tawo   *ang* kaabaw.
           moved   ACT   man   PAT   water.buffalo
           'The man moved the water buffalo.'

    b.   Gibalhin *ni*   Doro   *ang* kaabaw.
                     ACT.PN   PAT
           'Doro moved the water buffalo.'

    c.   Gibalhin *sa*   tawo   *si*   Doro.
                     ACT   PAT.PN
           'The man moved Doro.'

POSSESSABILITY is another respect in which classes of nouns in a language may be distinguished. Many languages have one or more of the following distinctions:

type 1: possessable vs. unpossessable nouns
type 2: obligatorily possessed vs. optionally possessed nouns
type 3: alienably possessed vs. inalienably possessed nouns

Maa (an Eastern Nilotic language) employs a type 1 system. In most dialects of Maa, many nouns cannot normally be grammatically possessed. Items that can be possessed include cows, houses, kin, goats, tools, wells, and money. Items that cannot easily be possessed include meat, water, rivers, mountains, land, rocks, wild animals, stars, etc. (examples courtesy of Doris Payne):

(12)   Non-possessable   Possessable
        ɛnkɔ́p   'land'/'dirt'   ɛnkɛ́ráí   'child'
        ??ɛnkɔ́p áí 'my land'   ɛnkɛ́ráí áí   'my child'

In many west African, Austronesian, and Native American languages there is a difference between obligatorily possessed vs. optionally possessed nouns. In these languages, all nouns can be possessed, but some absolutely must be. Obligatorily possessed nouns normally include body parts and kinship terms. The following examples are from Seko-Padang, a Western Austronesian language of South Sulawesi (examples courtesy of Tom Laskowske):

(13)   Optionally possessed   Obligatorily possessed
        kaya'-ku   'my shirt'   puso-ku   'my heart'
        kaya'-na   'his/her shirt' puso-na   'his/her heart'
        kaya'   'shirt'   *puso   (never occurs alone)

In some languages there are two grammatically distinct ways of expressing possession. All nouns can be possessed, but each noun can only be possessed in one of the two ways. Usually the two kinds of possession are termed **ALIENABLE** vs. **INALIENABLE** possession. Inalienable possession is used for roughly the same class of nouns that are obligatorily possessed in type 2 languages such as Seko Padang. The following examples are from Panare (Cariban, Venezuela). In this language, inalienable nouns (mostly body parts and kinship terms) are possessed via a possessive suffix and a prefix that agrees with the possessor (example 14). Alienable nouns, on the other hand, require the use of an additional word, called a "genitive classifier" (*ú'ku* in example 15):

(14)   Inalienable possession in Panare:
        matá   'shoulder'
        mátan   'my shoulder'
        amatán   'your shoulder'
        yɨmatán   'his/her shoulder'
        Tomán mátan   'Tom's shoulder'

(15)   Alienable possession in Panare:
        wanë   'honey'
        y-ú'ku-n   wanë   'my honey'
        1-CL.liquid-POS honey
        ayu'kún wanë   'your honey'
        yu'kún wanë   'his/her honey'
        Toman yú'kun wanë   'Tom's honey'

One interesting feature of Panare is that there exists both alienable/
inalienable and obligatory/optional possession. So the word *mata* 'shoulder,'
illustrated in example 14 may or may not be possessed, but if it is possessed,
it takes inalienable possession. One the other hand, the word *tamun*, 'husband,
uncle', always has the possessive suffix *-n* on it. In other words, the form **tamu*
does not exist:

(16)   tamún   '(someone's) husband, uncle'
        támun   'my husband'
        anantamún   'our (exclusive) husband(s)'
        atamún   'your husband'
        Achïm tamún   'Achïm's husband'

This illustrates that a language may have more than one distinction in the types
of possession it expresses.

Finally, languages often make a grammatical distinction between nouns that
refer to things that can be counted (**COUNT NOUNS**) and those that refer to
substances, like water, sand, air, wood, etc. (**MASS NOUNS**). In English, mass
nouns do not occur in the plural (except when they are used in a special, count,
sense). Furthermore, mass and count nouns take distinct, but partially overlapping,
classes of articles and quantifiers:

(17)   Mass nouns   Count nouns
        sand   house
        ?many sands   many houses
        much sand   ?much house
        some sand   ?some house
        ?a sand   a house
        ?some sands   some houses

This distinction is based on the meanings of these words (houses can be counted
but sand can't), but evidence that this semantic distinction is important consists
of formal properties. There is potentially an infinite number of "noun subclasses"
based on raw semantic properties, but subclasses are only significant for the
grammar if they have some formal consequences (e.g., whether the form takes
much or *many* as a quantifier).

Verbs

Prototypical **VERBS** are words that describe visible **EVENTS** that produce changes in the world, e.g., *die, run, break, cook, explode*. This characterization defines one extreme of a continuum, of which prototypical nouns occupy the other extreme. In determining whether a questionable form is a verb or not, one must determine how closely it matches the morphosyntactic pattern of prototypical verbs.

As is the case with nouns, and other major word classes, verbs are the semantic, and usually syntactic, heads of the clumps that they are a part of. What this means is that they *project* their distributional properties onto the Verb Phrase (VP). In chapter 6 we will see what this means in practice.

Conceptual categories likely to be expressed in verbs or verb phrases

Verbs or verb phrases tend to express the following conceptual categories:

- agreement/concord (with subject, object, and/or other nominal clause elements. See chapter 8)
- valence (chapter 9)
- **TENSE/ASPECT/MODE** (TAM)
- **EVIDENTIALS/VALIDATIONALS** (morphemes indicating the source or reliability of the information)
- location and direction
- **SPEECH-ACT MARKERS** (whether the clause is a question, an ASSERTION or a command, for example)
- verb(-phrase) **NEGATION**
- **SUBORDINATION/NOMINALIZATION**
- **SWITCH-REFERENCE** (chapter 10)

These categories, and many more, may be expressed by verb-phrase particles or any of the lexical or morphological processes described in previous chapters.

Semantic roles

Before discussing the various subclasses of verbs that may exist in a language, it is necessary to present a fuller discussion of the notion of semantic role. **SEMANTIC ROLES** are roles that participants play in the **MESSAGE WORLD**. The message world can be thought of as the shared imaginary[3] scenes being elaborated in any situation in which people are communicating. This world may correspond more or less closely to the "real world" (whatever that is), but may be entirely fictitious, abstract, or hypothetical. In any case, the message world is populated by participants and props whose properties, actions, and relationships form the content of linguistic messages. Elements of the message world, including semantic roles, are represented in the top half of the form–function composite introduced in chapter 1.

Though semantic roles influence morphosyntax profoundly, they are not primarily morphosyntactic categories. Ideally, semantic roles exist quite apart from linguistic expression. So, for example, if in some imagined situation (which may or may not correspond to objective reality), someone named Hiro purposely greets someone named Toshi, then Hiro is the AGENT and Toshi is the PATIENT of the greeting event, regardless of whether any observer ever utters a clause like *Hiro greeted Toshi* to describe that event. If anyone does care to describe this situation to someone else, they will definitely need to communicate who is the AGENT and who is the PATIENT. Thus every language provides grammatical tools for making that clear. Nevertheless, the roles themselves exist in the message world, and the means of expressing them belong to grammar.

Here we will describe some semantic roles most often expressed by the grammatical relations of subject, object, and indirect object in natural languages (see chapter 8 for a detailed discussion of grammatical relations). These are AGENT, THEME, FORCE, INSTRUMENT, EXPERIENCER, RECIPIENT, and PATIENT. Others, e.g., LOCATION, DIRECTION, SETTING, PURPOSE, TIME, MANNER, etc., are more likely to be expressed in **OBLIQUE** phrases (prepositional phrases in English) or **ADVERBIALS**.

An AGENT is "the typically animate perceived instigator of the action" (Fillmore 1968).[4] In scenes likely to be described by the following clauses, *Percival* would be the AGENT:

(18) a.   Percival ate beans.
     b.   Percival ran around the block.
     c.   That vase was broken by Percival.
     d.   Whom did Percival kiss?
     e.   It was Percival who deceived the President.

A prototypical AGENT is conscious, acts with **VOLITION** (on purpose), and performs an action that has a physical, visible effect. It is a powerful controller of an event. According to this characterization, *Percival* in 18a and c is a near prototypical AGENT. In 18b, although Percival is conscious and presumably acts with volition, there is no visible change in the message world that results from Percival's act. The same sort of observation can be made for 18d and e. Therefore, Percival is a less-than-prototypical AGENT in 18b, d, and e.

A FORCE is an entity that instigates an action, but not consciously or voluntarily. For example, *the wind* is a FORCE in the following clauses:

(19) a.   The wind is carrying us to freedom.
     b.   The wind blew and the waves crashed.
     c.   The sails are filled by the wind.
     d.   What did the wind knock over?
     e.   It was the wind that formed those rocks.

A THEME is a participant that moves, or is the locus of an action or property that does not undergo a change. For example, *Shaggy* is the THEME in the following clauses:

(20) a.   Shaggy fell into the well.
    b.   I'm Shaggy.
    c.   We love Shaggy.
    d.   Scooby looked at Shaggy.
    e.   Scooby forgot Shaggy.
    f.   It was Shaggy who seemed stand-offish.

An INSTRUMENT is something that causes an action indirectly. Normally an AGENT acts upon an INSTRUMENT and the INSTRUMENT accomplishes the action. For example, in the following clauses, *a hammer* is an INSTRUMENT:

(21) a.   I'll smash it with a hammer!
    b.   A hammer smashed the box.
    c.   That box was smashed by a hammer.
    d.   What did Uzma smash with a hammer?
    e.   It was a hammer that Uzma smashed it with.

An EXPERIENCER neither controls nor is visibly affected by an action. Normally an EXPERIENCER is an entity that receives a sensory impression, or in some other way is the locus of some event or activity that involves neither volition nor a change of state. For example, in the following English clauses, *Aileron* is an EXPERIENCER:

(22) a.   Aileron saw the bicycle.
    b.   Aileron broke out in a cold sweat.
    c.   The explosion was heard by Aileron.
    d.   What did Aileron feel?
    e.   It was Aileron who smelled smoke first.

Although THEME, FORCE, INSTRUMENT and EXPERIENCER are clearly semantically distinct from AGENT, languages often treat them the same as AGENT for purposes of grammatical expression. For example, in English, all of these roles are fairly commonly expressed as subjects. However, this is not necessarily true for all languages. Sometimes EXPERIENCERS appear in a different morphological case from AGENTS (see, for example, Guaymí cited in chapter 8).

A RECIPIENT is the typically animate destination of some moving object. The difference between RECIPIENT and GOAL is similar to the difference between AGENT and FORCE. Because RECIPIENT and GOAL are so similar, the forms used for GOALS tend to be similar to those used for RECIPIENTS. For example, English uses the preposition *to* to mark both roles:

(23) a.   I sent the book to Lucretia.   (Lucretia = RECIPIENT)
    b.   I sent the book to France.   (France = GOAL)

A prototypical PATIENT undergoes a visible, physical change in state. In the following clauses, *Joaquin* is the PATIENT (though not always a prototypical one):

(24) a.　　Montezuma stabbed Joaquin.
　　b.　　Joaquin fell from the third floor.
　　c.　　Joaquin was stung by a wasp.
　　d.　　Who washed Joaquin?
　　e.　　It was Joaquin that the republicans believed.

Semantically defined verb subclasses – scenes and argument structures

Verbs, like all words, are just vocal noises apart from their association with particular meanings. The meanings of verbs can be thought of metaphorically as idealized "scenes" that the verbs evoke in the minds of users of the language (Fillmore 1976, 1977. See chapter 9 for more discussion of this metaphor). Semantic features of such idealized scenes profoundly affect the *grammatical* features of individual verbs that evoke them. For example, scenes that inherently involve only one major participant tend to be expressed grammatically by verbs that require only one **ARGUMENT**, usually thought of as the **SUBJECT** (see chapter 8 for a discussion of subjects, objects, and other **GRAMMATICAL RELATIONS**). Any particular alignment of semantic roles and grammatical relations in a clause is sometimes called a **CASE FRAME**, or an **ARGUMENT STRUCTURE**.

For example, the verb *to grow* in English evokes an idealized scene that requires only one participant – a person or thing that grows. For this reason, clauses based on the verb *grow* only require one noun phrase, the subject. The argument structure (also known as the case frame) of this kind of clause can be represented schematically as follows:

(25)　　Scene:　　PATIENT　　GROW
　　　　　　　　　　↓　　　　　↓
　　　　Clause:　　NP$_{Subject}$　　Verb
　　　　　　　　　　The tulip　　grew.

In the case of *grow*, the only required participant is a semantic PATIENT – namely the person or thing that undergoes the change of state referred to by the verb. Many other noun phrases and other elements *may* occur, and usually do, in a clause constructed around the verb *grow*, but in order to qualify as an event of *growing*, only one participant is absolutely necessary. Verbs that evoke scenes that require only one participant are sometimes referred to as **INTRANSITIVE VERBS**, and clauses that require only one noun phrase are sometimes referred to as **INTRANSITIVE CLAUSES**.

Sometimes languages make grammatical distinctions among subclasses of verbs depending on the argument structures they occur in. For example, we have seen that the verb *grow* occurs in an argument structure that involves a PATIENT expressed as a subject argument. Other intransitive verbs occur in argument structures in which the subject is an AGENT (example 26), an EXPERIENCER (example 27), or any number of other possible semantic roles:

(26)   Scene: AGENT   WALK
                     ↓   ↓
        Clause: NP_{Subject}   Verb
                   My grandmother   walked.

(27)   Scene: EXPERIENCER   SNEEZE
                     ↓   ↓
        Clause: NP_{Subject}   Verb
                   Milton   sneezed.

It is hard to find syntactic properties that distinguish these classes of verbs in English, though there are some. For example, the past participle of intransitive verbs, like *grow*, that take a PATIENT as their subject can often be made into adjectives that modify the subject, whereas the past participles of other intransitive verbs generally cannot:

(28)   PAST PARTICIPLES FUNCTIONING AS ADJECTIVES

Patientive intransitive verbs:	Agentive/experiential intransitive verbs:
a *grown* child (a child that grew)	?a/my *walked* grandmother (a grandmother that walked)
a *fallen* log (a log that fell)	?a *sneezed* child (a child that sneezed)
some *melted* ice cream (ice cream that melted)	?a *jumped* athlete (an athlete that jumped)
a *changed* man (a man that changed)	?a *breathed* baby (a baby that breathed)

This test is rather subtle in English, but other languages make much more obvious and systematic grammatical distinctions among subclasses of intransitive verbs based on the semantic roles of their subjects. We will see some examples of these in chapter 8.

Even as the same picture can occur in different frames, the same message-world scene can occur in different argument structures (or "case frames")

In addition to intransitive verbs, all languages have verbs that evoke scenes that require more than one participant. For example, the verb *to eat* in English describes a situation in which two entities interact – an "eater" (prototypically a person or animal) and a thing that "gets eaten" (prototypically a food item). If you don't have these two participants, you don't have an event of "eating."

One major way that these semantic roles are expressed for the verb *eat* in English consists of an argument structure in which the AGENT is the subject and the PATIENT is the object. This structure, and a possible clause that instantiates it, is illustrated in 29:

(29)　　　Scene:　AGENT　EAT　PATIENT
　　　　　　　　　　↓　　　　↓　　　　↓
　　　　　Clause:　NP$_{Subject}$　Verb　NP$_{object}$
　　　　　　　　　　Aileron　　ate　　ice cream.

To a certain extent, argument structures are independent of individual verbs. For example, the verb *eat* perhaps normally occurs in an argument structure such as 29, but may in conversation occur in any number of other argument structures, depending on the communicative needs and creativity of the speaker. Here are some suggestive examples:

(30) a.　　She ate her way through her first year of college.
　　　b.　　I fished, I ate, I slept.
　　　c.　　This soup eats like a meal.
　　　d.　　The battery acid ate a hole in my jeans.

Good dictionaries typically list the major argument structure (or structures) for each verb but cannot possibly list all conceivable frames within which a verb might be used. On the other hand, the meaning of any verb does seem to limit the possible argument structures in which it may occur – verbs don't just randomly occur in any argument structure imaginable. Here is a comparison of some argument structures for the verbs *pound* and *eat*:

(31) a.　　subject = AGENT, object = PATIENT, oblique = INSTRUMENT:
　　　　　　She pounded the table with a hammer.
　　　　　　She ate the ice cream with a spoon.
　　　b.　　subject = AGENT, object = INSTRUMENT, oblique = PATIENT:
　　　　　　She pounded the hammer on the table.
　　　　　　*She ate the spoon on the ice cream.

There is something about the *meanings* of these verbs that make argument structure 31a work for both, while 31b works for *pound* and not *eat*. So we can see that possible argument structures are part of what every speaker of a language must know in order to use verbs understandably in conversations.

As we've seen, the meaning of a verb has a lot to do with the argument structures it can plausibly participate in. In particular, while many verbs can occur in both transitive and intransitive argument structures, they vary in how the transitive and intransitive frames relate to one another.

For example, the class of verbs illustrated by *grow* in 25 take a PATIENT as subject. These verbs can, for the most part, also occur in a transitive frame in which an AGENT is the subject and the PATIENT is the object:

(32)   a. subject = PATIENT   b. subject = AGENT, object = PATIENT
     melt   The ice melted.   Milton melted the ice.
     grow   The tomatoes grew.   Milton grew the tomatoes.
     change The city changed.   The mayor changed the city.
     break The stick broke.   Aileron broke the stick.
     move   The cow moved.   The cowboy moved the cow.
     burn   Dinner burned.   Mable burned dinner.

Other verbs that occur in argument structure b have AGENTS as subject when used intransitively:

(33)   a. subject = AGENT   b. subject = AGENT, object = PATIENT
     jump Milton jumped.   Milton jumped the burglar.
     run   Mable runs (to school).   Mable runs the program.

    c. subject = AGENT, object = THEME
     nod   Frank nodded.   Frank nodded his head.
     swim Maynard swims.   Maynard swam the channel.

Still other verbs are experiential when occurring in an intransitive argument structure. When these verbs occur in any kind of a transitive frame, they either express special metaphorical senses, or seem quite awkward:

(34)   subject = EXPERIENCER   TRANSITIVE FRAME?
    sneeze Jane sneezed.   Jane sneezed her head off.
    cry   The baby cried.   ?Milton cried the baby to sleep.
    sweat The athlete sweated.   Orual sweated the final exam.
    blush Martin blushed.   ?Everett blushed his cheeks.
    doze Alfred dozed.   Ilongo dozed the night away.

In addition to verb subclasses distinguished by their plausible argument structures, the verbs of a language may be subclassified according to other features of the idealized scenes that they evoke in the message world. For example, scenes that involve weather phenomena (*to rain*, *to snow*, *wind to blow*, etc.) are not likely to have any specific participants. Therefore, verbs that evoke such scenes may not have any arguments, or they may have a "dummy" argument that doesn't refer to any entity at all. This is the case in English clauses such as:

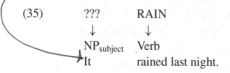

(35)   ???   RAIN
     ↓   ↓
   NP_{subject}   Verb
   It   rained last night.

What rained? What does *it* refer to? The weather? The sky? Nothing really. *It* is just there because English verbs have to have subjects.

The following list describes some situation types that linguists have found useful in categorizing the verbs of a language. These semantic properties tend to affect the grammatical behavior of individual verbs in characteristic ways, some of which will be discussed below. The categorization presented here is based largely on Chafe (1970), Talmy (1985), Jackendoff (1988) and others, though there are several semantic categorization schemes that may be useful in analyzing the grammatical structures of a language. In any given language, verbs that express different situation types may or may not be distinct from one another grammatically. If a language makes no grammatical distinction between the expression of two situation types, there is really no point in incorporating that distinction into the description of the language. What matters for grammar are grammatical properties. Nevertheless, there does seem to be a good deal of "clustering" of grammatical properties around particular areas of semantic space. Therefore, it is useful to consider verbs in terms of the semantics of scenes that they characteristically evoke.

States   NO CHANGE NO ACTION

States are situations in the message world in which there is no change, and no action. Consequently, verbs that prototypically evoke states in the minds of language users tend to not occur in constructions that imply progressive or other dynamic actions. For example, the **PROGRESSIVE ASPECT** in English is the construction that involves the auxiliary verb *be* plus another verb with the suffix *-ing*. This aspect is **DYNAMIC** in that it expresses events in progress, i.e., situations that inherently involve activity and change. Since states inherently *don't* involve activity or change, verbs that express states either sound awkward, or must be interpreted in a non-stative sense when they occur in the progressive aspect:

(36)   a. ?He is being tall.   c. ?They are knowing the answer.
           b. ?She is seeing the airplane. d. ?Sudha is having a cow.

All of these constructions can be used in the right context, but notice that the effect is to change a state into a dynamic event. If someone is *being tall* that seems to imply that he is doing something on purpose to make himself tall. This is quite different from the state described by a clause like *he is tall*. In some varieties of English *to have a cow* (36d) is an idiom meaning something like 'to react in an extremely emotional manner.' This is an extension of the expression *having a baby*, meaning 'giving birth.' Notice that giving birth, and reacting in an emotional way are highly dynamic events – something that involves activity and change. This is very different from the states normally evoked by clauses like *Sudha owns a cow* or *Aileron has three children*.

Stative clauses tend to require only one participant, since there is no action to transfer from one participant to another, though there may be a second, non-affected participant, e.g., the word *answer* in a stative situation like *she knew the answer*, or *mountain* in *she saw the mountain*. Stative concepts are often expressed via adjectives or nouns. However, many languages have a grammatically defined class of "stative verbs," with meanings such as *(be) hot/cold, broken, rotten, melted, skinned, dead, alive, born, unborn, to know, to have, to see.*

Processes

A process is a situation that involves change over time. Processes can be either involuntary or voluntary. In an involuntary process, there is only one participant, and that participant:

- undergoes a change in state,
- does not act with volition,
- does not necessarily move through space, and
- is not the source of some moving object.

For example, the intransitive senses of *grow, die, melt, wilt, dry up, explode, rot, tighten,* and *break* belong to this class.[5] (These verbs occur in answer to the question "What happened to X?", but less easily "What did X do?":)

(37)   What happened to Sylvan?   He died.
        What did Sylvan do?   ??He died.
        What happened to the mustard? It dried up.
        What did the mustard do?   ??It dried up.

Motion

The basic motion verb(s), *come/go,* may have different grammatical properties from motion verbs that express a particular manner, like *swim, run, walk, crawl, fly, jump,* etc. All of these verbs are voluntary, while the following are possibly involuntary movement activities: *fall, drop, flow, spew, squirt,* and others.

Some verbs of motion specify a portion of a trajectory of movement, rather than the whole trajectory. Such verbs include *depart* (specifies the beginning of a trajectory), *arrive* (specifies the end of a trajectory), *pass* (specifies a segment of a trajectory), and others. These may or may not be treated grammatically like other verbs of motion.

Sometimes verbs that describe TRANSLATIONAL MOTION (motion from one place to another) are grammatically distinct from verbs that describe simple motion. For example, translational motion verbs like *escape,* which means 'move from a place of captivity to freedom,' in English can be used adjectivally (38a, b, c), whereas simple motion verbs cannot (38d, e, f):

(38)   Translational motion: Simple motion:
        a. an escaped prisoner   d. *a gone student
        b. the deplaned passengers   e. *a flown bird
        c. a departed loved one   f. *a swum child

Position

Verbs that describe the static position of an object, e.g., *stand, sit, crouch, kneel, lie, hang,* tend to have morphosyntactic properties similar to verbs of motion. For example in English, verbs of position and motion can appear in PRESENTATIVE constructions. Other kinds of verbs cannot as easily be used in such constructions:

(39)	MOTION	Here comes my bus.
		Under the bed scurried the cat.
	POSITION	There sits my bus.
		Under the bed crouched the cat.
	OTHER	?There burns my bus.
		?Under the bed died the cat.

Actions

Actions are situations that are initiated by some conscious or unconscious force but do not *necessarily* involve an affected participant, e.g., *dance, sing, speak, sleep/rest, look (at), read, deceive, care for*. Note that actions can be either **DYNAMIC**, i.e., they involve change (*dance, sing, speak*), non-dynamic (*rest, look at*), or somewhere in between. These verbs may occur in answer to the question "What did X do?," but less easily "What happened to X?," unless a slightly ironic, sarcastic or extended meaning is desired:

(40)	What did Sally do?	She danced the tango.
	What happened to Sally?	?She danced the tango.
	What happened to the tango?	?Sally danced it.

(41)	What did Inigo do?	He read *War and Peace*.
	What happened to Inigo?	?He read *War and Peace*.
	What happened to the book?	?Inigo read it.

(42)	What did Carol do?	She cared for her son.
	What happened to Carol?	?She cared for her son.
	What happened to Carol's son?	?Carol cared for him.

Action-processes

Action-processes are situations initiated by some conscious or unconscious force, and which affect a distinct PATIENT, e.g., *kill, hit, stab, shoot, spear* (and other violent events), plus the transitive senses of *break, melt, crash, change*, and others. Verbs that express action-processes may occur in answer to both the questions "What did X do?" and "What happened to Y?":

(43)	What did Michael do?	He melted the ice.
	What happened to the ice?	Michael melted it.
	What did Aileron do?	She broke Trevor's nose.
	What happened to Trevor's nose?	Aileron broke it.

Factives

Factive verbs are those that describe the coming into existence of some entity, e.g., *build, ignite, form, create, make, gather* as in "a crowd gathered," etc. The semantic role of the entity that comes into existence is sometimes referred to as the PRODUCT, and sometimes as the THEME.

(44)   AGENT   PRODUCT   PRODUCT
          ↓   ↓   ↓
       NP_{subject} Verb NP_{object}   NP_{subject}   Verb
       a. Martin   built   three houses.   b. A crowd   gathered.

Cognition

Verbs of cognition express such concepts as *know*, *think*, *understand*, *learn*, *remember*, and *forget*. The only semantic role that is required for a cognition concept is an EXPERIENCER, though there also may be a SOURCE of the experience. In many languages all or many of these concepts are based on the name of an internal body part, e.g., *heart*, *liver*, *stomach*. For example, concepts expressed in English with the verbs *think*, *remember*, *remind*, *ponder*, and others are expressed in Yagua with verbs based on the root *jaachiy*, meaning 'heart':

(45)   jaachiy   'heart'
        jaachipíyąą   'to think/ponder'
        jaachííy   'to remember'
        jaachíítya   'to remind (cause to remember)'
        jaachipúúy   'to forget'

Sensation

Sensation (or sensory impression) verbs express concepts involving the senses, e.g., *see*, *hear*, *feel*, *taste*, *sense*, *observe*, *smell*, *perceive*, etc. As with concepts of cognition, there are two potential participants in a scene involving a sensory impression. One is the EXPERIENCER, and the other is the SOURCE of the sensation. Languages vary in how they treat these two participants grammatically. Sometimes the EXPERIENCER is treated grammatically like an AGENT of a transitive construction, as in English:

(46)   EXPERIENCER   SOURCE
              ↓   ↓
       NP_{subject} Verb   NP_{object}
       We   saw   you   at The Bronze.

Here the EXPERIENCER, *we*, is treated grammatically as the subject of the construction. Some languages, on the other hand, treat the SOURCE of the sensation as the subject, and the EXPERIENCER in some other manner. This is the case in Guaymí:

(47)   EXPER.   SOURCE
           ↓   ↓
       NP_{dative}   NP_{nominative}   Verb
       Davi-e   ru   hatu-aba.
       David-DAT   airplane.NOM   see-PAST

       'David saw the airplane.'

In this example, the person who sees the airplane (the EXPERIENCER) appears in the **DATIVE** case. This is the case that often expresses the recipient of a transferred object in a situation such as described by the verb *give* in English (see chapter 8). The SOURCE of the visual sensation is the airplane, which occurs in the nominative form.

Emotion

As with cognition concepts, concepts that refer to emotions, such as *fear*, *like/love*, *be angry/sad/mournful*, *be happy/joyful/pleased*, *grieve/mourn*, require an EXPERIENCER and are often based on a body-part noun such as *heart*, *liver*, or *stomach*. In Maa, body-part terms and color terms are often combined to express emotional states (Payne and Kotikash MS 2004):

(48) a. a-dɔ́(r)   ɔ́ŋ ʉ
         INF.SG-be.red   eye.NOM
         'to be fierce, angry and dangerous'

b. a-rɔk   ɔ́ŋ ʉ
    INF.SG-black   eye.NOM
    'to be envious'

c. a-rɔk   táʉ
    INF.SG-black   heart.NOM
    'to be taciturn (not expressing emotion)'

d. a-rok-ú   ɔ́shɔ́kɛ
    INF.SG-black-INCEP   stomach.NOM
    'to become angry'

Utterance

Utterance verbs, such as *speak*, *talk*, *say*, *tell*, *ask*, *answer*, *shout*, *yell*, *whisper*, *call*, *assert*, *imply*, *state*, *affirm*, *declare*, *murmur*, *babble*, *converse*, *chat*, *discuss*, and *sing*, only require an AGENT but may also involve a THEME referring to the content of the utterance. These verbs often exhibit irregular phonological, morphological, and/or syntactic properties. For example, utterance verbs often allow unusual word orders:

(49) a. "I'll be there in a minute," said John.
     b. "Where are we going?" asked Marilyn.
     c. "Pop!" went the toy.

In these clauses the grammatical subject follows the verb, even though with most other verb classes this is not allowed in English. Example 49c is particularly interesting in that we see the verb *go*, which prototypically expresses motion, being used as a verb of "utterance" (the toy "says 'pop'"). As such it follows the grammatical pattern of verbs of utterance by allowing the unusual Verb+Subject word order.

Manipulation

Manipulation verbs express concepts that involve an AGENT using physical or rhetorical force to get someone else to do something. Examples include *force, oblige, compel, urge, make, cause, let, allow*, and *permit. Forbid, prevent, prohibit*, and others are manipulative verbs that imply the use of force to *keep* someone from doing something (see chapter 9 on causative constructions).

The preceding section is meant to help you develop a sense for how semantic properties may influence the grammatical behavior of verbs. It is important to keep in mind that not all of these semantic classes of verbs will be distinguished by grammatical properties in every language. Furthermore, there are many more semantically based subclasses of verbs that a language may be sensitive to grammatically. The subclasses listed here represent "areas" of semantic space around which verbs with particular grammatical properties tend to cluster. However, the actual clustering of verbs will vary from language to language. Linguists are interested in the categorization that is relevant to the language, being careful not to impose a categorization scheme that may seem reasonable to the linguist, but for which there is no concrete grammatical evidence in the particular language being described.

Adjectives

An **ADJECTIVE** is a word that can be used in a noun phrase to specify some property of the head noun of the phrase, for example its color, size, shape, temperament, or other **PROPERTY CONCEPTS** (Thompson 1988). Another major function of adjectives is to express the main semantic content of a verb phrase, as in the following:

(50)   My holiday was *very long*.

The phrase *very long* is an Adjective Phrase (AP), because its distributional properties are determined (or projected) by the adjective *long* (see the discussion of syntactic headship of noun phrases above). This whole phrase, in turn, is a major part of the verb phrase *was very long*. The syntactic head of this verb phrase is the verb *was*. This is evidenced by the fact that the string *was very long* has all the distributional properties of verb phrases, and does not have the properties of adjective phrases. For example, you cannot modify a noun with the phrase *was very long* (example 51b), whereas you can modify a noun with the phrase *very long* (51a):

(51) a.   That *very long book* was fascinating.
    b.   *That *was very long book* was fascinating.

Another respect in which *was* is the syntactic head of the phrase *was very long* in example 50 is that it expresses all of the inflectional categories (tense, aspect, person, etc.) needed for this phrase. However, while it is clear that *was* is the syntactic head of its phrase, it is arguable that the adjective phrase, *very long*, is the semantic head, since it expresses the main semantic content of the VP. In a certain sense, the verb *was* (more accurately, *be*, in an appropriate inflectional form) is simply there to carry the inflectional information. It adds nothing substantive to the meaning. In fact many languages do not use a verb at all in this kind of clause.

Unlike nouns and verbs, adjectives cannot be characterized in terms of a prototype. This is because adjectives stand "between" nouns and verbs, evoking property concepts, rather than things or events. In fact, some languages have no grammatically distinct category of adjectives. In such languages, all property concepts are expressed as either nouns or verbs. Many other languages can express property concepts either as nouns or as verbs depending on how they are used in discourse (Thompson 1988).

Adj → no prototype [handwritten annotation]

English fairly clearly does have a distinct class of adjectives. This is because words that refer to property concepts for the most part have none of the grammatical properties of nouns or verbs. For example, properties of verbs in English include: (1) ability to take past tense (example 52a) and (2) agreement with a third-person singular subject in the present tense (52b). Properties of nouns include: (1) ability to take a plural marking (52c) and (2) ability to head noun phrases that take articles, modifiers, and quantifiers (52c and d):

(52)   a. He sang all evening.   e. *He sicked all evening.
       b. She sings every morning.   f. *She sicks every morning.
       c. We saw thirty-five patients.   g. *We saw thirty-five sicks.
       d. The patient is sitting on the sofa. h. *The sick is sitting on the sofa.

Adjectives in English have none of these properties (52e through h).[6] This is good evidence that English has a grammatically defined word class of adjectives.

Adverbs

Any full lexical word (see chapter 1) that isn't clearly a noun, a verb, or an adjective is often put into the class of **ADVERB**. Semantically, forms that have been called adverbs cover an extremely wide range of concepts. For this reason they cannot be identified in terms of individuation or any other well-defined semantic parameter. Also, some adverbs function on the clause or discourse level, i.e., their semantic effect (or **SCOPE**) is relevant to entire clauses or larger units rather than just to phrases. As with adjectives, there are no prototypical adverbs. Formally, adverbs can be characterized primarily in terms of their distribution. They are typically the most unrestricted word class in terms of their position in clauses. In the following subsections, English examples of various types of adverbs are presented. As mentioned with respect to verb subclasses described earlier, not every language exhibits all of these classes, and any language may have classes not represented here.

If it's not a N, V, or ADJ, probs an ADV. [handwritten annotation]

Manner

Manner adverbs usually constitute the largest subclass of adverbs in language. In English, manner adverbs are often formed from adjectives by the addition of the suffix -*ly*, e.g., *quickly, slowly, patiently, frequently.*

Time

Time adverbs include words such as *yesterday, today, tomorrow, next/last year/week/month, early, late,* etc.

Direction/location

Adverbs that express direction and/or location include the following: *up/downriver, up/downhill, up/down(ward), north(ward), south(ward), east(ward), west(ward), left(ward), right(ward), hither, thither,* etc.

Evidential/epistemic

EVIDENTIAL adverbs indicate the source of the information expressed in the clause (e.g., firsthand observation, secondhand observation, hearsay, inference, or pure conjecture). In English, evidential adverbs include *apparently, undoubtedly,* and *obviously.* English also uses what appear to be verbs of utterance or perception to accomplish this function, e.g., *I understand, they say, I hear, it seems, I guess,* etc.

EPISTEMIC adverbs indicate the degree to which the speaker is committed to the truth of the clause. Examples in English include: *maybe, possibly, surely, definitely,* and *really.* Sometimes there is a fine line, or a continuum, between epistemic adverbs and adverbs that serve a HEDGING function in discourse. Hedging is what speakers do when they are not sure how their utterances will be interpreted by the audience. It is a way speakers distance themselves from social commitment to the truth of their utterances. Good examples of hedging adverbs in English would be fixed expressions like *sorta, kinda,* and *nstuff.*

Other word classes

Nouns and verbs are almost always "open" word classes, in the sense that there is no theoretical limit to the number of nouns or verbs a language may have. New nouns and verbs are constantly being added to every language as speakers find they need to express new concepts. Most languages have thousands of nouns and verbs.[7] Many also have hundreds of adjectives, and adverbs, though these classes seem to be more limited than nouns and verbs. Some languages are reported to have no true adjectives, or perhaps only a handful. The same is true for adverbs.

Nevertheless, noun, verb, adjective, and adverb are usually considered to be the major word classes of any language. They express the main content of messages to be communicated. This is because they express complex and multidimensional ideas, such as *sincerity*, *absolutism*, and *underwear*. Words in minor classes, on the other hand, tend to express very limited and straightforward ideas. Sometimes words in major classes are described as expressing "lexical content," or "lexical meaning."

Languages also typically have several minor word classes, such as pronouns, AUXILIARIES, particles, conjunctions, and others. These classes express "grammatical" or "relational" meaning rather than lexical meaning. In other words their meaning is more restricted to very well-defined conceptual categories, like AND, SINGULAR, or PAST TENSE rather than complex lexical meanings like *mother* or *yesterday*. Minor word classes also tend to be "closed" in the sense that there is usually a limited, well-defined list of members for any given category. It is relatively difficult to add a member to a minor word class.

The following is a list of some of the minor word classes that may exist in a language, along with a few examples, mostly from English. Any given language may have fewer or more minor word classes than these.

Pronouns and anaphoric clitics

PRONOUNS are free forms (as opposed to affixes) that function alone to fill the position of a noun phrase in a clause. There are typically several "sets" of pronouns in a language. Here we will discuss PERSONAL PRONOUNS only. Other types, including RELATIVE PRONOUNS, POSSESSIVE PRONOUNS, DEMONSTRATIVE PRONOUNS and INTERROGATIVE PRONOUNS, will be discussed in later chapters. Table 4.1 presents the personal pronouns of most standard varieties of English.

Table 4.1 *Personal pronouns of English*

		Subject	Non-subject
Singular	1st person	I	me
	2nd person	you	you
	3rd person feminine	she	her
	3rd person masculine	he	him
	inanimate	it	it
Plural	1st person	we	us
	2nd person	you	you
	3rd person	they	them

Some varieties of English have added a pronoun (*y'all*, *you'ns*, *youse*, *youse guys*, *etc.*) in order to make up for the fact that second person plural is not distinguished from second person singular. However, such changes are very slow in becoming the norm and are certainly not as common as is the addition of new nouns and verbs.

For many languages it is difficult to distinguish **PRONOUNS** from **AGREE-MENT** (or concord) affixes. Here we will give strictly formal definitions, though it must be kept in mind that there is no necessary correlation between the function of a particular system in one language and formally similar systems in other languages. For example, free pronouns in English function roughly like person agreement marking does in Spanish. In Spanish the inflected form of a verb is sufficient to express a complete clause, e.g., *baila* 'he/she dances.' So we want to say that in Spanish, person marking on the verb is an **ANAPHORIC DEVICE**. That is, it counts as the only reference to the subject of the verb. In standard varieties of English, verb agreement cannot constitute the only reference to a participant, e.g., *dances* is not a well-formed clause, even though the *-s* suffix in some sense "refers to" a third-person singular subject. Therefore, we say that person marking on verbs in English is **NON-ANAPHORIC**.

Now, let us compare the pronouns. Spanish free pronouns are seldom used in discourse and are usually described as "emphatic" or "contrastive," whereas English pronouns are much more frequent. When we look at English personal pronouns more closely, however, we find that there are really two types – **STRESSED** and **UNSTRESSED**. Most personal pronouns in English discourse are unstressed. If they are stressed, they function very similarly to the Spanish pronouns, i.e., to express **CONTRASTIVENESS** of some sort. So a Spanish clause with a pronoun, e.g., *ellos vinieron*, roughly corresponds in function to an English clause with a stressed pronoun, *THEY came* (as opposed to someone else). The Spanish clause without a pronoun, *vinieron*, corresponds more or less to the English clause with an unstressed pronoun, *they came*. So it appears that English and Spanish each have two anaphoric devices functioning to refer to participants in events. Spanish person marking corresponds functionally to English unstressed pronouns while Spanish pronouns correspond to English stressed pronouns (roughly speaking). This illustrates that similar structures (e.g., pronouns in English and Spanish) can function very differently in discourse.

ANAPHORIC CLITICS kind of fall "in between" pronouns and agreement affixes. They are not free morphologically – they must attach to another word (see chapter 1). However, like personal pronouns they replace noun phrases. That is, typically either a determined noun phrase or a clitic, but not both, can refer to a participant in a given position in a clause. For example, in Yagua, a preverbal reference to a subject can be either a full noun phrase (example 53) or a proclitic (54), but not both (55):

(53)   Manungo   murráय.   'Manungo sings.'
        M.   sing

(54)   Sa-murrą́ą́y   'He sings.'
         3SG-sing

(55)   *Manungo sa-murrą́ą́y.

That *sa-* is not a pronoun is shown by the fact that it cannot stand alone. For example, you cannot answer a question like "Who's singing?" in Yagua simply with the form *sa*; there is a distinct third-person singular pronoun, *níí*, that is used in such contexts. Also, *sa-* can only appear immediately before the verb stem, whereas pronouns (such as *níí*) have the same distributional privileges as noun phrases (i.e., they can occur pretty much anywhere in a clause).

Furthermore, there is good morphological evidence that *sa-* must be bound to the verb that follows. For example, it is affected by morphophonemic rules that do not cross word boundaries.

The following are distinctions commonly reflected in pronoun/anaphoric clitic paradigms. Not all of these will be applicable to all languages, and there may be more that aren't mentioned here:

1.   PERSON. "First person" refers to the person who is speaking. "Second person" refers to the hearer (sometimes called the ADDRESSEE or audience). First and second persons are sometimes collectively referred to as SPEECH ACT PARTICIPANTS (or SAPs). "Third person" usually refers to any non-speech-act participant.[8]

       Many languages have an INCLUSIVE/EXCLUSIVE distinction within the class of first person. First person inclusive includes speaker and hearer and may or may not include a non-speech-act participant. First person exclusive excludes the hearer.

2.   NUMBER. Like nouns, pronouns and anaphoric clitics can vary for number. Usually, all the number classes in any language will be instantiated in the pronoun system, even if they are lacking for other types of nouns. For example, many languages have a DUAL class in the pronoun system, but not on full noun phrases. Also, classes that are expressed in the pronoun system may be "optional" on full nouns, or may occur only with certain classes of full nouns, e.g., animates.

3.   GENDER, or NOUN CLASS. Typical gender classes include masculine, feminine and neuter or inanimate. Many languages provide a much richer system for classifying nouns, typically in terms of shape, size, or function (see Craig 1986 and Aikhenvald 2000). This system often finds expression in pronouns, anaphoric clitics, and special morphemes called CLASSIFIERS.

4.   GRAMMATICAL RELATIONS. Subject, object, ergative, absolutive (see chapter 8).

5.   CASE or SEMANTIC ROLE. Agent, Patient, etc. (see the section on verbs above).

6.   IDENTIFIABILITY/SPECIFICITY. In many languages different pronouns are used for non-specific and/or non-identifiable referents.

For example, English employs the forms *whoever, whatever, wherever*, etc., as non-specific pronouns. Third-person plural forms (*they, them*) are often used to refer to non-specific or non-identifiable referents (see chapter 9 under impersonal passives).

7.   **HONORIFICS**. Very often different pronouns or anaphoric clitics are used depending on the relative social statuses of the speech-act participants. In English, there are some unusual situations where special forms are used in place of the standard second-person pronoun *you*. For example, when addressing a judge in a courtroom situation it is still customary to use the term *your honor*. Many other languages use honorifics on an everyday basis. For example, standard Spanish uses *tú* and *te* for the second-person subject and object pronouns when speaking in a familiar manner. In a more formal situation *Usted* and *le* are more appropriate.

Auxiliaries

AUXILIARIES (abbreviated AUX) are sometimes called "helping verbs." They are like verbs in that they tend to express the same sorts of conceptual categories that verbs do. However, they have a number of properties that distinguish them from prototypical verbs. First of all, the class of auxiliaries has all the properties of grammatical morphemes rather than full lexical words (see chapter 1, p. 15); auxiliaries are usually smaller than verbs in terms of numbers of phonemes, they constitute a smallish, closed class, and express relatively few semantic features. Auxiliaries also have different distributional properties than verbs do, so it makes sense to treat them as a word class distinct from verbs. One major feature that distinguishes auxiliaries from verbs is the fact that auxiliaries are the syntactic heads of the phrases they are a part of, but not the semantic heads (see above, p. 96, for a discussion of the difference between syntactic heads and semantic heads of phrases). Other verbs can typically be the syntactic and semantic heads of their phrases.

All elements that are syntactic heads of their phrases, but not semantic heads, must take a **COMPLEMENT**. The complement is the element that expresses the main semantic content. This makes sense, since, if something, like an auxiliary, only expresses grammatical meaning, it needs to rely on something else in order to express some communicational content. It needs something to "complete" it, hence the term "complement." For example, an auxiliary like *will* only expresses future time. We can't talk about future time in the abstract without imagining some scene that may occur in the future. In other words, a clause like the following must be understood as lacking some important information:

(56)   Frodo will.

Frodo will *what*? This could be a response to a question like *Who will challenge Sauron?* but in that case the complement *challenge Sauron* is understood. Frodo can't *will*, in the abstract, without willing *something*. So auxiliaries, as well as all other elements that are syntactic heads but not semantic heads of phrases, must have complements.

In English, auxiliaries come before their complements. In languages in which the verb usually comes at the end of the clause, such as Japanese, Turkish, Quechua, and many others, auxiliaries follow their complements.

In English, as in many languages, some verbs, notably *be*, *do*, and *have*, can be auxiliaries:

(57)   Slumbat *is* sleeping.
           Slumbat *does* need his rest.
           Slumbat *has* slept for three hours.

Though they can also be ordinary verbs:

(58)   Slumbat *is* a doctor.
           Slumbat *does* watercolors for a living.
           Slumbat *has* three pigs.

Another group of auxiliaries in English are sometimes called **MODALS**, or **MODAL AUXILIARIES**, because they express various speaker attitudes or evaluations of the information expressed:

(59)   Slumbat   *would*   encourage her to renunciate.
                     should
                     might
                     must
                     may
                     can
                     could
                     hasta ('has to')
                     oughta
                     will

Syntactically, the modal auxiliaries of English are really quite distinct from the auxiliary verbs (*be, do* and *have*), and in some frameworks are considered to be an entirely distinct word class. Grammatically, the "future-tense" auxiliary *will* falls into this class, though its function is very much in the range of tense marking (see, e.g., Payne 1997, chapter 8, for a fuller description of modal categories). In chapter 6 we will discuss the syntactic properties of auxiliaries in English in more detail.

Complementizers

COMPLEMENTIZERS are words that introduce a whole clause when it is a part of another clause or phrase. An example of a complementizer in English is the unstressed *that* that occurs in a sentence like:

(60)   I know *that* Elvis lives.

Notice that what follows *that* in this sentence is a clause in and of itself. "Elvis lives" is a perfectly well-formed sentence of English. We will have more to say about these kinds of **EMBEDDED CLAUSES** in chapter 10.

Adpositions

ADPOSITIONS, like auxiliaries, are another class of words that are syntactic heads of the phrases they are a part of, but are not normally the semantic heads. For this reason, adpositions must take a complement in order to express communicational content. An adposition expresses a relationship between its complement (sometimes called the *object* of the adposition) and the rest of the clause it appears in. Adpositions can be subdivided into prepositions and postpositions. English has **PREPOSITIONS**, such as *on*, *in*, *over*, *through*, and *above*. These are called PREpositions because they come before their complements:

(61)   *in* the basket   *under* the palace

Many other languages, including Japanese, have **POSTPOSITIONS** – adpositions which follow their complements:

(62) a.   biku   *no*   'of/inside/near the fishbasket'
             fishbasket in

     b.   kookyu *ue*   'Above the palace'
             palace above

We will have much more to say about adpositions and adpositional phrases in chapter 6.

Conjunctions

CONJUNCTIONS are small words that express relational ideas such as *and*, *but*, or *or*. Sometimes words that introduce **ADVERBIAL CLAUSES** are called **SUBORDINATING CONJUNCTIONS**. In English, these would be words or phrases like *because, though, therefore, even though,* and *although*. Clausal coordination and subordination will be discussed in chapter 10.

Determiners

As used in many linguistic theories, the term **DETERMINER** describes a position, or "slot," in a syntactic structure, rather than a word class (see chapter 6). The determiner position occurs near the beginning of a noun phrase in English, and several other Indo-European languages. However, a few theories have proposed that determiners must exist in all languages. Words that fill the determiner slot function to specify, identify, or quantify the following noun phrase. They can come from any number of word classes and can even be whole phrases. Here are some examples from English:

(63) a.	*a* system error; *the* system error	Articles: *a, the, an*
b.	Ø systematic errors; Ø clean air.	Zero (or "null") article for non-identified plural noun phrases, mass nouns and proper names
c.	*this* ridiculous textbook	Demonstratives: *this, that, these, those*
d.	*each* student	Quantifiers: *each, every, all, many, any, much, some, few*, etc.
e.	*either* end	
f.	*What* fingerprints?	Some question words
g.	*My* fingerprints, *Aileron's* fingerprints *The Queen of England's* crown	Possessive pronouns and noun phrases
h.	*You* linguists, *we* intellectuals	Some personal pronouns

Like auxiliaries and adpositions, determiners are arguably the syntactic heads of their phrases. The reason for this is that determined noun phrases (noun phrases with determiners) have different syntactic properties from "undetermined" noun phrases, in languages that make the distinction. See chapter 6, for further discussion of determiners and determined noun phrases in English).

Particles

PARTICLES are "small," uninflected words or clitics that normally express information having to do with tense, aspect, MODE, evidentiality, discourse structure, or other nuances of meaning. For example, there are a few particles that may occur within verb phrases (see chapter 6) in English:

(64)	You shine *up* like a new penny.	(*up* indicating action was fully accomplished)
	Aileron will *not* wear that dress.	(*not* as a negative particle)
	I want *to* raise turnips.	(*to* as an "infinitive particle")

Others function at the clause level:

(65)	That's her, *um*, friend.	(*um* as a "hesitation particle")
	So, what are you doing this summer?	(*so* as a discourse structuring particle)
	You're going to Toronto, *eh?*	(*eh* as a yes/no question particle)

In many languages, clause-level particles are used extensively in discourse to structure the flow of information. Such particles typically occur near the beginning of a clause, or at the very end. They can be very difficult to gloss in any consistent way (cf., the particle *so* in the usage exemplified in 65). For example, the following excerpt from a Yagua text illustrates three discourse-structuring particles, *jį́į́ta*, *niy*, and *dáy*:

(66) a. Núú   jį́į́ta   t̯a̯a̯ry-į́į́.   'One of them returned.'
         one   JIITA   return-NOM:ANIM

     b. Níí   niy   jį́į́ta   mísa   dáy.   'HE got well.'
         3SG   NIY   JIITA   heal   DAY

     c. Núú   jį́į́ta   jaa-ñuvį̃́į̃́   tḭ̀ḭtáju   roorí-vïïmú-ju̯.
         one   JIITA   enter-ARR1   all   house-inside-towards
         'One went right into the house.'

     d. Níí   NIY   jį́į́ta   dííy   tḭ̀ḭtáju.   'HE died completely.'
         3SG   NIY   JIITA   die   all

The use of *jį́į́ta* indicates that each clause describes an important sequential event in the story. The particle *niy* that appears in clauses 66b and 66d enforces the contrast between the two characters, similar to extra stress on pronouns in English. Finally, *dáy* in 66b divides the two parts of this excerpt in half. It clarifies that the speaker is contrasting not only two characters but also the two very different incidents that happened to each one. Because these meanings are difficult to "capture" in a concise morpheme-by-morpheme gloss, we have tentatively "glossed" these morphemes simply by repeating their forms, in small capital letters. This may be an acceptable interim practice for morphemes that are particularly unruly. However, as research on a language progresses, linguists always strive to provide concise and insightful glosses for all morphemes.

Conceptual outline of chapter 4

I.   Every language has major word classes and minor word classes. All languages have nouns and verbs (at least at the level of discourse). Most languages also have adjectives, and adverbs. Nouns, verbs, adjectives, and adverbs are the four major word classes. All languages also have several "smaller," or "minor," word classes, such as pronouns, conjunctions, and particles.

II.   Prototypical nouns are words which refer to *participants* in message-world events, and which tend to not change drastically over time. Nouns are defined grammatically by their grammatical properties.

       Nouns may be divided into semantically motivated subclasses. Typical semantic distinctions among noun subclasses include:
       • count vs. mass
       • proper vs. common
       • possessable vs. non-possessable
       • alienably possessed vs. inalienably possessed
       • animacy
       • gender

III.   Prototypical verbs are words which refer to *actions*, or *events*. Verbs are defined grammatically by their grammatical (distributional and structural) properties.

IV.   Semantic roles are the roles that participants play in message-world events, quite apart from any linguistic expression of those events. Verbs often fall into various "subclasses" based on the semantic roles of the participants in the scenes they express.

V.   Adjectives are words that typically express "property concepts" but are defined grammatically by their grammatical properties. Not all languages have a grammatically defined class of adjectives.

VI.   Adverbs are semantically rich content words that do not fall into any of the previous three major word classes.

Exercise 4.1: Chorti'

Adapted from England (1988)

1. kotor	'kneeling'	11. sitz'	'boy'
2. wa'rwa'r	'always standing'	12. ja'ja'	'soaked'
3. tzi'i'	'dog'	13. ji'	'sand'
4. rum	'dirt'	14. tuntun	'hard, like rock'
5. ja'	'water'	15. kotorkotor	'always kneeling'
6. lukurlukur	'always hanging'	16. pakarpakar	'always drunk'
7. pakar	'drunk'	17. ji'ji'	'full of sand'
8. sitz'sitz'	'like a boy'	18. wa'r	'standing'
9. rumrum	'full of dirt'	19. tzi'i'tzi'i'	'like a dog'
10. lukur	'hanging'	20. tun	'rock'

A.   What language family does Chorti' belong to?

B.   What morphological process do you see operating in these data? Be specific.

C.   There are three word classes represented in these examples. What are the three classes? Give your evidence for the classes, and for each class describe the conceptual category or categories expressed by the one morphological pattern evident in these data (in other words, the conceptual category expressed may be different, depending on the word class of the root).

Exercise 4.2: Apinajé

Ronnie Sim

1. kukrẽ kokoi   'The monkey eats.'
2. kukrẽ kra   'The child eats.'

3. ape kra.	'The child works.'
4. kukrẽ kokoi ratš	'The big monkey eats.'
5. ape kra metš	'The good child works.'
6. ape metš kra	'The child works well.'
7. ape ratš mɨ metš	'The good man works a lot.'
8. kukrẽ ratš kokoi punui	'The bad monkey eats a lot.'
9. ape punui mɨ piŋetš	'The old man works badly.'
10. ape piŋetš mɨ	'The man works a long time.'

A.   Where is Apinajé (also known as Apinaye) spoken? How many speakers are there?

B.   List and gloss all the morphemes in these data.

C.   How are adjectives and adverbs distinguished in Apinajé (if at all)?

Exercise 4.3: English word classes

Tom Payne

Below are ten stems in English. Your task will be to determine, as best you can, the number and identity of grammatically distinguished word classes and subclasses that these stems can be divided into. The ten stems that are the focus of this problem are:

1. destroy	4. suspicious	7. hair	10. cry
2. destruction	5. very	8. slice	
3. sympathy	6. owe	9. block	

The following data illustrate these stems in various morphosyntactic contexts, including many ungrammatical contexts (marked by an asterisk). These data will allow you to identify morphosyntactic properties that may distinguish word classes and subclasses. Use the analytical methods described in this chapter to identify the word classes and subclasses. It will be important to provide *evidence* for your analysis, since there may be more than one "correct" solution to this problem.

(1)
1. destroyed	12. ?three destructions
2. *destructioned	13. *three sympathies
3. *sympathied	14. *three suspiciouses
4. *suspicioused	15. three hairs
5. *haired	16. *three verys/veries
6. *veryed / *veried	17. *three owes
7. owed	18. three cries
8. cried	19. three slices
9. sliced	20. three blocks
10. blocked	21. *very destroy
11. *three destroys	22. *very destruction

23. *very sympathy
24. very suspicious
25. *very hair
26. *very owe
27. *very cry
28. *very slice
29. *very block
30. completely destroy
31. *completely destruction
32. *completely sympathy
33. completely suspicious
34. *completely hair
35. *completely very
36. ?completely owe
37. ?completely cry
38. completely slice
39. completely block
40. destroy an apple
41. *destruction an apple
42. *sympathy an apple
43. *suspicious an apple
44. *hair an apple
45. *very an apple
46. owe an apple (a dollar/a favor . . .)
47. *cry an apple (a dollar/a favor . . .)
48. slice an apple
49. block an apple (as it flies)
50. *a lot of destroy
51. a lot of destruction
52. a lot of sympathy
53. *a lot of suspicious
54. a lot of hair
55. *a lot of very
56. *a lot of owe

57. *a lot of cry
58. *a lot of slice
59. *a lot of block
60. She is destroying it.
61. *She is destructioning it.
62. *She is sympathying it.
63. *She is suspiciousing it.
64. *She is hairing it.
65. *She is verying it.
66. ?She is owing it.
67. *She is crying it.
68. She is slicing it.
69. She is blocking it.
70. *their destroy
71. their destruction
72. their sympathy
73. *their suspicious
74. their hair
75. *their very
76. *their owe
77. their cry
78. their slice
79. their block
80. *the obvious destroy
81. the obvious destruction
82. the obvious sympathy
83. *the obvious suspicious
84. the obvious hair
85. *the obvious very
86. *the obvious owe
87. the obvious cry
88. the obvious slice
89. the obvious block

Exercise 4.4: Maa word classes

Doris Payne and Tom Payne

Below are eleven roots in Maa, the language of the Maasai, Samburu and certain
other ethnic groups in Kenya and Tanzania, East Africa. Your task is to determine,
as best you can, the identity and number of grammatically distinguished word
classes and subclasses that the roots divide into. Rough English descriptions of
the concepts evoked by the roots are given as glosses, though some of the roots
cannot stand as full words by themselves. The eleven roots that are the focus of
this problem are:

1. ayíónì	'boy'	
2. dɔ	'red'	
3. duŋ	'cut'	
4. nyɔrr	'like, love'	
5. ŋirô	'grayish-brown'	
6. kɪtí	'small, young, little (amount or size)'	

7. olêŋ	'very'
8. or	'sweep'
9. Pir	'fat'
10. sídáí	'good'
11. títo	'girl'

The following data illustrate these roots in various morphosyntactic contexts, including some ungrammatical contexts (marked by an asterisk). Use the analytical methods described in this chapter to identify the word classes and subclasses evident in these data. It will be important to provide *evidence* for your analysis, since there may be more than one "correct" solution.

NOTES: *ɔ(l)-* and *o(l)-* are grammatically masculine gender prefixes. *ɛ(n)-*, *e(n)-*, and *ɛnk-* are grammatically feminine gender prefixes. *á-* means '1SG subject.' Any tone differences are irrelevant to the exercise.

(1)

1. ɛnkayíónì	'a little boy'
2. ɔlayíónì	'a boy'
3. entíto	'a girl'
4. oltíto	'a huge oafish girl' (offensive)
5. entíto ayíónì	'a boyish girl'
6. *entíto nayíónì	('a girl that is boyish')
7. *ɔlayíónì títo	('a girlish boy')
8. árá ɔlayíónì	'I am a boy'
9. *ɔlayíónì olêŋ	('a very boy')
10. esìdáí	'a good (fem.) thing'
11. osídáí	'a good (masc.) thing'
12. entíto sídáí	'a good girl'
13. *entíto násídáí	('a girl that is good')
14. *esídáí títo	('a good girl')
15. *osídáí ayíónì	('a good boy')
16. árá sídáí	'I am good'
17. sídáí olêŋ	'very good'
18. eŋirô	'donkey' / 'a brownish-gray one'
19. ɔlayíónì ŋirô	'a dirty boy'
20. *entíto naŋirô	('a girl that is dirty')
21. árá ŋirô	'I am brownish-gray'
22. etóŋírònò	'It became brownish-gray'

23. ŋirô olêŋ	'very brownish-gray'
24. ɛnkɪtí	'a small/young one'
25. entíto kɪtí	'a small/young girl'
26. *entíto nakɪtí	('a girl that is small/young')
27. ɛnkɪtí ayíónì	'a small/young boy'
28. árá kɪtí	'I am small/young'
29. kɪtí olêŋ	'very small'
30. *enduŋ / *olduŋ	('a cut/cutting')
31. *entíto duŋ	('a cutting girl')
32. entíto nádúŋ	'a girl that cuts'
33. *enduŋ títo	('a cut girl')
34. *árá duŋ	('I am cut'/'I am a cut thing'/'I am a section')
35. árá endúŋótó	'I am a section'
36. átúdúŋò	'I have cut it'
37. âdúŋítò	'I am cutting it'
38. *adúŋu	('I will start/begin to cut')
39. ádúŋ olêŋ	'I cut a lot'
40. *ɛnyɔrr	('a/the love')
41. *entíto nyɔrr	('a loving girl')
42. entíto nányɔ́rr	'a girl that loves'
43. *ɛnyɔrr títo	('a loving girl')

44.	*árá nyɔrr	('I am love/loving')	61. empirón	'fatness'
45.	árá ɛnyɔ́rrátá	'I am love'	62. *entíto pir	('a fat girl')
46.	átɔ́nyrrà ɔlayíónì	'I (have) loved the boy'	63. entíto nápír	'a girl that is fat'
			64. *ɛmpir títo	('a fat girl')
47.	*ányɔ́rrítà	('I am loving it')	65. *árá pir	('I am fat')
48.	enyɔ́rrù entíto	'She will begin to love the girl'	66. ápír	'I am fat'
			67. átópírò	'I have become fat'
49.	ányɔ́rr olêŋ	'I love a lot'		
50.	*endɔ / *ɔldɔ	('a red one')	68. *ápírítò	('I am being fat')
51.	*entíto dɔ	('a red girl')	69. ápírù	'I will become fat'
52.	entíto nádɔ́	'a girl that is red'		
53.	*endɔ títo	('a red girl')	70. ápír olêŋ	'I am very fat'
54.	*árá dɔ	('I am red')	71. eorét	'broom'
55.	ádɔ́	'I am red'	72. entíto náór	'the girl that sweeps'
56.	átɔ́dɔ́rɔ́	'I have become red'		
			73. átóórò	'I swept'
			74. áórítò	'I am sweeping'
57.	*ádɔ́rìtà	('I am being red')	75. *áórù	('I will start to sweep')
58.	ádórù	'I will become red'		
59.	ádɔ́ olêŋ	'I am very red'	76. áór olêŋ	'I sweep a lot'
60.	*empir / *ompir	('the fat one')		

Exercise 4.5: argument structures of English verbs

Tom Payne

A.   Give examples of three English verbs that can fit into each of the following frames (use nine different verbs altogether):

    a. Carlos   _____ his way through the PhD program.
    b.   _____
    c.   _____
    d. Aileron   _____ the tissue off the table.
    e.   _____
    f.   _____
    g. These papers   _____ easily.
    h.   _____
    i.   _____

B.   For examples a, d, and g, give the semantic role and grammatical relation of *Carlos, Aileron, the tissue,* and *these papers.*

C.   Now, for each of the nine verbs you have provided above, give one sentence that uses the verb in a *different argument structure.* In other words, use each verb with a different arrangement of semantic roles and grammatical relations from those used in the first nine examples. Indicate the semantic role of the subject and object arguments for each of your new examples.

Notes

1. Some linguists have argued that there are languages that don't make a distinction between noun and verb. It does appear to be true that for some languages few, if any, roots are *inherently* nouns or verbs. However, I believe all linguists would agree that noun and verb are important classes at the level of sentence structure in all languages. In other words, when a word is used in context it can be classified as a noun, a verb, or something else. For this reason, noun and verb are universally important notions. The point of view taken in this book is that word classes are distinguished by morphosyntactic properties of words in context. Sometimes roots can also be inherently classified, apart from any specific context, but this is not by any means essential or universal.

2. Though it is quite possible to use proper names as non-unique common nouns, for example "my Canada," "it's not the Canada I used to know," and "there are really two Canadas."

3. By "imaginary" I mean "consisting of mental images." This is not equivalent to "unreal," "false," or "unimportant." Every message ever communicated has to be imagined, i.e. conceptualized in someone's mind, before it can be expressed using language. If the conceptualizer chooses to communicate a concept using a linguistic utterance, the form of the utterance will depend on the roles and relationships in the conceptualized scene, just as the form of any tool depends on the function it is intended to accomplish. It is such conceptualized scenes that influence and/or determine the form of linguistic utterances, rather than any direct objective reality.

4. See DeLancey (1990) for an alternative definition of AGENT. I believe DeLancey's definition of AGENT as "the first CAUSE in the clause" is essentially compatible with Fillmore's definition plus the notion of "message world." That is, the clause is the linguistic unit within which message-world scenes are perspectivized. Insofar as the "instigator of the action" is equivalent to the "first CAUSE," and the message-world scene is equivalent to the "clause," the two definitions become near restatements of one another.

   Foley and Van Valin (1984) describe a functional continuum between two "macro-roles," ACTOR and UNDERGOER. The prototypical ACTOR is an AGENT and the prototypical UNDERGOER a PATIENT in the classic case grammar sense. This is their method of preserving an objectivist definition of AGENT and PATIENT while still accounting for the variability in grammatical expression of these roles.

5. The transitive uses of these verbs are causatives. These are action-processes, described below.

6. There are some situations in English in which an adjective is used as a noun, e.g., *The poor will always be with you* or in elliptical expressions, e.g., *Would you like to try the white or the red?*

7. Some languages, e.g., Tsafiki (Dickenson 2004) and Kalam (Pawley 1987), appear to be notable exceptions to this generalization. Both of these languages, and perhaps a few others around the world, are reported to have only a very limited class of verbs. Complex concepts are expressed by constructing strings of verbs, or using one of the small number of true verbs in combination with auxiliary or adverbial elements.

8. The term "fourth person" has been used in a variety of ways in the literature. None of the previous uses of this term describe a function that is not covered by some other term employed in this book. Therefore we will not attempt to survey the various uses of this term.

5   Exploring subclasses

As mentioned in the previous chapter, every language has subclasses within the major word classes. Subclasses exist when some stems in a class have different grammatical properties from others. There are many reasons why subclasses exist, and those reasons may not be obvious to a linguist who is learning the language for the first time, so it is a matter of grammatical analysis to determine what the subclasses are, and, if possible, determine their MOTIVATIONS, i.e., the reasons why they exist. As we will see in the next section, some subclasses are motivated by structure, and others by function. Some are motivated by a combination of structure and function, while still others have no apparent motivation whatsoever.

An example of a structure-based subclassification would be the three CONJU-GATION CLASSES of verbs in Spanish. Verbs in Spanish take different endings depending on whether the infinitive form of the verb ends in -ar, -ir, or -er. There is no meaning feature or set of features that correlates with the various classes. An example of a function-based subclassification would be certain zero-plural nouns in English, such as *deer, fish, elk, sheep*, etc. While there are no obvious structural similarities among nouns that take the zero plural, it turns out that there is a meaning, or functional, correlation – most of these nouns refer to animals that are traditionally hunted for food. Then again, the class of English nouns that take -en for the plural (*oxen, children*, and a few others) has neither a structural nor a functional motivation. It is just an historical relic from an earlier stage of English.

Systems of subclassification in the lexicon are usually quite "irregular" from a semantic point of view. This is because natural languages were not invented by linguists. As much as linguists are eager to provide neat categories and rules to describe structural patterns in languages, the reality is that language follows its own paths. Those paths are metaphorical, historical, and sometimes capricious. While a certain amount of regularity and predictability is necessary in order for communication to occur, real languages are seldom as regular as linguists, language teachers, and language learners would like them to be.

The gender system of Spanish is a good example of a subclassification of nouns that is "sorta structural," "sorta functional," and "sorta capricious." Traditional grammars say that most nouns in Spanish are categorized as either "masculine" or "feminine." This is a semantically based subclassification that works relatively well for animate referents that are inherently either male or female. However, it applies equally to inanimate referents that have no biological sex at all,[1] such as books, rocks, clouds, and floors. "Masculine" and "feminine" are important *grammatical* subclasses in Spanish because whether a noun belongs to the masculine or feminine subclass determines how adjectives, articles, and other elements in the noun phrase will agree with it, even though semantically it may or may not refer to something that has a biological sex. In fact, the grammatical gender of a word can be the opposite of the biological sex of the referent. The word *persona*, for example, is always grammatically feminine, even when referring to a male referent:

(1)   Él   es   un-a   person-a   buen-a.   'He is a good person.'
        3SG.MASC   is   a-FEM   person-FEM   good-FEM

So subclasses exist for many intersecting reasons. In this chapter we will walk through the process of analyzing the subclasses of linguistic units such as exist in all languages, and give some analytical methods and terminologies for identifying various kinds of subclasses.

Sometime subclasses of verbs are known as **CONJUGATION CLASSES**, and subclasses of nouns are called **DECLENSION CLASSES**. These are terms that come from the classical traditions (the study of ancient Sanskrit, Greek, and Latin) and are used in slightly different ways by various linguists and grammarians. It is important to be aware of these terms, though in this book we will pretty much stick with the terms "subclasses of nouns" and "subclasses of verbs." Other word classes may also have subclasses, but the principles relevant to analyzing subclasses of nouns and verbs apply to other word classes as well.

Methodology

When a linguist first looks at a range of data, one of the first items of business is to determine whether there are subclasses. Is there one pattern that holds for all the forms in the data, or do certain roots or stems in the data pattern one way, while others pattern another way? Words that differ significantly in terms of their grammatical properties probably belong to different classes or subclasses. After the grammatical properties of each subclass are identified, a **MOTIVATION**, or a reasonable hypothesis as to why the subclasses probably exist, may be construed. There are three broad groups of motivations for the existence of subclasses:

Structural motivations – motivations having to do with the forms (the consonants, vowels, **SYLLABLE STRUCTURES**, and autosegmental features) of the roots and other morphemes.

Functional motivations – motivations having to do with the meanings of morphemes, or how they are used in sentences and conversations.

Table 5.1 *Some minor class verbs of English*

'dive' class	'grow' class	'drink' class	'irregulars'
dive/dove	grow/grew	drink/drank	hit/hit, cut/cut, fit/fit
drive/drove	know/knew	sink/sank	eat/ate
strive/strove	throw/threw	sing/sang	is/was
ride/rode	blow/blew	ring/rang	go/went
write/wrote		sit/sat	win/won
smite/smote		swim/swam	run/ran
		stink/stank	fly/flew
			come/came
			lose/lost
			choose/chose

Capriciousness – actually, historical accident, but since everything in language is historical, "capriciousness" may be a more descriptive label for this range of factors. Languages just "like to be difficult," or so it seems.

In the following paragraphs we will illustrate how one goes about teasing out these various motivating factors, using some extended examples from English verbs and Russian nouns.

In modern English the largest subclass of verbs expresses the past tense via some form of the suffix spelled -*ed*. However, there are several smaller subclasses that take different past-tense forms. Table 5.1 illustrates some of these **MINOR CLASS** verbs.

The first thing you want to look for when faced with this kind of data is whether any of the apparently minor class stems can be derived from the major class stems by a morphophonemic rule, and therefore be incorporated into the major subclass. In other words, would it be possible, for example, to derive a form like *lost* /lɔst/ from *lose* /luz/ plus the major class past tense suffix {-d}? Perhaps there is a morphophonemic rule that changes the expected /luzd/ into /lɔst/, in the same way as the expected /lʊkd/ changes into /lʊkt/ by the morphophonemic rule called DEVOICING, discussed in chapter 3.

To make this work, we would need a rule that devoices both the stem-final /z/ of /luz/ and the /d/ of the past-tense suffix, then another one that changes the stem vowel from /u/ to /ɔ/. However, there is one very good reason for saying that these cannot be morphophonemic rules of English – namely, other verbs that also end in /-uz/ do not undergo this rule, e.g., the verbs *choose* /tʃuz/ and *bruise* /bruz/. Remember that if some variation is idiosyncratic (occurs in only one situation), it is not a pattern, and therefore cannot be a rule of the grammar of the language. Therefore, the past-tense form of *lose* must just be specified as a lexical (inherent) feature of that particular verb.

You might say that *lose/lost* is a minor class of verbs that has only one member. However, this doesn't help you much. Remember that grammatical analysis attempts to accurately represent or replicate the unconscious knowledge that speakers have about their language. Since people are basically lazy, it is unlikely that they would store in their memories two or three special rules needed to account for only one form. Why not just store the past-tense form directly and forget about the rules?

The minor class verbs in the first three columns do seem to follow patterns. Within each class there are regularities, though there is no natural way to derive the past-tense forms of the minor class verbs from their stems plus the regular past-tense suffix {-d}. Therefore, the minor class verbs must have special rules written just for them. At what point do we say a variation ceases to be idiosyncratic and starts to be a pattern? Two examples? Three?

There is no absolute answer to this question, though sometimes evidence can be gleaned by attempting to apply a suspected pattern to new, or nonsense forms. For example, it seems that the "drink class" of verbs follows a pattern that may be expressed as follows:

(2)   If the root vowel is ɪ in the present tense, it is æ in the past tense.

As mentioned in chapter 1, there is a logic to this pattern, as evidenced by the fact that children will apply this rule in situations where adults have learned not to: *I brang my new toy.* Also, if we invent a new verb that could be subject to this pattern, say *ming*, we can easily imagine the past tense being either *mang* or *minged.*

But how about the *grow* class? Is there a logic to the application of some rule that says "the root vowel /o/ becomes /u/ in the past tense"? Have you ever heard a child say *It snew last night!* (a hypothetical formation of *snow* to *snew* by analogy with *grow/grew*, *blow/blew*, etc.)? Or can we imagine a nonsense verb, say, *trow*, and derive the past tense *trew*? To my native English ear, this does not sound nearly as likely as *brang*, or *mang*, though this is perhaps debatable. If I am right, though, then the *grow* class does not exhibit a pattern and is therefore simply a list of individually memorized forms. The point of this exercise is simply to show that in fact there is a continuum between patterns and lists. Sometimes minor stem classes follow their own regular patterns, sometimes they consist of a list that has to be memorized, and sometimes they represent sort of a pattern, and sort of a list. Distinguishing the two is sometimes an art.

After you have checked to see if any of the minor stem classes can be eliminated by incorporating them into other classes, you look at the forms of the minor class stems to see if they have anything in common phonologically. If so, you try to

Table 5.2 *Some minor class nouns of English*

'mouse' class	'zero' class	'irregulars'
mouse/mice	fish/fish	child/children
louse/lice	sheep/sheep	person/people
	deer/deer	woman/women
	elk/elk	man/men
	moose/moose	ox/oxen
	antelope/antelope	
	buffalo/buffalo	

characterize the phonological commonality as explicitly as possible. For example, you will notice that verbs in the *dive* class are all one-syllable verbs in which the **DIPHTHONG** /ay/ is the nucleus, and which end in a consonant. However, not all verbs that have this form fall into the *dive* class, such as *bite/bit*, *light/lit*, *fight/fought*, *gripe/griped*, etc. So this is not entirely a phonologically determined class of verbs. Members of the class all end in /-ayC/ (where C is any consonant), but not all verbs of this form are in the class. Therefore each verb in this class must be marked specially in the lexicon. This means that speakers just have to memorize the special behavior of the past tenses of these verbs.

If you cannot find phonological commonalities in the members of a class of forms, you then look for semantic commonalities. In the case of the English verbs listed in table 5.1, I don't think you will find any semantic coherence to any of the classes. It is not the case, for example, that all verbs in one class are transitive, all intransitive, all movement verbs, all stative verbs, or anything like that.

However, there are some semantically based stem classes among English nouns. Table 5.2 lists some minor class nouns of English in their singular and plural forms.

We look at these classes and we notice that the only class that seems to have any phonological coherence is the *mouse* class (*mouse* and *louse* rhyme). However, there are apparently only two stems in this class, and many other nouns with similar form do not fall into this class, e.g., *grouse*, *blouse*, and *spouse*. The other two classes don't seem to have any phonological coherence. However, when we look at their meanings, we do see some intriguing patterns. For example "zero class" nouns all refer to animals. But not all nouns that refer to animals go into this class. In particular, *mouse*, *louse*, and *ox* do not, as well as many animal nouns that go into the major class (*cow*, *horse*, *duck*, *bird*, *dog*, *cat*, etc.). What kind of animals do take zero plurals? Well, to a certain extent they are animals that are traditionally hunted, or fished. Farm animals and non-game wild animals in general do not fall into this category. Well, what about *sheep*? Most sheep are domesticated animals, yet they seem to fall into the class of game animals for the purpose of plural formation. This may be considered an irregularity, or perhaps it is a throwback to an earlier stage of Anglophone culture in which sheep were primarily game animals.

It is common for semantically determined classes to have exceptions. Some of the exceptions may be MOTIVATED (they make sense), while others are not. For example, Yagua has a fairly clear morphological distinction between animate (things that are alive and which move, like animals and people) and inanimate things. However, pineapples, rocks, and brooms fall into the animate class. Though we want to keep looking for motivating factors, the reasons why pineapples, rocks, and brooms fall into the animate class in Yagua may be so lost in unrecorded history that we will never know the true reasons.

Once you've determined that you actually have bona fide subclasses (classes that can't be subsumed into other classes by morphophonemic rules), sometimes the term AFFIX SUPPLETION (also termed SUPPLETIVE VARIANTS, or SUPPLETIVE ALLOMORPHS) is used. These terms are similar to "stem suppletion," one of the kinds of lexical expression discussed in chapters 1 and 2. However, they really mean something quite different, though intriguingly related.

Stem suppletion, as a lexical expression type, is one way of expressing a conceptual category. You will remember, for example, that the conceptual category known as "past tense" is expressed by stem suppletion for the verb *go* in English. The past tense of this verb is *went*, which is completely distinct from the stem *go*. There is no way you can (reasonably) suggest that there is a morphophonemic rule that derives *went* from *go* + *-ed* (though some have tried).

The term "affix suppletion," on the other hand, refers to a situation where one conceptual category is expressed by two completely unrelated affixes in different subclasses. For example, the noun *ox* in English belongs to a very small subclass for which the plural suffix is |-ən|, *oxen*. The form |-ən| is an allomorph of the morpheme PLURAL, just as |-s|, |-ɨz|, and |-z| are. However, |-ən| cannot be related phonologically to the others at all. Therefore it is a *suppletive* allomorph – one that cannot be derived from the same "underlying form" as the others. The stems *go* and *went*, on the other hand, represent different conceptual categories (non-past and past tense), so they are *not* allomorphs of one another. They are simply suppletive stems.

So, the words "suppletion" or "suppletive" always refer to situations where one form is exchanged for another that is totally different phonologically. However, when the two forms express different conceptual categories, you have the lexical expression type known as stem suppletion. When two dissimilar affixes express the *same* conceptual category, but for different subclasses of stems, you have affix suppletion.

Now let's look at a problem dealing with noun declensions. Consider the following Russian words (transliterated into a roman-based alphabet – the symbol *y* represents a high, central, unrounded vowel, and *j* represents a palatal glide):

(3)   Russian singular nouns:

	Nominative case	Genitive case	Instrumental case	Gloss
a.	žénščina	žénščiny	žénščinoj	'woman'
b.	sýn	sýna	sýnom	'son'
c.	máma	mámy	mámoj	'mom'
d.	brát	bráta	brátom	'brother'

Don't worry too much about what the "cases" mean just yet. Just consider them labels for various conceptual categories at this point. As you look at these data, you'll notice that the cases are expressed by suffixes. However, for any given case, the suffixes are not the same for all the words, so you may suspect that you have stem classes. The first analytical step is to identify the formal properties that go with each class. Applying our familiar system of looking for correspondences between variation in form and variation in function, we come up with the following classes:

(4)

	Nominative:	Genitive:	Instrumental:
Class I (exs. 3a and c)	-a	-y	-oj
Class II (exs. 3b and d)	-Ø	-a	-om

We may informally think of these as the "a, y, oj class" and the "zero, a, om class."

Now that we have characterized the classes in terms of their forms, we want to see if we can reduce them to one class by some regular morphophonemic pattern. In order to do this, we would first have to come up with a rule that would delete the nominative -a in class II stems. But is there anything about class II stems that could conceivably make that -a delete? Not really. In particular, the stems of both examples 3a and b end in the same sound. If there were a rule that deleted the -a in 3b, why wouldn't it apply in 3a as well? Then we'd have to write rules that changed -y to -a (or vice versa depending on which one we decided was the underlying form), and -oj to -om (or vice versa). These all seem like pretty implausible rules. Well, it's possible we need more data, but I kind of doubt whether we are going to find morphophonemic motivations for these classes.

What about semantic motivations? Here we may have a possibility. What do the meanings of 'woman' and 'mom' have in common as against 'son' and 'brother'? Hello?! Biological sex is one of the most common semantic parameters that determines noun subclasses. We should not be at all surprised to find it in Russian, since Russian is an Indo-European language, and Indo-European languages usually do have a system of noun genders based on the sex of animate referents, albeit rather loosely.[2]

So we can (tentatively) rename class I as "feminine" and class II as "masculine." Another approach would be to say that the endings are portmanteau morphemes that express both gender and case.

Now let's take a look at some more Russian data. We will add the following to the words already discussed:

(5)   Russian singular nouns

	Nominative case	Genitive case	Instrumental case	Gloss
e.	vodá	vodý	vodój	'water'
f.	zakón	zakóna	zakónom	'law'
g.	paltó	paltó	paltó	'overcoat'
h.	vól	volá	volóm	'ox'
i.	kómnata	kómnaty	kómnatoj	'room'
j.	úgol	uglá	uglóm	'corner'
k.	čisló	čislá	čislóm	'number'
l.	pólʲe	pólʲa	pólʲem	'field'
m.	metró	metró	metró	'subway'
n.	rýba	rýby	rýboj	'fish'
o.	úzʲel	uzlá	uzlóm	'knot'
p.	posól	poslá	poslóm	'ambassador'
q.	derévnʲa	derévnʲl	derévnʲej	'village'
r.	učítʲelʲ	učítʲelʲa	učítʲelʲem	'teacher'
s.	línija	líniji	línijej	'line'

Do we see any "familiar faces" in these data? Do any of these words pattern the same way as the feminine or masculine nouns in 3? Well, examples 5i and n exactly follow the pattern of class I, or feminine, nouns. They are both "a, y, oj" verbs. Though there is nothing particularly feminine about rooms or fish, it does look like these nouns fall into the same declension class as the nouns meaning 'woman' and 'girl.' What about 5e? It is exactly like the other feminine nouns, except that STRESS falls on the ending. Stress, and other auto-segmental features, must always be taken just as seriously as other elements of structure, like consonants and vowels. It is quite possible that meaningful differences, or subclass distinctions, are expressed by stress. However, in this case, it looks like it is a lexical feature of the noun *vodá* 'water' in that it is always stressed on the last syllable (this isn't true for all the forms of this word, by the way, though it happens to be the case in all the forms cited in this exercise). So it looks like this is a consistent pattern, and 'water' can be grouped with the feminine nouns.

Two other examples in this set come close to the feminine pattern. These are 5q and s. Their pattern is *-a, -i, -ej*, rather than *-a, -y, -oj*. Since these patterns are quite similar, we want to look for some possible phonological conditioning factor that will allow us to avoid having to posit a third grammatical "gender" for these words. Is there some phonological feature of the stems *derévnʲ* and *línij* that might cause the different pronunciations of the case endings? Sure – a palatalized consonant or the palatal glide *-j* in stem-final position are exactly the kinds of sounds that are likely to cause a vowel to be fronted. So we can propose a tentative rule like the following that will subsume examples 5q and s into the class of feminine nouns:

(6) $V \rightarrow [front] / \begin{Bmatrix} j \\ C^j \end{Bmatrix}$—

This is a very natural rule, and captures the fact that both /y/ and /o/ are fronted when following a palatal or palatalized sound. This rule makes sense because palatal sounds are frontish themselves, and assimilation rules are the most common type of morphophonemic rule (see chapter 3). It also makes sense that a palatal sound does not change the /a/ vowel in the nominative case forms of examples 5q and s, because there is no [front] counterpart for the vowel /a/ in Russian – it's as front as it can get already (without undergoing some other change, like raising).

That seems to be all the candidates for the feminine class. What about the masculine class? Example 5f exactly fits the "Ø, a, om" prototype for this class, so we can fairly confidently call this a masculine noun. What about 5h? Its pattern is "Ø, á, óm." Is there any way to motivate this stress difference on the basis of the form of this root (*vól*)? Just looking at this data, it doesn't seem so. Perhaps the difference is because *vól* is a one-syllable word. However, *sýn* (example 3b) is also one syllable, and it takes unstressed suffixes in the genitive and instrumental cases. So it seems that the stress pattern of the forms of the noun *vól* just has to be memorized by speakers, and this must be another stem class. With additional data, we would eventually want to say that *vól* is in fact masculine, but that it belongs to a phonologically defined subclass of masculine nouns. However, just looking at these data, we can only guess that it might be masculine, but in the meantime treat it as a separate, possibly idiosyncratic, class.

The same is true for examples 5j, o, and p. These seem to represent variations on the pattern for masculine nouns, but it is hard to isolate phonological conditioning factors. Yes, they all end in /l/ but so does example r, and it doesn't exhibit quite the same pattern.

One interesting feature of examples 5j, o, and p is that there is variation *in the root* that accompanies the expression of the genitive and instrumental cases. Notice that a root vowel is dropped in these two declensions: the root *úgol*- becomes *ugl*-, *úz^jel*- becomes *uzl*-, and *posól*- becomes *posl*-. Other than that, these three stems seem to fall into the same subclass as *vól*. Since there is no regular, phonological rule that can account for this variation (at least not in the data we have available here), again this is just something that has to be memorized by speakers. This is an example of what we have called "weakly suppletive stems." They are "weakly" suppletive because the forms do bear some resemblance to each other, though the difference is not predictable by a regular rule. Using the terminology introduced in chapter 2, we may say that this is an example of weak stem suppletion *and* suffixation used to express one conceptual category.

Now before we leave the masculine class, what can we say about example 5r? It looks like a "Ø, a, om" verb, except that the instrumental suffix is *-em*. Does this look familiar at all? Of course. We saw that with feminine stems that end in the palatal glide *j* (or a palatalized consonant, Cʲ), the suffix vowels are fronted, if possible (remember that fronting is not possible with the vowel /a/ since there is no [front] counterpart to /a/ in the vowel inventory of Russian). So the same rule that we posited in 6 also applies here, and the word *učítjeľ* 'teacher' can be assigned to the masculine class.

We are now left with four stems still unaccounted for, repeated here for convenience:

(7)   Russian singular nouns

	Nominative case	Genitive case	Instrumental case	Gloss
g.	paltó	paltó	paltó	'overcoat'
k.	čisló	čislá	čislóm	'number'
l.	póľe	póľa	póľem	'field'
m.	metró	metró	metró	'subway'

Examples 7g and m clearly belong to a single class. What shall we call it? The "zero zero zero" class? These two nouns undergo no changes in the various cases. It may be tempting to say that nouns that end in a stressed /ó/ sound belong to this class, except when we look at 7k. Here is a noun that ends in /ó/ but does not belong to this class. So again, we have subclasses that just have to be memorized. Example 7k and l can be related to one another by the rule posited in 6. What, then, must the underlying root and suffix of the nominative case of 7l be? It must be *poľ* + *o*. So 7k and l represent a different declension pattern from any of the others: "o, a, om," and the variations *-e* and *-em* accounted for by a regular rule that we need anyway to account for several other forms. You may not have enough information here to decide what to call this class, but since it is not feminine, and not masculine, what would be a good guess? How about "neuter"? In fact, this is the label that is commonly given to this class by Russian grammarians. It does have some semantic basis, in that it is seldom, if ever, used for beings that have a biological sex.

Table 5.3 is a summary chart of the classes of Russian nouns in this exercise.

In summary, the steps in analyzing data that exhibit stem classes are the following:

> See if any apparently minor class stems can be combined with other classes by morphophonemic rules. If so, you can combine the two classes – the difference is predictable on the basis of ordinary morphophonemic rules, as discussed in chapter 3. If not, you have one form or another of "suppletion" (weak or strong, affix or stem) and you must go on to steps 2, 3, and 4.
>
> If any of the minor classes can be identified in terms of their phonological form, you have form-based stem classes.

Table 5.3 *A classification of some Russian nouns*

	Stem	Nominative	Genitive	Instrumental	Notes
Feminine:	žénščin- 'woman' mám- 'mom' vod- 'water'				Stress on final syllable
	kómnat- 'room' rýb- 'fish' derévnʲ- 'village' línij- 'line'	-a	-y	-oj	V → [front] / j __
Masculine:	sýn- 'son' brát- 'brother' zakón 'law'	-∅	-a	-om	
	vól- 'ox'				Stress on final syllable
	úgol-/ugl- 'corner'				Short stems in genitive and instrumental cases, plus stress on final syllable
	úzʲel/uzl- 'knot' posól-/posl- 'ambassador' učítʲelʲ- 'teacher'				V → [front] / ʲ __
Neuter:	čisl- 'number'	-o	-a	-om	Stress on final syllable
	pólʲ- 'field'				V → [front] / ʲ __
"Zero" class	paltó 'overcoat' metró 'subway'	-∅	-∅	-∅	

If any of the minor classes can be motivated in terms of their semantics, you have semantically based stem classes.

If there is no formal or semantic coherence to one or more stem classes, you just have arbitrary classes.

Always look for structural, i.e., phonological, conditioning factors first. If no structural patterns can explain the behavior of the minor class stems, then try to infer some semantic motivation for the class or classes. There is always the possibility that there is no discernible structural or semantic coherence to a given class of forms. In such cases, the lexical entries just have to specify the class for each stem. This is a "brute force" way of dealing with stem classes and is not preferred. However, because language is always changing, it is not uncommon for structural or semantic conditioning factors to be lost in history. In such cases, the classes will just seem random from the point of view of the contemporary, **SYNCHRONIC** grammar.

Conceptual outline of chapter 5

I. Languages tend to divide their major word classes into subclasses. These are sometimes called conjugation classes for verbs, or declension classes for nouns. In order to analyze the subclasses of any word class in a language, use the following procedure:

- Check to see if any of the classes can be subsumed by morphophonemic or regular phonological rules.
- If not, check to see if there is any formal coherence to any of the classes (e.g., one-syllable vs. multi-syllable stems, etc.).
- If not, check to see if there is any semantic coherence to any of the classes (e.g., animacy, gender, etc.).
- If not, then you just have arbitrary classes.

Exercise 5.1: Northern Tepehuan

Burt and Marvel Bascom

Meaning	Singular	Plural
1. 'rabbit'	toši	totoši
2. 'man'	kʌli	kʌkʌli
3. 'foreigner'	obai	obai
4. 'tree'	uši	uši
5. 'son'	mara	mamara
6. 'stone'	odai	oxodai
7. 'friend, relative'	aduni	aaduni
8. 'arrow'	uyi	uxuyi
9. 'turkey'	tova	totova
10. 'elder brother'	šiʌgi	šišiʌgi
11. 'species of bird'	adatomali	aadatomali
12. 'needle'	oyi	oxoyi
13. 'younger brother'	sukuli	susukuli
14. 'species of fish'	aaši	aaši
15. 'rat'	dʌgi	dʌdʌgi
16. 'water jar'	ayi	axayi

A.   Where is Northern Tepehuan spoken?

B.   Organize these nouns into classes depending on how they form their plurals. For each class, describe in prose how the plural is formed from the singular. How many classes are there? Try to motivate the classes.

Exercise 5.2: Lamnso

Vernyuy Francis Ndzenyuy and Tom Payne

The following are some words in Lamnso. Tone is very important in Lamnso and is marked as follows: A vowel with no diacritic carries low tone. A vowel with an acute accent (á) carries high tone. A vowel with an overbar (ā) carries mid tone.

1.	ntīr	'advice'	14.	mbōm	'shape'
2.	biˈ	'to argue'	15.	ntāv	'strong person'
3.	táv	'to be strong'	16.	kúr	'to tie'
4.	bóm	'to build'	17.	kúv	'to treat'
5.	ŋkūr	'bundle'	18.	nsān	'twin'
6.	mbuy	'chimpanzee'	19.	mbiˈ	'argument'
7.	kem	'to disagree'	20.	shún	'to vaccinate'
8.	sán	'to give birth to twins'	21.	fin	'to lock'
9.	buy	'to go wild'	22.	nshūn	'vaccination'
10.	nsə̄ˈ	'joint'	23.	sə́	'to join'
11.	mfin	'lock'	24.	ŋkem	'disagreement'
12.	fiˈ	'to measure'	25.	mfiˈ	'measurement'
13.	ŋkūv	'medication'	26.	tír	'to advise'

A.   Where is Lamnso (or Lam Nso) spoken?

B.   How many speakers are there?

C.   There is one conceptual category illustrated in these data. Organize the words into columns with related words side by side. One column should contain unaffixed words and the other one affixed words.

D.   Describe the conceptual category that is expressed by the affixed words.

E.   Describe, as explicitly as possible, the morphological pattern that expresses the category. Be sure to account for any variations in the pattern.

Exercise 5.3: Kannada

Mirjam Fried

Kannada is a major language of India, spoken by more than 25 million people, primarily in the South. It is a very old language and it uses its own writing system. Hint: There is no Kannada form corresponding to English 'the.'

Nominative case:			Dative case:	
1.	mane	'house'	manege	'to (the) house'
2.	peeṭe	'market'	peeṭege	'to (the) market'
3.	tande	'dad'	tandege	'to dad'
4.	roṭṭi	'flat bread'	roṭṭige	'to (the) flat bread'

rule   i/e → ṣe
(persona → kke) *(a → hiṣe)*

5. chaṭni	'chutney'	chaṭnige	'to (the) chutney'
6. hakki	'bird'	hakkige	'to (the) bird'
7. taayi	'mother'	taayige	'to mother'
8. joola	'corn'	joolakke	'to (the) corn'
9. pustaka	'book'	pustakakke	'to (the) book'
10. simha	'lion'	simhakke	'to (the) lion'
11. kalkatta	'Calcutta'	kalkattakke	'to Calcutta'
12. manushya	'man'	manushyanige	'to (the) man'
13. amma	'mom'	ammanige	'to mom'
14. huḍuga	'boy'	huḍuganige	'to (the) boy'
15. sneehita	'friend'	sneehitanige	'to (the) friend'
16. hamsa	'swan'	hamsakke	'to (the) swan'
17. akka	'older sister'	akkanige	'to (the) older sister'
18. tangi	'younger sister'	tangige	'to (the) younger sister'

A. Fill in the missing Kannada words.

B. Describe the rule for forming the dative case in Kannada.

Exercise 5.4: Rotokas

Adapted from Merrifield et al. 1987, problem #50

1. avaravere	'I'll go.'	25. puraavere	'I'll make it.'
2. avauvere	'You'll go.'	26. purarivere	'You'll make it.'
3. avarovere	'He'll go.'	27. purarevere	'He'll make it.'
4. avaraepa	'I went.'	28. puraava	'I made it.'
5. avauepa	'You went.'	29. purariva	'You made it.'
6. avaroepa	'He went.'	30. purareva	'He made it.'
7. puraravere	'I'll say it.'	31. ruiparavere	'I'll want it.'
8. purauvere	'You'll say it.'	32. ruipauvere	'You'll want it.'
9. purarovere	'He'll say it.'	33. ruiparovere	'He'll want it.'
10. puraraepa	'I said it.'	34. ruiparaepa	'I wanted it.'
11. purauepa	'You said it.'	35. ruipauepa	'You wanted it.'
12. puraroepa	'He said it.'	36. ruiparoepa	'He wanted it.'
13. pauavere	'I'll build it.'	37. vokaavere	'I'll walk.'
14. paurivere	'You'll build it.'	38. vokarivere	'You'll walk.'
15. paurevere	'He'll build it.'	39. vokarevere	'He'll walk.'
16. pauava	'I built it.'	40. vokaava	'I walked.'
17. pauriva	'You built it.'	41. vokariva	'You walked.'
18. paureva	'He built it.'	42. vokareva	'He walked.'
19. tapaavere	'I'll hit it.'	43. pauravere	'I'll sit.'
20. taparivere	'You'll hit it.'	44. pauuvere	'You'll sit.'
21. taparevere	'He'll hit it.'	45. paurovere	'He'll sit.'
22. tapaava	'I hit it.'	46. pauraepa	'I sat.'
23. tapariva	'You hit it.'	47. pauuepa	'You sat.'
24. tapareva	'He hit it.'	48. pauroepa	'He sat.'

A.   List and gloss all the morphemes in these data. Group the verbs by verb class.

B.   Is there a semantic basis for the verb classes? If so, what is it?

Exercise 5.5: "irregular" verbs

Tom Payne

A.   Fill in the following charts using phonetic transcription for the English verbs 'be' and 'go.' You may consult with a native speaker if necessary.

	1SG	2SG	3SG	1PL	2PL	3PL	
1. 'be'							NON-PAST
							PAST
							PAST-PARTICIPLE

	1SG	2SG	3SG	1PL	2PL	3PL	
2. 'go'							NON-PAST
							PAST
							PAST-PARTICIPLE

B.   Make a chart of the forms of the verbs meaning 'be' (if there is one) and 'go' in another language you know well. If there is no verb meaning 'be,' then use the verb meaning 'say.' Don't use more than two tenses, even if the language has more. Try to include all of the person and number categories, though. If the verbs do not express these conceptual categories morphologically, include the relevant pronouns, and tense particles, as appropriate.

C.   Are the paradigms you have charted in B regular or irregular? In one short paragraph, describe how they differ from paradigms of regular verbs.

Exercise 5.6: Kiowa

Adapted from Merrifield et al. 1987, problem #46
Note: The symbol ":" indicates vowel length on the preceding vowel. A cedilla (ָ) under a vowel indicates nasalization.

1. àbáːnmà̰	'I go.'	16. yá̰táy	'I wake up.'
2. èmbáːnmà̰	'You go.'	17. gyáttáy	'You wake up.'
3. báːnmà̰	'She goes.'	18. á̰ntáy	'She wakes up.'
4. gyàtkhɔ́ːmɔ̰̀	'I read.'	19. gyàthíːnmɔ̰́	'I dig.'
5. bátkhɔ́ːmɔ̰̀	'You read.'	20. báthíːnmɔ̰́	'You dig.'
6. gyátkhɔ́ːmɔ̰̀	'She reads.'	21. gyáhíːnmɔ̰́	'She digs.'
7. gyàtpḭ́ɔ̰́ːmɔ̰̀	'I cook.'	22. yá̰yáy	'I'm busy.'
8. bátpḭ́ɔ̰́ːmɔ̰̀	'You cook.'	23. gyátyáy	'You're busy.'
9. gyápḭ́ɔ̰́ːmɔ̰̀	'She cooks.'	24. á̰nyáy	'She's busy.'
10. yá̰tɔ̰́ːzáːnmà̰	'I talk.'	25. àpɔ́ttɔ̀	'I eat.'
11. gyáttɔ̰́ːzá · nmà̰	'You talk.'	26. èmpɔ́ttɔ̀	'You eat.'
12. á̰ntɔ̰́ːzáːnmà̰	'She talks.'	27. pɔ́ttɔ̀	'She eats.'
13. àphɔ̰́	'I stand up.'	28. gyàtgúttɔ̀	'I write.'
14. èmphɔ̰́	'You stand up.'	29. bátgúttɔ̀	'You write.'
15. phɔ̰́	'She stands up.'	30. gyágúttɔ̀	'She writes.'

A.   Where is Kiowa spoken, and how many speakers are there?

B.   List and classify all the verb stems in these data. Give the subject prefix paradigms for each class. Describe any plausible morphophonemic rules that may allow you to collapse some of the classes.

C.   After you have reduced your classes to the bare minimum, try to "motivate" the remaining classes in terms of semantics.

Exercise 5.7: German

Adapted from Cowan and Rakušan (1998:82)

	Singular	Plural	English Gloss	Underlying form
1.	aːʀt	aːʀtən	'kind'	—
2.	ait	aidə	'oath'	—
3.	beʀk	beʀgə	'mountain'	—
4.	diːp	diːbə	'thief'	—
5.	dʀuk	dʀukə	'printing'	—
6.	felt	feldəʀ	'field'	—
7.	fiŋk	fiŋkən	'finch'	—
8.	flek	flekən	'stain'	—
9.	fluːt	fluːtən	'flood'	—
10.	gelt	geldəʀ	'coin'	—
11.	geʃtalt	geʃtaltən	'shape'	—
12.	hiːp	hiːbə	'blow'	—
13.	lump	lumpən	'scoundrel'	—
14.	ʃtaik	ʃtaigə	'footpath'	—
15.	taːk	taːgə	'day'	—
16.	tyːp	tyːpən	'type'	—
17.	ziːp	ziːbə	'sieve'	—

A.   Give the underlying form of each noun stem in these data.
B.   Can you write rules to determine what form of the plural morpheme
       is used for each noun? What are your observations?

Exercise 5.8: French

Cowan and Rakušan (1998:96)

	Feminine	Masculine	English		Feminine	Masculine	English
1.	vɛʁt	vɛʁ	'green'	11.	movɛz	movɛ	'bad'
2.	gʁ̥ad	gʁ̥a	'big'	12.	ɛtɛliʒat	ɛtɛliʒa	'intelligent'
3.	blaʃ	bla	'white'	13.	kuʁt	kuʁ	'short'
4.	fɔʁt	fɔʁ	'strong'	14.	almad	alma	'German'
5.	gʁos	gʁo	'fat'	15.	aglɛz	aglɛ	'English'
6.	bas	ba	'low'	16.	famøz	famø	'famous'
7.	dus	du	'sweet'	17.	fos	fo	'false'
8.	øʁøz	øʁø	'happy'	18.	fʁɛʃ	fʁɛ	'fresh'
9.	pətit	pəti	'small'	19.	ot	o	'high'
10.	tut	tu	'all'				

A.   List the root forms for all of these French adjectives.
B.   Which type of morphological process is involved in the difference
       between feminine and masculine adjectives in French?
C.   Write a morphological rule that describes this process.

Exercise 5.9: Southern Barasano

Adapted from Merrifield et al. 1987, problem 107

	Singular	Plural	Sg. diminutive	Pl. diminutive	Gloss
1.	aya	aya	ayaka	ayaka	'snake'
2.	bicibą	bici	bicibąka	biciaka	'vine'
3.	bitia	biti	bitiaka	bitiaka	'bead'
4.	cotɨ	cotɨri	cotɨaka	cotɨriaka	'pot'
5.	ga	ga	gaka	gaka	'eagle'
6.	gia	gi	giaka	giaka	'louse'
7.	goaro	goa	goaroaka	goaka	'bone'
8.	gu	gua	guaka	guaka	'turtle'
9.	habo	haboa	haboaka	haboaka	'armadillo'
10.	hoabą	hoa	hoabąka	hoaka	'hair'
11.	kabyro	kaby	kabyroaka	kabyaka	'bench'
12.	kacabo	kacabori	kacaboaka	kacaboriaka	'platform'
13.	kahea	kahe	kaheaka	kaheaka	'eye'
14.	kįa	kį	kįaka	kįaka	'cassava'
15.	ohoro	oho	ohoroaka	ohoaka	'banana'

16. race	racea	raceaka	raceaka	'toucan'
17. wi	wiri	wiaka	wiriaka	'house'
18. widiro	widi	widiroaka	widiaka	'pile'
19. wiha̧i	wiha̧iri	wiha̧iaka	wiha̧iriaka	'shelter'
20. yai	yaia	yaiaka	yaiaka	'tiger'

A.   Where is Southern Barasano spoken?

B.   Group the noun stems into subclasses, taking care to reduce the number of classes as much as is reasonably possible.

C.   List and gloss the underlying forms of each noun root and suffix.

D.   Write rules that derive the surface forms for each class.

E.   Try to "motivate" the classes.

Exercise 5.10: Isthmus Zapotec

Velma Pickett

1. ri'ree	'goes out'	17. ka'za	_____
2. ri'bani	'wakes up'	18. za'bani	'will wake up'
3. bi'ree	'went out'	19. ru'yubi	_____
4. zu'kaa	'will write'	20. za'za	_____
5. ku'yubi	'is looking for'	21. ri'niʔ	'talks'
6. ka'dzela	'is finding'	22. bi'kaa	_____
7. ri'za	'walks'	23. gu'ni	_____
8. ri'dzela	'finds'	24. zu'žoone	_____
9. gu'za	'walked'	25. bi'dzela	_____
10. bi'žoone	'ran'	26. ka'niʔ	'is talking'
11. zu'yubi	'will look for'	27. ku'kaa	_____
12. ka'ree	_____	28. bi'bani	_____
13. ru'kaa	_____	29. za'niʔ	_____
14. ku'žoone	_____	30. za'ree	_____
15. ka'bani	_____	31. bi'yubi	_____
16. ru'žoone	_____	32. za'dzela	_____

A.   Fill in all the English translations.

B.   How many stem subclasses are there in these data, and how are they distinguished?

C.   List and gloss all the morphemes (stems and affixes) for each class that you find.

D.   Is there any semantic motivation to the classes? If so, describe it as best you can.

Notes

1. We will use the term "sex" to refer to the biological differentiation between male and female, and the term "gender" to refer to a grammatical classification of nouns.

Sometimes the term "gender" is used in linguistics to refer to any semantically based subclassification of nouns, not just those whose semantic basis is biological sex.

2. In fact, in Russian the semantic basis for the genders is even less exact than it is in many other Indo-European languages. For example, even the word for 'man' is feminine! It is important to recognize that grammatical gender is determined by grammatical properties (like agreement), and not directly by semantic categories, such as female and male.

6   Constituent structure

As linguistic structures become larger and more complex, prose, position-class diagrams, and process rules begin to lose their effectiveness as means of representing and analyzing them. In particular, structures known as **PHRASES** and **CLAUSES** typically have a great deal of internal complexity that is not amenable to the same kind of analysis as words are. Units within such larger structures may vary in their positions, and units in the same position may have a much wider range of functions than elements of word structure tend to have. For this reason linguists usually make a fairly major distinction between morphology (the study of the shapes of words) and syntax (the study of how words clump together in phrases and clauses).

Of course, this distinction is really a continuum. What is a syntactic pattern at one historical stage of a language may become morphological at a later stage (seldom the reverse). Since language change over time rarely proceeds in quantum leaps, there are many situations in which a syntactic pattern is "becoming" morphological. In such cases either a syntactic or a morphological analysis may be useful. Furthermore, as we have seen in earlier chapters, functions that are accomplished in the syntax of one language may be accomplished morphologically in another. So in reality the distinction between morphology and syntax is not always absolutely clear, though it is often very useful.

In this chapter we will discuss how phrases and clauses tend to be organized in the world's languages, and will present a couple of methods for analyzing these larger spans of patterned linguistic behavior.

A note about syntactic formalisms

Since this is primarily a methods text, before we discuss analytical methods for dealing with syntactic structure, it may be helpful to say something about the place of formal representations, or **FORMALISMS**, in linguistics.

There are a number of frameworks, models, or theories that can be useful for understanding syntactic structure. In fact, there are far too many to begin to discuss them all in one book. One famous linguist, James McCawley, even wrote a book called *Thirty million theories of grammar* (1982). While McCawley may have been exaggerating a little bit, his point is clear – there are many ways of thinking about and analyzing grammar. Each theory has its own system of formalisms – ways of rendering simple but insightful representations of syntactic structures and idealized patterns. When you get to know a particular system of formalism well, you can use it as you ponder the syntactic structures of a language you are doing research on. You can, for example, "sketch out" different hypotheses about how a phrase or clause is put together. This task can help you conceive of additional data that may be needed to check your ideas, and thereby lead to a deeper understanding of how the language works.

Every system of formalisms is no more than a metaphor for the actual syntactic facts of a language, or of languages in general. Some formalisms may be particularly useful for expressing certain kinds of facts, or dealing with certain kinds of languages, but all of them are simply metaphors. Like all metaphors, a syntactic formalism is something simple ("hah!" you say) that is used to communicate something more complex, with the expectation that the metaphor will lead to greater insight into the phenomenon communicated. If the metaphor becomes more complex than what it is trying to represent, then it loses its value as a metaphor. So I encourage linguistics students not to get too enchanted by any particular formal method of representing linguistic structure, because there is bound to be a point where the formalism fails.

With this caveat in mind, we will present some formalisms that are used extensively in the linguistics literature. These formalisms are good ways of making sense of the hierarchical structure that is found in every human language. The formalisms we will employ in this chapter are **PHRASE STRUCTURE RULES** and **TREE DIAGRAMS**. These stem from work in **GENERATIVE GRAMMAR** (Chomsky 1965, 1995; Radford 1988, 1997, *inter alia*). This is intended to be an introduction only – enough to lay the groundwork for an advanced course in linguistic theory, but there are many theoretical concepts, arguments, and problems that will necessarily be left out. The emphasis in this chapter will be on methods for analyzing syntactic structures, not on the nuances of any particular linguistic theory.

Syntax

Part of what you know when you know a language is how words can combine to form larger units, such as phrases and clauses. **LINEAR ORDER**, **CONSTITUENCY** (which we will also refer to as **SYNTACTIC MERGER**, "grouping" or "clumping"), and **HIERARCHICAL STRUCTURE** (also referred to as "nesting") are the major features of the **SYNTAX** of all human languages. All of these features provide important clues to a speaker's intended meaning.

The basic building blocks of syntactic structure are called **SYNTACTIC CATEGORIES**. These are very different from conceptual categories, discussed in earlier chapters. There are two subtypes of syntactic categories: **LEXICAL CATEGORIES** and **PHRASAL CATEGORIES**. Lexical categories are very similar to what we have described as word classes in previous chapters. They consist

Table 6.1 *Syntactic categories used in this book*

Lexical categories (abbrev.)	Phrasal categories (abbrev.)
Noun (N)	Noun Phrase (NP or "N-bar")
Verb (V)	Verb Phrase (VP or "V-bar")
Adjective (Adj)	Adjective Phrase (AdjP)
Determiner (D)	Determiner Phrase (DP)
Adverb (Adv)	Adverb Phrase (AdvP)
Adposition (P)	Adpositional Phrase (PP)
Auxiliary (Aux)	Inflected Verb Phrase (IP)

of units that do not have internal syntactic structure themselves. For example, a noun may have morphological structure (prefixes, suffixes, etc.) but is not made up of syntactically distinct units. Phrasal categories, on the other hand, may have internal syntactic structure. For example, a noun phrase must contain a noun, but may also contain adjectives and many other units that "clump together" with the noun. It is important to note that a phrasal category may consist of only one unit. For example, a noun like *Lucretia* may also be a noun phrase. This is because it has the same distributional properties as a noun phrase (see chapter 4). Table 6.1 lists all of the syntactic categories we will be dealing with in this book, along with their common abbreviations.

The largest category in phrase structure is a special category, sometimes symbolized by the letter S. In earlier versions of Generative Grammar this was a mnemonic for "Sentence"; however, we will continue to refer to it as "clause," or "the clause level." It is generally assumed in Generative Grammar that linguistic structure above the S level is not amenable to phrase structure analysis; though some theoreticians, notably Van Dijk (1972), pointedly disagree with this assertion. More recent versions of Generative Grammar (in particular, **MINIMALISM**) have eliminated the need for this special category altogether, having subsumed it under the phrasal category labels. However, for our purposes it will be convenient to continue to use the S label. In more advanced formal syntax courses you will learn about the fascinating theory-internal reasons for why S is no longer needed.

We can consider a clause to be the grammatical expression of a **PROPOSITION**. A proposition is a semantic notion, whereas a clause is a grammatical notion. In other words, a proposition has to do with entities in the message world and semantic relations among them, whereas a clause has to do with syntactic categories and the syntactic relations among them. We can informally think of a proposition as consisting of a "complete thought." It consists of one or more entities (sometimes referred to as "participants"), and a property or relation. For example, the semantic notion *IAGO BETRAYS OTHELLO* consists of two entities, *IAGO* and *OTHELLO*, and a relationship of *betraying* that relates them. This proposition may be expressed in any number of grammatical clauses, e.g.:

(1) a.   Iago betrays Othello.
   b.   Othello is betrayed by Iago.
   c.   Othello is who Iago betrays.
   d.   Iago traiciona a Otelo.
   etc.

It is fairly clear that a good portion of human thought and communication is propositional, in the sense that it consists of such entities and relations. However, recent research (see, e.g., Lakoff and Johnson 1999) is beginning to show that *images*, rather than simply propositions, may be much more relevant to human thought and communication than has previously been thought. Nevertheless, most linguistic theories, in particular Generative Grammar, are primarily concerned with the propositional component of linguistic communication.

In the following sections we will discuss the universal properties of syntactic structure that any syntactic theory or framework must be able to take into account.

Linear order

Because linguistic units, such as words, are pronounced one after another in time, differences in order can be exploited to express differences in meaning. For example, in the following English clauses, linear order is the only signal of the difference in meaning:

(2) a.   Aileron saw the duke.
   b.   The duke saw Aileron.

The observation that the order of words can be adjusted to express this kind of difference in meaning may seem obvious to native speakers of English; but as we have seen in earlier chapters, not every language uses linear order in exactly the way English does. However, it is probably safe to say that variations in linear order are used to express *some* important meaning distinction in every language. Linear order is just too strong and obvious a structural variable for languages not to use it in some way to accomplish important communicative work.

Constituency

If linear order were the only respect in which units in the linguistic stream could be related to one another, language would be very simple indeed. Utterances would be short, and the ideas expressed would be quite limited. In fact, this kind of language would be very similar to several animal communication systems that have been studied by zoologists. One characteristic that seems to distinguish human languages from other natural communicative systems is that human language exhibits constituency and hierarchical structure. Constituency means that linguistic units "clump together," or "merge" (Chomsky 1995) in discourse. This is a fact that all language users unconsciously know about their language. For example, the following two phrases have exactly the same words in identical linear order. Nevertheless, the meaning can vary depending on how the hearer clumps the words. In these examples, constituents (clumps) are indicated in brackets:

(3) a.   [Good girls] and boys
    b.   Good [girls and boys]

In 3a *good girls* is treated as a constituent which is then combined with *boys* to form a complex phrase that refers to a set of good girls plus boys that may be good, bad or neither. In 3b, *girls and boys* forms a constituent that is modified by the adjective *good* to yield a complex phrase that refers to a set of good girls and good boys only.

Of course, in actual conversation, intonation and many other factors help a hearer infer the precise constituent structure intended by the speaker in a particular context. This example simply illustrates that constituency, or how linguistic units are clumped, is a significant factor in the use of language. Linear order and constituency are two important variables that any syntactic analysis of a language must be able to describe.

Hierarchical structure

HIERARCHICAL STRUCTURE refers to the fact that linguistic units and clumps tend to "nest" within one another. Hierarchical structure is good, because it makes life easier. Psychological experiments (as well as common sense) have shown that the human mind can only deal with a small number of things at a time, from four to six at the most. Have you ever been given an important phone number but you had no pen or paper to write it down with? What did you do? First you probably tried to repeat it several times to get it "ingrained" in your mind (this is sometimes called "overlearning"). Then you probably unconsciously "clumped" it into two or more parts: 928, 4056, or maybe 92, 84, 056. When you memorize clumps in a series like this, you effectively convert the clumps into units (undivided pieces) in your memory. Once they are units, you can clump them again at a higher level to form even larger units. Once you have overlearned a clump, you no longer have to think about its internal complexity – you can just deal with it as a whole, "from the outside," as a unit equivalent to other units of the same type.

Telephone companies are very aware of this cognitive fact, and for this reason they usually present phone numbers in clumps. Also, country codes, and city or area codes are other clumps that enter into the hierarchical structure of more complex phone numbers. Imagine how difficult it would be to remember phone numbers if they were all 12 random digits in length, with no structure as to which digits represented the country, the area, or the city code!

Hierarchical structure in language is a natural consequence of this same fact of human cognition. A **NOUN PHRASE**, for example, is a unit that can have very simple or very complicated internal structure:

(4) a.   Simple noun phrase: the dog

b.   Complicated noun phrase: the big black dog that always barks at me as I try vainly to sneak past the junkyard on my way home from my piano lesson

The phrase in 4b has quite a bit of internal complexity, and therefore requires a lot of mental processing. However, once it is processed, it can enter into larger structures as easily (well, almost as easily) as simple structures such as 4a. They are both just noun phrases as far as the structure of the larger clause is concerned:

(5) a.   [The dog] attacked the postman.

b.   [The big black dog that always barks at me as I try vainly to sneak past the junkyard on my way home from my piano lesson] attacked the postman.

The bracketed noun phrase in 5b itself contains several clumps, including a complete clause (*I try vainly to sneak past the junkyard...*). But once you have treated the entire bracketed portion as a noun phrase, you do not have to be concerned with its internal structure. It is just a unit, like any number of others, that is available for deployment in larger structures. This ability to nest symbolic units within other units is a very important feature of human cognition that has a great effect on the way languages are put together.

Grammaticality

Judgments of grammaticality constitute some of the most important data that linguists of all theoretical persuasions rely on for testing syntactic analyses. Typically, a linguist will present a string of words to a native speaker of a language and ask the speaker whether someone may reasonably be expected to utter such a string in a conversation. The speaker then makes a judgment, "yea," "nay," or "maybe," that must be interpreted by the linguist in order to build a model of the unconscious linguistic knowledge of the speaker.

Here is an analogy that may help elucidate the process of constructing a model of a speaker's knowledge of a language. Imagine that you know nothing about chess, but you are involved in a chess game with someone who knows the game perfectly. Your opponent has no way of communicating with you, other than to say "That is a permissible move," or "That is not a permissible move." Eventually, after much trial and error, you would learn the game, just by trying this move and that move and being told that this was right, and that was wrong.

Ideally,[1] building a model of a grammar is something like this, though of course the rules of a language are much more complicated than the rules of chess. Native speakers of a language know these "rules" perfectly, but do not know how to describe them directly. All they know is what works and what doesn't. It is the job of the linguist to infer from these judgments what the unconscious "rules of the game" are.

Every language has certain **CONVENTIONALIZED** behavioral patterns (or rules) for constructing clumps of linguistic units. In this chapter, we will be using examples primarily from English, though of course the same general principles (not the exact rules), apply to any language. Certain clumps of words are consistent with the conventionalized patterns of a language and certain other clumps are not, just like certain chess moves are consistent with the rules of chess and certain other moves are not. For example, there is a type of clump in English that consists of a Determiner (D), and a Noun:

(6)   [D]   [N]
         the   tree
         a   dog
         my   chair
         that   cat
                television

This simple pattern, plus four determiners and five nouns, represents twenty possible clumps: "Choose one from column A and one from column B." It is *useful* to have this kind of pattern because it makes our lives more predictable; once we hear a determiner, we know that what will come next will most likely be a noun (actually, a noun phrase – see below). In addition to being basically lazy, humans also prefer predictability over randomness. Because constituent structure helps make life more predictable, all people make use of it, whether they are writing down telephone numbers, chatting with friends or producing multi-volume works of literature.

As a pattern such as 6 proves useful, we develop ways of incorporating new words into it. Eventually it becomes a "rule" of our internalized grammar that a D comes before a N. A sequence of N+D is not a part of that internalized, ingrained, grammar:

(7)   *tree my, *dog the, *chair that, etc.

An asterisk (*) before a sequence of units indicates that it is not consistent with the conventionalized grammatical patterns of the language. Sometimes such sequences are termed "ungrammatical." This doesn't mean you *can't* say these things. Such sequences may accidentally come together in a discourse, but they would not form a clump, i.e., a constituent that functions as a unit at a higher level of structure. Also, there may come some point in the history of English when people, for some unpredictable reason, start using these word combinations as clumps, perhaps under the influence of some other language or social group, or perhaps because someone coins a new expression that "catches on." It's just that at this point in the history of English, speakers don't have an established, well-oiled mental habit pattern of producing N+D clumps.

Tests for constituent structure

Now we have seen that the major facts that any theory, or framework, for depicting syntactic structure must take into account are linear order, constituency, and hierarchical structure. Judgments of grammaticality regarding sequences of linguistic units constitute the available evidence for building a model of that structure. Of course, some features of syntactic structure are more easily observed than others. For example, linear order is not a problem. Even if you are listening to (or reading) a language you have no knowledge of, you can tell fairly easily what order the sounds are arranged in. There are no special "tests" needed to determine this property of syntactic structure.

The other two properties, constituency and hierarchical structure, are more difficult to determine just by looking at, or listening to, the language. As illustrated earlier, a sequence of units like *good girls and boys* can have more than one constituent structure. Also, native intuition, while helpful, is not reliable in determining the constituent structure of longish strings, such as 5b above. Therefore, we need ways of "probing and poking" syntactic structures in order to determine how units clump together, where the boundaries between units and clumps are, and how clumps nest within one another. This section will describe some of the tests that linguists commonly use to analyze the constituent structure of any language, even languages for which the linguist has no native intuitions.

I have asserted that the pair of words *the dog* can be a clump, but if we have a longer string, like 8, how do we know whether *the dog* is a constituent, as opposed to, maybe, *dog watched*, *watched a fluffy*, or some other random sub-string of this string of words?

(8)   The dog watched a fluffy cat.

There are two major tests and three secondary tests that can be used to reveal the constituent structure of a string such as this. The two major tests are:

- Movement
- Substitution

The three secondary tests are:

- Interposition
- Coordination
- Omissibility

We will briefly discuss each of these tests in the following paragraphs. Then we will attempt a constituent structure analysis of some simple English data.

Movement

Every language allows some constituents to appear in various positions in a syntactic structure. Such variable positioning is often metaphorically referred to as "movement." For example, in English, Determined Noun Phrases (DPs) can be placed in unusual positions for purposes of asking questions or making statements with some kind of special focus:

(9) a.   Beans I like.   (Object, *beans*, placed before subject.)
   b.   What does Frieda want?   (Object, *what*, placed before auxiliary.)
   c.   Here comes my bus.   (Subject, *my bus*, placed after the verb.)

A good test for whether an element is part of a phrase or not, then, is if it moves with the head when the head moves. So, in example 8, if *the dog* is a constituent, we should be able to move it around, contrast it, etc. without affecting the grammaticality of the clause. The sequence *the dog* does pass this test for constituency:

(10)   *The dog* is what watched a fluffy cat.
         What watched a fluffy cat is *the dog*.

Since these are both grammatical strings of English, this is evidence that *the dog* is a constituent.

However, what about *dog watched a* in example 8? Is it possible to treat this as a constituent for purposes of movement? Let's try:

(11)   **Dog watched a* is the what a fluffy cat.
         **The what a fluffy cat is *dog watched a*.

Clearly *dog watched a* fails this test for constituency.

Now let's try one that is a little trickier. What about *watched a fluffy cat*? Is there any clumping or nesting structure in this sequence of words? Consider the following examples:

(12) a.   *Watched a fluffy cat* is what the dog did.
    b.   **Watched* is what the dog did a fluffy cat.

Example 12a is evidence that *watched a fluffy cat* can move to the front of the clause as a unit, and therefore it is a constituent. This constituent we will call an **INFLECTED VERB PHRASE**, or IP. Example 12b shows that the verb *watched* cannot be moved out of this constituent. Of course, it is possible for an IP to consist only of a verb (13a), in which case the verb alone can be moved (13b):

(13) a.   Finkelstein *sweated*.
    b.   *Sweated* is what Finkelstein did.

But if there are other elements in the IP, they all must be fronted together with the verb.

Now consider the following:

(14)   *A fluffy cat* is what the dog watched.
         What the dog watched is *a fluffy cat*.

The examples in 14 prove that *a fluffy cat* is a constituent. But we just saw that *watched a fluffy cat* is also a constituent. How can this be? The answer, of course, is hierarchical structure! Constituents may "nest" within other constituents. These kinds of examples show that the noun phrase that follows the verb (often called the **OBJECT** in English – see chapter 8) is a constituent that is nested within the verb phrase. In other words, the correct bracketing arrangement for the inflected verb phrase in 8 is as given in 15a rather than 15b:

(15) a. Correct syntactic analysis: [watched [a fluffy cat]]
     b. Incorrect syntactic analysis: [watched] [a fluffy cat]

Now consider the following:

(16) a. Finkelstein sweated the final exam.
     b. Sweated the final exam is what Finkelstein did.
     c. The final exam is what Finkelstein sweated.
     d. *Sweated is what Finkelstein did the final exam.
     e. *Final is what Finkelstein sweated the exam.
     f. *Exam is what Finkelstein sweated the final.
     g. *The is what Finkelstein sweated final exam.
     h. *The final is what Finkelstein sweated exam.

These examples show that *the final exam* or *sweated the final exam* are the only parts of the inflected verb phrase that can be moved out (or **EXTRACTED**). It is not possible to move *sweated, the, final, exam* or any sub-group of these out of this structure. So it seems that *sweated the final exam* is a constituent, and *the final exam* is another constituent embedded within it. The inflected verb phrase is, in turn, embedded within the whole clause *Finkelstein sweated the final exam*. One way of expressing embedding relationships is with multiple bracketing, as follows:

(17)   [Finklestein [sweated [the final exam]]]

Notice that there are just as many left-hand brackets as there are right-hand brackets. Sometimes each bracket can be labeled (usually with small subscripts) to make it clear which left-hand bracket goes with which right-hand bracket:

(18)   [$_1$ Finklestein [$_2$ sweated [$_3$ the final exam]$_3$]$_2$]$_1$

The labeling makes it clear that clump 1 is the "largest" clump in this structure. The others are contained within it. The clump labeled 3 is the smallest clump (so far) in this structure. It is contained within clump 2 and clump 1.

Finally, the brackets are sometimes given meaningful labels, corresponding to the syntactic category of the clump they represent. Example 19 shows how this labeling may work (see table 6.1 above for an explanation of the abbreviations). In later sections we will try to explain why these particular labels are useful for English. Different labeling conventions may be appropriate for other languages:

(19)   [$_s$ Finklestein [$_{ip}$ sweated [$_{dp}$ the final exam]$_{dp}$]$_{ip}$]$_s$

Substitution

The second major test for constituency is **SUBSTITUTION**. This refers to the fact that a constituent may be replaced by a substitute like a pronoun, or the expression *(so) do*, whereas other random strings of units may not. The substitute words are sometimes called **PRO-FORMS**, of which pronouns and the

PRO-VERB *(so) do* in English are subtypes. For example, *so do* can substitute for the verb *escape* in the following:

(20)   The Duke escaped and *so did* Aileron.

This means that Aileron also escaped. Therefore *escape* is a constituent all on its own. Well, what happens when a phrase like *a fluffy cat* follows a verb? Does *so do* substitute for just the verb, or the verb plus the noun that follows?:

(21) a.   The dog watched a fluffy cat and *so did* the elephant.
     b.   *The dog watched a fluffy cat and *so did* the elephant a scruffy mouse.

These examples show that *so do* substitutes for the whole string *watched a fluffy cat*, rather than just the verb *watched*. This is yet more evidence that *watched a fluffy cat* is a constituent, and that the clump *a fluffy cat* must be a part of the phrase that contains *watched*.

Movement and substitution are the main tests for constituency. The other three tests, interposition, coordination and omissibility, can also be used to confirm or refine hypotheses made on the basis of movement and substitution.

Interposition

INTERPOSITION is based on the fact that elements that affect a whole clause, such as adverbs, can more easily be inserted between constituents than inside of other constituents. This can be a way of determining constituent boundaries. For example, in English the adverb *surreptitiously* can only be inserted in certain places in a clause:

(22) a.   Surreptitiously the dog watched the fluffy cat.
     b.   *The surreptitiously dog watched the fluffy cat.
     c.   The dog surreptitiously watched the fluffy cat.
     d.   ?The dog watched surreptitiously the fluffy cat.
     e.   *The dog watched the surreptitiously fluffy cat.
     f.   *The dog watched the fluffy surreptitiously cat.
     g.   The dog watched the fluffy cat surreptitiously.

It turns out that the only places this adverb can naturally appear in a clause are at the beginning (22a), at the end (22g), and at the major constituent boundary between the main determined noun phrase and the inflected verb phrase (22c). It can possibly occur after the verb, but this is highly unnatural (indicated by the question mark at the beginning of 22d).

Coordination

The next secondary test for constituency is **COORDINATION**. This test is based on the universal linguistic principle that only units that are of the same category can normally be linked together by the syntactic construction known as coordination – often expressed with the word *and* in English. For example, the following are acceptable coordinate structures in English:

(23) a.   A boy and a girl
    b.   The boys and girls
    c.   The scruffy dog and fluffy cat
    d.   over the river and through the woods
    e.   ... saw a fluffy cat and cried
    f.   Aileron cleaned the house and Slumbat watched television.

The fact that we can coordinate two clumps is evidence that the clumps belong to the same syntactic category. If we were to try to coordinate two distinct syntactic categories, for example a DP and a PP, a DP and a VP, or a VP and a Clause, an ungrammatical sequence would result:

(24)   *the boys and over the river
        *a scruffy dog and saw a fluffy cat
        *cleaned the house and Slumbat watched television

These sequences cannot be grammatical constituents in English, though they may occur as random, non-clumped sequences, for example:

(25)   I shouted at the boys and over the river they jumped.
        She heard a scruffy dog and saw a fluffy cat.
        Aileron cleaned the house and Slumbat watched television.

However, movement and substitution will clearly reveal that the sequences in 24 cannot be clumps:

(26)   *the boys and over the river is what I shouted at they jumped
        *a scruffy dog and saw a fluffy cat is what she heard
        *cleaned the house and Slumbat watched television is what Aileron did

Therefore, coordination can be a way of confirming what phrasal category a clump belongs to, or whether it is a clump at all. However, it can't be the major way of determining constituent structure.

Omissibility

Every language allows **ELLIPSIS** – the omission of certain words or phrases when it is obvious from the context what those words or phrases would be. This is most easily illustrated in answers to questions. For example, the following yes/no question may elicit any number of affirmative responses:

(27)   Q: Do you always begin conversations this way?
        Response a: Yes, I always begin conversations this way.
        Response b: Yes, I always do ~~begin conversations this way~~.
        Response c: Yes, ~~I always begin conversations this way~~.

Response 27a does not leave anything out of the original question. Response b leaves out the phrase *begin conversations this way*, and response c leaves out the whole clause *I always begin conversations this way*. This is evidence that the omitted portions are constituents. There are certain other sequences that are not comfortably omitted in such a response:

(28)   Q: Do you always begin conversations this way?
Response d: *?Yes, I always begin ~~conversations this way~~.
Response e: *Yes, I always ~~do begin~~ conversations this way.
Response f: *Yes, ~~I always begin~~ conversations this way.
etc.

Response 28d is not ungrammatical, in the sense described above. It is an utterance that is sanctioned by the grammatical patterns of the language. However, it is just not an appropriate response to the question. It does not constitute a reduced form of the full response *Yes, I always begin conversations this way*. Responses e and f are more clearly ungrammatical, as well as inappropriate answers to the question. These examples are evidence that the omitted portions of the responses are not syntactic constituents.

Omissibility needs to be used with caution for a couple of reasons. First of all, in practice just about anything can be omitted from a clause if the speaker believes the omitted portion can be recovered by the hearer in the context. Consider the following:

(29) a.   Been there, done that.
b.   How many on board, Mr. Murdoch?

In example 29a, the sequence *I have* has been omitted twice. Yet the major tests for constituency show that *I have* is not a constituent:

(30)   ??Been there *I have*.   (*I have* moved to end of clause)
*I have been there and *so* been here too.   (*So* substituted for *I have*.)

Similarly, 29b can be considered a reduction of *How many people are on board, Mr. Murdoch?* Again, the omitted portion, *people are*, clearly is not a constituent:

(31)   *People are* how many on board, Mr. Murdoch? (*People are* moved to beginning of clause)
*How many *people are* on board, and so/such/do on shore, Mr. Murdoch? (Various possible pro-forms substituted for *people are*.)

The second reason why omissibility should be used with caution is that, at least in English, it is only reliable in distinguishing certain constituent boundaries, and not others. For example, we have seen that there are major constituent boundaries between the subject of a clause and the verb. Also there is definitely a syntactic boundary between a verb and its object. Finally, we will also see below that there is a "small" constituent boundary between a determiner and the remainder of a determined noun phrase. None of these boundaries is testable using the omissibility criterion:

(32)   Q: Did you see the gnarly tree?
Response a: *Yes, I ~~saw the gnarly tree~~.
Response b: *?Yes, I saw ~~the gnarly tree~~.
Response c: *Yes, I saw the ~~gnarly tree~~.

The fact that a, b, and c are not comfortable responses to the question seems to indicate that the omitted portions are not constituents. However, the major tests for constituency show that, at some level, these all must be considered constituents. Therefore, omissibility, along with the other "minor" tests for constituency, must be used with caution. The minor tests are ways of "poking" a syntactic string in order to derive clues as to its internal structure, but they are not necessarily applicable in every situation, and should be used only as a supplement to the major tests.

Phrase structure rules

One method that linguists use to represent, or model, the conventionalized syntactic patterns in languages is called **PHRASE STRUCTURE RULES**. In this section we will briefly present the basic principles of phrase structure rules, using English as the example language. Recent versions of Generative Grammar have eliminated the necessity for phrase structure rules in a formal grammar. However, such rules can be useful ways of thinking about generalizations over wide classes of constructions, if not for analyzing individual clauses.

Phrase structure (or PS) rules are one way of representing idealized patterns of constituent structure that are part of speakers' unconscious knowledge of their language. They consist of a label for the idealized clump (either a phrase or a clause) being represented, followed by an arrow, and then a specification of the possible contents of the clump:

(33)   LABEL → CONTENTS

For example, the simple pattern described in 6 can be represented by the following PS rule:

(34)   NP → D N

The way this rule would be pronounced is "A noun phrase may consist of a determiner followed by a noun."

Notice that the arrow (→) in PS rules is quite different from the arrow that appears in phonological and morphophonemic rules. There is no change involved in PS rules. The arrow simply indicates that the **PHRASAL CATEGORY** on the left is made up of the string of elements on the right. The sequence on the right is a more detailed, "inside" view of the phrasal category named on the left. In this sense the arrow in a PS rule is more similar to an equals sign (=) than to an arrow in some kind of process rule.

More complex phrase structure rules may employ additional notational conventions, to be discussed below. All PS rules, however, consist of a label for the clump, an arrow, and the contents of the clump.

This is all we will have to say about phrase structure rules for now. You now know the basic principles of how they are written, and why they are important.

Now we will turn to another notational system, which is a more common way of representing the structure of individual linguistic strings.

Constituent structure trees

We have just seen examples of phrase structure rules. These attempt to represent, in a mathematically explicit way, regular patterns of behavior that all speakers must have developed in their minds as a result of having learned a language. Such patterns of behavior "sanction" the basic clauses and phrases of a language, and "disallow," or "exclude," sequences of elements that are not a part of that language. They are like the "building codes" that many communities enact in order to instruct builders as to what counts as an acceptable building for that community (Radford 1988:132).

Now we will consider another metaphor – **CONSTITUENT STRUCTURE TREES** – that is particularly useful for depicting the structure of individual sentences. Constituent structure trees (also called "phrase markers") are like architectural plans of individual buildings, rather than building codes that specify what counts as an acceptable building and what doesn't. Constituent structure trees are "evaluated," "validated," or "sanctioned" by phrase structure rules, in the same sense as building plans are evaluated in relation to building codes. These two modes of representation serve quite different purposes – phrase structure rules present general patterns, while constituent structure trees are graphic representations of the constituent structure of individual phrases and clauses.

Here is an example of how constituent structure trees work. A clump like *the dog* consists of a D plus a Noun. We have already used labeled brackets to represent this structure:

(35) $[_{np}$ D N $]_{np}$
              the dog

The brackets indicate that the D and N are "merged" (Chomsky 1995) into a constituent, or "clump," and the small subscript labels indicate the phrasal category of the clump. Larger structures can be represented with multiple labeled brackets, as in 19. Another method of displaying this structure is a "tree":

(36)   NP
             /\
          D   N
          | |
         the dog

In this tree, the phrasal category is written at the top (NP), while the parts of the phrase are written underneath. They are linked to the phrasal category label by lines, called **BRANCHES**. Each labeled point is called a **NODE**. **PHRASAL NODES** are nodes that designate phrasal categories (NP in this example), and **TERMINAL NODES** are the nodes at the bottom of the tree – the ends of the branches (D and N in this example). Terminal node labels designate lexical categories (see table 6.1 above).

You will probably notice that this does not look much like a tree at all. This way of drawing trees is really more like an upside down tree, or the root system of a biological tree. In fact, constituent structure trees are sometimes written the other way – with the phrasal category label at the bottom and the branches extending upwards to the lexical category labels as "leaves." However, the rather odd, upside down way of presenting syntactic trees is more common.

As we have seen above in the discussion of tests for constituency, things get a little more complicated when we are dealing with clumps of more than two words. Consider the following:

(37)   The gnarly tree

This is clearly a clump, because, for one thing, a pronoun can substitute for the whole string (major test for constituency #2):

(38) a.   The gnarly tree fell down.
      b.   It fell down.

However, what about internal constituency? Is there any reason to argue for or against any of the following possible constituency relationships among the elements of this simple phrase?:

(39) a.   [the gnarly tree]   (All one clump – no internal constituency)
      b.   [[the gnarly] tree]
      c.   [the [gnarly tree]]

These three possible constituent analyses can be represented with three different trees (we'll add labels to all the nodes in a minute):

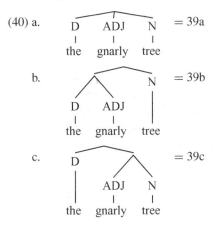

How can we "probe and poke" this structure to see which of these analyses is best? We can apply the tests for constituency to see if *the gnarly* or *gnarly tree* is a constituent. If neither one is a constituent, then analysis 40a must be correct.

What about movement? Well, the examples below show that movement doesn't tell us anything:

(41) a.   *The gnarly is what tree fell down.
     b.   *Gnarly tree is what the fell down.

What about substitution? Consider the following:

(42)   You like this gnarly tree and I like that *one*.

The word *one* in this example is used as a non-specific pronoun. What does it substitute for? I think most English speakers agree that it stands for *gnarly tree*, and not simply *tree*. This is one small piece of evidence that *gnarly tree* is a clump.

Here is some more poking and probing that involves substitution:

(43) a.   *The gnarly tree* that it is, I still love it.
     b.   *The gnarly* that it is, I still love it.
     c.   *Gnarly tree* that it is, I still love it.

What does this show? (I'm sure you can figure that out for yourself.)

What about interposition? Well, I think you can place adjectives on either side of *gnarly* in this phrase, so I don't think interposition helps.

(44) a.   The old gnarly tree
     b.   The gnarly old tree

How about coordination? Consider the following expressions:

(45) a.   The gnarly and rotten tree
     b.   The gnarly tree and rotten log
     c.   The gnarly tree and the rotten log
     d.   ?The gnarly and the rotten tree

Example 45a shows that *gnarly and rotten* can form a clump, but this is not surprising, since they are both fairly clearly adjectives. Remember that coordination shows that the two coordinated elements are of the same syntactic category, so it makes sense that two adjectives can be coordinated. What does 45b show? This shows that *gnarly tree* and *rotten log* can be coordinated. In other words, it shows that something like the following tree is the appropriate analysis for 45b:

(46)

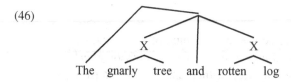

The   gnarly   tree   and   rotten   log

In this example, the X symbols just indicate that the two clumps, *gnarly tree* and *rotten log*, must belong to the same category (if they didn't, you wouldn't be able to coordinate them like this), without making a commitment yet as to what that category is.

This is some more evidence that an ADJective and a Noun can clump together, separately from the Determiner within a phrase.

Example 45c shows that *the gnarly tree* and *the rotten log* belong to the same category, and therefore can be coordinated. This, again, is not surprising at all, since we have already determined that such strings are clumps.

Example 45d is a little problematic. It seems as though it is trying to coordinate *the gnarly* and *the rotten*, leaving *tree* out. This would show that the following is a conceivable tree structure for this phrase:

(47)

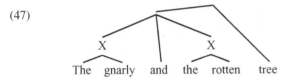

However, the fact that many native speakers reject this phrase indicates that maybe it's not all that grammatical. Even those English speakers who accept this phrase as grammatical will agree that 45b sounds "better" somehow. Actually, if we think a little more about this phrase, we find that it sounds a little better if the noun is plural:

(48)   The gnarly and the rotten trees.

What does this tell us? It seems to make more sense if we are talking about a grove of trees, some of which are rotten and some of which are gnarly. If they were all gnarly and rotten, we would be more likely to say *the gnarly and rotten trees*. Example 45d would be a reduction from something like *the gnarly trees and the rotten trees*, with the first instance of *trees* just elliplted. Therefore, it can be seen as another example of the kind of structure illustrated in 45c, but with one of the nouns eliminated, because it is the same as another noun in the same phrase:

(49)

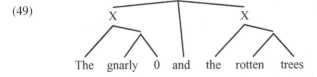

All of this poking and probing has given us some evidence that within the simple three-word phrase *the gnarly tree*, there is clumping, first between *gnarly* and *tree*, and then between this clump and the determiner *the*. In other words, the tree in 40c above is more consistent with the syntactic facts of English than the tree in 40b.

Now let's consider how to label the tree in 40c. When we look at the whole grammar of English, we notice that determined noun phrases, i.e., noun phrases that begin with one of the many possible English determiners,[2] have different distributional properties than "undetermined" noun phrases. We've already seen some examples of this above. Other examples include the fact that subjects of verbs must be determined:

(50) a.   The tree fell down.
    b.   That tree fell down.
    c.   Farmer John's tree fell down.
    d.   *Tree fell down.
    e.   *Gnarly tree fell down.

Note that *gnarly tree*, without the determiner, can appear in examples like 43c, but the same phrase cannot occur in examples like 50e. Therefore, it is clear that NPs with a determiner and those without one have different syntactic properties. Since the presense of a determiner governs the syntactic properties of the whole phrase, it makes sense to think of the determiner as being the syntactic HEAD of the phrase. By the projection principle (syntactic heads project syntactic properties onto their phrasal categories), it is reasonable to consider the whole determined noun phrase a **DETERMINER PHRASE**, or DP. A noun phrase, then, would be the part that doesn't include the determiner. Under this analysis, the complete tree diagram of our famous phrase would be the following:[3]

(51)

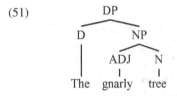

In this tree, there are two phrases – a determiner phrase with a noun phrase embedded within it. The terminal nodes, D and N, represent the syntactic heads of these two phrases respectively. A common convention is that phrases will generally have the same label as their syntactic heads, with the addition of a P (for Phrase). So D is the syntactic head of a DP, and N is the (syntactic and semantic) head of an NP.

Another convention you may run across in the literature is a bar placed over the label of a major word class to indicate a phrase that is the projection of that category. So, for example, a Noun Phrase is a projection of an N, so you may see N̄ (pronounced "N-bar") instead of NP. There are good theory-internal reasons for doing it this way, but for our purposes, it will be sufficient to use the terms NP, DP, etc.

Now let us look at an even more complex structure. Consider the example in 8, repeated here for convenience:

(52)   The dog watched a fluffy cat.

Given the constituent structure analysis presented earlier in this chapter, plus our analysis of determined noun phrases above, we come up with the following labeled bracket analysis and tree diagram of this clause (again, we are about to work on the category labels, so be patient!):

(53)   [s [dp [d The]d [np [n dog]n]np]dp [vp? [v watched]v [dp [d a]d [np [adj fluffy]adj [n cat]n]np]dp]vp?]s

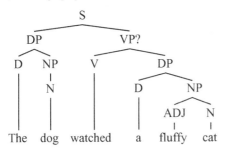

As you can see, constituent structure trees are logically equivalent to labeled brackets, though trees are often easier to read, especially when more complex structures are involved.

Before we conclude this section, let's take a look at another common phrasal category – the verb phrase. Consider the following clauses:

(54) a.   My daughter is reading an Igbo dictionary.
     b.   Is my daughter reading an Igbo dictionary?

The major question here is "What is the syntactic status of the Auxiliary element *is*?" Is it part of a clump that includes *reading an Igbo dictionary*, one that includes *my daughter*, or neither? In fact, there are at least five possible syntactic analyses of example 54a. These are given below in 55. In these trees, the triangles are simply abbreviations for structures that are not relevant to the current discussion:

(55) a.

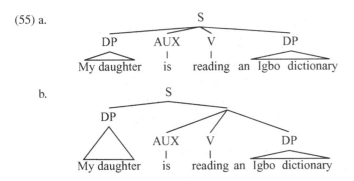

c.

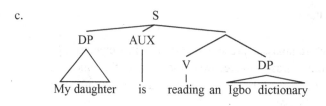

d.

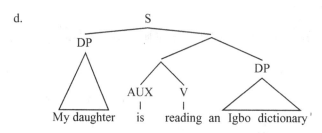

e.

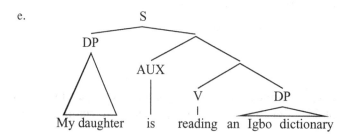

We have already dealt with noun phrases and determiner phrases, so we don't need to complicate our discussion by worrying about the internal structure of these elements anymore. Our focus now is on the external relationships of the DPs, as well as the syntactic status of the AUX and the V. Also, we have left some nodes unlabeled, because these analyses are only possibilities at this point. We need to "probe and poke" the structure a bit to see which of these is most consistent with the facts of English. After we've done that, we'll worry about the category labels.

Analyses like 55a are sometimes referred to as **FLAT STRUCTURES**. In a flat structure, there is no syntactic merger between any of the elements under the S node. This kind of structure would suggest that the order of these elements may be fairly "free" (though there still may be a "basic," or "normal," constituent order). Some languages (e.g., Naga, mentioned in chapter 1, Warlbiri, and many others) have been claimed to exhibit a very flat syntactic structure.

We will test this structure for English by applying the now familiar tests for constituency. Example 54b shows that the AUX can move to the front by itself, therefore it is a constituent on its own at some level. This would seem to eliminate possibilities 55b and 55d immediately, since in these structures the AUX is merged directly with other lexical categories. We would expect that if the AUX moved, its "sisters" would move too, but they don't:

(56)   Trying to move *is reading an Igbo dictionary* as a clump:

    | *Is reading an Igbo dictionary | my daughter.

    Is reading an Igbo dictionary is what my daughter does.
    etc.

(57)   Trying to move *is reading* as a clump:

    | *Is reading | my daughter an Igbo dictionary.

    Is reading is what my daughter an Igbo dictionary does.
    etc.

The other tests also show that *is reading an Igbo dictionary* (example 55b) and *is reading* (55d) cannot be constituents; therefore we can eliminate these two analyses and concentrate on 55a, c, and e.

Analysis 55a suggests not only that *is* can be moved independently (and 54b shows that it can) but also that *reading* should be able to so move also. This is not the case:

(58)   Trying to move *reading* independently:
    Reading my daughter is an Igbo dictionary.
    Reading is what my daughter is an Igbo dictionary does.
    etc.

Therefore we can pretty confidently conclude that analysis 55a is out, for English. So we are left with 55c and e. These two structures, one with the AUX attached directly to the S node, and the other with the AUX connected at a lower level to the semantically main verb, are in fact the two most commonly proposed basic syntactic structures for English clauses. For many years 55c, with the AUX attached directly to the S node, was the favored analysis for English. In recent years, however, analyses more similar to 55e have been preeminent. In the following discussion, we will "probe and poke" this structure a little more to see which analysis seems best, from the point of view of the tests for constituency provided above. Then we will briefly discuss the controversy that these two possible analyses have stimulated. The point of this discussion, however, is simply to illustrate how constituent structure trees and the tests for constituency can be used to determine the hierarchical structure of linguistic units – not to argue conclusively for one particular analysis or another of English.

We have seen in example 56 that the sequence *is reading an Igbo dictionary* cannot move as a clump. This is one piece of evidence for analysis 55c. What about substitution? Consider the following:

(59)   Trying to substitute *(so) do* for *is reading an Igbo dictionary*:
    *My daughter is reading an Igbo dictionary and *so does* my son.

Rather, it seems much easier to substitute *so* alone for the sequence *reading an Igbo dictionary*, leaving the AUX in place:

(60)   Substituting *so* for *reading an Igbo dictionary*:
         My daughter is reading an Igbo dictionary and *so* is my son.

Furthermore, in answer to a question like "What is your daughter doing?" it is
reasonable to expect an answer like 61a, but not b:

(61) a.   Reading an Igbo dictionary.
     b.   *Is reading an Igbo dictionary.

Interposition similarly seems to show that there is a major constituent boundary
after *is*, but perhaps somewhat less major boundaries before *is* and after *reading*:

(62) a.   My daughter is avidly reading an Igbo dictionary.
     b.   ?My daughter avidly is reading an Igbo dictionary.
     c.   ?My daughter is reading avidly an Igbo dictionary.

This seems to argue in favor of analysis 55c, in which the boundary between
AUX and V is at the highest level.

Finally, coordination also provides evidence that *reading an Igbo dictionary* is
a constituent, whereas *is reading an Igbo dictionary* is not:

(63) a.   My daughter is reading an Igbo dictionary and chewing gum.
     b.   ?My daughter is reading an Igbo dictionary and is chewing gum.

In summary, both of the major tests for constituency, and some of the minor
tests as well, seem to point to the tree structure in 55c as the most reasonable
analysis for this English clause (and presumably for all other English clauses
with auxiliaries, though each would need to be tested to make sure).

Now let us briefly consider why, in more recent theoretical work, analysis 55e
is considered more appropriate. The reasoning is that the AUX in a structure like
54a is the syntactic head of the rest of the clause. What is the evidence that AUX
is a syntactic head? First, the particular AUX chosen determines the form of the
verb that follows. Consider the following:

(64) a.   Frodo is leaving the Shire.
     b.   Frodo has left the Shire.
     c.   Frodo will leave the Shire.
     d.   Frodo ought to leave the Shire.

The examples in 64 illustrate four distinct auxiliaries *be*, *have*, *will*, and *ought*,
respectively. Each of these requires a distinct form of the verb that follows. Example 64a shows that the auxiliary *be* takes an "*-ing* form" (traditionally called a
PRESENT PARTICIPLE) of the following verb. Example 64b shows that the
auxiliary *have* takes a **PAST PARTICIPLE** form (*left*) of the following verb.
Example 64c shows that the auxiliary *will* is followed by the **BARE FORM**
(*leave*) of the semantically main verb. Finally, example 64d shows that the auxiliary *ought* requires an **INFINITIVE** form (*to leave*) of the main verb. These
facts are evidence that the AUX plus the verb have a close syntactic relation to
one another. In particular, they provide one piece of evidence that the AUX is the

syntactic head of the verb, since the grammatical properties (the particular verb form) of the semantically main verb depend on the AUX. Another way of saying this is that the AUX GOVERNS the semantically main verb that follows.

The second piece of evidence that the AUX is the head of a phrase that includes the following verb is that the AUX takes the major inflectional information (tense and agreement) for the whole phrase. For example, consider the following:

(65) a.   Frodo is leaving the Shire.
    b.   Frodo was leaving the Shire.
    c.   Frodo and Bilbo are leaving the Shire.
    d.   Frodo and Bilbo were leaving the Shire.

In these examples, *leaving the Shire* is clearly the main action that is being described. Nevertheless, the auxiliary *be* (*is*, *was*, *are*, and *were*) is what varies for tense and for the number of the subject. The semantically main verb, *leaving*, remains the same in all examples. This is a major defining property of auxiliaries in English – they express the inflectional information that is relevant to the semantically main verb that follows. Consider these additional auxiliaries:

(66)   a. I have seen the lady.   c. I can only eat organic food.
        b. I had seen the lady.   d. I could only eat organic food.

These examples show that the auxiliaries *have* and *can* also take the tense inflection for the whole clause, even though the verbs *see* and *eat* respectively express the main semantic content.

In summary, while the traditional tests for constituency seem to argue for a three-way branching under the S node in English (analysis 55c), it is clearly the case that the AUX is more tightly related to the verb to its right than it is to the DP to its left. Another way of looking at this is to say that the relationships among the three major constituents of the S (the first DP, the AUX, and the VP) are *asymmetrical*. That is to say, the AUX is syntactically "closer" to the verb than to the subject of the sentence.

Since we have argued that the AUX is the syntactic head of a constituent that includes the following verb, you might think that a reasonable label for this constituent would be Auxiliary Phrase, AP, or maybe AuxP (to help distinguish this phrasal category from Adjective Phrases and Adverb Phrases). This would be analogous to the way we use the term "Determiner Phrase" to refer to a phrase whose head is a determiner.

Nevertheless, most recent accounts use the term INFLECTIONAL PHRASE (IP) to refer to the kind of structure that is headed by an auxiliary. There are good theoretical reasons for this that we will only touch on here. Briefly, not all constituents that have the syntactic properties of inflectional phrases have auxiliaries in them. For example, consider clauses like the following:

(67) a.   Frodo ought to leave the Shire.
    b.   Frodo has to leave the Shire.

While the auxiliaries *ought* and *has* govern the form of the whole constituent that follows, there is a sense in which the particle *to* governs the form of the verb *leave* – the verb following *to* always must be in its bare form (no inflection or any other kind of affixation) following the particle *to*, no matter what the auxiliary is. This suggests that the syntactic analysis of 67 would be the following:

(68)

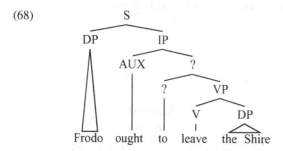

The usual analysis of this type of structure is that the constituent under the first IP node is another IP. This would be consistent with the fact that auxiliaries and *to* govern the constituent to their right. However, we can't say that *to* is an auxiliary. Why? Because it doesn't have the syntactic properties of an auxiliary. In particular, it doesn't take inflectional information:

(69)   *Frodo to-s leave the Shire.
            *Frodo and Bilbo to leave the Shire.
            *Frodo to-d leave the Shire, etc.

The label that is usually used for the particle *to* in this kind of structure is **INFINITIVE PARTICLE**, and the abbreviation for this category is simply "I." So the final tree diagram for example 67a would be 70:

(70)

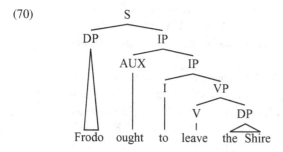

The possibility of nesting inflectional phrases within other inflectional phrases is consistent with the fact that auxiliaries and the infinitive particle govern the constituent to their right. It also allows for **AUXILIARY STACKING**, which is a very notable fact of the syntax of English and many other languages. Consider the following clauses:

(71) a.   The winning side has paid you much better.
     b.   The winning side would have paid you much better.
     c.   The winning side would have been paying you much better.

We've already seen that the auxiliary *have* governs the past participle form of the verb that follows. In 71a and b, *have* precedes the verb *pay*, and therefore the past participle form, *paid*, is required. In 71c, the auxiliary *have* precedes the auxiliary *be*. And, lo and behold, *be* occurs in the past participle form, *been*, while *pay* appears in the present participle form, *paying*. Why is this? Because in this example *pay* is governed by the auxiliary *be*, rather than the auxiliary *have*.

What governs the form of *have* in example 71b? The auxiliary *would* does. If it didn't, then the form of *have* would be the same as it is in 71a – *has*. Therefore, we see that there is good evidence for a structure in which either an AUX or the infinitive particle *to* recursively governs the element to its right (its complement). These facts of the grammatical knowledge of English speakers can be nicely captured in the following kind of tree diagram:

(72)

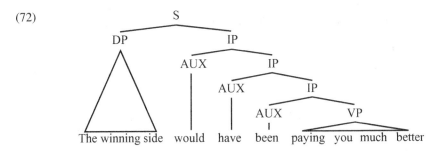

The last few clauses we have diagrammed consist of a DP plus an IP at the highest level. If we were to translate this generalization into a phrase structure rule, the rule for S would be:

(73)   S → DP IP

This rule would capture a general principle of English syntax that (just about) any clause may consist of a DP plus an IP. However, what about sentences that don't have an overt auxiliary or infinitive particle? The way we have described IPs so far, such sentences, like the following, would not contain an IP:

(74)   He roped himself a couple of sea turtles.

Since there is no auxiliary in this clause, we may want to diagram it as in 75:

(75)

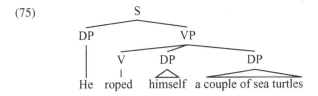

If this were the proper tree for this clause, we would need to complicate the PS rule for the S node to include the possibility of a VP instead of an IP appearing at the highest level:

(76) $S \rightarrow DP \quad \begin{Bmatrix} IP \\ VP \end{Bmatrix}$

The "curly brackets" in this rule are similar to the curly brackets we used in chapter 3 in discussing morphophonemic rules. They mean that the items inside constitute a choice – either an IP or a VP.

There are a couple of reasons why this kind of analysis would not be very satisfying. First, the rule in 76 is more complex than the rule above that includes only an IP. Remember that the best analyses are those that involve the simplest apparatus (the **MINIMALIST CRITERION**). Second, if IP really stands for "Inflectional Phrase," then *roped himself a couple of sea turtles* should also be included, since it certainly is inflected (it expresses the past tense). It's just that the inflection in this phrase is part of the verb, rather than being expressed in a separate auxiliary. What if we treat the inflection as an "invisible category," that migrates to the verb whenever there is no auxiliary to receive it? This analysis may be diagrammed as follows:

(77)

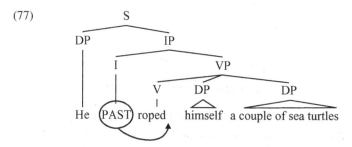

This kind of analysis preserves the generalization that clauses consist of a DP plus an IP, though it does require a node whose logical (understood) content is expressed as part of a word that is under a different node. If we are going to posit an abstract analysis such as this, it would be more convincing if it could do more for us than simply eliminate the need for a more complex phrase structure rule, like 76. After all, if you reduce the complexity of the analysis in one area, only by increasing complexity in another, you haven't really made your grammar simpler overall. In this particular case, it would help us evaluate the invisible category hypothesis if we could show that this analysis is needed to capture some other fact or facts of English syntax. Well, consider the rule that is sometimes referred to as **SUBJECT–AUX** inversion in English.

Subject–aux inversion happens in various kinds of questions in English. For example, if you want to ask someone a question, based on the statement *I can't have a normal boyfriend*, you may say:

(78)   Why can't I have a normal boyfriend?
            Can't I have a normal boyfriend?

Notice what happens to the auxiliary, *can't*, in these questions. In both examples, it precedes the subject, *I*, rather than follows it, as in the statement. This inversion of subject and auxiliary in questions is completely regular, for all auxiliaries in English.

Now, we may ask what happens to a clause like 74 when you apply subject–aux inversion. After all, it looks like there is no auxiliary in this clause, right? Well, check this out:

(79)   Why did he rope a couple of sea turtles?
         Did he rope a couple of sea turtles?

Voilà, the abstract inflectional element appears in the form of the auxiliary *do*, which then takes the tense inflection. Meanwhile, the semantically main verb, *rope*, goes back to its bare form. It's almost as though the auxiliary were there all along, lurking within the inflected verb. The inversion construction simply flushes it out into the open.

There are a couple of additional constructions in English that reveal the invisible inflectional element in an auxiliaryless inflectional phrase. Consider the standard negation construction. When there is an auxiliary in the affirmative, the negative particle, *not*, follows the auxiliary:

(80)   Negative: Affirmative:
         I am *not* being fired.   I am being fired.
         I can *not* see why you would be upset.   I can see why you would be upset.
         You would *not* believe how much I weigh.   You would believe how much I weigh.

In modern Englishes, it is not common for the negative particle to follow the verb:

(81)   *I am being *not* fired.
         *I can see *not* why you would be upset.
         *You would believe *not* how much I weigh.

Well, what happens when you negate an affirmative clause that does not have an auxiliary?

(82)   Negative: Affirmative:
         I do *not* feel like parting with it.   I feel like parting with it.
         I do *not* even exercise.   I even exercise.
         I do *not* even have a picture of him.   I even have a picture of him.

Again, the auxiliary *do* automatically appears. One could say it appears *so that* the negative particle can follow it. This is yet another piece of evidence that something like the invisible element analysis of auxiliaryless inflected verb phrases in English is correct.

That's probably enough on tree diagrams and tests for constituency for now. Of course, there are many more considerations, and important theoretical principles that we are glossing over here, but this should give you a general idea of how the formalisms of early twenty-first century Generative Grammar work. The important ideas to remember at this point are:

> Linguistic formalisms are metaphors designed to help us analyze and understand the internal grammatical knowledge that every speaker of a language must have.

Phrase structure rules provide one way of understanding and modeling internal grammatical knowledge.

Constituent structure trees provide a way of representing possible constituent structure analyses of individual linguistic strings.

There are certain tests for constituency that linguists use to "probe and poke" a linguistic string in order to understand its constituent structure better.

Ambiguity

Some linguistic utterances are ambiguous. This simply means that they may be interpreted in more than one way. **AMBIGUITY** describes the property of expressing more than one possible meaning. There are several reasons why a linguistic string may be ambiguous. Perhaps the most obvious kind of ambiguity is **LEXICAL AMBIGUITY**. There's a bank in my town that plays on this kind of ambiguity in its advertising:

(83)   The right bank is on your left.

Right can mean either 'correct,' or 'the opposite of *left*.' This ambiguity is resolved by the PP *on your left* in 83 – the directional meaning of *right* is negated. The bank can't be both 'on your left' and 'the opposite of left.' Here's another example that plays on the ambiguous word *bank*:

(84)   Let's try another bank.

In the context of fishermen looking for a good place to fish, it means one thing. In the context of people who are tired of the institution where they keep their money, it means something else. This is called lexical ambiguity because the two different interpretations are both associated with the same noise, [bæŋk].

STRUCTURAL AMBIGUITY arises when one sequence of words can have more than one meaning because it has more than one possible phrase structure. This is the kind of ambiguity exhibited by a phrase like *good girls and boys*, illustrated at the beginning of this chapter. The ambiguity of this phrase is not because any of the words are ambiguous, but rather because there are two distinct tree structures that can be applied to it:

(85) a.   b.

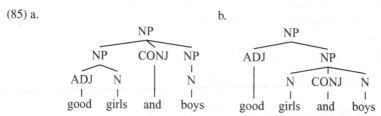

In example 85a, the two NPs, *good girls*, and *boys*, are conjoined by the conjunction *and*. In this case, the Adjective, *good*, only applies to *girls*. In example 85b, on the other hand, the Nouns *girls* and *boys* are conjoined, and the Adjective *good* applies to the entire conjoined NP.

Here is another famous example:

(86)   Lincoln wrote the Gettysburg address while traveling from Washington to Gettysburg on the back of an envelope.

Why does this utterance (purported to be an actual sentence from a student essay) strike us as funny? There are two possible phrase structure analyses: *on the back of an envelope* might be a modifier of *traveling* or a modifier of *wrote*. The utterance means something different in each case. The writer meant to clump it with *wrote*, but readers commonly clump it with *traveling* because *traveling* is closer.

Here is another ambiguous example:

(87)   They are moving stairways.

Perhaps the first meaning you might think of is the one in which some workers are in the process of physically moving some stairways. This would be an answer to the question: "What are they doing?" Example 88 gives the constituent structure tree of this meaning:

(88)

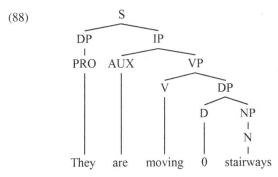

There is another possible meaning to the clause in 87. Can you figure out what it is? The word *moving* might be an ADJective inside an NP headed by the Noun *stairways*. In other words the clause might mean: "Those things over there are stairways that are moving." Here is the constituent structure tree for this meaning of example 87:

(89)

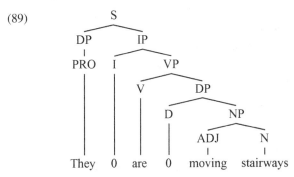

Notice that the surface form is the same for both meanings. The only thing that differs is the constituent structure. This is called structural ambiguity, because the ambiguity is due to two possible phrase structures being applied to the same sequence of words. In the exercises at the end of this chapter, you will have a chance to analyze several types of structural ambiguity.

Conceptual outline of chapter 6

I.   Part of what every speaker of a language implicitly knows are the patterns involved in putting words together into phrases and clauses. This part of grammatical knowledge is called syntax.

II. Linguists have developed several systems of formalisms for representing syntactic structures. Formalisms are metaphors that help linguists understand the facts of a language or of Language in general. Each formalism has its strengths and weaknesses.

III. The universal properties of syntactic structure that any formalism must be able to account for are:
   • linear order
   • constituency ("clumping" or "merger")
   • hierarchical structure ("nesting" or "embedding")

IV. It makes sense that human languages exhibit these properties for the following reasons:
   • the nature of the vocal apparatus (linguistic noises follow one another in sequence)
   • the nature of the human mind (people can only attend to four to six things at once)
   • the complexity of the ideas humans have the ability and need to express

V.   Linguists have developed several methods, or "tests," in order to determine the syntactic structure of a linguistic string. These tests are ways of "probing and poking" that are analogous to methods a chemist may use to analyze an unknown chemical compound.

VI. "Grammaticality judgments" are used to evaluate hypotheses concerning syntactic structures. Structures that are "probed and poked" using the tests for constituency are presented to native speakers for evaluation. If native speakers agree that a string is a possible utterance of the language, then the string is considered to be "grammatical," i.e., sanctioned by the grammatical patterns of the language.

VII. Three methods for representing syntactic structures include:
   labeled bracketing
   phrase structure rules (PSRs)
   constituent structure trees ("tree diagrams" or "phrase markers")

VIII. PSRs are ways of representing the general syntactic patterns of a language. These can be helpful, though they are no longer (early twenty-first century) considered to be necessary in a formal description of a language. Labeled bracketing and constituent structure trees are ways of representing the constituency and hierarchical structures of individual linguistic strings.

IX. Linguistic strings can have more than one valid syntactic structure. In such a case, the string will be structurally ambiguous. This is different from lexical ambiguity, which is ambiguity due to multiple meanings of one word. The notion of structural ambiguity illustrates the reality of constituency relations, and the usefulness of constituent structure analysis.

Exercise 6.1: translating bracketing into trees

Tom Payne

"Translate" the following labeled and bracketed strings into constituent structure trees. Be sure to label each node correctly.

a. $[_x [_y A [_z B]_z [_x C]_x]_y [_w [_z D]_z [_z E]_z]_w]_x$

b. $[_x [_y [_z A]_z [_z B]_z C]_y [_w [_y [_z D]_z E]_y F]_x$

c. $[_s [_{dp} [_d \emptyset]_d [_{np} [_n \text{Death}]_n]_{np}]_{dp} [_{ip} [_i \text{cannot}]_i [_{vp} [_v \text{stop}]_v [_{dp} [_d \emptyset]_d [_{np} [_{adj} \text{true}]_{adj} [_n \text{love}]_n]_{np}]_{dp}]_{vp}]_{ip}]_s$

d. $[_s [_{dp} [_d \emptyset]_d [_{np} [_n \text{Wesley}]_n [_{conj} \text{and}]_{conj} [_n \text{Buttercup}]_n]_{np}]_{dp} [_{ip} [_i \emptyset]_i [_{vp} [_v \text{raced}]_v [_{pp} [_p \text{along}]_p [_{dp} [_d \text{the}]_d [_{np} [_n \text{ravine}]_n [_n \text{floor}]_n]_{np}]_{dp}]_{vp}]_{ip}]_s$

Exercise 6.2: tree diagrams

Tom Payne

A. Draw a possible constituent structure tree for the following English clause. Be sure to include all phrasal and terminal nodes:

The scruffy dog watched the fluffy cat through the window.

B. The following English clause is structurally ambiguous. Draw two constituent structure trees, one for each of the possible structures that underlie this clause:

She saw a man with a telescope.

Exercise 6.3: phrase structure rules

Tom Payne

A. List all the sentences that the following Phrase Structure (PS) rules and lexicon will sanction:

PS rules:

S → VP NP

NP → D N

VP → V (NP)

Lexicon:

N → dog, cat, mouse

D → the

V → chased, bit

B.   Write a PS rule that will sanction each of the following strings (one rule for each example). You may assume the word classes are the same as the English glosses – this is, in general, not a good assumption to make, but you may do so for the purposes of this exercise:

1. Isthmus Zapotec (Southern Mexico):
   čupa   ležu   wiini   'two little rabbits'
   two   rabbit   little

2. Apinajé (Jé, Brazil):
   ape   kra   'the child works'
   works child

3. Tlingit (Athabaskan, Alberta, Canada):
   hit   yix'   'in the house'
   house in

4. Malagasy (Austronesia, Madagascar)
   manasa lamba Rashu   'Rasoa washes clothes'
   wash   clothes Rasoa

Exercise 6.4: syntactic argumentation

Tom Payne

Consider the first verse of the Lewis Carroll poem quoted on p. 5:

'Twas brillig, and the slithy toves
Did gyre and gimble in the wabe;
All mimsy were the borogoves,
And the mome raths outgrabe.

There are two possible constituent structures for the last clause: *The mome raths outgrabe* (ignore *and* for the purposes of this exercise).

A.   Draw two tree diagrams corresponding to the two possible structures.

B.   Give evidence for why one structure is more plausible in this context than the other.

     Note: No special knowledge of the "meanings" of any of the words (except maybe *the*) is needed to complete this exercise. In other words, you are not being asked to give the "official" analysis of this clause, which is in fact provided in the original book. Just given your knowledge of English, what constituent structure analyses are possible for the string *The mome raths outgrabe*, and why would you choose one over the other? The official analysis may actually confuse the issue.

Exercise 6.5: Ewe phrase structure

Adapted from Yule (1996)

The following is a "toy" (i.e., tiny, incomplete) phrase structure grammar and lexicon for Ewe ([ɛ́βɛ́]), a language spoken in Ghana, West Africa. Use these rules to write out at least six well-formed Ewe sentences:

Phrase structure rules:

S → DP VP
DP → N (D)
VP → V NP

Lexicon:

Nouns	Determiners	Verbs
oge	ye	xa
ika	la	vo
amu		

Exercise 6.6: Scottish Gaelic phrase structure

Yule (1996)

Here are some simplified phrase structure rules for Scottish Gaelic:

S → V NP NP

NP → { D N (ADJ) / PN }

Lexicon:

Determiner	Noun	Proper Noun	ADJective	Verb
an	cu	Tearlach	beag	chunnaic
	gille	Calum	mor	bhuail

Only two of the following strings would be considered well-formed, according to the rules above. First, identify the ill-formed sentences, using the asterisk (*) symbol. Second, draw tree diagrams for the two well-formed sentences:

*1. Calum chunnaic an gille.
2. Bhuail an gille mor an cu.
*3. Bhuail an beag cu.
4. Chunnaic Tearlach an gille.

Exercise 6.7: Iraqi Arabic

Adapted from Cowan and Rakušan (1998)

1. ilbinit tigdar tiʃtiri ilkitaab.	'The girl can buy the book.'
2. haay ilbibit triid tiʃtiri ilkitaab.	'This girl wants to buy the book.'
3. ilbibit tiʃtiri ilkitaab	'The girl buys the book.'
4. iʂʂabi raah ʕal beet.	'The boy went to the house.'
5. haaða iʂʂabi raah ʕal masdʒad.	'This boy went to the mosque.'
6. ilbinit ilbibit raaħit ʕal mustaʃa.	'The girl went to the hospital.'
7. haay ilbibit iʃtarit xubuz.	'This girl bought bread.'
8. ðaak irradʒdʒaal maat.	'That man died.'
9. ðiitʃ ilbinit maatit.	'That woman died.'

A.   Provide a lexicon of this corpus of Iraqi Arabic, including a word class label and English gloss for each word.

B.   Give phrase structure rules, based on your lexicon, that will sanction all of the examples in this corpus.

C.   Give two additional clauses, not found in the corpus, that your phrase structure rules sanction.

Exercise 6.8: constituency

Tom Payne

A.   Bracket the DPs, and underline the VPs in the following excerpt (from "The ice palace" by F. Scott Fitzgerald). Remember that there may be multiple embeddings, i.e., phrases within other phrases.

> The sunlight dripped over the house like golden paint
> over an art jar, and the freckling shadows
> here and there only intensified the rigour of the
> bath of light.

B.   Circle the "semantic head" and underline the "syntactic head" of the following phrases:

a. the Queen of England's crown
b. a bunch of flowers
c. a lot of apples
d. the attorney general of the United States
e. a sensitive but not too brilliant boyfriend
f. a decorated camel-litter, which carried the daughters of the sheikh
g. a hole in the wall
h. a tall, spare, weatherbeaten man of few words
i. the tribal equivalent of regimental colors

j. a large number of people
k. one of my best friends
l. the entrance to the building

Exercise 6.9: tree diagrams

Tom Payne

Choose two sentences from a newspaper or magazine article. You may shorten the sentences if necessary, but do not invent them – use ones you actually find in a real text. If you shorten a sentence, it should still be grammatical after you shorten it.

One sentence must be transitive and contain explicit reference to the direct object. The other sentence must be intransitive. Either or both sentences should contain:

A prepositional phrase.
An adverb.
A modified noun phrase.

Draw syntactic tree diagrams for both sentences.

Exercise 6.10: structural ambiguity

Tom Payne

The following English sentences are structurally ambiguous. Draw a tree diagram for each possible meaning of each sentence.

1. The mother of the boy and the girl left early.
2. Visiting relatives can be boring.
3. The police killed a man with a knife.
4. I saw her duck.
5. The missionary is ready to eat.

Notes

1. The term "ideally" is crucial here. In fact, there is now a fairly large body of literature showing that grammaticality is not an "either/or" notion. All languages have "core" construction types – those syntactic patterns that are clearly part of the grammatical knowledge of all native speakers – and "peripheral" constructions – those that resemble the core constructions to a greater or lesser degree (Goldberg 1995). There are also a number of reasons why native speakers may reject a particular string of linguistic units, ranging from ungrammaticality in the traditional generative sense implied in this text, to embarrassment. A particular sentence may be perfectly well formed grammatically, but just not make sense, or be too embarrassing to utter in the presense of a linguist, or be unacceptable for some other reason. Nevertheless, linguists seem to have a love/hate

relationship with grammaticality judgments: while many modern approaches eschew them as a legitimate source of data regarding syntactic knowledge, the notions of grammaticality and ungrammaticality are widely used, if not acknowledged, by linguistic researchers in all theoretical traditions.

2. Including zero in certain cases, such as proper names, indefinite plurals and mass nouns. We'll see some examples of these in a minute.

3. The idea that nominal constituents are projections of a determiner (either overt or null) in many languages, including English, is widely referred to as the DETERMINER PHRASE HYPOTHESIS, or DP HYPOTHESIS (Radford 1997:98). Many linguists find this idea unconvincing, and it certainly cannot be supported as a universal characteristic of languages. In many, perhaps most, languages, as we will see in later chapters, the appropriate phrasal category for nominal constituents is simply Noun Phrase. However, postulating a node that contains modifiers and nouns under the node that includes the determiner is necessary for English, given syntactic tests such as those described in this section. Whether one calls the larger constituent a Determiner Phrase or some other term is a matter of individual preference. Some terms that have been used include NP" and NP^{max}.

7   Language typology

A **TYPOLOGY** is simply a categorization of some range of phenomena into various types. To "typologize" something is to group its parts into types. For example, we often hear jokes like the following: "There are three kinds of people – those who can count, and those who can't." Typological linguists are people who like to group languages into well-defined and useful types.

But what makes a typology useful? A typology is useful when it makes "predictions" about multiple characteristics of the items being typologized. For example, suppose we were to typologize motorized vehicles. Which would be the most meaningful typology, A or B?:

- Typology A: bus, van, automobile, tractor
- Typology B: red ones, green ones, blue ones, white ones

If you know that a motor vehicle is a bus, what else do you know about it? Quite a lot actually – it is probably going to be a large vehicle, with lots of seats, designed primarily to carry people, etc. If, on the other hand, you know some random motor vehicle is blue in color, there is not much else you can guess about its characteristics. Therefore, typology A is more useful, because it reflects "clusters" of structural and functional characteristics that go together, rather than simply indicating isolated properties.

Turning to a linguistic example, we could say that there are two kinds of languages in the world – those that have the sound [r] in their phonetic inventory and those that don't. However, knowing whether a language has an [r] is not likely to have many repercussions in other parts of the language, therefore this is not a particularly interesting or useful typology. However, there are several other linguistic typologies that have been very helpful to people interested in exploring the characteristics of the human mind. These are typologies that identify *clusters* of characteristics that languages are likely to possess.

The value of typologizing languages is that it helps linguists understand the range and limits of possible variation among human languages. If logically possible types are found to be very rare or nonexistent, that may provide some insight into how the human mind works. Thus language typology can give us a "window" on the mind and communication. To extend our non-linguistic example, if we typologized all the motorized vehicles in the world according to number of wheels, we might find that there are no, or extremely few, vehicles with five wheels. This fact would invite us to investigate *why* motorized vehicles are restricted in exactly this respect. What is it about the origin, history, or function of motor vehicles that seems to rule out the existence of five-wheeled vehicles?

Several typologies of language have been proposed in the history of linguistic science. In this chapter, we will discuss morphological and syntactic typology. In later chapters we will discuss a typology of grammatical relations (chapter 8), voice and valence (chapter 9), and clause combining (chapter 10). Syntactic typology has proven particularly fruitful in stimulating the subfields of **TYPOLOGICAL LINGUISTICS**, and **FUNCTIONAL LINGUISTICS**.

Morphological typology

There are two parameters by which the morphological typology of a language may be measured. These are described by Comrie (1989) as the **INDEX OF SYNTHESIS** and the **INDEX OF FUSION**. The index of synthesis refers to how many morphemes tend to occur per word in a language, while the index of fusion refers to how many meanings tend to be associated with each morpheme.

The index of synthesis defines a continuum from **ISOLATING** languages at one extreme to highly **POLYSYNTHETIC** languages at the other. Figure 7.1 illustrates this continuum.

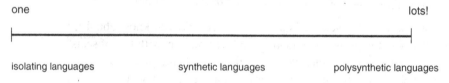

one   lots!

isolating languages   synthetic languages   polysynthetic languages

Figure 7.1 *The index of synthesis (the number of morphemes per word)*

A strictly isolating language is one in which every word consists of only one morpheme. The Chinese languages come close to this extreme. A highly polysynthetic language is one in which words tend to consist of several morphemes. The Quechuan and Eskimo-Aleut languages are good examples of highly polysynthetic languages. The following is an example of a polysynthetic structure in Central Yup'ik (thanks to Eliza Orr):

(1)   Tuntussuqatarniksaitengqiggtuq
           tuntu-ssur-qatar-ni-ksaite-ngqiggte-uq.
           reindeer-hunt-FUT-say-NEG-again-3SG.IND
           'He had not yet said again that he was going to hunt reindeer.'

The index of fusion (figure 7.2) describes a continuum between highly **AGGLUTINATIVE** languages to highly **FUSIONAL** languages. A highly agglutinative language is one in which most morphemes express one and only one meaning. A highly fusional language (sometimes called "inflectional," but since this has other connotations, we will use the term fusional) is one in which morphemes often express several meanings. For example, in Spanish the suffix -*ó* in a word like *habló* expresses at least five conceptual categories: indicative mood, third person, singular, past tense, and perfective aspect. If any one of these conceptual

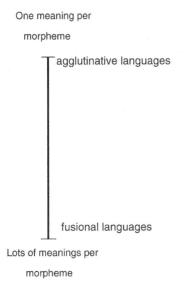

One meaning per

morpheme

agglutinative languages

fusional languages

Lots of meanings per

morpheme

Figure 7.2 *The index of fusion*

categories changes, the form of the suffix must change. Turkish is a language for which each lexical meaning and conceptual category is, in general, expressed by its own morpheme. Therefore, Turkish is a highly agglutinative language. For highly isolating languages, the index of fusion just doesn't apply. If anything, English is agglutinative rather than fusional, e.g., in *anti-dis-establish-ment-ari-an-ism* each morpheme has a specific and fairly clear meaning. But then, such words in English are mostly of Latin origin. Fusion is apparent in English in the present tense, third person, singular suffix *-s*, as in *he walks the line*, and in the paradigm for the verb *be*, but not much else.

There is no generally accepted quantitative method for precisely establishing the indices of synthesis and fusion for a given language. A rule of thumb for the index of synthesis is that if the language can express a whole sentence with just a verb, it is polysynthetic. If it can't, then it is isolating. Adjectives such as "somewhat" or "highly" can then be added in order to give a sense of where a language falls on each continuum, e.g., English is "somewhat isolating," Mandarin is "highly isolating." Turkish is "somewhat polysynthetic and highly agglutinative" while Yup'ik is "highly polysynthetic and somewhat fusional." Knowing something about the morphological typology of a language helps linguists make better hypotheses about the likely meanings of various structures and helps tremendously in understanding the historical roots and development of a language.

Syntactic typology

Linguists have long noticed that some languages tend to place the verb at the end of a clause, others at the beginning, still others place it somewhere in the middle. Finally, many languages seem to place the verb just about anywhere.

Among the nominal ("noun-like") elements in a clause, an important distinction has traditionally been made between subject and object (abbreviated S and O in early typological research).[1] In terms of tree diagrams, you can think of the subject as the DP that is directly under the S node, and the object as the DP that is directly under the VP node:

(2)

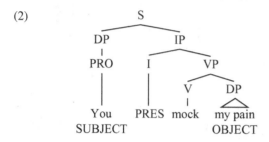

It turns out that there is a very major **TYPOLOGICAL** distinction between languages in which the object follows the verb (VO languages), and those in which the object precedes the verb (OV languages; Greenberg 1963, inter alia). In terms of phrase structure rules, this can be thought of as a distinction between languages, like English, in which the VP rule has an optional DP following the head verb, and others, like Japanese, in which the optional DP precedes the head verb:

(3)   VP → (DP) V   OV Languages (Japanese, Finnish, Hindi . . .)
         VP → V (DP)   VO Languages (Mandarin, Indonesian, English . . .)

What is interesting about this typology is that the order of object and verb in the verb phrase tends to correlate with other aspects of the syntax of the language. For example, if a language has OV order, it will almost certainly have postpositions, rather than prepositions. Conversely, if a language has VO order, it will almost certainly have prepositions. Also, in OV languages, inflected auxiliaries almost always come after the verb, whereas in VO languages, auxiliaries usually precede the verb. In short, there are, generally speaking, two major types of languages in the world: those in which syntactic heads normally precede their complements, and those in which syntactic heads follow their complements:

(4)

		VO languages:		OV languages:	
		Head	Complement	Complement	Head
VP	→	V	DP	DP	V
IP	→	AUX	VP	VP	AUX
PP	→	P	DP	DP	P
DP	→	D	NP	NP	D

Because every language is always in a state of change, and the order of head and complement in a particular phrasal category is one variable that may change over time, these correlations are not absolute. However, they are highly significant from a statistical point of view. It is certainly not mere coincidence that languages correlate in this way. The problem for linguistic theory is *why* this should be the case. Many linguists have approached this problem from different directions, and

Table 7.1 *Summary of Greenberg's Universals (from appendix 2 of Greenberg 1963)*

Greenberg's Universal	Parameter	correlation	
#1	Main clauses	V-O	O-V
#3,4	Adpositions	Prepositions	Postpositions
#2	Genitive (possessor) and head noun	N-G	G-N
#17	Head noun & adjective	N-Adj	Adj-N
#24	Relative clauses and head noun	N-RelCL	RelCL-N
#22	Comparatives	Adj-Mkr-Std	Std-Mkr-Adj
#16	Inflected auxiliaries	Aux-V V-Aux	
#9	Question particles	Sentence-initial	Sentence-final
#12	Question words	Sentence-initial or elsewhere	Sentence-initial
#27	Affixes	Prefixes	Suffixes

we will not try to summarize these here. Rather, we will simply present the findings of some very important foundational research, and then give some examples of languages that represent each of the major types.

The foundational work in syntactic typology was done by Joseph Greenberg in the early 1960s. Greenberg compared the syntactic characteristics of thirty languages and found several interesting correlations. In particular, he noticed that the languages in his sample tend to have a basic, or unmarked, syntactic structure, and that the order of certain elements in this basic structure correlate with the orders of other elements. Table 7.1 summarizes the correlations that Greenberg (1963) observed for VO and OV languages. These have come to be known as "Greenberg's Universals," since they were assumed to represent correlations that hold true universally, i.e., for all languages.

It is important to recognize that Greenberg simply observed certain correlations. He did not attempt to provide a reason for (i.e., to "motivate") those correlations, or even to test them for statistical significance. In this sense, Greenberg did not attempt to *predict* constituent orders in as yet unstudied languages. Since 1963, much research has revealed problems with Greenberg's original typology. Significant revisions, criticisms, and extensions of Greenberg's work are found in Hawkins (1983), D. Payne (1985), Mithun (1987), Dryer (1988, 1992), and Hawkins (1994). In an important correction, Dryer (1988) shows that Greenberg's Universal number 17 (the order of adjective and head noun) does not hold when a larger sample of languages is considered. Nevertheless, Greenberg's work stimulated the field of typological linguistics and has continued to be very influential.

In the following sections we will explain and illustrate some of the correlations described in table 7.1, using examples from two typologically distinct languages – Japanese and Malagasy.

Examples of an OV and a VO language

Japanese and Malagasy are two languages that conform to Greenberg's observations very closely. Most languages are not this ideal, but these will suffice to exemplify a rather remarkable recurring pattern in the syntactic structures of the world's languages.

The following example illustrates OV constituent order in Japanese. In this clause, the inflected VP is in brackets. Notice that the object, *inu*, precedes the Verb, *mita*:

(5)   O V: Taro   ga   [inu   o   mita   ]   'Taro saw a dog.'
                Taro   NOM   dog   ACC   saw

Here is a possible tree diagram of this clause:

(6)

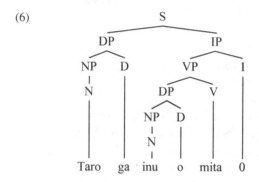

Notice that under the IP node, the tree "branches" to the left. The syntactic head of each phrasal category is on the right, and its complement branches off to the left. In tree diagrams of English sentences, you will notice that the branching tends to extend to the right (see, e.g., example 72, in chapter 6). For this reason, languages like Japanese are sometimes called **LEFT-BRANCHING** languages, in contrast to English and other VO languages, which can be termed **RIGHT-BRANCHING** languages. Other terms sometimes used for these two language types are head-final and head-initial languages, respectively, or complement+head and head+ complement languages, respectively.

In the next Japanese example, we see that the possessor, *hito*, precedes the possessed item, *inu*, in a noun phrase. The grammatical relation that corresponds most closely to the functional notion of "possessor" is GENitive. Therefore, in Greenberg's terminology, Japanese employs GENitive+Noun order in the noun phrase:

(7)   GEN N: Taro   ga   [hito   no   inu   o   ]   mita
                          NOM   man   GEN   dog   ACC   saw
                    'Taro saw the man's dog.'

In example 8 the word *ookii*, meaning 'big,' comes before the noun that it modifies. Therefore, Japanese exhibits ADJective + Noun order in noun phrases:

(8)   ADJ N: Taro   ga   [ookii inu   o]   mita.   'Taro saw a big dog.'
                           NOM   big   dog   ACC   saw

In both of the above examples we see again that branching extends to the left in Japanese. Here are some corresponding tree diagrams:

(9)

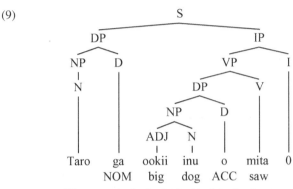

'Taro saw (or looked at) a/the big dog.'

(10)

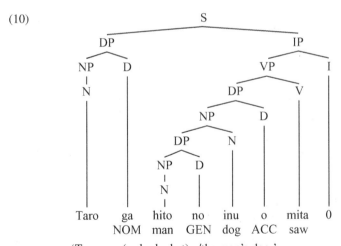

'Taro saw (or looked at) a/the man's dog.'

Notice that under the IP node of example 10, there is a VP, then a DP, then an NP, then another DP. Among many other facts, this diagram captures the important fact that genitive nouns (those for which the determiner in Japanese is *no*) are nested within other NPs. In other words, genitive nouns are a kind of modifier, or optional complement, of other nouns.

Example 11 illustrates a **RELATIVE CLAUSE** in Japanese. Relative clauses are clauses that modify nouns and are embedded within noun phrases. We will have much more to say about relative clauses in chapter 10. For now, just notice that the Relative Clause (bracketed by {curly braces}) comes before the Noun it modifies, *inu*:

(11)   RC N: Taro   ga   [{niku   o   tabeta}   inu o]   mita
                          NOM   meat ACC ate   dog ACC   saw
                 'Taro saw the dog that ate the meat.'

Japanese has *post*positional phrases rather than *pre*positional phrases. This is another common characteristic of verb-final languages. In 12 we see the POST-position *kara* following the Noun it is related to:

(12)   N Postposition: Taro   ga   [mado   kara] inu   o   mita
                                  NOM   window from   dog ACC saw
                 'Taro saw a dog from the window.'

AUXiliaries in Japanese also follow the main Verb:

(13)   V AUX: Taro-ga   inu   o   [miru bekida]
                     -NOM dog ACC   see   should
                 'Taro should see a dog.'

Here is a plausible tree diagram of a Japanese clause with a postpositional phrase and an inflectional element (something like an auxiliary) following the verb:

(14)

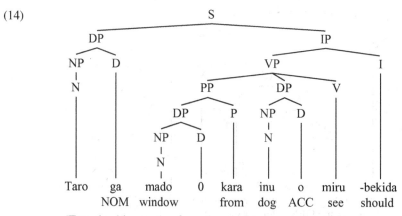

'Taro should see a dog from the window.'

Now we will look at some examples from Malagasy, a language that in many respects exhibits syntactic structure that is the "mirror image" of Japanese.

In Malagasy the verb normally comes first in the clause. Then comes the O, and finally the subject (examples courtesy of Andoveloniaina Rasolofo):

(15)   V O: [Nahita   alika]   Rashu.   'Rasoa saw a dog.'
                    saw   dog   Rasoa

In the noun phrase, the GENitive (possessor) follows the possessed Noun:

(16)   N GEN: Nahita   [ni   alika   n'ilai   rangahi]   Rashu
                  saw   the   dog   the   man   Rasoa
                  'Rasoa saw the man's dog.'

Also, ADJectives follow their head Nouns:

(17)   N ADJ: Nahita   [alika   be]   Rashu   'Rasoa saw a big dog.'
                  saw   dog   big   Rasoa

Auxiliaries in Malagasy come before the Verb:

(18)   AUX V: [afaka   maita]   alika   be   Rashu   'Rasoa can see a big dog.'
                  can   see

Again, Malagasy is exactly the opposite of Japanese in placing relative clauses after their head Nouns. In this example, the head noun is *alika*, 'dog,' and the Relative Clause which modifies it follows:

(19)   N RC: Nahita   ilai   [alika   { nihinana   ilai   hena }]   Rashu
                 saw   the   dog   ate   the   meat   Rasoa
                 'Rasoa saw the dog that ate the meat.'

Finally, Malagasy exhibits PREpositions rather than postpositions:

(20)   PREP N: Nahita   alika   [avi   varavarana kely]   Rashu
                   saw   dog   through   door   small   Rasoa
                   'Rasoa saw a dog through the window.'

Thus we see that Malagasy exhibits exactly the mirror image of Japanese in terms of basic syntactic structure. Here is a possible tree diagram of a Malagasy clause that illustrates all of the phrasal structures we have mentioned:

(21)

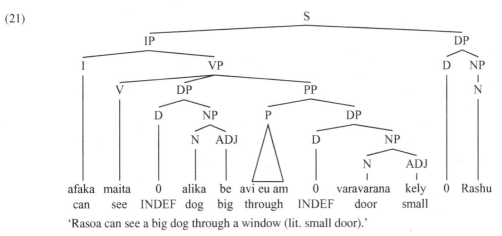

'Rasoa can see a big dog through a window (lit. small door).'

Notice that in this diagram the branches under the IP node extend to the right, rather than the left. In this respect, Malagasy can be considered a "right-branching" language.

It is important to emphasize two facts about the pioneering work of Greenberg. First, most languages are not as consistent with Greenberg's general findings as Japanese and Malagasy are. Second, Greenberg's sample was quite inadequate in a number of respects. More recent work (e.g., Dryer 1988, 1992) has shown that some of Greenberg's observations simply cannot be sustained when a larger, more statistically significant, sample of languages is taken into account.

Pragmatic constituent order languages

While the work of Greenberg (1963) and other early typologists was instrumental in establishing the fields of typological and functional linguistics, there were several conceptual problems with this early work. In particular, one of the assumptions was that all languages employ constituent order to express grammatical relations. In other words, the very use of the terms SVO, SOV, and others to describe language types takes it for granted that "Subject" and "Object" are the relevant terms that determine the order of words in languages. This does hold true for English and many other languages, but is it necessarily true for all? Could it be the case that a language may use the order of words in a clause to express some other communicationally important information? What would such a language be like?

As a thought experiment, imagine a language that uses word order to express relative size rather than grammatical relations. In this language, when a clause describes two participants interacting, the larger participant is mentioned first, and the smaller one is mentioned later, regardless of which one is subject and which is object. Therefore, a clause like the following would be ambiguous:

(22)   HYPOTHETICAL DATA: Bear kill man.

By putting *bear* early in the clause, the speaker is asserting only that the bear is larger than the man, not whether the bear is the subject or the object of the clause. This sentence could conceivably mean 'The bear kills the man' or 'The man kills the bear.'

This kind of ambiguity is not often tolerated in languages, because it is dysfunctional – expressing who acts and who or what is acted upon is such an important communicative task that it is not likely to be ignored by the morphosyntax of any natural language. Therefore, if the language is determined to use word order to distinguish size, it would probably come up with some other solution to the problem of expressing which participant is the actor, and which one is the affected participant.

How about a morphological solution? This is the kind of solution illustrated in chapter 1 with the Naga language:

HYPOTHETÍCAL DATA:

(23) a.   Bear-a kill man.   'Bear kills man.'   (A suffix -a marks the AGENT.)
     b.   Bear kill man-a.   'Man kills bear.'

(24) a.   Bear kill man-p.   'Bear kills man.'   (A suffix -p marks the PATIENT.)
     b.   Bear-p kill man.   'Man kills bear.'

(25) a.   Béár kill màn.   'Bear kills man.'   (High tone marks AGENT; low
                                                      tone marks PATIENT.)
     b.   Bèàr kill mán.   'Man kills bear.'

The examples in 23, 24, and 25 illustrate three possible solutions to the problem of how to express the AGENT and PATIENT if word order is used for some other purpose. Of course, any of the morphological, lexical, or syntactic expression types discussed in chapters 1 and 2 may be used. These are just random possibilities, out of an infinite number. We will have a lot more to say about how languages actually do express grammatical relations and semantic roles in chapters 8 and 9.

As you may suspect by now, there are in fact languages that use word order for purposes other than to express grammatical relations. There are probably none that use word order to express relative size, though such a language is conceivable. What is much more common are languages that use the linear order of words in clauses to express **PRAGMATIC** information, such as **IDENTIFIABILITY**, **TOPICALITY**, **REFERENTIALITY** and others. In this section we will give a few examples from such languages, and then present some suggestions for how to analyze pragmatically based constituent order languages.

In Ngandi (Heath 1978:206 as cited in Mithun 1987), constituent order is governed by the following principle:

(26)   New, indefinite, or otherwise "newsworthy" information is placed early in the clause. Given, definite, or otherwise already introduced information is placed later.

In example 27 from Ngandi, we see subject-verb order when the subject refers to a non-specific, newly mentioned participant (27a), and verb-subject order when the subject refers to a specific identified item (27b):

(27) a.   Subject   Verb
        Načuweleñ-uŋ   gu-jark-yuŋ   gu-ja-walk, . . .
        then-ABS   GU-water-ABS   GU-now-go:through
        'Then water passes through,' (first mention of water)

     b.   Verb   Subject
        Načuweleñ-uŋ   gu-ja-geyk-da-ni   gu-jark-yuŋ
        then-ABS   GU-now-throw-AUG-PR GU-water-ABS
        'Then the water rushes through,' (subsequent mention of water)

Coos (Frachtenberg 1913:7) also follows this "indefinite early" principle. In example 28a, the matting is the affected participant, and it comes before the verb when it is mentioned for the first time. In 28b, the matting is again the affected participant, but this time it comes after the verb, because in this clause the matting has already been mentioned in the discourse, and therefore can be taken as GIVEN INFORMATION:

(28) a.

Object	Subject	Verb
TE tc!i'cil	yüL is	yö'qat . . .
that matting	we two	split:it

'Let's split this mat.' (first mention of mat)

(they did so, and went down to examine the earth. The earth was still not solid, even . . .)

b.

			Verb		Object
i	lau	tci	uxhi'touts	hE	tc!icil.
when	that	there	they:two:put:it:down	the	matting

'after they had put down the mat,' (subsequent mention of mat)

In both of these languages, the positions of all nominal clause constituents (i.e., subject, object, and other elements) are determined to a large extent by pragmatic factors.

For some languages, one nominal element exhibits a fairly fixed position (variable only under extreme pragmatic pressures), while another is more variable. Some languages that operate in this way are:

- Spanish. Fairly fixed verb-object, pragmatically variable subject (Bentivoglio 1983).
- Guaymí (Chibchan, Costa Rica, and Panama). Fixed object-verb, pragmatically variable subject.
- Panare (Cariban, Venezuela). Fixed verb-subject, pragmatically variable object.
- Apuriná (Arawakan, Brazil). Fixed subject-verb, pragmatically variable object (Aberdour 1985).

The areas of the world in which languages seem particularly sensitive to pragmatic ordering principles are the Americas, Australia, and to a lesser extent Austronesia and South Asia. Not enough studies of constituent order in discourse have been conducted in Africa to allow generalizations regarding the sensitivity of African languages to pragmatic principles in constituent ordering (though some interesting work has been done; see, e.g., Watters 1979 and Dooley and Levinsohn 2001). The Slavic languages tend to be the most pragmatically sensitive in the Indo-European family.

It should be emphasized, however, that pragmatic factors influence constituent order in all languages to one degree or another. It is just that in some languages pragmatic factors are so dominant that it is difficult or impossible to describe the "basic" constituent order in terms of subject and object. On the other hand, even languages in which pragmatics dominates may show sensitivity to grammatical relations to some extent.

Finally, some languages have pragmatically determined constituent order that is overridden by syntactic considerations only when ambiguity would result. To understand how this might work, let's extend our thought experiment a little. Imagine the hypothetical language represented in example 22, without any of the morphosyntactic expressions of semantic roles proposed in examples 23 through 25. In this language, would a sentence like the following be ambiguous?:

(29)   Car drove Lucretia.

Remember that physical size determines the order of constituents, therefore, *car* comes first because it refers to a participant that is larger than Lucretia. Nevertheless, quite apart from word order there is good reason to guess that *Lucretia* refers to the actor, and *car* refers to the affected participant. What is that? Hello?! People drive cars, but cars don't drive people! This is a pragmatic fact about the world that everyone (at least those who understand what cars and people are) implicitly know. When you think about it, the vast majority of two-participant clauses that we use are of this sort – only one of the participants is the pragmatically plausible AGENT. For many common activities, such as reading books, eating apples, preparing meals, cleaning house, sweeping floors, carrying suitcases, etc., morphosyntactic signals are not even needed to distinguish which participant acts and which is acted upon. It is only in those relatively rare situations in which either participant could fulfill either role that ambiguity may result. It is in those cases only that morphosyntax may be needed to express the distinction. For example people both control and are affected by activities such as chasing, insulting, hugging, slapping, etc., therefore clauses that describe these kinds of activities are more likely to be ambiguous in our hypothetical language:

(30)   Hypothetical language in which largest participant comes first:
   a.   Apollo chased Daphne.
   b.   Cyclops insulted Sinbad.
   c.   Goliath killed David.

These examples would all be ambiguous in our hypothetical language in which size determines constituent order, whereas an example like the following would not be:

(31)   Camel rode Ali.

Why not? Because the examples in 30 describe activities in which either participant could conceivably be the AGENT. In 31, on the other hand, Ali (a man's name) can plausibly ride a camel, but a camel can't plausibly ride Ali. Therefore there may be (and actually are) some languages that invoke a morphosyntactic solution to the problem of distinguishing participant roles only in situations like 30, but don't bother in situations like 31, because in these cases context and common sense are sufficient to make the intended meaning clear.

How to analyze the syntactic typology of a language

Most linguists would consider the "basic" constituent orders of a language to be exhibited at least in **PRAGMATICALLY NEUTRAL** clauses. Pragmatically neutral clauses are those that do not present any part of the clause as being unusually highlighted, emphasized, or contrasted. For example, a clause like 32 is not pragmatically neutral in English:

(32)   O   S   V
          Beans   I   like.

A clause like this places special contrast on the O argument, as illustrated in a context such as *Beans I like*; *rice I hate*. We would not want to analyze the syntactic typology of English based on this kind of clause. If we did, we would probably say that English is an OV language, which is clearly incorrect. Similarly, we wouldn't want to use sentences like the following:

(33)   V   S
      a.   Once there was a Hobbitt.   **EXISTENTIAL CLAUSE**
                        O   S   V
      b.   Whom did Frodo see?   Question
                        V   S   O
      c.   Have you a match?   Question

All of these structures are **PRAGMATICALLY MARKED**. That is, they are used only in special circumstances in a conversation, such as when participants are being brought onto the discourse stage for the first time, or when some specific piece of information is being questioned. As you can see, these English clauses express unusual constituent orders (VS, OSV, and VSO). For this reason, we would not want to use examples such as these to determine the "basic" syntactic typology of a language. Instead we want to use pragmatically neutral clauses.

However, identifying one clause type as pragmatically neutral is often difficult. A general way to approach this problem is to start with a large corpus of texts (stories, transcribed conversations, or other discourse types) and eliminate from consideration clause types that are known to exhibit marked constituent orders in some languages. These would include:

- Dependent clauses (see chapter 10)
- Clauses that introduce participants onto the discourse stage (33a)

- Questions (33b, c)
- Negative clauses
- Clearly contrastive clauses (e.g., 32)
- Clauses in which a pronoun is used to express O and/or S (i.e., basic constituent order concerns order of **FULL NOUNS** and verbs).

Here is an example from Spanish to show that clauses with pronouns can exhibit unusual orders. In Spanish, the basic order when S and O are full nouns is SVO (34a). However, as is the case in many Romance languages, when O is expressed as a clitic pronoun, it comes right before the inflected verb (34b):

(34) a.	Frodo	vió	a	Gandolfo.	'Frodo saw Gandolph.'
	Frodo	see.PAST.3SG	DAT	Gandolph	
b.	Frodo	*lo* vió.	(*Frodo vió lo).		'Frodo saw him.'
		3SG			

Once all the clause types listed above have been eliminated from consideration, it is probable that the clauses that remain are largely pragmatically neutral. If in these remaining clauses there are examples of transitive verbs with full NPs expressing S and O, *and* if those NPs exhibit a consistent order relative to the verb, then that order can be considered basic. Unfortunately, in reality this is a rare situation. Once you have eliminated all of the clause types listed above, you are often left with very few clauses indeed. Such clauses as are left often lack overt expression of one or more **CORE ARGUMENTS** (S or O in Greenberg's terms). D. Payne (1986) has observed that pragmatically neutral clauses tend to consist of a verb and one or fewer noun phrases. In many languages use of any full nouns in discourse is pragmatically marked.

If you can't decide on a basic constituent order using the above criteria, the language is probably one of the many languages of the world that employs constituent order to express pragmatic status. In this case you will need to conduct a statistical study of the use of the various constituent order possibilities in discourse. Analytical methods for conducting such studies lie outside the scope of the present book. However, if you go on in linguistics you will undoubtedly have opportunities to take courses in discourse analysis. In those courses you will learn, among other things, how to conduct a study to determine the pragmatic principles that underlie the ordering of constituents in any language.

There is one last point that needs to be made concerning how to determine the basic constituent order of a language. The orders of elements within verb phrases, noun phrases, or adpositional phrases is not evidence for a particular order in main clauses. For example, Greenberg observed that languages with postpositions are always (in his sample) of the OV type. However, if we know the language has postpositions rather than prepositions, we cannot use Greenberg's observations to claim that the basic order in main clauses must be OV. Greenberg did not make predictions – only observations based on a very small sample. Languages are too often inconsistent for us to take non-main-clause orders as evidence for main-clause constituent order.

Conceptual outline of chapter 7

I.   Languages can be typologized (classified into types) according to a number of parameters. The most interesting typological parameters are those that describe "clusters" of grammatical properties. The two typologies discussed in this chapter are:
 • Morphological typology
 • Syntactic typology (also known as "constituent order typology")

II.   Morphological typology consists of two parameters:
 • The index of synthesis (the number of morphemes per word)
 • The index of fusion (the number of meanings per morpheme)

III.   There are three broad types of languages according to their syntactic typology:
 • Languages in which syntactic heads follow their complements (called OV languages, left-branching languages, head-final languages, or complement+head languages).
 • Languages in which syntactic heads precede their complements (variously termed VO languages, right-branching languages, head-initial languages, or head+complement languages).
 • Languages for which constituent order is determined by some principle other than grammatical relations.

IV.   In the last type of language, pragmatic statuses such as referentiality, identifiability, and contrastiveness are the functional variables most likely to be expressed by constituent order. In these languages, the semantic roles of participants must be expressed in some other morphosyntactic way, at least in those situations where more than one participant could plausibly be an AGENT.

V.   In order to determine the "basic constituent order" (if any) of a language, it is important to isolate pragmatically neutral clauses.

Exercise 7.1: Yagua

Tom Payne and Matthew Dryer

Yagua is a **LANGUAGE ISOLATE** spoken by about 4,000 people in northeastern Peru.

A.   On the basis of the examples on the following page, identify whether Yagua is basically an O-V or a V-O language, and whether it is S-V or V-S. Give the evidence for your claims.

B.   List the other constituent order characteristics of Yagua illustrated in
these data. For each characteristic, indicate whether it is expected,
unexpected, or neither, given the basic order of V and O identified
above. Cite examples that illustrate each of your claims.

O – V
V – O
S – V
V – S

S . O

1. a. Sa-munaa-dee   Alchíco.   'Alchico's placenta.'
      3SG-placenta-DIM   Alchico

   b. Alchíco munaadee.   'Alchico's placenta.'
      *Munaadee Alchíco, *Alchíco samunaadee.

   c. Samunaadee.   'His placenta.'

2. Jirya munaadee.   'This placenta.'
   *Munaadee jirya.

3. Tinkii munaadee.   'One placenta.'
   *Munaadee tinkii.

4. Samunaadee kúútya.   'His placenta whispers.'
   *Kúútya samunaadee.

5. Sakúútya Alchíco munaadee   'Alchico's placenta whispers.'

6. Jíryoonú   sų́ų́y-anú   sa-roori-myú   Alchíco-níí
   bushmaster   bite-PAST   3SG-house-LOC   Alchico-3SG
   'A bushmaster (snake) bit him in Alchico's house.'
   *Jíryoonú sasų́ų́yanuníí. ('A bushmaster he bit him.')

7. Sa-sų́ų́y-anú   jíryoonu   Alchico   roori-myú-níí
   3SG-bite-PAST   bushmaster-3SG   Alchico   house-LOC-3SG
   'A bushmaster (snake) bit him in Alchico's house.'

8. sạ-ạ   rą́ą́-kyu.   'He will jump!'
   3SG-FUT   jump-POT
   *rą́ą́kyu sạạ, *sarą́ą́kyu sạạ, *sarą́ą́kyu ạ.

9. Sa-niy   suvú-tyạa jiñu   munátya sų-ymuteẹsá
   3SG-MALF   fear-INTS this   ancestor 3SG-behind

   munaa   játiy sa-reẹ-ñíí.
   placenta   REL   3SG-jump-3SG
   'This ancestor is really afraid behind the placenta that makes him jump.'

10. Rạ-a   ją́ą́-charatá jiyu-dáy   koodí-vyiimú.
    1SG-FUT   fall-might here-DAY   snake-inside
    'I might fall here inside a snake.'

Exercise 7.2: Tshangla

Eric Andvik

1. Ja-ga   ata   yigi   ringmu thur   dri-ba.
   1SG-DAT   eld.brother letter long   one   write-PAST
   'My elder brother wrote one long letter.'

2. Ro-ka   gari   otha   phai   yanglu   jap-kai   tsuk-pa cha.
   3SG-DAT   car   that   house green   behind-ABL   put-PAST is
   'His car is parked behind that green house.'

3. Ja-ga   usin-ga   chharo   nan-gi   ye-khan
   1SG-DAT   young.sis-DAT   friend   2SG-ERG   speak-REL
   echha   ngo-le   re-be.
   book   buy-NPAST   can-NPAST
   'My younger sister's friend can buy the book that you talked about.'

A.   Where is Tshangla spoken? What is its genetic affiliation? How many
     speakers are there?

B.   Describe the head and complement orders in the various syntactic
     constituents illustrated. In what respects do these data conform to
     Greenberg's (1963/1966) observations, and in what respects do they
     not conform? Note any ambiguous or problematic data.

Exercise 7.3: Shugnan

M. E. Alexeev, adapted by Tom Payne

Here are some noun phrases in Shugnan and their translations into English:

1. kuzaa hats   'jar of water'
2. chalak zimaadj   'bucket of dirt'
3. tambal byuyun   'beard of a lazybones'
4. biig dyuyunaa   'pot of corn'
5. kuzaa gjev   'lid of a jar'
6. beechoraa zimaadj   'dirt of a beggar'

A.   What language family does Shugnan belong to, and where is it
     spoken?

B.   Translate into Shugnan:

7. 'bucket of water'
8. 'corn of a beggar'
9. 'jar of a lazybones'

C.   What determines the order of genitive and head noun in Shugnan?

Exercise 7.4: translating trees into bracketing

Tom Payne

The following are constituent structure trees from three typologically distinct
languages.

A.   "Translate" each tree into a labeled and bracketed string.

B.   For each language, indicate its syntactic type (head+complement or complement+head).

a. Panare: 'I took the sugar cane out of the room.'

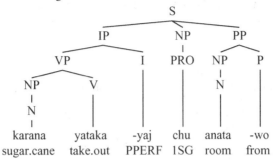

Labeled, bracketed string: Karana   yataka   -yaj   chu   anata   -wo
Language type: _____

b. Yup'ik: 'Nuk'aq and father are using my boat.'

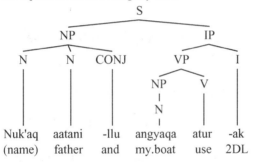

Labeled, bracketed string: Nuk'aq   aatani   -llu   angyaqa   atur   -ak
Language type: _____

c. Thai: 'The girl will ask for your number.'

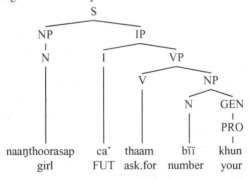

Labeled, bracketed string: naaŋthoorasap   ca'   thaam   bïï   khun
Language type:

X

Exercise 7.5: translating bracketing into trees

Tom Payne

The following are labeled and bracketed sentences from three typologically distinct imaginary languages.

A.   "Translate" these strings into constituent structure trees. Be sure to label each node correctly.

B.   Give a plausible gloss and free translation for each example.

a. [s [ip [aux vro]aux [vp [v olin]v [dp [np [n fim]n]np [d gron]d]dp]vp]ip| [dp [np [n smu]n [adj nid]adj]np [d rad]d]dp]s

b. [s [np[n olnik]n]np [ip [np [adjiops]adj [n poms]n]np [vp [v anterrettim]v]vp [aux bim]aux]ip]s

c. [s [ip [i e]i [vp [v apa'a]v [dp [d ek]d [np [n eliam]n [adj gib]adj]np]dp [pp [p iva]p [dp [d ila]d [np [ni' ot]n]np]dp]pp]vp]ip [dp [d ila]d[np [nanar]n [adj ipso]adj]np]dp]s

Exercise 7.6: a small grammar of Japanese – an OV language

Mitsuyo Hamaya, Naoaki Tai, and Tom Payne

A.   Fill in the missing translations of clauses 12 (Japanese) and 13 (English).

B.   Write phrase structure rules and a lexicon that will sanction all of the following clauses of Japanese.

C.   Give three more clauses that your rules and lexicon allow, and three strings that would be ungrammatical.

1. Taro ga hashitta.	'Taro ran.'
2. Taro ga ookina inu o mitsuketa.	'Taro found the big dog.'
3. Mitsuyo ga neta.	'Mitsuyo slept.'
4. Taro ga ookina koen de hashitta.	'Taro ran in the big park.'
5. Mitsuyo ga boru o nageta.	'Mitsuyo threw the ball.'
6. Taro ga boru o koen de nageta.	'Taro threw the ball in the park.'
7. Taro ga nageta.	'Taro threw (something).'
8. Taro ga inu to hashitta.	'Taro ran with the dog.'
9. Taro ga Mitsuyo ni ookina boru o nageta.	'Taro threw the big ball to Mitsuyo.'
10. Mitsuyo ga inu ni gohan o koen de ageta.	'Mitsuyo gave rice to the dog in the park.'
11. Mitsuyo ga inu ni hone o ageta.	
12. ———	'Taro gave the ball to the dog.'
13. Taro ga Mitsuyo ni inu o ageta.	

Exercise 7.7: Hungarian

A. N. Zhurinsky, adapted by Tom Payne

Here are six Hungarian sentences (in the official alphabet) and their translations into English:

1. Az asztalon a térkép van.	'The map is on the desk.'
2. Az asztalokon a térképek vannak.	'The maps are on the desks.'
3. A füzetnél az újság van.	'The newspaper is near the notebook.'
4. Az újságokon a füzetek vannak.	'The notebooks are on the newspapers.'
5. Az ablakoknál a pad van.	'The bench is near the windows.'
6. A székeken a kasok vannak.	'The baskets are on the chairs.'

A. Translate the following English sentences into Hungarian (Hints: Remember that Hungarian has vowel harmony. There is no irregularity in this problem):

7. The notebook is on the desk.
8. The newspapers are on the notebook.
9. The chairs are near the desk.
10. The benches are near the chairs.
11. The basket is on the window.

B. Describe the difference in usage between *a* and *az* in Hungarian.

C. What do you know about the basic constituent orders of Hungarian, just based on these data? Is this consistent or inconsistent with Greenberg's (1963) observations?

Note

1. It is perhaps an unfortunate fact of the history of linguistics that multiple terminologies have been used in the domain of grammatical relations. The focus in the present chapter is Greenberg's (1963) pioneering work on syntactic typology. In that work, and in much subsequent research, the terms S, O, and V were used to refer to the notions of Subject, Object, and Verb respectively. It is important for all students of linguistics to be aware of these terms, and be able to use them confidently. However, later work revised this terminology significantly, and we will be discussing the newer terminologies starting in chapter 8. It is also important not to confuse the term S as a syntactic category (the "highest level" category label) with S as an abbreviation for "subject."

8   Grammatical relations

Grammatical relations (GRs) are structurally defined relations between words in phrases and clauses. Common terms used to refer to particular grammatical relations are **SUBJECT, DIRECT OBJECT, INDIRECT OBJECT, ERGATIVE, ABSOLUTIVE, GENITIVE**, and **OBLIQUE**. Sometimes the oblique relation (discussed below) is considered to be the *absence* of a grammatical relation. Like other structural notions, GRs are *defined* independently of function (such as semantics or topicality), though they clearly have communicative functions. Even as the structure of any tool is logically distinct from (though intimately connected to) its function, so GRs are logically distinct from the functions that they perform. Nevertheless, it is important to recognize that GRs play a significant role in expressing meaningful distinctions, such as who is acting upon whom, what is topical, and so on.

A second important fact about GRs is that they are essentially *relational* concepts. In other words, they don't exist unless there are two elements that are related. A nominal element by itself does not "have" a grammatical relation. It is only when it occurs in a structure with a verb that we can say that it is a "subject" or an "object," etc. In fact, it may be better to always say "subject of" or "object of" since these terms make it clear that there must be another element in the construction. The grammatical properties that identify GRs are determined by syntactic constructions, and not simply by semantic properties of individual nouns or verbs.

Here is an analogy from real life. A concept like "boy" is not inherently relational, because it depends solely on the characteristics of the individual. The concept of "brother," on the other hand, is relational, because someone can't be simply a *brother* without reference to someone else. Getting back to grammar, a category like plurality is non-relational, because it usually depends on the semantic characteristics of the individual referent of a noun. This semantic characteristic is reflected structurally in many languages by some kind of "plural marking." Subject, on the other hand, is a category that depends on the structure of the whole clause. A nominal element can only be the "subject of" some other grammatical element.

Sometimes the term **ARGUMENT** is used to refer to any nominal that has a grammatical relation to a verb, or to another noun. This sense of the term "argument" is borrowed from mathematics where an argument is an independent variable in a function; in other words, a thing that has a property, or has a relation to some other thing. A nominal that doesn't have a grammatical relation to some other word is called either a "non-argument," or an oblique.

GRs can be reflected structurally by any number of features. The three main structural features that often reflect grammatical relations in a clause are the following:

- Case marking on nouns
- **PARTICIPANT REFERENCE** marking on verbs (agreement, concord)
- Constituent order

In the following pages, we will see examples of how different languages use these structural features (and a few others) to organize systems of grammatical relations, and will present some methods for analyzing them.

Grammatical relations within noun phrases

The simplest illustration of a grammatical relation is the genitive relation that may hold between nouns in a noun phrase. In an English Determined Noun Phrase (DP) like:

(1)   Caitlin's quilt

the word *Caitlin's* refers to a person the speaker is portraying as someone who, in some broad sense, is closely associated with the quilt. Although we intuitively think of genitive arguments (*Caitlin* in this example) as expressing "possession," in fact the actual relation between the message-world person referred to by the name *Caitlin* and the message-world item referred to by the word *quilt* is in fact quite open ended. The quilt may be the one that Caitlin made, e.g., in the context of a contest in which homemade quilts are being judged, even though she already sold it to someone else. Or it may be the quilt that Caitlin happens to be using right now, though she is not its legal owner. It may be the quilt that Caitlin just bought, or the one she likes best. There are many examples of genitive-plus-noun constructions in which the genitive noun cannot reasonably be considered the "owner" of the other noun. For example:

(2) a.   Hiro's mathematics professor
   b.   Milicent's favorite political party
   c.   the car's color
   d.   Madaline's home town
   e.   the book's main point

Even though the semantic relations between the genitive and the head noun are very different in all of these examples, the morphosyntactic (grammatical) features that express the relation in English are the same. Namely, the "possessor" comes before the head noun and is marked by the suffix spelled *'s*. These *grammatical* features constitute evidence that the two nouns have a *grammatical* relation to one another. This relation constrains, to a certain extent, the range of semantic relations likely to be inferred, but the grammatical properties themselves (linear order and case marking) are logically independent of the semantic relations. For this reason, we use the neutral, grammatical term "genitive" to refer to the grammatical relation between *Caitlin* and *quilt* in example 1 rather than a semantically loaded term such as "possessor."

Like all grammatical relations, a genitive relation can be expressed in many different ways in different languages. In some languages, the relation is marked on the head noun, rather than the genitive noun. These are sometimes called **HEAD-MARKING** languages (Nichols 1986). For example, in Panare, a suffix goes on a noun when the noun refers to something that is possessed by something else. We will use the abbreviation HGEN, for "head of a noun phrase that contains a genitive noun," for this suffix:

(3) a. matá   'shoulder'
    b. matá-n   'someone's shoulder'
        shoulder-HGEN

    c. Tomán máta-n   'Tom's shoulder'
        Tom shoulder-HGEN

    d. a-matá-n   'your shoulder'
        2-shoulder-HGEN

In Panare, the possessor may be understood from the context (3b), expressed by a full noun (3c), or expressed simply by a prefix on the head. In all of these examples, the genitive relation is marked on the head noun, 'shoulder,' rather than on the genitive noun itself.

Occasionally we will use the cover term G to refer to a noun in a genitive relation, regardless of how it is expressed grammatically. This is illustrated for Panare and English in example 4:

(4)   G   HEAD
    a.   Toman   máta-n   'Tom's shoulder'
         Tom   shoulder-HGEN

             G   HEAD
    b.   Caitlin-'s quilt
         Caitlin-GEN

There are many other ways that languages express a genitive relation between nouns. We will see examples of some of these in the exercises at the end of this chapter. Now we turn to grammatical relations that hold within clauses.

Grammatical relations in clauses

The simplest illustration of a grammatical relation in a clause is probably the subject relation that may hold between a noun and a verb (more accurately, a noun phrase and a verb phrase). For example, in all of the following English clauses, the pronoun *I* is the subject:

(5) a.   I exercise every evening.
    b.   I can see the Statue of Liberty already!
    c.   I carry nothing.
    d.   I hate pills.
    e.   I was smeared by the *New York Times*.

The semantic role of the referent of the pronoun *I* and the rest of the clause in each of these examples is quite different. In 5a, *I* refers to an AGENT – someone who controls the action described by the verb and does it on purpose (see chapter 4 for discussion of semantic roles). In 5b, *I* refers to an EXPERIENCER – someone who receives a sensory impression but does not control the event, or perform it on purpose. In 5c, *I* refers to someone who does not do anything with respect to the following verb. In 5d, *I* refers to someone who has an emotional response that is most likely not purposeful, or controlled. Finally, in 5e, *I* refers to something like a PATIENT.

In spite of these very different semantic roles, in each case the grammatical relation of *I* to the rest of the clause is the same. How do we know this? We look at the grammatical properties that commonly distinguish grammatical relations (sometimes we will call these "structural features"). These are repeated here for convenience:

•   case marking on nouns or pronouns
•   participant reference marking on verbs (agreement, concord)
•   constituent order

In English, the subject relation is expressed partially by the case of personal pronouns. Other noun phrases are not morphologically marked for the subject relation in English. The pronoun *I* in English specifically refers to first-person singular *subjects* only. If a first-person singular participant is not a subject, another form of the pronoun is used, either *me* or *my*:

(6) a.   Mr. Frodo's not going anywhere without *me*.
    b.   American girls would seriously dig *me* . . .
    c.   . . . with *my* cute British accent.
    d.   Do you mean you wish to surrender to *me*?

These forms are ungrammatical in the subject position:

(7) a.   *Me* exercise every evening.
    b.   *Me* can see the Statue of Liberty already!
    c.   *My* carry nothing.
    d.   *My* hate pills.
    e.   *Me* was smeared by the *New York Times*.

Correspondingly, *I* is ungrammatical in other grammatical positions:

(8) a.   *Mr. Frodo's not going anywhere without *I*.

   b.   *American girls would seriously dig *I* . . .

   c.   * . . . with *I* cute British accent.

   d.   *Do you mean you wish to surrender to *I*?

This is one grammatical property of subjects in English: pronouns appear in the subject case (*I*, *we*, *they*, etc.) when they function as subject.

What about participant reference marking on verbs (agreement)? English does have a system of verb agreement, though it is rather impoverished compared to agreement systems of many other languages, even within the Indo-European family. In the present tense of English major class verbs, there is a suffix spelled -*s* (without the apostrophe) that appears when the subject is third-person singular:

(9)   He hates pills.

When the subject is a different person, or a different number, this -*s* goes away (at least in standard Englishes):

(10) a.   They hate pills.   *They hates pills.

   b.   We hate pills.   *We hates pills.

   c.   You hate pills.   *You hates pills.

The -*s* does not change when other nouns or pronouns in a clause change:

(11)   a. She digs me.   c. She digs him.

          b. She digs us.   d. She digs them.

Therefore, this -*s* is an expression of verb agreement with the subject, and is another grammatical property of the relational notion of *subject* in English.

Finally, what about constituent order? In English, constituent order does help us distinguish the subject from other nouns in a clause, but we need to be careful how we state the generalization. We may be tempted to say something like "the subject is the first NP in the clause." This usually is true, but not always. Consider the following:

(12) a.   The King's stinking son fired me.

   b.   Fezzik, are there rocks ahead?

   c.   On the horizon appeared a ship.

   d.   "A giant!" yelled Frodo.

   e.   What house do you live in?

The first noun phrase in each of these examples is *the king*, *Fezzik*, *the horizon*, *a giant*, and *what house*. None of these have the other grammatical properties of subjects, and none of them would be considered the subject according to any respectable linguistic theory. Therefore, we need to qualify our statement concerning the position of subjects in English somehow.

How about "the subject is the nominal element that appears right before the main verb or auxiliary"? We can see from the examples in 12 that this generalization isn't always true either. In 12b *Fezzik* appears right before the main verb, *are*. In 12c, d, and e the noun phrase that comes right before the verb or auxiliary is also not a subject.

In spite of these problems in determining the position of the subject in the clause, we still have this common-sense idea that the "subject comes first." Why is that? The reason is that it very frequently *does* come early in the clause, normally right before the verb or auxiliary. This is a well-oiled habit pattern of English. This pattern can be varied for special purposes, such as questions (12b and e), **PRESENTATIVES** (12c), and **QUOTATIVES** (12d). These are all **PRAGMATICALLY MARKED** constructions, in the sense that they are used in special contexts, e.g., when information is being requested, when new participants are being introduced into the discourse, etc. Clauses in which the subject comes right before the verb or auxiliary are pragmatically neutral (see chapter 7). So, to describe the position of the subject in English, we need to clarify that we are only talking about pragmatically neutral clauses:

(13)   The subject is the noun phrase or pronoun that immediately precedes the verb or auxiliary in pragmatically neutral clauses.

While you may be able to think of apparent counterexamples to this statement, it is a reasonably good generalization regarding subject position in English.

We've seen that grammatical relations, like subject, are identified by grammatical properties (like case, agreement, and linear order), rather than semantic roles (AGENT, EXPERIENCER, etc.). This fact can be illustrated even with the same verb. Consider the following English examples:

(14) a.   I opened the door with the key.   SUBJECT = AGENT
     b.   The key opened the door.   SUBJECT = INSTRUMENT
     c.   The door opened.   SUBJECT = PATIENT

In these clauses the formal category of subject (as identified by preverbal position, pronominal form, and potentially verb agreement in English) expresses three distinct semantic roles, AGENT, INSTRUMENT, and PATIENT. Furthermore, *the key* does not have a direct grammatical relation in 14a (it is an oblique) but in 14b it is the subject, even though it fills the same semantic role in both clauses. Similarly, *the door* is the direct object in 14a and 14b, but subject in 14c, even though it is the semantic PATIENT in all three clauses. The determination of which participant becomes subject, then, is a matter of **PERSPECTIVIZATION** (Fillmore 1976). That is, clauses 14a, b, and c could all be descriptions of the same message-world situation, but from different perspectives.

While all languages use a small number of grammatical relations to express a large number of semantic roles, some languages seem to be more sensitive to semantic roles than others. For example, in Guaymí (a Chibchan language of Costa Rica and Panama), there is a grammatical case for AGENTs, and other semantic roles that are very "AGENT-like." This case is marked by a zero suffix, as illustrated by the word *Toma* in example 15:

(15)   Toma-∅   Dori   dëma-e.   'Tom greets Doris.'
         Tom   Doris   greet-PR

EXPERIENCERs, on the other hand, appear in the dative case:

(16)   Davi-e   Dori   gar-e   'David knows Doris.'
         David-DAT Doris   know-PR

(17)   Toma-e   Dori   tïr-i̇.   'Tom remembers Doris.'
         Tom-DAT   Doris   remember-PR

(18)   Ti-e   ru   hatu-aba.   'I saw the airplane.'
         1SG-DAT   airplane see-PAST

(19)   Ti-e   timëna   nib-i.   'I feel thirst.' ('I'm thirsty.')
         1SG-DAT   thirst   feel-PR

Certain other Guaymí verbs that describe involuntary actions place one of their core arguments in a LOCATIVE case:

(20) a. José-**biti** Maria   köinigwi-ani-nggö.   'José forgot Maria.'
         José-LOC   Maria   forget-PAST1-ASP

    b.   Köinigwit-ani-nggö   ti-**biti.**   'I forgot it.' (lit: 'It was
         forget-PAST1-ASP   I-LOC   forgotten upon me.')

(21)   Davi-**bötö**   Dori   hurö   rib-aba.   'David was afraid of Doris.'
         David-LOC   Doris   fear   feel-PAST2

(22)   Ti-**bötö**   kö   nib-i   tibo.   'I'm cold.'
         I-LOC   place   feel-PR cold

So we see that grammatical relations are one major way that languages express semantic roles, even though it is not possible to identify grammatical relations purely on the basis of semantic roles. It would be a mistake, for example, to define the notion of subject as "the noun that refers to the AGENT" for any language. As we have seen, many subjects are not AGENTS, and AGENTS can be expressed in other ways than via the subject relation. In fact, if subject could be defined as the AGENT or vice versa, there would be no need for both terms.

Systems for organizing grammatical relations

In order to insightfully discuss systems of grammatical relations within a clause, it is convenient to identify three basic "semantico-syntactic roles" termed S, A, and O (Dixon 1972, 1979, 1994). Similar terms are used by Comrie (1978) and Silverstein (1976). These terms assume two prototypical clause types:

(23) a.   S   V
         Single argument: 'Bob   left.'

    b.   A   V   O
         Multi-argument: 'Bob greeted Aileron.'

The S is defined as the only nominal argument of a single-argument clause. This is quite different from the S used by Greenberg in his characterization of constituent order typology, as discussed in chapter 7, or the S used in earlier versions of Generative Grammar to refer to the highest node in constituent structure. While the term S often reminds us of the grammatical relation subject, S as used in this chapter refers informally to the "Single" argument of a single-argument clause. Sometimes this type of clause is referred to as an **INTRANSITIVE** clause.

The A is defined as the most AGENT-like argument of a multi-argument clause. Sometimes this type of clause is referred to as a **TRANSITIVE** clause. If there is no argument that is a very good AGENT, the A is the argument that is treated morphosyntactically in the same manner as prototypical AGENTs are treated. Usually there will be one argument in every verbal clause that exhibits this property, though there may not be. More complex systems are described below.

O is the most PATIENT-like argument of a multi-argument clause (see chapter 4). While the term O often reminds us of the grammatical relation 'object,' O refers informally to the "Other" argument of a multi-argument clause. Again, if none of the arguments is very much like a PATIENT, then the argument that is treated like a prototypical PATIENT is considered to be the O.

In this schema, the grammatical relation of **SUBJECT** can be defined universally (i.e., for all languages, rather than for one particular language) as S together with A, while **DIRECT OBJECT**, or simply "object," can be defined as O alone. Some languages pay more grammatical attention to these notions than do others. In the following extended discussion, we will discuss the various morphosyntactic systems for expressing S, A, and O.

Languages may treat S and A the same morphosyntactically, and O differently. The following English examples illustrate this system with pronominal case forms – one form, *he*, is used for third-person singular masculine pronouns in both the S and the A roles. A different form, *him*, is used for third-person masculine singular pronouns in the O role:

(24) a.   He left.
     b.   He greets him.

nominative | accusative

(Subject)   (Object)

The extended circle around S and A in this diagram indicates that S and A are treated by the grammar of English as "the same," as demonstrated by the subject properties discussed above (use of the subject case form, *he*, in 24, immediately before the verb). The distinct circle around O indicates that O is treated differently, insofar as a different pronominal form, *him*, is used to refer to it. *Him* also appears in a different position in the clause, namely after the verb. This system is often referred to as a **NOMINATIVE/ACCUSATIVE** system. The morphosyntactic grouping of S and A together can be called the **NOMINATIVE** case, while the distinct morphosyntactic treatment of the O role is the **ACCUSATIVE** case.

The Quechuan languages (a group of languages spoken throughout the Andes mountains in South America) employ the same arrangement. However, in addition to pronominal forms and constituent order, the Quechua languages express this system in morphological case marking on free noun phrases. In the following examples from Huallaga Quechua (Weber 1989) the same case marker, Ø (zero), occurs on noun phrases in both the S (example 25a) and A (25b) roles. A distinct case marker, -*ta*, occurs on noun phrases in the O role (25b) (all Quechua examples courtesy of David Weber, p.c.):

(25) a.   S
         Juan-Ø   aywan.   'Juan goes.'
           -NOM   goes

     b.   A   O
         Juan-Ø   Pedro-ta   maqan.   'Juan hits Pedro.'
           -NOM   -ACC   hits

Nominative/accusative systems usually seem very reasonable to speakers of Indo-European languages since most of these languages exhibit this kind of system.[1]

The following examples from Yup'ik (Alaska) illustrate another system for grouping S, A, and O:

(26) a.   S
         Doris-aq   ayallruuq.   'Doris traveled.'
           -ABS   traveled

     b.   A   O
         Tom-am   Doris-aq   cingallrua. 'Tom greeted Doris.'
           -ERG   -ABS   greeted

In these examples the case marker -*aq* occurs on the S argument of an intransitive clause (26a) and the O argument of a transitive clause (26b). The case marker -*am* marks only the A of a transitive clause. If any morphological case marks A alone, it can be called the **ERGATIVE** case. Similarly, any morphological case that marks both S and O can be termed the **ABSOLUTIVE** case:

(27)

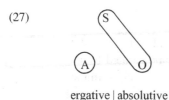

ergative | absolutive

This arrangement, known as an **ERGATIVE/ABSOLUTIVE** system, is sporadic in European and African languages. However, it is common in other areas of the world. Ergativity occurs as a basic system for organizing grammatical relations in many languages of Australia, Central Asia, and the Americas. It occurs as a partial case marking system in South Asia and in many other languages of the Americas. Many Austronesian languages have also been claimed to exhibit this system.

In addition to morphological case marking on pronouns or full noun phrases, languages may manifest ergative/absolutive or nominative/accusative systems in person marking on verbs, and/or constituent order.

We have seen above that Quechua manifests a nominative/accusative system in case marking of noun phrases. Quechua also manifests a nominative/accusative system for organizing grammatical relations in person marking on verbs. Consider the following examples:

(28) a.   S
           Aywa-n.   'He goes.'
           go-3SG

    b.   S
           Aywa-a.   'I go.'
           go-1SG

    c.   O A
           maqa-ma-n.   'He hit me.'
           hit-1SG-3SG

In example 28a the third-person singular S of an intransitive verb is referred to by the suffix -*n*. In 28b the first-person S argument is expressed by the suffix -*a* (actually length on the final vowel of the root). Example 28c shows that the suffix -*n* is also used for third-person A arguments of transitive verbs. Hence, A and S are treated morphologically alike by the person-marking system of Quechua. The fact that, in 28c, the first-person suffix for O arguments is -*ma* rather than -*a* illustrates that O and S are treated as different. Again, this way of treating S and A alike and O differently constitutes a nominative/accusative system.

As might be expected, languages can also manifest an ergative/absolutive GR system in person marking on verbs. Yup'ik will again serve as our example of such a system:

(29) a.   S
           Ayallruu-nga.   'I traveled.'
           traveled-1SG

    b.   S
           Ayallruu-q.   'He traveled.'
           traveled-3SG

    c.   A O
           Cingallru-a-nga.   'He greeted me.'
           greeted-3SG-1SG

In example 29a the suffix *-nga* indicates a first-person singular S argument of an intransitive verb. In 29b the suffix *-q* marks the third-person S. In 29c the suffix *-nga* marks the first-person O argument of a transitive clause. Since this is the same marker that is used for first-person S arguments, this suffix groups S and O together morphologically into an absolutive category. The third-person singular A argument of a transitive clause is expressed by a suffix *-a*. Since this suffix is different from the third-person S suffix, it can be said to identify ergative arguments. Again, this treatment of S together with O as distinct from A constitutes an ergative/absolutive system.

Since constituent order is universally one major means of expressing grammatical relations, one might ask whether ergative/absolutive and/or nominative/accusative systems can be manifested in constituent order. Of course, the answer is "yes." English, consistent with its strong nominative/accusative orientation, treats S and A alike in that the S of intransitive verbs and the A of transitive verbs most neutrally occur in preverbal position. The O of transitive verbs, on the other hand, is treated differently in that it occurs in post-verbal position.

In some verb-medial languages the verb and the O argument form a "tight" constituent in transitive clauses, and the verb and the S argument form an analogous constituent in intransitive clauses. In Kuikúro, a Cariban language of Brazil, SV (intransitive) and OV (transitive) are very rigid structures. The most neutral position for the A argument is following the OV complex (example 30b) (examples from Franchetto, 1990):

(30) a.

	S	V	
	karaihá	kacun-tárâ	'The non-Indian is working.'
	non-Indian	work-CONT	

b.

	O	V		A
	kuk-aki-sâ	ta-lâîgo	léha	karaihá-héke
	1INC-word-POS	hear-FUT	ASP	non:Indian-ERG
	'The non-Indian will hear our words.'			

In 30a the S argument of an intransitive verb occurs in preverbal position. In 30b the O argument of a transitive verb occurs in preverbal position, and the A argument occurs in post-verbal position. Since both S and O occur in the same position, we can say that this language manifests an ergative/absolutive system in constituent order.

One language, Sanuma (a variety of Yanomamɨ spoken in Brazil and Venezuela), is a verb-final language that is reported to exhibit constituent order ergativity. In this language, SV and OV form tight constituents. In transitive clauses A precedes O and V, but if there is any other constituent, call it X, it must occur after A. Thus the orders are AXOV and XSV (Borgman 1990, as reported in Dixon 1994:52). Since A is treated distinctly by being separable from the OV complex, this pattern can be considered to be a kind of constituent order ergativity.

In summary, any system that treats S and A alike as opposed to O is a nominative-accusative system for organizing grammatical relations. Any system that treats S and O alike as opposed to A is an ergative/absolutive system. The following section will provide some suggestions for how to approach the analysis of grammatical relations.

Analyzing grammatical relations systems

In this section we will walk through a couple of basic problems in analyzing systems of grammatical relations. First we will look at some data from classical Latin. Then we will look at a slightly more complex problem from Managalasi, a language spoken in Papua New Guinea. Here are the Latin data:

(31) a. puella columbam liberat   'The girl is freeing the dove.'
     b. puellae columbam liberant   'The girls are freeing the dove.'
     c. puella arat   'The girl is plowing.'
     d. puellae arant   'The girls are plowing.'
     e. puella columbas liberat   'The girl is freeing the doves.'
     f. columba volat   'The dove is flying.'
     g. columbae volant   'The doves are flying.'
     h. columba puellam amat   'The dove loves the girl.'
     i. columbae puellam amant   'The doves love the girl.'
     j. columba puellas amat   'The dove loves the girls.'

Since grammatical relations are most directly reflected in (1) case marking on NPs, (2) verb agreement, and (3) constituent order, we want to look at all three of these domains to see if we have any evidence for grammatical relations. One way to approach this task is to make a three-column chart and list the ways in which S, A, and O are expressed in each column:

	S	A	O
case marking			
verb agreement			
constituent order			

You will want to leave lots of room under each heading, since you don't know ahead of time how many different forms you will have to insert in each column.

Now we just list the forms that express the S, A, and O roles. As we do our standard comparison of form and meaning, we notice very quickly that this appears to be a language in which clauses are structured in AOV order. In fact, constituent order in Latin is highly pragmatically based. Nevertheless, even if it were consistently AOV, we would not be able to rely on constituent order to express a system for organizing grammatical relations. Why is that? Well, if the orders of elements in transitive and intransitive clauses are AOV and SV, which argument of the transitive clause is treated like the S of the intransitive clause? You could say that the A is treated like the S because both occur at the beginning of their respective clauses. On the other hand, you could also say that the O is treated like the S because they both occur immediately before the verb! This shows that in this type of language, constituent order just doesn't work as a way of determining the system for organizing grammatical relations.[2] Since constituent order cannot be relied upon for expression of grammatical relations in Latin, we can eliminate that row in our chart.

We see in example 31a that the form meaning 'girl' must be *puella*. Since this word is functioning in the A role, we put this form in the column under A:

	S	A	O
case marking		puella 'girl'	
verb agreement			

The next noun in sentence 31a is *columbam*, which must mean 'dove.' When we look at the free translation, it appears that 'dove' is functioning in the O role. In 31b, *puellae* must mean 'girls,' which is functioning in the A role, and again we have *columbam* functioning in the O role. Examples 31c and 31d are single-argument clauses, therefore they have S arguments, but no A or O arguments. The S argument of 31c is *puellae* and the *S* argument of 31d is *puella*. In this way we work through all the data and fill in the top row of the chart:

	S	A	O
case marking	puella 'girl' puellae 'girls' columba 'dove' columbae 'doves'	puella 'girl' puellae 'girls' columba 'dove' columbae 'doves'	puellam 'girl' puellas 'girls' columbam 'dove' columbas 'doves'
verb agreement			

We notice that the forms are the same under S and A, and different under O. Therefore this must be a nominative/accusative case-marking system. The best analysis of the case endings, given these data, is the following:

(32)   Nominative singular: -Ø   (zero, i.e., no marker)
         Nominative plural: -e
         Accusative singular: -m
         Accusative plural: -s

Now let us look at the verbs. In examples 31a and 31b the verb ending changes from -*t* to -*nt*. The only meaning difference between the two clauses is plurality of the A argument. Therefore it looks like -*t* is used when the A is singular and -*nt* is used when the A is plural:

	S	A	O
case marking	puella 'girl' puellae 'girls' columba 'dove' columbae 'doves'	puella 'girl' puellae 'girls' columba 'dove' columbae 'doves'	puellam 'girl' puellas 'girls' columbam 'dove' columbas 'doves'
verb agreement		-t SG -nt PL	

Just looking at 31a and 31b we cannot tell whether the verb changes with the plurality of the O, since the O is singular in both examples. However, 31a and 31e are identical except for the plurality of the O. And, voilà, the verb does not change. Therefore it appears from these data that the O is not marked on the verb at all. When we look at all the examples (crucially 31c and 31d), we can fill in the rest of the chart as follows:

	S	A	O
case marking	puella 'girl' puellae 'girls' columba 'dove' columbae 'doves'	puella 'girl' puellae 'girls' columba 'dove' columbae 'doves'	puellam 'girl' puellas 'girls' columbam 'dove' columbas 'doves'
verb agreement	-t SG -nt PL	-t SG -nt PL	-0 SG -0 PL

Again we see that S and A are treated alike, and O differently. Therefore this language exhibits a nominative/accusative system in verb agreement as well as case marking on nouns.

Split systems

We have seen that grammatical relations can be organized according to a nominative/accusative or an ergative/absolutive system. We have also seen that there are three structural features that most directly identify GRs: case marking, participant reference marking on verbs (verb agreement), and constituent order. In this section, we will look at some examples of languages which illustrate both nominative/accusative and ergative/absolutive systems, depending on the context. Such languages are sometimes said to exhibit a "split" system for organizing grammatical relations. In most such splits, the appearance of one system or the other is related either to the semantics/pragmatics of intransitive clauses (**SPLIT INTRANSITIVITY**), or to the semantics/pragmatics of transitive clauses (**SPLIT ERGATIVITY**). Further information on split intransitivity can be found in Merlan (1985) and Mithun (1991). Further information on split ergativity can be found in Silverstein (1976), DeLancey (1982) and the references on ergativity cited above.

Split intransitivity

Some languages express S arguments of intransitive verbs in two or more morphologically distinct ways. Such languages are sometimes said to exhibit **SPLIT INTRANSITIVITY**. The most common split intransitive systems express some S arguments in the same way as A arguments and others in the same way as O arguments. Other terms that have been used for such systems include **STATIVE/ACTIVE**, **ACTIVE**, **SPLIT-S**, and **FLUID-S** systems, among others. Split intransitivity is most commonly exhibited in verb agreement, though we will illustrate a marginal case of split intransitivity in case marking below (Guaymí). Examples 33a, b, and c illustrate basic transitive clauses in Lakhota (examples quoted in Mithun 1991, or provided by Walter and Delores Taken Alive of Little Eagle, South Dakota):

(33) a.   a-ma-ya-phe   'you hit me'
           DIR-1SG-2SG-hit

     b.   wa-ø-ktékte   'I kill him'
           1SG-3SG-kill

     c.   ø-ma-ktékte   'he kills me'
           3SG-1SG-kill

Examples 33a and c illustrate that the prefix *ma-* refers to the first-person singular O argument of a transitive clause. Example 33b illustrates that the prefix *wa-* refers to the first-person A argument of a transitive clause. Some intransitive verbs, such as those meaning 'fall,' 'die,' and 'shiver,' take the O prefix *ma-* to refer to first-person S arguments:

(34) a.   ma-hîxpaye   'I fall'
           1SG-fall

     b.   ma-t'e'   'I die'
           1SG-die

     c.   ma-č'âča   'I shiver'
           1SG-shiver

Other verbs, e.g., those meaning 'play,' 'swim,' and 'sing,' take the A prefix, *wa-*, for first-person S arguments:

(35) a.   wa-škate   'I play'
           1SG-play

     b.   wa-nûwe   'I swim'
           1SG-swim

     c.   wa-lowâ   'I sing'
           1SG-sing

Therefore, we can say that there are two kinds of S arguments in Lakhota: S_a arguments are those S arguments that are treated grammatically like transitive A arguments (examples 35a, b, and c), while S_o arguments are those S arguments that are treated like O arguments. This kind of system may be diagrammed as follows:

(36)   intransitive non-volitional, or stative, clauses

transitive clauses

intransitive volitional, or active, clauses

Usually there is a fairly obvious semantic basis for the distinction between the two types of S arguments, though the basis is apparently not the same for every language (Mithun 1991). For example, in modern colloquial Guaraní (Paraguay) intransitive verbs that describe events that involve change fall into the S_a class, while those that describe states fall into the S_o class. A few languages have been shown to exhibit split intransitivity based on discourse pragmatics. For example, in Yagua, certain verbs of motion (specifically **TRANSLATIONAL MOTION** verbs; see chapter 4) can take S_a or S_o subjects, depending on the discourse context:

(37) a.   Muuy   sii-myaa-si-ñíí   'There he rushed out.'
           there run-COMPL-out-3:O

     b.   Sa-sii-myaa-síy   'He rushed out.'
           3:A-run-COMPL-out

In example 37a the S is expressed by an enclitic -níí. This is the form that is used for O arguments of transitive verbs. In 37b the S is expressed by a prefix sa-. This is the form used for A arguments of transitive verbs. It is clear that this distinction is not based on semantics since the S arguments of both clauses are understood to be equally as agentive, volitional, etc. An empirical study of narrative text shows that S_o subjects occur at scene changes and episodic climax (37a), whereas S_a subjects occur elsewhere (37b) (T. Payne 1992). Similar observations have been made for Pajonal Campa (Heitzman 1982), and Asheninca Campa (J. Payne and D. Payne 1991). Both of these languages are spoken in the same geographic region as Yagua, but they are not genetically related to Yagua.

Split ergativity

If a language exhibits a nominative/accusative system in one part of the grammar, and an ergative/absolutive system in another part, that language can be said to exhibit split ergativity. Among such languages, there are two main factors that may condition the split: one is the semantic and/or pragmatic character of the arguments, and the other is tense/aspect. We will briefly describe these two types of split ergativity in the following sections.

The first type of split-ergative system is one in which some kinds of nominal arguments participate in a nominative/accusative system, whereas others participate in an ergative/absolutive system. To illustrate this kind of system, we will

take an extended look at another language, Managalasi, spoken in Papua New
Guinea:

(38) a.   a   va'-ena   'You will go.'
           2SG   go-FUT.2SG

     b.   na   va'-ejo   'I will go.'
           1SG   go-FUT.1SG

     c.   nara   a   an-a'-ejo   'I will hit you.'
           1SG   2SG   hit-2SG-FUT.1SG

     d.   ara   na   an-i'-ena   'You will hit me.'
           2SG   1SG   hit-1SG-FUT.2SG

Again, we notice that this is a verb-final language, therefore we will be concerned only with nominal case marking and verb agreement. Examples 38a and
38b are intransitive (single-argument) clauses, therefore they have S arguments
only. The S arguments in both examples are pronouns, which we can place in the
chart as follows:

	S	A	O
pronouns	a 2SG		
	na 1SG		
verb agreement			

In example 38c the 1SG pronoun is *nara*. Since, according to the free translation,
the 1SG argument (*I*) is the most AGENT-like, we will put *nara* in the A column.
The other argument in this clause is 2SG, *a*, therefore we will put *a* in the O
column. In 38d the 2SG argument, *ara*, is the most AGENT-like, so we will put
ara in the A column. The other argument in 38d is *na*, therefore we will put *na*
in the O column, thus completing the first row of the chart:

	S	A	O
pronouns	a 2SG	ara 2SG	a 2SG
	na 1SG	nara 1SG	na 1SG
verb agreement			

Since the forms in the S and O columns are the same, and the forms in the A
column are different, this represents an ergative/absolutive case-marking system.
The case endings may be analyzed as follows:

(39)   Ergative case marker: -ra
            Absolutive case marker: -Ø (zero)

Now let us look at verb agreement. It is evident from the glosses in 38 that in
this language, verb agreement is combined with future tense. Since the tense is the
same in all the examples, we need not be concerned specifically with tense – all
the variation in the suffixes must be due to variation in the person of the arguments.

Since the suffixes are different in 38a and 38b, we know that the verb must agree with the S. In 38c the verb agrees with the 1SG A argument, and in 38d the verb agrees with the 2SG A argument. We also notice that the suffix -*a'* refers to a 2SG O argument, while -*i'* refers to a 1SG O argument. Therefore we can complete the second row of the chart as follows:

	S	A	O
pronouns	a 2SG	ara 2SG	a 2SG
	na 1SG	nara 1SG	na 1SG
verb agreement	-ena 2SG	-ena 2SG	-a' 2SG
	-ejo 1SG	-ejo 1SG	-i' 1SG

In the second row we notice that the S and A columns are identical, while the O column is the odd one out. Therefore, in terms of verb agreement, this language illustrates a nominative/accusative system. Our conclusion is that this language has a split-ergative system in which pronouns exhibit an ergative/ absolutive system and verb agreement exhibits a nominative/accusative system.

The second type of split ergativity is one based on tense and/or aspect. In all such languages, the ergative/absolutive system occurs in the past tense or perfective aspect, while the nominative/accusative system occurs in the non-past tense(s) or imperfective aspect (DeLancey 1982). The following example is from Georgian, the national language of the Republic of Georgia (Comrie 1989):

(40) a. Student-i   midis.   'The student goes.'
              -NOM goes

    b. Student-i   ceril-s   cers.   'The student writes the letter.'
              -NOM letter-ACC writes

    c. Student-i   mivida.   'The student went.'
              -ABS went

    d. Student-ma ceril-i   dacera.   'The student wrote the letter.'
              -ERG letter-ABS wrote

In these examples, the case marker -*i* marks S and A nominals in the "present" tense (examples 40a and b). Therefore, it is appropriate to refer to this case marker as marking nominative case. The same case marker, however, marks S and O nominals in the "past tense" (examples 40c and d).[3] In these clauses, then, it is appropriate to describe -*i* as an absolutive case marker. The following table summarizes the Georgian system:

Georgian	S	A	O
case marking: present tense	-i	-i	-s
case marking: past tense	-i	-ma	-i

This table illustrates clearly that S and A are treated alike and O differently in the present tense, thus manifesting a nominative/accusative system. At the same time, S and O are treated alike and A differently in the past tense, thus manifesting an ergative/absolutive system. This is a classic split-ergative system based on tense/aspect.

Before leaving the topic of split systems for organizing grammatical relations, we will present one interesting example of a combination split-intransitive/split-ergative case-marking system. This is from Guaymí of Panama and Costa Rica. Guaymí has a straightforward split-intransitive case-marking system in past tenses. This is illustrated in 41a, b, and c. The ergative case marker -*gwe* can only occur on the A arguments of transitive verbs or S arguments of agentive intransitive verbs in one of the past tenses. The marker -*gwe* may not occur on the S argument of 41b because the verb *ŋat*-, 'die,' is non-volitional; it is something that happens to the dog, rather than something the dog does on purpose. These examples show that a split-intransitive system for organizing grammatical relations can be manifested in nominal case marking as well as in verb agreement:

(41)	a.	Dori-gwe	blit-ani.		'Doris spoke.'
		Doris-ERG	speak-PAST 1		
	b.	Nu	ŋat-ani.		'The dog died.'
		dog	die-PAST 1		
	c.	Toma-gwe	Dori	dëma-ini.	'Tom greeted Doris.'
		Tom-ERG	Doris	greet-PAST 1	
	d.	Dori	blit-e.		'Doris speaks.'
		Doris	speak-PR		
	e.	Toma	Dori dëma-e.		'Tom greets Doris.'
		Tom	Doris greet-PR		
	f.	Nu	ŋat-e.		'The dog dies.'
		dog	die-PR		

However, -*gwe* never occurs, regardless of the semantics or transitivity of the verb in the present, or any tense other than past (41d, e, and f). One could say that Guaymí has two quite distinct case-marking systems, a split-intransitive system in the past tense and a neutral system in the present:

(42)   Split system for organizing grammatical relations in Guaymí:

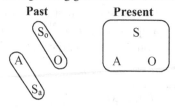

The exercises at the end of this chapter will give you practice in recognizing the different ways in which languages organize their grammatical relations.

Conceptual outline of chapter 8

I.   Languages typically treat each nominal element in a clause in one of about three or four morphosyntactic ways. These morphosyntactic means of treating nominal elements are called grammatical relations. Terms used for various grammatical relations that have been proposed include genitive, subject, (direct) object, indirect object, oblique, ergative, and absolutive. The structural features that most directly express grammatical relations are:
  • case marking on nouns
  • participant reference marking on verbs (agreement, concord)
  • constituent order (usually not helpful in verb-final or verb-initial languages)

II. There are different possible "systems" for organizing grammatical relations. The systems discussed in this chapter are:
  • nominative/accusative systems
  • ergative/absolutive systems
  • split-intransitive systems
  • split-ergative systems

III. There are two basic types of split-ergative systems in the world's languages, though combinations may occur:
  • split-ergative systems based on the ways arguments are expressed (verb agreement vs. pronouns vs. full NPs)
  • split-ergative systems based on tense and/or aspect

IV. A method for analyzing the system for organizing grammatical relations of any language is presented.

Exercise 8.1: Iraqi Arabic

Adapted from Cowan and Rakušan (1998:100)

1. ilwalad yiʃuuf ilbeet.   'The boy sees the house.'
2. ilwalad yihibb ilbinit.   'The boy loves the girl.'
3. ilwalad yiktib ilmaktuub.   'The boy writes the letter.'
4. ilbinit tiʃuuf ilwalad.   'The girl sees the boy.'
5. ilbinit tiktib iddaris.   'The girl writes the lesson.'
6. ilwalad yigi.   'The boy is coming.'

A.   How would you say: 'The girl loves the boy' in Iraqi Arabic?

B.   Describe the system for organizing grammatical relations in Iraqi Arabic. What kind of system is manifested here? Be sure to consider all structural features that express grammatical relations.

Exercise 8.2: Gujarati

Tom Payne

1.	Ramesh pen khəridto həto.		'Ramesh was buying the pen.'
	(male name) pen (fem)		
2.	Rameshe pen khəridyi.		'Ramesh bought the pen.'
3.	Ramesh awyo.		'Ramesh came.'
4.	Sudha awyi.		'Sudha came.'
	(fem. name)		
5.	Sudha awti həti.		'Sudha was coming.'
6.	Ramesh awto həto.		'Ramesh was coming.'
7.	Sudhae pen khəridyi.		'Sudha bought the pen.'

A.   What structural features distinguish grammatical relations in Gujarati?

B.   What system or systems for organizing grammatical relations does it use? Give evidence for your claims.

Exercise 8.3: Avar

Yakov Testelets

1.	Vas vigiana.	'The boy got up.'
2.	Vas vegana.	'The boy lay down.'
3.	Yas yigiana.	'The girl got up.'
4.	Yas yegana.	'The girl lay down.'
5.	Vasas yas yettsana.	'The boy praised the girl.'
6.	_____	'The girl praised the boy.'

A.   What language family does Avar belong to?

B.   What is the probable translation of number 6 in Avar?

C.   What structural features reflect grammatical relations in Avar?

D.   Describe the system for organizing grammatical relations in Avar. Give all of the evidence.

Exercise 8.4: Endo

Tom Payne

1.	Kícho Pëëlyòn	'Elephant came.'
2.	Kícho Kíplêkwà	'Hare came.'
3.	Kílëchí Kíplêkwà Pëëlyón	'Hare told Elephant . . .'
4.	Kílëchí Pëëlyón Kíplêkwà	'Hare told Elephant . . .'
5.	Kílëchí Kìplêkwà Pëëlyòn	'Elephant told Hare . . .'

6. Kílëchí Pëëlyòn Kìplêkwà	'Elephant told Hare . . .'
7. Kípka pííč	'People came.'
8. Kíro pííč	'People saw (him/her/it).'
9. Kíro pîíč	'He/she saw people.'
10. Kíro Kìplêkwà	———
11. Kíro Kíplêkwà	———

A.   Where is Endo spoken? What language family does it belong to?

B.   What structural features distinguish grammatical relations for full noun phrases in Endo?

C.   What system for organizing grammatical relations is employed?

D.   Translate numbers 10 and 11.

Exercise 8.5: Swahili, Safi dialect, part I

David Perlmutter, Mary Rhodes, and Paul Thomas

1. Mtoto alipoteka.	'The child got lost.'
2. Kitabu kilipoteka.	'The book got lost.'
3. Watoto walipoteka.	'The children got lost.'
4. Vitabu vilipoteka.	'The books got lost.'
5. Mtoto aliona kisu.	'The child saw a knife.'
6. Mtoto anaona kisu.	'The child sees a knife.'
7. Mtoto aliona vitabu.	'The child saw books.'
8. Watoto walileta vitabu.	'The children brought books.'
9. Wewe ulileta kitabu.	'**You** brought a book.'
10. Mimi ninataka vitabu.	'**I** want books.'
11. Sisi tulipoteka.	'**We** got lost.'
12. Nilipoteka.	'I got lost.'
13. Aliona visu.	'He saw knives.'

The use of verb prefixes other than the ones given would be ungrammatical, for example:

    14. a. *Mtoto kilipoteka.   ('The child got lost.')
         b. *Mtoto walipoteka.
          etc.

The use of no prefix at all would also be ungrammatical.

Give a position-class diagram of the verb based on these data. In the diagram, list and gloss all morphemes.

Exercise 8.6: Swahili, Safi dialect, part 2

David Perlmutter, Mary Rhodes, and Paul Thomas

(This is a continuation of the previous exercise. In answering the questions below, be sure to keep the data in exercise 8.5 in mind.)

15. Mtoto alimwona mganga.   'The child saw the doctor.'
16. Mtoto aliwaona wanyama.   'The child saw the animals.'
17. Watoto wanakitaka kitabu.   'The children want the book.'
18. Mtoto anavitaka vitabu.   'The child wants the books.'
19. Mimi niliwaona wao.   '**I** saw them.'
20. Yeye aliniona mimi.   '**He** saw me.'
21. Mgeni alivileta visu.   'The visitor brought the knives.'
22. Watoto wanakipenda kitabu.   'The children like the book.'
23. Watoto waliwupenda wewe.   'The children liked you.'
24. Watoto waliwapenda waganga.
25. Mganga anamleta mtoto.
26. _____   'The visitors brought the knives.'
27. _____   '**I** like the child.'
28. _____   'The visitors like the children.'
29. _____   'I like books.'
30. _____   'They see knives.'

A. Fill in the English for examples 24 and 25 and the Swahili for 26–30.
B. Revise the chart that you made for exercise 8.5 to incorporate these data.
C. State any morphophonemic rules that apply.
D. What system is used for organizing grammatical relations in these data?

Exercise 8.7: Guugu Yimidhirr

John Haviland

1. Ngayu nhangu nhaadhi.   'I saw him/her.'
2. Gudaangun yarrga nhaadhi.   'The dog saw the boy.'
3. Nyulu nganhi nhaadhi.   'He/she saw me.'
4. Yarrgangun gudaa nhaadhi.   'The boy saw the dog.'
5. Ngayu dhadaa.   'I am going to go.'
6. Gudaa dhadaa.   'The dog is going to go.'
7. Nyulu dhadaa.   'He/she is going to go.'
8. Yarrga dhadaa.   'The boy is going to go.'
9. Ngayu yarrga gunday.   'I hit the boy.'
10. Yarrgangun nganhi gunday.   'The boy hit me.'

A. Where is Guugu Yimidhirr spoken? What language family does it belong to? How many speakers are there?
B. List and give a meaning for each morpheme in the above data.
C. In what respects are grammatical relations in Guugu Yimidhirr organized on an ergative/absolutive basis, and in what respects are they organized on a nominative/accusative basis? Is this consistent or inconsistent with universal expectations?

Exercise 8.8: Russian

Sam Hanchett and Deborah Fink

1. d'évačka ísit sabáku   'The girl is looking for the dog.'
2. sabáku ísit d'évačka   'The girl is looking for the dog.'
3. sabáka ísit b'élku   'The dog is looking for the squirrel.'
4. ísit sabáka b'élku   'The dog is looking for the squirrel.'
5. ísit b'élku d'évačka   'The girl is looking for the squirrel.'
6. p'ísit d'évačka   'The girl is writing.'
7. sabáka lájit   'The dog is barking.'
8. ísit sabáka d'évačku

A.   What structural features distinguish grammatical relations in Russian?
B.   What system for organizing grammatical relations does Russian employ? Give evidence for your claims.
C.   Translate example 8.

Exercise 8.9: Ho

John and Sally Mathai

There are two ways of saying each of the following sentences in Ho. Other possibilities are ungrammatical.

1. I am going.	senɔṭanaɲ	/	aɲ senɔṭana
2. You are going.	senɔṭanam	/	am senɔṭana
3. He/she is going.	senɔṭanae	/	aʔe senɔṭana
4. I am beating you.	ṭammeṭanaɲ	/	ameɲ ṭammeṭana
5. I am beating him.	ṭamiː ṭeneɲ	/	aʔeɲ ṭamiː ṭene
6. You are beating me.	ṭamiɲṭenem	/	aɲem ṭamiɲṭene
7. You are beating him.	ṭamiː ṭenem	/	aʔem ṭamiː ṭene
8. He is beating me.	ṭamiɲṭene	/	aɲeʔe ṭamiɲṭene
9. He is beating you.	ṭammeṭanae	/	ameʔe ṭammeṭana
10. He is beating him.	ṭamiː ṭene	/	aʔeʔe ṭamiː ṭene
11. I went.	senɔjanaɲ	/	aɲ senɔjana
12. You went.	senɔjanam	/	am senɔjana
13. He/she went.	senɔjanae	/	aʔe senɔjana
14. I beat you.	ṭamkeḍmijaɲ	/	ameɲ ṭamkeḍmija
15. I beat him.	ṭamkijeɲ	/	aʔeɲ ṭamkije
16. You beat me.	ṭamkidiɲem	/	aɲem ṭamkidiɲe
17. You beat him.	ṭamkijem	/	aʔem ṭamkije
18. He beat me.	ṭamkidiɲe	/	aɲeʔe ṭamkidiɲe
19. He beat you.	ṭamkeḍmijae	/	ameʔe ṭamkeḍmij
20. He beat him.	ṭamkije	/	aʔeʔe ṭamkije

A.   Where is Ho spoken? What language family does it belong to?
B.   List and gloss all the morphemes illustrated in these data.
C.   Using concise English prose, describe the system that Ho uses for expressing S, A, and O arguments.

Exercise 8.10: Kurmanji Kurdish

Nick Bailey

The Kurdish people number at least 25 million. Kurdish is an important member of the Iranian branch of the Indo-European language family. The variety known as Kurmanji Kurdish is spoken by about 15 million people living in Turkey, Iran, Iraq, Syria, and the former USSR. This variety is normally written in Cyrillic script (as is Russian) but is presented here in a modified Latin script:

1. ez diçim   'I am going.'
2. tu diçî   'You (sg.) are going.'
3. ew diçe   'He/she/it is going.'
4. ew diçin   'They are going.'
5. gulistan diçe   'Gulistan is going.'
6. ez çûm   'I went.'
7. tu çûyî   'You (sg.) went.'
8. ew çû   'He/she/it went.'
9. ew çûn   'They went.'
10. gulistan çû   'Gulistan went.'
11. ez gulistanê dikişînim   'I am pulling Gulistan.'
12. tu gulistanê dikişînî   'You (sg.) are pulling Gulistan.'
13. ew gulistanê dikişîne   'He/she/it is pulling Gulistan.'
14. ew gulistanê dikişînin   'They are pulling Gulistan.'
15. gulistan min dikişîne   'Gulistan is pulling me.'
16. gulistan te dikişîne   'Gulistan is pulling you (sg.).'
17. gulistan wî dikişîne   'Gulistan is pulling him.'
18. gulistan wê dikişîne   'Gulistan is pulling her.'
19. gulistan wan dikişîne   'Gulistan is pulling them.'
20. min gulistan kişand   'I pulled Gulistan.'
21. te gulistan kişand   'You (sg.) pulled Gulistan.'
22. wî gulistan kişand   'He pulled Gulistan.'
23. wê gulistan kişand   'She pulled Gulistan.'
24. wan gulistan kişand   'They pulled Gulistan.'
25. min ew kişand   'I pulled him/her/it.'
26. min ew kişandin   'I pulled them.'
27. min tu kişandî   'I pulled you (sg.).'
28. te ez kişandim   'You (sg.) pulled me.'
29. te ew kişandin   'You pulled them.'
30. gulistanê ez kişandim   'Gulistan pulled me.'

A.   What structural features distinguish grammatical relations in Kurdish?

B.   What kind of system does Kurmanji Kurdish use to organize gram-
            matical relations? Please provide charts of all the relevant forms
            (a separate sheet of paper will be necessary for this part of the
            exercise).

Exercise 8.11: Samoan II

Olga Uryupina, adapted by Tom Payne
Samoan is spoken by 38,700 people in American Samoa and 153,000 in Western
Samoa, an independent country. About 162,000 additional Samoan speakers live
in New Zealand, Hawaii, Fiji and on the West Coast of mainland USA. Samoan
is a Polynesian language

     1. 'Ua lafi le pua'a.   'The pig hid.'
     2. 'Ua tutuli e tagata maile.   'The people chased away the dogs.'
     3. 'Ua pupu'e e le pusi 'isumu. 'The cat caught the mice.'
     4. 'Ua pu'e e le tama le pusi.   'The boy caught the cat.'
     5. 'Ua fefefe teine.   'The girls got scared.'
     6. 'Ua fasi e tama le 'isumu.   'The boys killed the mouse.'

A.   Translate from Samoan into English:

     7. 'Ua fefe le pusi.
     8. 'Ua tuli e 'isumu le pusi.

B.   Translate from English into Samoan:

     9. 'The boys hid.'
     10. 'The mice caught the dog.'
     11. 'The girl killed the pigs.'

C.   What system or systems does Samoan employ for organizing gram-
            matical relations? Give your evidence.

Notes

1. The terms nominative and accusative are from the traditional grammars of classical
   languages. To a large extent their use in those grammars corresponds to the definitions
   given here. However, the terms in the classical languages refer strictly to morphological
   cases. The markers that signal those cases are often used in many other ways in addition
   to marking A, S, and O arguments. For example, the accusative case in Latin marks
   objects of certain prepositions. Here we are using the terms nominative and accusative to
   describe expressions of grammatical relations, no matter how those roles are instantiated
   in the morphosyntax. So we may, for example, refer to a particular noun phrase as a
   nominative noun phrase if it is an S or an A argument, whether or not it is marked by
   a distinct nominative case marker.
2. Note that this is not the same thing as saying that constituent order does not distinguish
   grammatical relations. In an AOV language, the relative position of A and O clearly may

help identify which is which. However, a *system* of organizing grammatical relations must involve intransitive clauses as well, and, as mentioned in the text, there is no consistent way of grouping A with S or O with S in terms of constituent order in an AOV/SV language.

3. "Past tense" is actually a simplification of the meaning of this conceptual category in Georgian, but for our purposes it will suffice.

9   Voice and valence

Every language has constructions that affect the alignment between semantic roles and grammatical relations in clauses. Such constructions are sometimes referred to as **VOICES**. For example, in a typical **ACTIVE VOICE** construction in English an AGENT is the subject of the clause and a PATIENT is the object. The **PASSIVE VOICE** creates a different argument structure, one in which the PATIENT bears the subject relation and the AGENT appears in an oblique role:

(1) a.   ACTIVE: Orna baked these cookies.   Subject = AGENT
                                                      Object = PATIENT
    b.   PASSIVE: These cookies were baked by Orna. Subject = PATIENT
                                                      Oblique = AGENT

In this chapter we will use the concept of **VALENCE** to explore constructions that affect the relationship between grammatical relations and semantic roles. These include constructions that traditionally fall under the heading of voice, though there are several valence-related constructions that are not normally considered voices. Nevertheless, because of their functional similarities, and because many languages treat valence-related constructions in structurally similar ways, it is often convenient to group them together for analytic or expository purposes.

VALENCE can be thought of as a semantic notion, a syntactic notion, or a combination of the two. **SEMANTIC VALENCE** refers to the number of participants in the message-world scene normally expressed by a verb (see chapter 4 on verbs and their argument structures). For example, the verb *eat* in English has a semantic valence of two, since for any given event of eating there must be two participants – something that eats and something that gets eaten. If one of these is missing from the scene itself, then it is hard to imagine describing the scene as an event of eating.

GRAMMATICAL VALENCE (or **SYNTACTIC VALENCE**) refers to the number of arguments present in any given clause (see chapter 8 for discussion of the term "argument"). The verb *eat* in English may occur in a clause with a grammatical valence of 1 or 2 depending on how the verb is used. In a clause like *Calvin already ate* there is no direct object, so the only core argument of the verb refers to the "eater." Nevertheless, in the scene expressed by this clause, it is understood that something is eaten. It's just that the identity of the eaten thing is not known or is unimportant for the particular communicative task at hand.

This can be represented in terms of argument-structure diagrams, introduced in chapter 4, as follows:

(2)   EVENT OF EATING (semantic valence = 2):   AGENT   PATIENT
                                                          ↓   ↓
                                                          S   Ø
            (grammatical valence = 1):   Calvin already ate Ø.

Similarly, in a clause like *She ate away at the bone* there is only one core argument of the verb. *Bone* is an oblique and therefore is not a core argument:

(3)   EVENT OF EATING (semantic valence = 2): AGENT   PATIENT
                                                       ↓   ↓
                                                       S   OBLIQUE
            (grammatical valence = 1):   She ate away <u>at the bone.</u>

Valence-adjusting constructions are morphosyntactic constructions that affect the *semantic* and/or *grammatical* valence of a clause.

Before we go any further, we need to discuss an important difference between the omission of a verbal argument and use of a **ZERO PRONOUN**. In a clause like 2, there is arguably a "zero" (the absence of an expected noun or pronoun) following the verb *ate*. In 4 there is another kind of "zero" preceding the verb *grabbed*:

(4)   EVENT OF GRABBING (semantic valence = 2):   AGENT   PATIENT
                                                           ↓   ↓
            (grammatical valence = 2):   S   O
                              Calvin came in and Ø grabbed Hobbes.

In this example the zero preceding the verb *grabbed* is an **ANAPHORIC DEVICE**. It *refers* to a specific participant that is mentioned in the previous clause. It is so obvious who that participant is that you would hardly ask *who grabbed Hobbes?* after someone utters this sentence. Therefore the second clause in example 4 still has a grammatical valence of 2, as well as expressing a situation that has a semantic valence of 2.

On the other hand, example 2 represents a valence-decreasing construction (object omission). It has a grammatical valence of 1, while expressing a situation that has a semantic valence of 2. The zero after *ate* is not anaphoric; it does not refer to any particular entity. You could very naturally ask *What did he eat?* after someone says *Calvin already ate*. So there are at least two kinds of "zeros" in language – zero pronouns, which are anaphoric, i.e., they refer to participants on the discourse stage, and omitted arguments, which are non-anaphoric. Omitted arguments don't refer to anything in particular.

In many languages, zero pronominalization (also referred to at times as "zero anaphora," or "pro-drop") is much more common than it is in English. In such languages it may be difficult to distinguish constructions with reduced grammatical valence from those with zero pronouns. In the extreme case of languages with no morphological means of expressing grammatical relations, and few restrictions on zero anaphora, the only way to decide is to examine the discourse context.

But then, for such languages, it is largely a moot point whether a particular construction constitutes reduced valence or not. The concept of grammatical valence is valuable insofar as it leads to an understanding of alternative arrangements of grammatical relations (e.g., alternative case-marking patterns, verb agreement, or constituent order). If the language provides few such alternatives, then grammatical valence is not much of an issue.

The notion of valence is closely connected with the traditional idea of **TRANSITIVITY**, i.e., a **TRANSITIVE** situation is a relation between two participants such that one participant acts toward or upon the other. An **INTRANSITIVE** situation is a property, state, or other situation involving only one participant. Sometimes intransitive situations are called **UNIVALENT**, i.e., they have a semantic valence of one. Similarly, transitive situations such as *He killed a bear* are called **DIVALENT**. **TRIVALENT** situations are those that involve three core participants, e.g., *He gave us the gate key*. Sometimes trivalent situations are, perhaps confusingly, called **DITRANSITIVE**, or **BITRANSITIVE**. These terms are based on the fact that verbs like *give* can take two objects – the given thing, and the recipient. Valence theory is more general, however, looking at all the possible arguments – not just objects. From this point of view there are potentially three core arguments, including the subject, for a verb like *give* that expresses a trivalent situation.

Many studies (principally Hopper and Thompson 1980) have taken the term "transitivity" to be a relative notion, referring to the degree to which an event carries over from an active, volitional AGENT to a PATIENT. Nevertheless, it is common to find the term used in the traditional way.

Perhaps unfortunately, linguists do not always distinguish semantic valence from grammatical valence. So, for example, there are some who would say that *eat* is always a transitive verb – you don't have an event of "eating" if you don't have an "eater" and an "eaten thing." These linguists use the term transitive in the sense we are using the term semantically transitive. Others would say *eat* is sometimes transitive and sometimes intransitive. These linguists are most likely referring to syntactic transitivity. Still others would say that there are two related verbs *eat* in the lexicon of English, one of which is transitive and the other intransitive. However, in order to understand valence-adjusting constructions (a major portion of the grammatical system of most languages – Bybee 1985:31), it is very useful to make a clear distinction between semantic valence and grammatical valence.

One metaphor that is particularly useful in understanding valence theory, and which has been used extensively by linguists, is that of *communication as a play*. Much research on discourse comprehension and production has used some form of this metaphor to make substantive hypotheses and claims about how people communicate. For example, Fillmore (1976) suggested that verbs with their unique argument structures activate **SCENES** in the minds of language users. Lakoff's (1987) notion of **COGNITIVE MODEL** is also related to the notion of scenes. Scenes and cognitive models are idealized mental structures, "pictures" if you will, that the human mind uses to categorize, store, and communicate experience and knowledge. These approaches capture the fact that all knowledge is acquired and stored with reference to a context. One way of thinking about such a context is in terms of the metaphor of a **DISCOURSE STAGE**.

Valence-related constructions can be categorized in terms of how they affect the idealized scene evoked by particular verbs. The communicative effect of increasing syntactic valence can be characterized most generally as bringing a participant that is normally not part of a scene, or on the margin of a scene, onto "center stage." The effect of decreasing syntactic valence, on the other hand, is to downplay a normally center-stage participant to marginal status, or eliminate it from the scene altogether. Furthermore, the participants brought onto or taken off center stage can be controllers, i.e., AGENTs or Agent-like participants, affected or Patient-like participants, or they may have any number of other peripheral roles, such as RECIPIENTS, INSTRUMENTS, or BENEFACTEES (see chapter 4 on semantic roles).

With the metaphor of the "discourse stage" in mind, we can begin to sketch out a functional typology of valence-adjusting constructions. Following this, we will briefly discuss this typology and introduce analytical methods for modeling argument structures and the adjustments that they may undergo. **A functional typology of valence-adjusting constructions:**

Valence-decreasing constructions:

Those that "combine" controlling and affected participants into a single participant:	REFLEXIVES RECIPROCALS MIDDLES
Those that downplay a controlling participant:	SUBJECT OMISSION PASSIVES
Those that downplay an affected participant:	OBJECT OMISSION ANTIPASSIVES OBJECT DEMOTION OBJECT INCORPORATION

Valence-increasing constructions:

Those that add a controlling participant:	CAUSATIVES
Those that upgrade a peripheral participant:	APPLICATIVES DATIVE SHIFT POSSESSOR RAISING DATIVE OF INTEREST

Valence-decreasing constructions

Languages can employ lexical, morphological, and syntactic expression types for reducing valence. In the following subsections we will describe and give examples of how various valence-decreasing constructions can be expressed by each of the three expression types.

Reflexives and reciprocals

The first group of valence-decreasing construction types we will consider are those which reduce valence by "combining," metaphorically speaking, the two core arguments of a transitive clause. These types are: reflexive, reciprocal, and middle constructions. In this section we will discuss reflexives and reciprocals only. Middle constructions will be discussed in the following section.

A **REFLEXIVE** construction is one in which A and O are the same entity, e.g., *She saw herself*. All true reflexive constructions reduce the semantic valence of a transitive clause by specifying that there are not two separate entities involved. Rather, one entity fulfills two semantic roles and/or grammatical relations. With lexical and morphological reflexives and reciprocals, the reduction in semantic valence is reflected in a corresponding reduction in grammatical valence. Syntactic reflexives and reciprocals do not reduce grammatical valence, as we will see below.

A **LEXICAL REFLEXIVE**[1] is one which is tied to the lexical meaning of a particular verb. For example, the English verbs *to get dressed*, *wash up*, *shave*, etc., when used intransitively, all imply that the AGENT and PATIENT are the same entity, e.g.:

(5)   Calvin shaved, washed, and got dressed.

This sentence implies that Calvin shaved himself, washed himself, and got himself dressed. If some other object is intended, it must be explicitly mentioned, e.g.:

(6)   Calvin shaved Hobbes.

The argument structure of a lexical reflexive can be expressed as follows:

(7)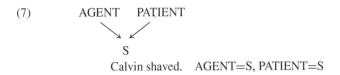

        Calvin shaved.   AGENT=S, PATIENT=S

In other words, the semantic roles of AGENT and PATIENT are both expressed by the only argument of a one-argument clause.

Certain actions are highly likely to be accomplished reflexively, primarily "grooming" activities such as *wash*, *shave*, and *dress*. These concepts are typically expressed with the simplest (i.e., phonologically smallest, and least complex) kind of reflexive construction available in the language. Often this is the lexical reflexive.

A **MORPHOLOGICAL REFLEXIVE** is expressed by one of the morphological processes discussed in chapter 2. English has no morphological reflexives. The most well-known examples of morphological reflexives are probably those of Romance languages. However, the writing systems of these languages tend to obscure the fact that the reflexive morphemes are actually bound clitics rather than free words. For example, in Spanish a reflexive is formed from a transitive verb by the addition of the proclitic *se* (example 9):

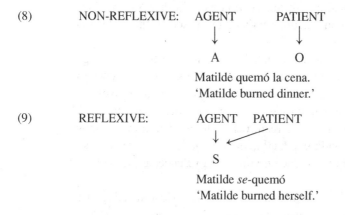

(8)   NON-REFLEXIVE: AGENT   PATIENT
                          ↓   ↓
                          A   O

            Matilde quemó la cena.
            'Matilde burned dinner.'

(9)   REFLEXIVE: AGENT   PATIENT
                       ↓
                       S

            Matilde *se*-quemó
            'Matilde burned herself.'

All semantically transitive verbs must take a reflexive proclitic to be understood as reflexive in Spanish. There are no lexical reflexives of the English variety:

(10) a.   Matilde lavó el carro.   'Matilde washed the car.'
           Matilde se-lavó.   'Matilde washed (herself).'
           *Matilde lavó.

     b.   Horacio afeitó el tigre.   'Horace shaved the tiger.'
           Horacio se-afeitó.   'Horace shaved (himself).'
           *Horacio afeitó.

     c.   Aleida vistió al niño.   'Aleida dressed the boy.'
           Aleida se-vistió.   'Aleida got dressed.'
           *Aleida vistió.

The Spanish morphological reflexive is sometimes called a **HARMONIC REFLEXIVE**. This is because the reflexive marker "harmonizes" with the person (and number for non-third persons) of the S argument. Notice that in example 11 the reflexive proclitic is *se* only for third persons (11a). When the S is first-person singular, the proclitic is *me* (11b), and when it is second-person singular, the proclitic is *te* (11c):[2]

(11) a.   Milton *se* mordió.   'Milton bit himself.'
    b.   Yo *me* mordí.   'I bit myself.'
    c.   Tu *te* mordiste.   'You bit yourself.'

Russian offers additional examples of morphological reflexives. In Russian, a reflexive is formed by the addition of a suffix -*ся* (-*s'a*) (example 13):

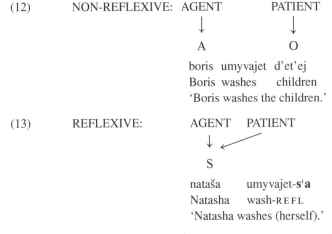

(12)   NON-REFLEXIVE: AGENT   PATIENT
                             A   O

                             boris umyvajet d'et'ej
                             Boris washes   children
                             'Boris washes the children.'

(13)   REFLEXIVE: AGENT   PATIENT
                             S

                             nataša   umyvajet-**s'a**
                             Natasha   wash-REFL
                             'Natasha washes (herself).'

In contrast to Spanish, the morphological reflexive in Russian is **NON-HARMONIC** in that the form -*s'a*, does not vary according to any features of the S argument:

(14) a.   я   умываю-съ.   'I wash myself.'
         ja   umyvaju-*s'*
         1SG   wash.PR.1SG-REFL

    b.   Ты   умываеш-ся.   'You wash yourself.'
         ty   umyvaješ-*s'a*
         2SG   wash.PR.2SG-REFL

    c.   Мы   умываем-ся.   'We wash ourselves.'
         my   umyvajem-*s'a*
         1PL   wash.PR.1PL-REFL

The last type of reflexive construction we will discuss is **ANALYTIC REFLEXIVES**. In English, analytic reflexives are expressed by the **REFLEXIVE PRONOUNS** *myself, yourself, himself, herself, ourselves, yourselves, themselves* and *itself*. For example:

(15)   AGENT   PATIENT
                                          A   O
         Do you have any control over how creepy you allow *yourself* to get?

This is an analytic reflexive because reflexivity is expressed via a separate word that is distinct from the verb. From a purely syntactic point of view, the analytic reflexive construction of English is not a valence-decreasing construction. This is because there are still two syntactic arguments – *you* and *yourself*. We may want to say, however, that this clause is semantically intransitive because the two syntactic arguments refer to a single entity.

Often languages will have more than one type of reflexive construction. We have already seen lexical and analytic reflexives in English. Russian is one of the many languages that has morphological (ex. 14) and analytic reflexives. The analytic reflexive pronoun is *себя* (*seb'a*), which is transparently related to the reflexive suffix -*ся* (*-s'a*):

(16)   Она   поднимает   себя.   'She lifts herself.'
        ona   podnimajet   seb'a
        3SG.F   raise.PR.3SG   REFL.PN.ACC

Like the morphological reflexive in Russian, the analytic reflexive is non-harmonic. That is to say, the reflexive pronoun does not vary for person and number (though it does vary for case). Again, the analytic reflexive does not decrease syntactic valence, since there are still distinct A and O arguments.

A **RECIPROCAL** construction is very similar conceptually to a reflexive. For this reason, reciprocals and reflexives are expressed identically in many languages. A prototypical reciprocal clause is one in which two participants equally act upon each other, i.e., both are AGENT and PATIENT. For example, *they saw each other* is a reciprocal in English. Reciprocals are conceptually similar to reflexives in that both indicate that AGENT and PATIENT are **COREFERENTIAL** (they refer to the same person), though for different reasons.

LEXICAL RECIPROCALS are verbs for which reciprocity is a built-in component of their meaning. Some lexically reciprocal verbs in English are *kiss*, *meet*, and *shake hands*, e.g., *Matilde and Mary kissed* usually means *Matilde and Mary kissed each other*. This can be diagrammed as follows. Notice that both *Matilde* and *Mary* refer to the AGENT and the PATIENT:

(17)   AGENT   PATIENT

            Matilde and Mary kissed.

If some other situation is to be communicated, the object must be explicitly mentioned, e.g., *Matilde and Mary kissed Grandma*.

Many languages that have morphological reflexives also have **MORPHO-LOGICAL RECIPROCALS**. These languages often express reflexives and reciprocals with the same morphemes. Here we will provide examples from Spanish.

(18)   REFLEXIVE: Matilde   se-quemó.   'Matilde burned herself.'
                     M.   REFL-burn.3SG.PAST

(19)   Matilde y   María   se-conocieron   en Lima.
        M.   and   M.   REFL-meet.3PL.PAST   in Lima
        'Matilde and Maria met (each other) in Lima.'

(20)   Matilde y   María   se-quemaron.
        M.   and   M.   REFL-burn.3PL.PAST
        'Matilde and Maria burned themselves.' *or* 'Matilde and Maria burned each other.'

Often such constructions are technically ambiguous, as in examples 19 and 20 above. Each of these could be construed in a reflexive or a reciprocal sense. However, there are some ways of resolving the ambiguity. When the subject is singular, the reflexive construal is demanded (e.g., 18). However, when the subject is plural, both reflexive and reciprocal construals are possible. In such cases, the context helps. So example 19 would probably not mean *Matilde and Maria met themselves*, as this represents a logically bizarre, though conceivable, interpretation. Example 20, on the other hand, is truly ambiguous out of context.

In Seko Padang (an Austronesian language spoken in Sulawesi, Indonesia) reflexives are analytic (21), but reciprocals are morphological, being expressed via a verb prefix *si-* (22) (examples courtesy of Tom Laskowske):

(21)   na-kakoang-i   kalai-na   'He called himself.'
        3-call-APL   body-3POSS   (Lit: 'He called his body.')

(22)   si-kakoang-i   'They called each other.'
        RECIP-call-APL

In English, there are analytic reflexives and reciprocals, but they are not identical. Reflexives use the reflexive pronouns, described above, whereas reciprocals use the special anaphoric expression *each other*:

(23)   Melinda and Stephanie saw *each other*.

We have just described a sample of the major types of reflexive and reciprocal constructions in the world's languages. In addition to prototypical reflexive and reciprocal functions, many languages also use reflexive and reciprocal structures to accomplish other tasks. In the following paragraphs we will briefly discuss some of these "extended" uses of reflexive and reciprocal morphosyntax.

In some languages, the reflexive/reciprocal morphology also occurs in noun phrases to indicate coreference between the possessor of the noun and an argument of the verb. This can be called **COREFERENTIAL POSSESSION**. Guaymí provides a ready example of this phenomenon. First we will give an example of a non-reflexive, transitive clause (24), then an example of a morphological reflexive construction (25), and finally an example of reflexive possession (26):

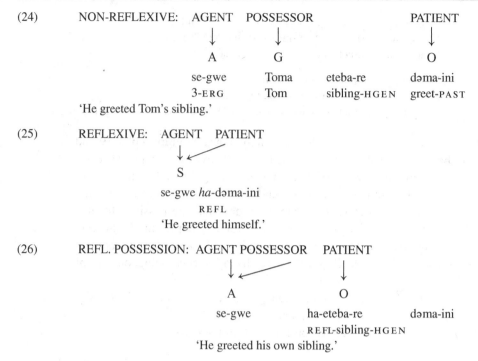

(24)   NON-REFLEXIVE: AGENT   POSSESSOR   PATIENT

                                     ↓   ↓   ↓

                                     A   G   O

                               se-gwe   Toma   eteba-re   dəma-ini
                               3-ERG   Tom   sibling-HGEN   greet-PAST
               'He greeted Tom's sibling.'

(25)   REFLEXIVE: AGENT   PATIENT

                                 ↓ ↙

                                 S

                         se-gwe *ha*-dəma-ini
                                   REFL
                         'He greeted himself.'

(26)   REFL. POSSESSION: AGENT POSSESSOR   PATIENT

                                        ↓ ↙   ↓

                                        A   O

                               se-gwe   ha-eteba-re   dəma-ini
                                               REFL-sibling-HGEN
                         'He greeted his own sibling.'

In 26, the reflexive prefix *ha-* appears on the noun that refers to the O argument of the clause. This prefix indicates that the possessor of the O is coreferential with the A argument. This prefix can be glossed as "reflexive" because it is the same morpheme used in (non-harmonic) morphological reflexives, such as 25. Notice that the commonality between the two uses of *ha-* is that in both cases it links two semantic roles to one surface argument. In example 25, this results in a reduction in syntactic valence, whereas in 26 it does not. This is because in 26 there are still two core arguments, an A and an O, expressed in the clause.

Another common extended use of reflexive/reciprocal morphosyntax is to indicate a special kind of emphasis. For example, in English and many other languages, reflexive pronouns are used to emphasize that a reference is to a particular participant alone:

(27)   Edsel washed the car *himself*.
            Mercedes washed the car all by *herself*.
            Porsche *herself* washed the car.

(28)   The car *itself* is worth $10,000.
            Celica paid $10,000 for the car *itself*.

Middle constructions

The term **MIDDLE** or **MIDDLE VOICE** has been used in a variety of ways. What all such constructions have in common is that they involve a reduction in valence. The motivation for the term is that these constructions are neither passive nor active – they are in between, or "middle." We will consider a middle construction to be one that expresses a semantically transitive situation in terms of a process undergone by a PATIENT, rather than as an action carried out by a distinct AGENT.

A prototypical middle construction is one which is expressed by some special verb form (see examples below). However, many languages have verbs that can be used in a middle sense without any special morphological marking. These can be considered to be **LEXICAL MIDDLE** verbs. Sometimes verbs of this class are called **LABILE VERBS** (Haspelmath 1993). We will use the term "middle verb" simply to capture the functional similarity between intransitive constructions formed with these verbs and morphological middle constructions in other languages. The verb *change* in English is a good example of a middle verb. Used transitively, *change* typically expresses an AGENT in the A role and a PATIENT in the O role. When used intransitively, however, the PATIENT rather than the AGENT is the S:

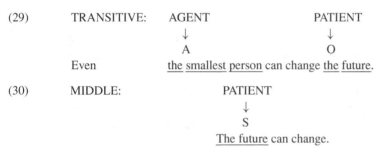

```
(29)    TRANSITIVE:    AGENT                   PATIENT
                         ↓                        ↓
                         A                        O
        Even          the smallest person can change the future.

(30)    MIDDLE:                     PATIENT
                                       ↓
                                       S
                        The future can change.
```

This property distinguishes verbs like *change*, *break*, and *grow* from other verbs that can be either transitive or intransitive (probably the majority of verbs in English). For example, the verb *hit* can also be used either transitively or intransitively, but when it is used intransitively the S argument is the AGENT, rather than the PATIENT. Compare these argument-structure diagrams for *hit* with 29 and 30:

```
(31)    TRANSITIVE:   AGENT  PATIENT
                        ↓       ↓
                        A       O
                      Fezzik hit the door.

(32)    "MIDDLE" (ungrammatical):   PATIENT
                                       ↓
                                       S
                        *The door hit.

(33)    INTRANSITIVE:   AGENT
                          ↓
                          S
                        Fezzik hit.
```

English also employs a syntactic middle construction. Almost any transitive verb that can reasonably be modified with a manner adverbial can be used in a middle construction, if an adverb or prepositional phrase expressing the manner follows:

(34) a.   This soup eats *like a meal* (*by children).
  b.   These trousers *wear well* (*by women).
  c.   That old Volvo of his drove *like a tank* (*by him).
  d.   Chomsky's books read *easily* (*by psychologists).

These are *syntactic* middle constructions because separate words – the manner adverbial element, italicized in these examples – must be present for this construction to be grammatical (c.f. **this soup eats*, **his Volvo drove*, etc.).

There is significant functional similarity between middle constructions and passives (discussed in more detail below). The only difference is that a passive treats the situation as an action carried out by an AGENT, but with the identity of the AGENT downplayed. A prototypical middle construction, on the other hand, treats the situation as a process, i.e., it ignores the role of the AGENT entirely. Notice that the S in the examples in 34 is the participant that undergoes the action expressed by the verb, rather than the AGENT. However, these cannot be passives, because the AGENT may not be expressed in a "*by* phrase." Any causal action on the part of a distinct AGENT is not part of the scene evoked by middle constructions.

Because passive and middle functions are so similar, many languages use the same morphology to express both. In Koiné Greek, for example, middle and passive constructions are the same in all tense/aspects except aorist (examples from Swetman 1998):

(35)	Verb	λύω		'to loose'
(present)	active	λύω	lúo	'I let (someone) loose.'
	passive	λύομαι	lúɔmai	'I am let loose (by someone).'
	middle	λύομαι	lúɔmai	'I become loose'/'I let myself loose.'
(aorist)	active	ἐλυσα	élusa	'I let (someone) loose.'
	passive	ἐλύσην	ɛlúsēn	'I was let loose (by someone).'
	middle	ἐλυσάμην	ɛlusámēn	'I became loose.'/'I let myself loose.'

Some other languages, however, consistently treat middle constructions as distinct from passives. The following are examples from Panare:

(36)	Verb	*amaika*	'to keep':	
		active	amaika	'keep'
		passive	amaikasa'	'be kept'
		middle	samaika	'stay/sit/remain'

Frequently, middle constructions express the notion that the subject is both the controller and the affected participant. However, this feature does not distinguish the function of middle constructions from the function of reflexives. Indeed, in many languages reflexives and middles are expressed by the same morphosyntax. In order to consistently distinguish middle and reflexive functions, we must employ the notion of *process* versus *action*. Middle constructions express a scene as a process whereas reflexives and passives express a scene as an action.

Sometimes morphological middle constructions are called **ANTICAUSA-TIVES**. This is because they are the logical opposite of causative constructions (see the discussion of causative constructions later in this chapter). Instead of starting with a non-causative frame and adding a verbal affix to make a causative, a middle construction starts with an inherently causative frame and results in a non-causative frame. Consider the following Yagua examples:

(37) a.　　Sa-supatá-ra.　　　　'He pulled it out.'
　　　　　　3sG-pull.out-INAN
　　　b.　　Rá-supáta-*y*.　　　　'It came out.'
　　　　　　INAN-pull:out-MID

The simple verb stem *supata* 'pull out' (37a) contains the notion of CAUSE as part of its lexical entry, i.e., the gloss can be paraphrased 'cause to come out.' The morphological middle construction (37b) adds a morpheme which effectively *subtracts* the notion of cause from the lexical meaning of the verb.

Subject omission

　　　　The easiest way to downplay the centrality of a controlling entity in a clause is simply not to mention it. This strategy does not work well for languages with nominative/accusative systems for organizing grammatical relations. The reason is that if you omit a nominative argument from a transitive clause in a nominative/accusative language, you are left with a verb plus an accusative argument. This is usually an unacceptable arrangement for languages such as English:

(38)　　　　Transitive clause:　　Hobbes greeted Calvin.
　　　　　　Subject omission:　　*Greeted Calvin.

However, in languages with ergative/absolutive systems for organizing grammatical relations, if you omit an A argument of a transitive clause, you are left with a verb plus absolutive argument. This is the normal arrangement for intransitive clauses, therefore subject omission is often fully grammatical in such languages. The following examples are from Guaymí:

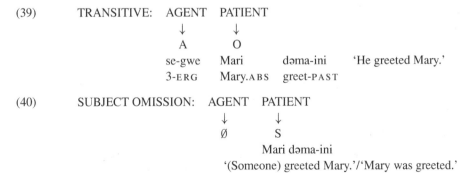

(39)　　　　TRANSITIVE:　AGENT　PATIENT
　　　　　　　　　　　　　　　↓　　　　↓
　　　　　　　　　　　　　　　A　　　　O
　　　　　　　　　　　　　se-gwe　Mari　　dəma-ini　　'He greeted Mary.'
　　　　　　　　　　　　　3-ERG　Mary.ABS　greet-PAST

(40)　　　　SUBJECT OMISSION:　AGENT　PATIENT
　　　　　　　　　　　　　　　　　↓　　　　↓
　　　　　　　　　　　　　　　　　Ø　　　　S
　　　　　　　　　　　　　　　Mari dəma-ini
　　　　　　　　　　　'(Someone) greeted Mary.'/'Mary was greeted.'

Notice that the only difference between 39 and 40 is that in 40 the A argument is omitted.

Passives

A prototypical **PASSIVE** construction is characterized in terms of both its morphosyntactic form and its discourse function. Morphosyntactically, a prototypical passive is a semantically transitive (two-participant) construction which has the following three properties:

- The A is either omitted (not zero-pronominalized, see above) or demoted to an OBLIQUE role.
- The other core argument (the O) becomes an S.
- The verb becomes grammatically intransitive.

In terms of discourse function a prototypical passive is used in contexts where the A is relatively low in topicality with respect to the O. In the following paragraphs we will first discuss prototypical passives, sometimes called "personal passives." Then we will briefly discuss some less prototypical passive constructions, such as **IMPERSONAL** and **ADVERSATIVE PASSIVES**.

PERSONAL PASSIVES are constructions for which some specific agent is implied, but either is not expressed or is expressed in an oblique role. Personal passives can be lexical, morphological, or syntactic. Examples of each type, along with argument-structure diagrams, are provided below.

A **LEXICAL PASSIVE** is any clause headed by a verb that is inherently passive in character. To be inherently passive, the verb must express a scene that includes the presence of a causing AGENT, but the PATIENT must be the grammatical subject. A verb such as *break* in English is not a lexical passive because when used intransitively it does not automatically evoke a scene in which some AGENT acts upon some PATIENT, e.g., *The window broke*.

Several Niger-Congo languages in West Africa (Mande and Senoufo families, at least) have fairly prototypical lexical passives. The following example from Maninka of Kankan illustrates active and passive constructions based on the verb meaning 'cook' (examples from Grégoire, 1985:193):

(41) a. músó   bàra   kínin   tíbi   ACTIVE
         woman   AUX   rice   cook
         'The woman cooked the rice.'

    b. kínim   bàra   tíbi   (músó bòlo)   PASSIVE
        rice   AUX   cook   woman by
        'The rice was cooked (by the woman).'

The construction in 41b can be analyzed as a passive rather than a middle construction for two reasons: First, although the AGENT may be omitted, it is still understood that there is a causal agent involved in the event. This is not true of a middle construction like *the stick broke*. Second, the AGENT may be expressed as an oblique. This is also not true of prototypical middles (**The stick broke by Mary*). Example 41b represents a lexical pattern, rather than a morphological or syntactic one, because there is no extra morphology, or syntactic elements added.

It is a case of isomorphism (see chapter 2) between the active and passive forms of the verb.

MORPHOLOGICAL PASSIVES are very common. Passive morphemes are sometimes derived from **PERFECT ASPECT** morphemes, **COPULAS**, or **NOMINALIZERS**. Consider the following examples from Kalam Kohistani, a Dardic language spoken in Northwestern Pakistan (Baart 1999:98):

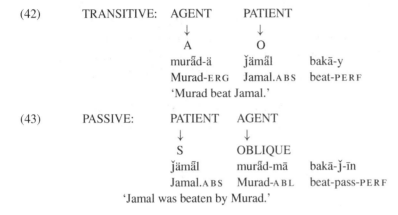

(42)   TRANSITIVE: AGENT   PATIENT
                          ↓   ↓
                          A   O
                       murãd-ä   jǎmãl   bakã-y
                       Murad-ERG   Jamal.ABS   beat-PERF
                       'Murad beat Jamal.'

(43)   PASSIVE: PATIENT   AGENT
                          ↓   ↓
                          S   OBLIQUE
                       jǎmãl   murãd-mã   bakã-ǰ-īn
                       Jamal.ABS   Murad-ABL   beat-pass-PERF
                   'Jamal was beaten by Murad.'

Example 42 illustrates a standard transitive clause in Kalam Kohistani. Example 43 illustrates a morphological passive. Notice that the verb carries a suffix -ǰ that is lacking in 42. The effect of adding this suffix is to change the argument structure of the construction. Instead of an AGENT expressed as A and PATIENT expressed as O, the passive verb is intransitive and takes a PATIENT expressed as S. If the AGENT is expressed at all, it may be mentioned in an oblique phrase, marked by the ablative postposition *mã*.

The following examples from Tariana, an Arawakan language spoken in the Vaupés river basin in Brazil and Colombia (Aikhenvald 2003:258–59), illustrate something of a hybrid morphological/analytic passive. The passive morphology on the verb consists of a "relative" prefix (a kind of nominalizer) *ka-* and a passive suffix *-kana* (examples 45 and 46):

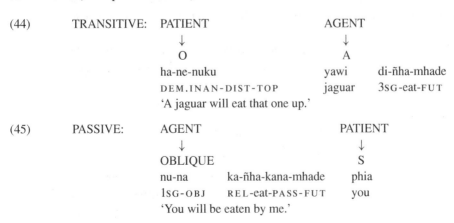

(44)   TRANSITIVE: PATIENT   AGENT
                          ↓   ↓
                          O   A
                       ha-ne-nuku   yawi   di-ñha-mhade
                       DEM.INAN-DIST-TOP   jaguar   3SG-eat-FUT
                       'A jaguar will eat that one up.'

(45)   PASSIVE: AGENT   PATIENT
                          ↓   ↓
                       OBLIQUE   S
                       nu-na   ka-ñha-kana-mhade   phia
                       1SG-OBJ   REL-eat-PASS-FUT   you
                       'You will be eaten by me.'

(46)   PASSIVE: PATIENT   AGENT
                         ↓   ↓
                         S   Ø
                      ha-ne   ka-ñha-kana-mhade   di-a
                      DEM.INAN-DIST   REL-eat-PASS-FUT   3SG-AUX
                      'It will be eaten.'

Notice that in 45 the *ka-* and *-kana* affixes are the only indication of passive voice. Therefore this can be considered a prototypical morphological passive construction. Example 46, on the other hand, contains an auxiliary *dia* after the verb meaning 'eaten.' Therefore this construction has an analytic, as well as morphological, component. According to Aikhenvald (2003:258), this auxiliary is optional.

English, and many other languages, have **ANALYTIC PASSIVES**. In English passives, a **COPULAR VERB** (*be* or *get*) plus the past participle of the active verb must be used:

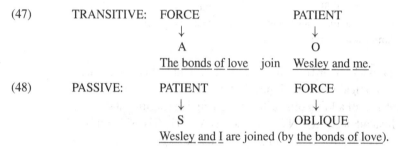

(47)   TRANSITIVE: FORCE   PATIENT
                            ↓   ↓
                            A   O
                         The bonds of love   join   Wesley and me.

(48)   PASSIVE: PATIENT   FORCE
                            ↓   ↓
                            S   OBLIQUE
                         Wesley and I are joined (by the bonds of love).

Example 48 is an analytic passive because it requires the presence of a distinct word – the copula *be* (of which *are* is one form). It is also somewhat morphological in that the verb, *join*, occurs in the **PAST PARTICIPLE** form. However, because this construction *requires* a separate auxiliary, and the past participle form appears in many other constructions, this is primarily an analytic passive. The Tariana example, on the other hand, only optionally takes an auxiliary and does involve one affix, *-kana*, that only appears in passive constructions. Therefore example 46 is primarily a morphological passive, though it has an analytic component as well.

Many languages possess more than one passive construction. For example, English has the common *be* passive (see above) and the slightly less common *get* passive:

(49) a.   I *got* well paid for it on both occasions.
     b.   We are *getting* bogged down by this textbook.
     c.   *Get* paid more interest by First National Bank!

Get passives imply that the PATIENT retains some degree of control over the event. This is evidenced by the fact that a *get* passive can be used in the imperative (example 49c). *Be* passives, on the other hand, cannot easily be used in the imperative. This is obviously due to the pragmatic fact that you can't command someone to do something they have no control over:

(50) a.   ??*Be* well paid!
    b.   ??*Be* bogged down by this textbook!

In other languages different passives may have other functional differences. For example, Yup'ik has at least three morphological passives. These are illustrated below (Reed *et al.* 1977):

(51)   TRANSITIVE: AGENT   PATIENT
                           ↓   ↓
                           A   O
                 carayag-pi-im   tuntuva-k   nere-llru-a
                 bear-real-ERG   moose-ABS   eat-PAST-3SG/3SG
                 'The real bear ate the moose.'

(52)   ADVERSATIVE PASSIVE:
         PATIENT   AGENT
            ↓   ↓
            S   OBLIQUE
         tuntuva-k   nere-sciu-llru-u-q   (carayag-mun)
         moose-ABS   eat-PASS-PAST-INTRNS-3SG bear-OBL
         'The moose was eaten (by a bear).'

(53)   ABILITATIVE PASSIVE: keme-k   ner-narq-u-q   (yug-nun)
                                  meat-ABS   eat-PASS-INTRNS-3SG   person-OBL
                                  'Meat can be eaten by people.'

(54)   NEGATIVE ABILITATIVE PASSIVE:
         tauna   ner-nait-u-q   (yug-nun)
         this.ABS   eat-PASS-INTRNS-3SG   person-OBL
         'This one cannot be eaten (by people).'

The adversative passive (example 52) expresses an event that happens to the detriment of the subject argument. In this case, being eaten is definitely something detrimental to the moose.

Japanese and a few other languages allow passive morphology to appear on semantically intransitive verbs for specific purposes. This construction is termed the **ADVERSATIVE** in Japanese grammar, though it is typologically quite different from the Yup'ik adversative passive illustrated above. Example 55b illustrates the normal morphological passive, expressed by the morpheme -*rare*:

(55)   TRANSITIVE: a. Hanako-ga   Taro-o   kabat-ta.
                              -NOM   -ACC   support-PAST
                         'Hanako supported Taro.'
         PASSIVE: b. Taro-ga   (Hanako-ni)   kaba-rare-ta.
                              -OBL   -DAT   support-PASS-PAST
                         'Taro was supported (by Hanako).'

Example 56b illustrates that with an intransitive verb -*rare* indicates that the event occurred to the detriment of the subject, and the agent of the detrimental action is expressed in an oblique case, just like the agent of a normal passive clause:

(56)   INTRANSITIVE: AGENT
                           ↓
                           S
         Tomodachi-ga   ki-ta   'His friend came.'
         friend-NOM   come-PAST

(57)   ADVERSATIVE PASSIVE: PATIENT   AGENT
                                  ↓   ↓
                                  S   OBLIQUE
         Taro-ga   tomodachi-ni   ki-rare-ta
         Taro-NOM   friend-OBL   come-PASS-PAST
    'Taro was arrived by his friend (to Taro's disadvantage).'

Many languages have a construction or constructions that can be termed **IMPERSONAL PASSIVES**. Like personal passives, impersonal passives downplay the centrality of an AGENT-like participant. However, in impersonal passives, the downplayed participant is not a specific individual. It is usually a non-identifiable, unknown and/or vague entity. Impersonal passives can sometimes be formed from semantically intransitive as well as transitive verbs. For example, in an intransitive impersonal passive clause like the German 'dancing takes place here' (ex. 58 below), the identity of the dancers is not central to the speaker's communicative goal; only the fact that dancing takes place:

(58)   IMPERSONAL PASSIVE: AGENT
                                 ↓
         Ø   Es   wird   hier   ge-tanzt.
              it   be   here   PASS-dance
              'Dancing takes place here.'

The following English examples are close functional approximations to impersonal passive constructions in languages that have them. However, the English examples are based on other clause patterns, namely an ordinary active verb with a third-person plural subject for 59a and an existential construction in 59b:

(59) a.   *They* say it can puncture the skin of a rhino.
     b.   *There* will be dancing in the streets.

Spanish uses reflexive morphology in one kind of impersonal passive:

(60)   Spanish: *Se*   caen   mucho   acá.   'They fall a lot here.'
                  REFL   fall.3PL a.lot   here

In this example, the 3PL S argument marked on the verb does not refer to any particular "they," but just "people" in general.

I know of no languages that employ specific morphology just for impersonal passives. This is not particularly surprising, as the same is almost true for personal passives as well – both morphological and analytic personal passives tend to "borrow" structures whose basic function is either: (1) perfect aspect marking, (2) copulas, or (3) patient nominalizers (past participles). Similarly, impersonal passives tend to employ morphology common to (1) reflexive/reciprocal constructions, (2) existential constructions, (3) third-person plural anaphoric devices (*they, them*), and personal passives.

Antipassives

Like passives, **ANTIPASSIVES** are valence-decreasing constructions. They downplay the centrality of one participant in a scene by downgrading the syntactic status of the verbal argument that refers to that participant. Unlike passives, however, antipassives downplay the centrality of an O argument rather than an A argument. Prototypical antipassives have the following formal characteristics:

- The A becomes an S.
- The O argument is omitted or appears in an oblique case.
- The verb becomes grammatically intransitive.

The following examples are from Yup'ik:

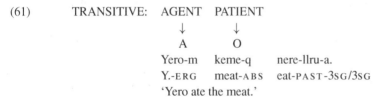

(61)   TRANSITIVE: AGENT   PATIENT
                          ↓   ↓
                          A   O
                Yero-m   keme-q   nere-llru-a.
                Y.-ERG   meat-ABS   eat-PAST-3SG/3SG
                'Yero ate the meat.'

(62)   ANTIPASSIVE: AGENT   PATIENT
                          ↓   ↓
                          S   (OBLIQUE)
                Yero-q   (kemer-meng)   nere-llru-u-q.
                Y. -ABS   meat-INST   eat-PAST-INTRNS-3SG
                'Yero ate (meat).'

In 62, the patient *kemermeng*, 'meat,' appears in the instrumental case, the verb takes the intransitive suffix *-u*, and the AGENT goes into the absolutive case.

The clearest examples of antipassives are found in morphologically ergative languages, i.e., those that have a morphologically defined absolutive case. In non-ergative languages, object demotion or omission (see below) serves essentially the same function.

Object demotion and omission

Like antipassive, **OBJECT DEMOTION** constructions downplay the centrality of a O argument. In fact, some linguists (e.g., Heath 1976) have treated object demotion and **OBJECT OMISSION** as types of antipassivization. The crucial difference, if it is necessary to draw a distinction between object demotion/omission and antipassive (e.g., if a given language has both), is that in antipassives the verb takes some specific marker of antipassivization or intransitivity, whereas in object demotion/omission no such verbal marker occurs. Consider the following examples from Bzhedukh, a Northwest Caucasian language:

(63)   TRANSITIVE: AGENT   PATIENT
                              ↓   ↓
                              A   O
                 čʔaalya-m   čʔəgʷo-ər   ya-žʷoa
                 boy-ERG   field-ABS   3SG-plows
                 'The boy plows the field.'

(64)   OBJECT DEMOTION: AGENT   PATIENT
                                   ↓   ↓
                                   S   OBLIQUE
                      čʔaalya-r   čʔəgʷo-əm   ya-žʷoa
                      boy-ABS   field-OBL   3SG-plows
                      'The boy is trying to plow the field.'

In 63 the interpretation is that the field is in fact being plowed, whereas in 64 the field may or may not actually be affected by the action of the boy. So we can say that the PATIENT is "less involved" in the activity of plowing in 64 than in 63. The only reason we would probably not want to call 64 an antipassive is that there is no special marker on the verb.

Object demotion and omission also occur in non-ergative languages. For example:

(65)   TRANSITIVE: The hunter shot the deer.

(66)   OBJECT DEMOTION: The hunter shot at the deer.

(67)   OBJECT OMISSION: The hunter shot.

As in Bzhedukh, the English object demotion construction tends to express a situation in which the PATIENT-like participant is less involved or less affected by the action of the verb than in the transitive argument structure. Similarly, object omission suggests that the identity of the PATIENT-like participant, if any, is totally irrelevant.

Object incorporation

Noun INCORPORATION is a construction in which an argument of a transitive clause becomes "attached to" or "incorporated into" the verb. Incorporation exhibits all the characteristics of compounding, namely: (1) a stress pattern characteristic of words rather than phrases, (2) possibly unusual word order, (3) morphophonemic patterns characteristic of words rather than phrases, (4) possibly special morphology, and (5) meanings that are more specific than the meanings of the individual parts.

Object **INCORPORATION** is more common than other types of noun incorporation in the world's languages. In English, A and O incorporation occur,
but neither is very productive (in these examples the abbreviation INC refers
to an incorporated element that has lost its status as an independent verbal
argument):

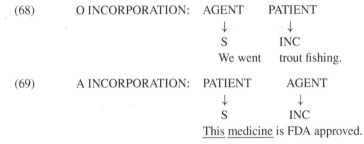

(68)   O INCORPORATION: AGENT   PATIENT
                                ↓   ↓
                                S   INC
                            We went   trout fishing.

(69)   A INCORPORATION: PATIENT   AGENT
                                ↓   ↓
                                S   INC
                        This medicine is FDA approved.

Evidence that the INC element in each of these examples is not an independent
argument of the verb includes the fact that they have none of the properties
of independent noun phrases. For example, they cannot take plural marking,
determiners, etc. (examples 70a, b). Also, they may not be promoted to subject
status in a passive (70c):

(70) a.   *We went the trout fishing.
    b.   *We went trouts fishing.
    c.   *Trout was gone fishing by us.

Incorporated forms in English are either lexicalized expressions, such as *baby
sit*, or they are severely restricted with respect to their syntactic possibilities, e.g.,
to trout fish can only be used in the progressive aspect: **I trout fished all morning*,
or **I trout fish for a living*.

Formally, object incorporation is a valence-decreasing construction when the
object ceases to function as an independent argument and becomes part of a
formally intransitive verb. Object incorporation is common in many parts of the
world, in particular in Amerindian and Siberian languages. Consider the following
examples from Chukchee:

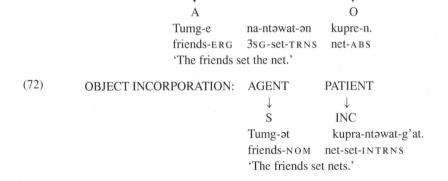

(71)   TRANSITIVE: AGENT   PATIENT
                           ↓   ↓
                           A   O
                         Tumg-e   na-ntəwat-ən   kupre-n.
                         friends-ERG   3SG-set-TRNS   net-ABS
                         'The friends set the net.'

(72)   OBJECT INCORPORATION: AGENT   PATIENT
                                       ↓   ↓
                                       S   INC
                               Tumg-ət   kupra-ntəwat-g'at.
                               friends-NOM   net-set-INTRNS
                               'The friends set nets.'

The evidence that 'net' has been incorporated in 72 is (1) there is a morpho-phonemic rule that changes the stem meaning 'net' from *kupre* into *kupra*. This rule applies within a word, but not between words. (2) The verb in 72 is formally marked as intransitive (the suffix *-g'at*). This suggests that *kupra* in this example is not an independent O argument, but rather is a part of the verb complex.

Valence-increasing constructions

Causatives

CAUSATIVE CONSTRUCTIONS are very common in the world's languages. Prototypical examples express an ordinary event or situation with the addition of a causer, i.e., an AGENT that is external to the situation itself. By "external" I mean the AGENT of a causative is not an essential part of the caused event. The event can be fully described even with no mention of the causal AGENT. For example, consider the following clause:

(73)   Calvin broke the vase.

This is a kind of causative because the AGENT (Calvin) is the causer of an event of breaking, yet the event still would be complete if the AGENT were not present on the scene:

(74)   The vase broke.

Now consider the following:

(75)   Cortez ate possum.

This clause expresses an event that has an AGENT (Cortez). However, this clause would not adequately describe an event of eating if the AGENT were left out. You don't have an event of "eating" if you don't have an eater! So 75 is not a causative – Cortez did not cause the possum to eat. We can make a causative out of 75 by adding a separate verb that expresses the idea of cause:

(76)   Montezuma made Cortez eat possum.

This is a causative because it takes the event expressed in 75 and adds an external causer, Montezuma.

The parts of a causative construction are:

- The effect: *eat possum* in example 76.
- The cause: *made* (something happen) in example 76.
- The causee (or AGENT of effect): *Cortez* in example 76.
- The causer (or AGENT of cause): *Montezuma* in example 76.

Causatives can be expressed by any of the three expression types mentioned in chapters 1 and 2: lexical, morphological, and syntactic/periphrastic/analytic. All causative constructions increase semantic valence, in that they add one participant (a causer) to a scene. Morphological causatives also increase grammatical valence, in that they add one argument (an A) to the argument structure. In the following paragraphs we will give examples and argument-structure diagrams of all three types.

LEXICAL CAUSATIVES: Most, if not all, languages have some lexical causatives. There are at least three subtypes of what we will term lexical causatives. The unifying factor behind all of these types is the fact that in each case the notion of cause is wrapped up in the lexical meaning of the verb that expresses the effect. There is no distinct morpheme or morphemes involved. The three types are:

Isomorphism (no difference between non-causative and causative verb):

(77) a.   NON-CAUSATIVE: The vase broke.
     b.   CAUSATIVE: Calvin broke the vase. (i.e., Calvin caused the vase to break.)

Weak suppletion (some idiosyncratic difference between verbs):

(78) a.   NON-CAUSATIVE: The tree fell. (verb = 'to fall')
     b.   CAUSATIVE: Bunyan felled the tree. (verb = 'to fell')

(Strong) suppletion (completely distinct verbs):

(79) a.   NON-CAUSATIVE: Inigo's father died.
     b.   CAUSATIVE: You killed Inigo's father.
           also: see/show, teach/learn, etc.

Morphological causatives. Morphological causatives involve a productive change in the form of the verb.

Turkish (Altaic) has two very productive morphological causatives. The suffix *-dür* (the vowel varies depending on the context) can be applied to virtually any intransitive verb to form a causative of that verb (Comrie 1989):

(80)   INTRANSITIVE: PATIENT
                            $\downarrow$
                            S
                         Hasan   öl-dü   'Hasan died.'
                         H.   die-PAST

In example 80, the only argument of the intransitive verb *öl* happens to be a PATIENT – dying is something that "happens to" someone, rather than something that someone "does" willingly. Therefore the basic argument structure for this verb consists of a PATIENT functioning as S. When the suffix *-dür* is added, a new argument – a causal AGENT – occurs in the argument structure. This new argument becomes the A, and the PATIENT in the intransitive structure becomes the O in the newly derived transitive construction:

(81)   CAUSATIVE: AGENT$_{cause}$ PATIENT
                         $\downarrow$ $\downarrow$
                         A   O
                       Ali   Hasan-t   öl-*dür*-dü
                         A.   H.   -ACC   die-CAUSE-PAST
                    'Ali killed Hasan.'

In this example, we have labeled the semantic role of the A argument as
AGENT$_{cause}$ (read AGENT of cause) in order to indicate that this is the argument that is added to the scene by the causative derivation (signaled by *-dür*).

To form a causative of a transitive construction, the suffix *-t* is used
(example 83):

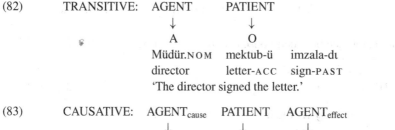

(82)   TRANSITIVE: AGENT   PATIENT
                          ↓   ↓
                          A   O
                      Müdür.NOM   mektub-ü   imzala-dı
                      director   letter-ACC sign-PAST
                      'The director signed the letter.'

(83)   CAUSATIVE: AGENT$_{cause}$ PATIENT AGENT$_{effect}$
                          ↓   ↓   ↓
                          A   O   DATIVE
                      Dişçi   mektub-ü   müdür-e   imzala-*t*-tı
                      dentist.NOM letter-ACC director-DAT sign-CAUSE-PAST
                      'The dentist made the director sign the letter.'

Notice that in 83 there are two AGENTs. This sets up a potential conflict. You
are probably familiar with situations in which two different people both thought
they were the leader of some group, committee, or government. The conflicts
that result can be pretty serious. In the case of languages, these kinds of conflicts
are usually resolved amicably. In Turkish, we see that the AGENT of effect
(AGENT$_{effect}$), in this case the director who signs the letter, takes a **DATIVE**
case marker, while the AGENT of cause takes the A role, and is marked with
the nominative case. Other languages deal with this kind of argument structure
conflict in different ways.

One noteworthy fact about morphological causatives is that they usually express
a range of meanings in addition to ordinary causation. These other notions often
include permission or enablement. Georgian exhibits one such construction (from
Comrie 1978:164):

(84)   Mama   shvil-s   ceril-s   acer-*ineb*-s.
         father son-DAT   letter-ACC write-CAUSE-3SG
         'Father makes/helps/lets his son write the letter.'

Many morphological causatives can only be used with intransitive stems (like
Turkish *-dür* above). The following examples from Central Yup'ik Eskimo illustrate a typical range of meanings often associated with morphological causative
constructions that are restricted to intransitive stems (Reed *et al.* 1977:177):

(85)   Intransitive stem   Causative stem
         tuqu-   'die'   tuqute-   'kill'
         tai-   'come'   taite-   'bring'

uita-	'stay'	uitate-	'let stay / leave alone'
tatame-	'be startled'	tamate-	'startle'
ane-	'go out'	ante-	'put outside'
itr-	'go in'	iterte-	'put in/insert'
atrar-	'go down'	atrarte-	'take down'
mayur-	'go up'	mayurte-	'put up'

You can see that the stems in the right-hand column all in some sense express the idea of 'cause to V' where V is the corresponding verb stem in the left-hand column. Yup'ik also has distinct causative suffixes that function with intransitive or transitive stems. The first of these is -*vkar*, illustrated in 86 and 87:

(86)   CAUSATIVE OF INTRANSITIVE STEM (go up):
          AGENT$_{cause}$ AGENT$_{effect}$
               ↓   ↓
               A   O
               Ø   Qetunra-ni   tage-*vkar*-aa
              (3SG)   son-ABS.HGEN   go:up-CAUSE-3SG>3SG
          'He makes/lets his own son go up.'

In this diagram you'll notice that there is an A argument, but that the A argument is not expressed with a noun or free pronoun. How do we know that this clause in fact is transitive, and that it has an A and an O argument? Why can't 86 just be an example of "subject omission" as discussed in the previous section (example 40)? Couldn't an appropriate English translation be 'His son was made to go up'? The reason this analysis is not appropriate for example 86 is that the verb is clearly marked as transitive. The suffix -*aa* indicates that a specific third-person argument (*he*) is acting upon another third-person argument (*his son*). Grammatically, there is an A argument in the clause, though there is no separate noun or pronoun that refers to it. This is very different from omission of an argument (as discussed early in this chapter).

In 87 we again see the morphological causative suffix -*vkar*, but this time it appears on a transitive stem, *nere*-, 'eat':

(87)   CAUSATIVE OF TRANSITIVE STEM (eat):
          AGENT$_{cause}$ AGENT$_{effect}$ PATIENT
               ↓   ↓   ↓
               A   OBLIQUE   O
            Arnam   irnia-mi-nun   neqerrlu-ut   nere-*vkar*-ai.
          woman-ERG   child-POS-OBL   dryfish-ABS.PL   eat-CAUSE-3SG>3PL
          'The woman makes/lets her child eat the dryfish.'

Yup'ik has yet another morphological causative, -*cet* (also -*cess*), that may appear on both intransitive and transitive stems. The choice of whether to use -*vkar* or -*cite* to express causation seems to depend on the verb stem:

(88)   CAUSATIVE OF INTRANSITIVE STEM (go):

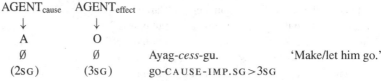

AGENT~cause~	AGENT~effect~		
↓	↓		
A	O		
Ø	Ø	Ayag-*cess*-gu.	'Make/let him go.'
(2SG)	(3SG)	go-CAUSE-IMP.SG>3SG	

In example 88, both A and O arguments are expressed on the verb, rather than with free pronouns or noun phrases. The verb ending *-gu* is a portmanteau suffix that means imperative mood, singular A acting on third-person singular O. The A is understood as second person for all imperative mood clauses. Example 89 illustrates a transitive verb stem suffixed with the same causative morpheme *-cet*. Adding *-cet* to a verb affects the argument structure in the same way as *-vkar* does – the AGENT of cause becomes the A, the PATIENT becomes the O, and the AGENT of the effect (or causee) becomes an oblique:

(89)   CAUSATIVE OF TRANSITIVE STEM (dry):

AGENT~cause~	AGENT~effect~		PATIENT
↓	↓		↓
A	OBLIQUE		O
Nukalpia-m	aana-mi-nun	kenir-*cet*-aa	kemek
young:man-ERG	mother-POS-OBL	dry-CAUSE-3SG>3SG	meat:ABS
'The young man made/let his own mother dry the meat.'			

Quechua uses the same morphological causative for both intransitive (example 91) and transitive (93) stems:

(90)   INTRANSITIVE STEM (sleep):   AGENT

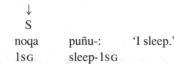

	↓	
	S	
noqa	puñu-:	'I sleep.'
1SG	sleep-1SG	

(91)   CAUSATIVE OF INTRANSITIVE STEM (sleep):

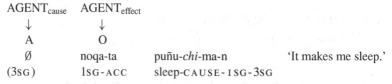

AGENT~cause~	AGENT~effect~		
↓	↓		
A	O		
Ø	noqa-ta	puñu-*chi*-ma-n	'It makes me sleep.'
(3SG)	1SG-ACC	sleep-CAUSE-1SG-3SG	

(92)   TRANSITIVE STEM (hit):

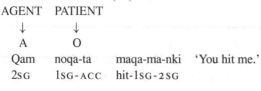

AGENT	PATIENT		
↓	↓		
A	O		
Qam	noqa-ta	maqa-ma-nki	'You hit me.'
2SG	1SG-ACC	hit-1SG-2SG	

(93)   CAUSATIVE OF TRANSITIVE STEM (hit):

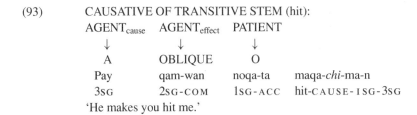

            AGENT_cause   AGENT_effect   PATIENT
                ↓   ↓   ↓
                A   OBLIQUE   O
            Pay   qam-wan   noqa-ta   maqa-*chi*-ma-n
            3SG   2SG-COM   1SG-ACC   hit-CAUSE-1SG-3SG
            'He makes you hit me.'

The above examples illustrate a very common pattern with morphological causatives of semantically transitive verbs: the causee appears in an oblique role. In Turkish and Georgian, this is the dative case, in Yup'ik it is the terminalis (a kind of directional locative abbreviated simply as OBL) and in Quechua it is the **COMITATIVE**. In all of these languages, the PATIENT of the effected situation (if there is one) remains in the accusative or, in Yupi'k, the absolutive case. Another possibility is for the causative of a transitive verb to allow two accusatives. The following examples are from Sanskrit (Comrie 1974:16):

(94) a.   Rama-m   veda-m   adhyapa-yate.
            Rama-ACC   Veda-ACC   learn-CAUSE
            'He teaches Ram the Veda.'

    b.   Batu-m   odana-m   bhoja-yati.
            boy-ACC   food-ACC   eat-CAUSE
            'He makes the boy eat food.'

In these two causative constructions, we see that the AGENT of the caused event (*Rama* in 94a and *Batu* in 94b) appears in the accusative case.

Before we leave the topic of morphological causatives, I want to present at least one example in which the causative morpheme is not a suffix. In many languages, in particular Austronesian languages, a morphological causative construction is expressed by a verbal prefix. In Cebuano (the major language of the southern Philippines), that prefix is *pa-*. It forms causatives of both intransitive (example 96) and transitive (98) clauses:

(95)   INTRANSITIVE (leave): AGENT

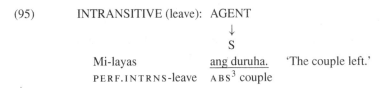

                                      ↓
                                      S
            Mi-layas   ang duruha.   'The couple left.'
            PERF.INTRNS-leave   ABS³ couple

(96)   CAUSATIVE OF INTRANSITIVE (leave):

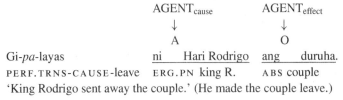

                            AGENT_cause   AGENT_effect
                                ↓   ↓
                                A   O
            Gi-*pa*-layas   ni   Hari Rodrigo   ang   duruha.
            PERF.TRNS-CAUSE-leave   ERG.PN king R.   ABS couple
            'King Rodrigo sent away the couple.' (He made the couple leave.)

(97)   TRANSITIVE (know/meet):

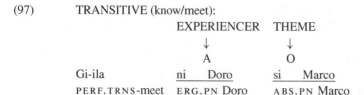

	EXPERIENCER	THEME
	↓	↓
	A	O
Gi-ila	ni Doro	si Marco
PERF.TRNS-meet	ERG.PN Doro	ABS.PN Marco

'Doro met Marco.'

(98)   CAUSATIVE OF TRANSITIVE (know/meet):

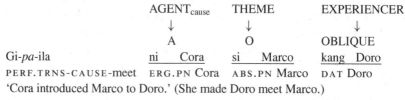

	AGENT$_{cause}$	THEME	EXPERIENCER
	↓	↓	↓
	A	O	OBLIQUE
Gi-*pa*-ila	ni Cora	si Marco	kang Doro
PERF.TRNS-CAUSE-meet	ERG.PN Cora	ABS.PN Marco	DAT Doro

'Cora introduced Marco to Doro.' (She made Doro meet Marco.)

Cebuano is a verb-initial language (see chapter 7), so in many respects it exhibits syntactic structure that is the "mirror image" of the verb-final languages illustrated above. In particular, the verbs take prefixes, and case markers come before the nouns. It is not surprising, then, that the morphological causative is a verbal prefix rather than a suffix in this language.

Analytic causatives: Most causatives in English are analytic in that they involve a separate causative verb, e.g., *make*, *cause*, *force*, *compel*, etc.

(99)   He made me do it.
         Gloucester caused Aileron to die.
         Melinda forced her hairdresser to relinquish his position.
         Marie compelled Taroo to dance with her.

In most cases analytic causatives consist of a **MATRIX VERB** (expressing the notion of CAUSE) whose complement (see chapter 10) refers to the caused event. They are not normally considered to be valence-increasing constructions, because they do not increase the grammatical valence of a single clause. Rather, they accomplish the task of adding a controlling AGENT by adding a verb (the matrix verb) that contributes its own arguments to the valence of the whole construction. Therefore you may say that analytic causatives increase the semantic valence of a scene, but not the syntactic valence of an individual clause.

Applicatives

Some languages have constructions in which a normally peripheral participant is expressed as a direct object. Here we will refer to such constructions as **APPLICATIVES**, though they are also called **ADVANCEMENTS** or **PRO-MOTIONS** to direct object. The "new" direct object is sometimes referred to as the **APPLIED** object. For verbs that already have one direct object, either

the applicative results in a three-argument (ditransitive) verb, or the original
direct object is demoted to a peripheral role, or omitted. In the latter case, the
applicative cannot be considered a valence-increasing construction, since the
original and the resulting verb have the same number of arguments. Rather, the
applicative simply ascribes a new, formerly peripheral, semantic role to the direct
object.

Yagua has an applicative that does increase valence, whether used with
a basically intransitive or transitive verb. The applicative suffix *-ta* indicates
that a locative or instrumental participant is in direct object position. The
following argument-structure diagrams illustrate a simple intransitive clause
(100), with an oblique participant ('it,' which refers to a magic flute in
the folktale in which this example occurs), and a transitive clause (101) in
which the oblique participant has become an O argument in an applicative
construction:

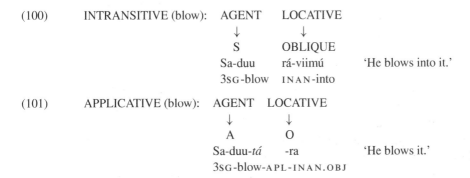

(100)   INTRANSITIVE (blow):   AGENT   LOCATIVE
                                      ↓   ↓
                                      S   OBLIQUE
                                   Sa-duu   rá-viimú   'He blows into it.'
                                   3SG-blow INAN-into

(101)   APPLICATIVE (blow):   AGENT   LOCATIVE
                                     ↓   ↓
                                     A   O
                                  Sa-duu-*tá*   -ra   'He blows it.'
                                  3SG-blow-APL-INAN.OBJ

Notice that in 101 the locative argument has become a direct object. This is
evidenced by the fact that the enclitic *-ra*, referring to inanimate direct objects,
appears on the verb. In effect the *-ta* applicative suffix changes an intransitive
verb, *duu*, into a transitive verb, *duuta*, that means something like 'to blow (into)
something.' The communicative effect of this applicative construction is to assert
that the locative participant is more directly and completely affected by the action
of blowing. In other words, the location, which is often only a peripheral part of a
communicated scene, can be brought more onto "center stage" by an applicative
construction.

The same suffix *-ta* can be used with transitive verbs, in which case it increases
valence from 2 to 3:

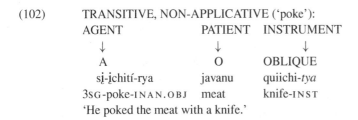

(102)   TRANSITIVE, NON-APPLICATIVE ('poke'):
          AGENT   PATIENT   INSTRUMENT
            ↓   ↓   ↓
            A   O   OBLIQUE
          sị-ịchití-rya   javanu   quiichi-*tya*
          3SG-poke-INAN.OBJ   meat   knife-INST
          'He poked the meat with a knife.'

(103)   TRANSITIVE APPLICATIVE ('poke-with'):

AGENT	INSTRUMENT	PATIENT
↓	↓	↓
A	O	?
si-ichití-*tya*-ra	quiichiy	javanu
3SG-poke-TA-INAN.OBJ	knife	meat

'He poked meat with the knife.'

In 102, the postposition that marks a nominal as having the semantic role of INSTRUMENT is the same form as the applicative verbal suffix (-*tya* and -*rya* are phonologically conditioned allomorphs of -*ta* and -*ra* respectively). Notice that in 103 the INSTRUMENT no longer takes this postposition. Rather, it has all the grammatical characteristics of direct objects – it appears directly after the verb, and the -*ra* enclitic agrees with it. The syntactic status of the PATIENT, however, is a bit muddier, hence the question mark in place of a semantico-syntactic role for this clause element in 103. In fact, this argument has *some* properties of direct objects, but not *all* of them. Neither does it clearly possess grammatical properties of oblique participants. In some frameworks, notably **RELATIONAL GRAMMAR** (Perlmutter 1980), clausal elements of this sort, those that have been "kicked out" of their normal position in the clause, are termed CHÔMEURS. This is a French word that means "unemployed." The idea is that this noun phrase has been "fired" from its position as direct object, and is now just drifting along, functioning neither as a direct object nor as an oblique.

One way of thinking about this kind of applicative construction is as a way of transforming a verb that means "poke" into a verb with the complex meaning "poke-with." Since English does not employ applicative constructions, many verbs, like *poke*, can occur in multiple argument structures with no special morphology whatsoever. In 104 the object argument is the INSTRUMENT, or THEME, of poking, rather than the PATIENT:

(104)   She poked her fork into the cabbage.

Here's another potentially helpful example. I once heard a child use an English expression that sounded very much like an applicative to me. The expression was the following:

(105)   Mommy, Billy messupped my picture!

This is not a grammatical sentence in any Standard English; however, it does have a logic to it, and the logic is similar to the logic behind applicative constructions. The particle *up* that usually follows the verb in an expression like *he messed up my picture* is incorporated into the verb in 105, thus forming a complex verb for which the picture is the direct object. The evidence that the particle has become part of the verb is that the tense marker, -*ed*, follows the particle. This isn't quite like the "poke-with" literal translation of example 103, but maybe it helps illustrate the concept of an applicative.

Some languages have more than one applicative construction, depending on the semantic role of the peripheral participant that is brought onto center stage.

Kinyarwanda, a Bantu language of Rwanda (examples from Kimenyi 1980:32ff), has at least three applicative suffixes, depending on the semantic role of the applied object. The following two examples illustrate two of these applicative suffixes, along with argument-structure diagrams. In each case the participant that fills the O position would be an oblique element if the verb did not carry the applicative suffix:

(106)   BENEFACTIVE APPLICATIVE:

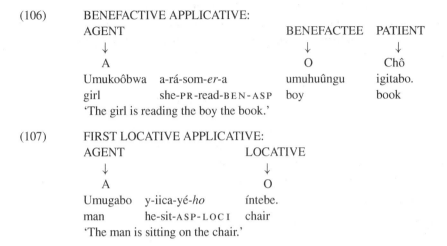

(106)
AGENT   BENEFACTEE   PATIENT
  ↓   ↓   ↓
  A   O   Chô
Umukoôbwa   a-rá-som-*er*-a   umuhuûngu   igitabo.
girl   she-PR-read-BEN-ASP   boy   book
'The girl is reading the boy the book.'

(107)   FIRST LOCATIVE APPLICATIVE:
AGENT   LOCATIVE
  ↓   ↓
  A   O
Umugabo   y-iica-yé-*ho*   íntebe.
man   he-sit-ASP-LOC I chair
'The man is sitting on the chair.'

In example 106 the suffix *-er* indicates that the first object after the verb has the semantic role of BENEFACTIVE. There are syntactic tests in Kinyarwanda that show that this normally peripheral element really is a syntactic direct object of the verb (Kimenyi 1980). However, notice that the PATIENT in 106 now has the syntactic status of Chômeur. This is because it has been "fired" from its position as direct object of the verb. In example 107, the suffix *-ho* indicates that the first object is a LOCATIVE. Again, syntactic tests show that this participant now has the syntactic status of direct object. It has been "promoted" or "advanced" from oblique to direct object position.

Example 108 illustrates two applicative suffixes occurring on the same verb. In this case the benefactive applicative suffix *-er* advances the BENEFACTEE to the O position, then the locative applicative suffix *-mo* advances the LOCATIVE participant, 'car,' to the O position. The argument structure of such multiple-layered valence-related constructions can be represented in a complex argument-structure diagram, as illustrated in 108:

(108)   BENEFACTIVE APPLICATIVE PLUS SECOND LOCATIVE APPLICATIVE:

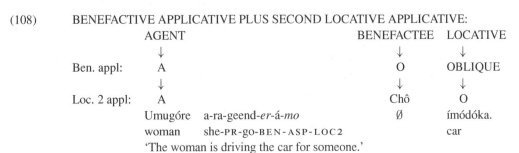

                        AGENT   BENEFACTEE   LOCATIVE
                          ↓   ↓   ↓
Ben. appl: A   O   OBLIQUE
                          ↓   ↓   ↓
Loc. 2 appl: A   Chô   O
            Umugóre   a-ra-geend-*er*-á-*mo*   Ø   ímódóka.
            woman   she-PR-go-BEN-ASP-LOC2   car
            'The woman is driving the car for someone.'

Much more complicated systems of applicatives can be found in some languages of the world. For example, in Nomatsiguenga, a Pre-Andine Maipuran Arawakan language of the Eastern Peruvian foothills, there are at least nine applicative suffixes that "advance" a variety of peripheral semantic roles to direct object position (Wise 1971).

Another interesting fact about applicatives is that the instrumental applicative is often the same as a causative. For example, in Kinyarwanda, the causative and the instrumental applicative are expressed by the same morpheme, *-iiš*. The functional basis for this parallelism is apparent in the following pair of examples (Kimenyi 1980:164):

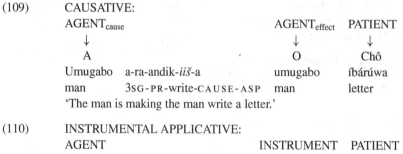

(109)   CAUSATIVE:

AGENT$_{cause}$		AGENT$_{effect}$	PATIENT
↓		↓	↓
A		O	Chô
Umugabo	a-ra-andik-*iiš*-a	umugabo	íbárúwa
man	3SG-PR-write-CAUSE-ASP	man	letter

'The man is making the man write a letter.'

(110)   INSTRUMENTAL APPLICATIVE:

AGENT		INSTRUMENT	PATIENT
↓		↓	↓
A		O	Chô
Umugabo	a-ra-andik-*iiš*-a	íkárámu	íbárúwa
man	3SG-PR-write-APL-ASP	pen	letter

'The man is writing a letter with a pen.'

The only real difference between these two clauses is the animacy of the causee. In 109 the causee is animate and therefore retains some control over the effect, whereas in 110 the "causee" is inanimate, and therefore has no control independent of the AGENT's acting upon it. In both cases a causer acts on something or someone to accomplish some action. In 109 the thing he acts on is another human, whereas in 110 the thing he acts on is a pen. Other languages in which the same kind of isomorphism obtains are Yagua (see example 102 above), Malay and Dyirbal (Croft 1990:242), and Maa (Tucker and Mpaayei 1955). In many other languages the causative and instrumental applicatives are different morphemes.

In Seko Padang, a Western Austronesian language, the suffix *-ing* has a benefactive applicative function when used with transitive verbs (111b), but a causative function when used with certain intransitive verbs (112b) (examples courtesy of Tom Laskowske):

(111)a. Yeni   mang-ala   kinanne:
         Jenny   TRNS-get   rice
         'Jenny is getting rice.'

     b. Yeni   mang-ala-*ing*   kinanne: adi-nna
         Jenny   TRNS-get-APL   rice   brother-3:POS
         'Jenny is getting rice for her brother.'

(112)a.   jambu   mi-rène'
           guava   INTRNS-fall
           'Guava fell.'

   b.   Matius   mar-rène'-*ing*   jambu
           Matthew   TRNS-fall-APL   guava
           'Matthew dropped guava.'

Example 111b cannot mean 'Jenny is making her brother get rice' even though this is a pragmatically plausible concept one may want to express. It is just part of the meaning of the -*ing* suffix that it expresses an applicative with transitive stems, and causative with intransitive stems.

Dative shift

Many languages have two alternative morphosyntactic means of expressing a trivalent situation. Trivalent situations often involve an AGENT, a THEME (an item that moves from one place to another), and a RECIPIENT, GOAL, or EXPERIENCER. Some English verbs that often express trivalent propositions are *show*, *give*, and *send*, though many other verbs can be used in a trivalent frame (see, e,g., Goldberg 1995). In an English trivalent construction the RECIPIENT, GOAL, or EXPERIENCER occurs sometimes in the dative case, marked by the preposition *to*, and sometimes with no case marker. The construction in which the RECIPIENT does not take a preposition may be termed a **DATIVE-SHIFT** construction:

(113)   'to' construction: a. Ugarte gave the exit visas *to Rick*.
         Dative shift: b. Ugarte gave *Rick* the exit visas.

Dative shift can be considered a valence-increasing construction because it is a means of bringing a participant with a peripheral semantic role, e.g. RECIPIENT, onto center stage, in addition to whatever participants may already be there.

There are two rather subtle differences between applicative and dative shift constructions: (1) applicatives involve some marking on the verb whereas dative-shift constructions do not, and (2) dative-shift constructions typically allow only RECIPIENTs, GOALs, and EXPERIENCERs to become direct objects whereas applicative constructions usually advance other roles as well, such as INSTRU-MENTs or LOCATIVEs.

It is important to note that in many languages the normal way of expressing RECIPIENTs, GOALs, and EXPERIENCERs in trivalent constructions is the same as patient-like arguments of ordinary transitive clauses. They are never expressed as a dative or oblique argument. In such languages it doesn't make sense to talk about "dative shift" because nothing "shifts"! For example, Huichol (a Uto-Aztecan language spoken in Northern Mexico) is one of these languages (Comrie 1982:99, 108). In 114a, we see an example of an ordinary transitive clause, with an A and an O. Example 114b illustrates a trivalent construction which involves an AGENT ('I'), a THEME ('the man'), and a RECIPIENT ('the girls'). Notice that the plural RECIPIENT in 114b is expressed on the verb, with the 3PL prefix *wa-*. This is the same prefix used for the THEME, 'children,' in 114a:

(114)a. Uukaraawiciizɨ tɨɨri   me–wa–zeiya.
         women   children 3PL–3PL–see
         'The women see the children.'

   b.   Nee uuki uukari ne–wa–puuzeiyastì.
         1SG girls man   1SG–3PL–show
         'I showed the man to the girls.'

The fact to note about these examples is that there exists no construction in Huichol in which the RECIPIENT of a trivalent verb is treated grammatically as an indirect object, or oblique. Dryer (1986) terms this kind of system a **PRI-MARY/SECONDARY OBJECT** system, rather than a direct/indirect object system. The grammatical relation that expresses PATIENT-like arguments of ordinary transitive clauses (such as 114a) and the RECIPIENT of trivalent clauses (such as 114b) is called the **PRIMARY OBJECT**. The other object of a trivalent clause ('man' in 114b) is called the secondary object.

Dative of interest

Some languages allow an animate participant that is associated with the event in some way to be referred to with a dative pronoun. In some traditions (e.g., Ancient Greek), this may be called the **ETHICAL DATIVE**. Spanish is one well-known language that employs a dative of interest construction:

(115)   Se   *me*   quemó   la   cena.
         REFL 1SG   burn.3SG.PAST DEF.FEM.SG   dinner
         'Dinner burned on me.' (valence = 2)

This clause might be translated 'dinner burned with respect to me,' or 'dinner burned for me.' Dative of interest constructions are distinct from applicatives and dative-shift constructions in that the argument that is added to the clause is expressed as a dative participant, i.e., as the third argument in a trivalent construction. With applicatives and dative-shift constructions, the additional argument appears as a direct object. With transitive verbs, the dative of interest sometimes indicates that the participant referred to with a dative pronoun is the *possessor* of the direct object:

(116)   *Me*   cortó el   pelo.
         1DAT   cut   the   hair
         'She cut hair (with respect to/on/for) me.' (i.e., 'She cut *my* hair.')

This last construction is sometimes called **POSSESSOR RAISING, POSSES-SOR ASCENSION**, or **EXTERNAL POSSESSION**. However, all of these terms assume that the dative participant is at some deep level a syntactic possessor of the direct object, as in the English translation equivalent. However, there is no particular reason to make this assumption for Spanish in light of the fact that Spanish has a fully productive dative of interest construction type. In fact, in most varieties of Spanish, it is possible, though a bit odd-sounding, for the object in an example like 116 to remain possessed:

(117)   Me   cortó   mi   pelo.
         1DAT   cut   my   hair
         'She cut **my** hair (on/to/for me).'

Example 117 (used for special emphatic purposes) shows that the dative pronoun is not a raised possessor, since the possessor remains in place as part of the noun phrase *mi pelo*. The *me* in this example is grammatically the same as a dative of interest, as illustrated in example 115. In other languages, however, there may be formal evidence that a genitive argument has been upgraded to status as a subject, direct object, or dative argument, as we will see in the next section.

Possessor raising or external possession

In some languages possessor raising may in fact be a distinct pattern from dative of interest or other valence-increasing constructions in the language. For example, in Chickasaw and Choctaw (Munro 1984), the possessor of the object of a clause can be expressed as the grammatical direct object of the clause. The verb then takes the dative prefix. This is sometimes termed **RAISING** because in a syntactic tree the node that dominates the possessor of the direct object is lower on the tree than the node that dominates the object itself (examples courtesy of Pam Munro):

(118)   Naahollo   i-tobi-ya   apa-li-tok.   NO POSSESSOR RAISING
         Anglo   3HGEN-bean-NS   eat-1SG-PAST
         'I ate the white man's beans.' ('White man's beans' = green peas)

In 118, *naahollo itobiya* is a noun phrase meaning literally 'white man's beans,' with *naahollo* as the possessor, and *tobi* marked with the non-subject suffix *-ya*. Here is a possible syntactic tree for example 118:

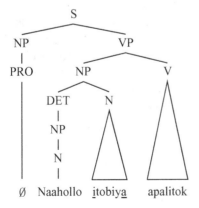

(119)   Naahollo-ya   tobi   im-apa-li-tok.   POSSESSOR RAISED
          Anglo-NS   bean   3DAT-eat-1SG-PAST
          'I ate the white man's beans/green peas.'

Notice that in 119 the possessor, *Naahollo*, takes the *-ya* suffix. Also *tobi*, 'beans,' is now without the HGEN prefix, showing that it is no longer the head of a possessed noun phrase. This is evidence that *naahollo* is no longer a constituent of the NP headed by *tobi*; rather it has been "raised" to the level of the VP, and has become a syntactic argument of the verb:

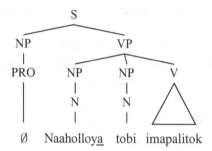

In 119, the verb now takes the dative prefix. If this were a dative of interest construction comparable to 115 above in Spanish, one would expect that it could be interpreted to mean 'I ate beans for the white man.' However, this meaning is not possible. The noun phrase meaning 'white man's beans' is an idiomatic expression that means 'green peas,' even when the possessor is raised to direct object status, as in 119. The fact that this is still the only possible meaning indicates that *naahollo* is still semantically a possessor. Munro (1984) includes additional arguments that show that possessor raising in Chickasaw and Choctaw must be distinct from a more generic dative-of-interest construction.

Combinations of valence-related constructions

We have already seen at least one example of a clause in which two distinct valence-related constructions interact. This was the example of the "double applicative" in Kinyarwanda, illustrated in 108. Occasionally, a language will allow other combinations of valence-related constructions to occur. For example, imagine a language (we'll call it "Morpho-English") that happens to have the same vocabulary as Real English, but employs a morphological causative suffix, *-cause*, and a morphological passive suffix, *-pass*. In this language, a morphological causative construction creates a grammatically transitive clause by adding a causal AGENT:

HYPOTHETICAL "MORPHO-ENGLISH" EXAMPLES:

(120)   You laugh-cause-d me.   'You made me laugh.'

Then, a passive construction may take that same grammatically transitive clause and make it intransitive again by demoting the causal AGENT to oblique status.

(121)   I laugh-cause-pass-ed (by you).   'I was made to laugh (by you).'

Or, a causative construction like 120 may itself be causativized, creating a trivalent "double causative" clause:

(122)   He laugh-cause-cause-d me to you.
         'He made you make me laugh.'

Of course, in Real English, only analytic causative and passive constructions exist. Nevertheless, the Real English translations of these Morpho-English examples show that multiple instances of valence-related constructions, such as causatives and passives, are logically possible even in highly analytic languages. In this section, we will briefly illustrate one way to represent structures that combine valence-related constructions.

Consider the following data from Ebembe, a Bantu language spoken in Central Africa. The first example is glossed for you (examples courtesy of Myra Adamson):

1.	A-toc-ile.	'He/she asked.'
	3SG-ask-PAST	
2.	Abatocile bana.	'He asked the children.'
3.	Twabatocile bana.	'We asked the children.'
4.	Twamtocile Atondo.	'We asked Atondo.'
5.	Twamtocile Atondo na bana.	'We asked Atondo for the children.'
6.	Twabatocilile bana Atondo.	'We asked Atondo for the children.'
7.	Twatocanile.	'We asked each other.'
8.	Twatocanile na bana.	'We asked each other for the children.'
9.	Twabatocanilile bana.	'We asked each other for the children.'

Since you have gotten this far through this book, you should already be familiar with how clauses in Bantu languages tend to be put together. You have seen several examples and problems in Swahili, Kinyarwanda, and maybe some others. As you go through these data you notice that there are prefixes referring to S, A, and O, and a past-tense suffix. The verb structure of examples 1 through 5 can be represented most insightfully in a position-class diagram (see chapter 2) as follows:

S/A	O	ROOT	TENSE
a- 3SG twa- 1PL	m- 3SG ba- 3PL	toc 'ask'	-ile PAST

So far so good. But what is happening in 6 through 9? Examples 5 and 6 seem to have the same meaning, yet there are some structural differences between the two Ebembe clauses. In particular, in 5 there is a prefix *m-* in the O position that must refer to *Atondo* (a man's name). However, in 6 the prefix *ba-*, referring to a third-person plural argument, appears in the O position. This must refer to *bana*, 'children.' We also notice that in 5 the name *Atondo* immediately follows the verb, while *bana* follows what seems like a preposition, *na*. This *na* disappears in 6, and *bana* appears in the position immediately following the verb. Finally, there is an extra syllable, *-il*, in the verb, yet to be accounted for in our position-class diagram. What can we conclude from these facts? It seems that *Atondo* is the object and *bana* is an oblique in example 5, whereas in 6 *bana* is the object, and *Atondo* has been "kicked out" of his position as object, and so must have some other grammatical status. This hypothesis can be represented using our famous argument-structure diagrams as follows:

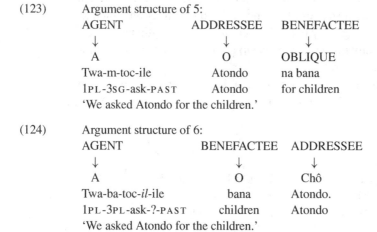

(123)   Argument structure of 5:

AGENT	ADDRESSEE	BENEFACTEE
↓	↓	↓
A	O	OBLIQUE
Twa-m-toc-ile	Atondo	na bana
1PL-3SG-ask-PAST	Atondo	for children

'We asked Atondo for the children.'

(124)   Argument structure of 6:

AGENT	BENEFACTEE	ADDRESSEE
↓	↓	↓
A	O	Chô
Twa-ba-toc-*il*-ile	bana	Atondo.
1PL-3PL-ask-?-PAST	children	Atondo

'We asked Atondo for the children.'

Since examples 5 and 6 "mean the same thing,"[4] the same set of semantic roles must be "on stage" in both clauses – at the level of semantic roles they describe the same scene. The differences seems to be in how those semantic roles are expressed grammatically – which one or ones are on "center stage" and which are peripheral.

We see that example 6 has "perspectivized" or "advanced" or "upgraded" an oblique participant to object status. What valence-related construction does that? Correct – applicative! In particular, this applicative advances a BENEFACTEE. It may advance other semantic roles as well, but the only evidence we have indicates that it advances BENEFACTEES. The extra morpheme *-il* in the verb is what signals that the clause has a special argument structure. Without *-il* in 6, hearers would probably assume that the children were the ADDRESSEE of the question, rather than the BENEFACTEE. Therefore we can tentatively gloss *-il* as BENEFACTIVE APPLICATIVE, or BEN.APL.

Now let's go on to 7. In this example, there seems to be only one grammatical argument – there is no prefix in the O position, and there is no noun phrase following the verb. Yet the scene involves two participants that function equally as A and O. What kind of construction is this? Yes, reciprocal! Here is the argument-structure diagram for 7, according to the reciprocal hypothesis:

(125)   Argument structure of 7:   AGENT   ADDRESSEE

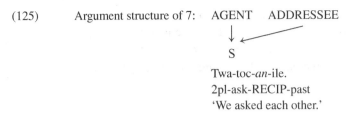

                                           S

                   Twa-toc-*an*-ile.
                   2pl-ask-RECIP-past
                   'We asked each other.'

The only structural clue that this clause is a reciprocal is the suffix -*an* in the verb. Without this -*an*, the clause would probably mean 'We asked,' with simply no reference to the addressee of the act of asking. Therefore, R E C I P is a reasonable gloss for the verb suffix -*an*.

Now let us go on to 8. This example is the same as 7, except that it has an additional oblique argument referring to a BENEFACTEE, the children. But what happens in 9? It has the "same meaning" as 8 but seems to have a different argument structure. The BENEFACTEE is no longer an oblique, but has been "advanced" to object status, as evidenced by the *ba-* object prefix on the verb. Further, perhaps most interestingly, there are two, count 'em *two*, valence-related suffixes on the verb, -*an* and -*il*. So, example 9 involves two "layers" of valence-adjusting constructions – a reciprocal and an applicative. Here is one way of representing this kind of argument structure:

(126)   Argument-structure diagram for example 9:

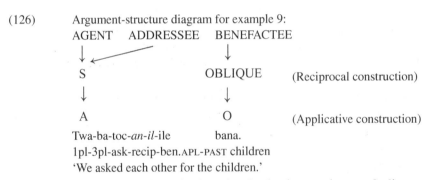

                   Twa-ba-toc-*an-il*-ile   bana.
                   1pl-3pl-ask-recip-ben.APL-PAST children
                   'We asked each other for the children.'

So we see that example 9 can be thought of as having two layers of adjustments to its argument structure. It "starts out" as a transitive clause ('we ask someone'), then becomes intransitive by the reciprocal construction ('we ask each other'), and finally becomes transitive again by the applicative construction ('we ask each other for the children').

Conceptual outline of chapter 9

I.   Part of the grammatical knowledge that speakers have about their languages consists of morphosyntactic patterns for adjusting the relationships between semantic roles and grammatical relations. These patterns are sometimes referred to as "voice" or "valence-adjusting" constructions, and they allow speakers to present their messages from various "perspectives." Valence-adjusting constructions allow speakers to "perspectivize" (bring into perspective or remove from perspective) different participants in the scene evoked by a verb.

II. Valence adjustments (increasing, decreasing, or rearranging) can be accomplished:
- lexically
- morphologically
- syntactically (analytically or periphrastically)

III. Valence-decreasing constructions include:
- reflexives and reciprocals – these often employ the same morphosyntactic patterns.
- middles
- subject omission – a way of deperspectivizing a controller, usually available only in morphologically ergative languages.
- passives – another way of deperspectivizing a controller.
  - personal passives
  - impersonal passives
  - adversative passives
- antipassives – these and object demotion, object omission, and object incorporation are ways of downplaying, or "deperspectivizing," the O argument of a grammatically transitive clause. Antipassives are the logical "mirror image" of passive constructions. They are most common in morphologically ergative languages.
- object demotion and omission – these differ from antipassives in that they do not exhibit special marking on the verb.
- object incorporation – a construction that deperspectivizes an O argument by making it a part of the verb.

IV. Valence-increasing constructions include:
- causatives – these increase valence by adding a causer to the scene evoked by the verb.
- applicatives – these increase valence by adding an O argument to the scene evoked by the verb. They register this change by marking the verb with a special applicative morpheme.
- dative shift – these express a recipient as a core argument, and do not involve special marking on the verb.
- dative of interest – these make some other participant into a core argument, without requiring special morphology on the verb.
- possessor raising or external possession – these perspectivize a possessor of one of the clausal arguments by making it a core argument of the verb.

V. Languages may allow more than one valence-adjusting construction to apply to the same clause. In this case, valence-adjusting constructions can be thought of as applying in "layers."

Exercise 9.1: argument-structure diagrams

Tom Payne

A.   Provide argument-structure diagrams for the following examples provided earlier in this chapter (be sure to diagram the language of the example, and not the English free translations):

1. Example 1b: These cookies were baked by Orna.
2. Example 11c: Tú te mordiste.   'You bit yourself.'
3. Example 16:   Она поднимает себя.   'She lifts herself.'
4. Example 22:   sikakoangi   'They called each other.'
5. Example 34:   This soup eats like a meal.
6. Example 41b: kínim bàra tíbi mùsó bòlo.   'The rice was cooked by the woman.'
7. Example 84:   Mama shvils cerils acerinebs.   'Father makes/helps/lets his son write the letter.'
8. Example 105:   Mommy, Billy messupped my picture!

B.   Find an example of one each of the following constructions in an English newsmagazine or newspaper. Provide an argument-structure diagram for each one:

1. A reciprocal construction.
2. A causative construction.
3. A passive construction.
4. An object omission, object demotion, or object incorporation construction.

Exercise 9.2: English valence-decreasing constructions

Tom Payne

Each of the following pairs of English clauses contains an intransitive (INTR) clause which may or may not be construed as a valence-decreased version of the transitive (TR) clause in the pair. Your tasks are:

A.   Indicate which valence-decreasing construction, as discussed in this chapter, is represented by the intransitive member of the pair.

B.   Indicate whether the intransitive member of the pair can be construed as a valence-decreased version of the transitive member or not ("Yes" or "no" are fine answers).

C.   Indicate the kind of expression involved in this construction (lexical, morphological, or analytic/periphrastic). Occasionally more than one kind of strategy is used. Indicate at least the main strategy.

TR: Marsha and Akim hugged themselves.   A:
INTR: Marsha and Akim hugged.   B:
                                             C:

TR:	A matatu ran over Dedan.	A: *passive*
INTR:	Dedan got run over.	B:
		C:

TR:	Akim burned dinner.	A:
INTR:	Dinner burned.	B:
		C:

TR:	Akim and Michelle kicked each other.	A:
INTR:	Akim and Michelle kicked.	B:
		C:

TR:	We hunted impala.	A:
INTR:	We went impala hunting.	B:
		C:

TR:	Bildad escaped Lodwar Prison.	A:
INTR:	Bildad escaped.	B:
		C:

TR:	We finished the assignment.	A:
INTR:	We were finished by the assignment.	B:
		C:

Exercise 9.3: Yagua #1

Tom Payne

1. Sarííy.   'She shouts.'
2. Riryííy.   'They (3 or more) shout.'
3. Naadarííy.   'They (2) shout.'
4. Sasuutaríy.   'She washes them (3 or more).'
5. Sasuutára.   'She washes it.'
6. Richuutaníí.   'They (3 or more) wash her.'
7. Sasuutaníí.   'She washes her.'
8. Sasuutáyu.   'She washes herself.'
9. Richuutáyu.   'They wash each other.'
                  or 'They wash themselves.'

A. Describe the system for organizing grammatical relations that is exhibited in these data. Give evidence.

B. What is the function or are the functions of -*yu* in Yagua? Again, give evidence for your claims.

C. State all morphophonemic rules that apply in these data.

Exercise 9.4: Yagua #2

Tom Payne

This is a continuation of exercise 9.3. Be sure to take your solution to 9.2 into account as you consider the following additional data from Yagua.

Note: The subscripts i, j, and k in the free translations indicate reference relationships. Expressions with the same subscript are coreferential, while those with different subscripts must be non-coreferential.

10.	Rooríy sámirya.	'The house is good.'
11.	Sarooríy sámirya.	'Her house is good.'
12.	Riryooríy sámirya.	'Their house is good.'
13.	Sasuuta vaturára	'The girl washes it.'
14.	Sasuuta vaturaníí	'The girl washes her.'
15.	Sasuuta vaturáyu	'The girl washes herself.'
16.	Sasuuta vatura roorimyuníí	'The girl$_i$ washes her$_j$ in the house.'
17.	Sasuuta vatura roorimyúyu	'The girl washes herself in the house.'
18.	Sasuuta roorimyúyu	'She washes herself in the house.'
19.	Sasuuta saroorimyuníí	'She$_i$ washes her$_j$ in her$_k$ house.'
20.	Sasuuta saroorimyúyu	'She$_i$ washes her$_j$ in her$_j$ house.' *or*
		'She$_i$ washes herself$_i$ in her$_j$ house.'
21.	Roorimyú sasuutára.	'In the house, she washes it.'
22.	Saroorimyú sasuutáyu	'In her$_i$ house, she$_j$ washes herself$_j$,' *or*
		'In her$_i$ house, she$_j$ washes her$_i$.'
23.	Saroorimyú sasuutaníí	'In her$_i$ house, she$_j$ washes her$_k$.'

A.   What additional function or functions do we see -*yu* serving in these data? Give evidence.

B.   Can we say that -*yu* always indicates a decrease in syntactic valence in Yagua? Why or why not?

Exercise 9.5: Dyirbal

From Dixon (1972, 1994)

1.	ŋuma banagan^{y}u yabugu	'Father returned to mother.'
2.	yabu banagan^{y}u	'Mother returned.'
3.	ŋana banagan^{y}u ŋumangu	'We all returned to father.'
4.	n^{y}urra banagan^{y}u	'You all returned.'
5.	n^{y}urra ŋanana buran	'You all saw us.'
6.	ŋana n^{y}urrana buran	'We all saw you all.'
7.	yabu ŋumaŋgu buran	'Father saw mother.'
8.	ŋuma yabuŋgu buran	'Mother saw father.'
9.	n^{y}urrana yabuŋgu buran	'Mother saw you all.'
10.	ŋanana ŋumaŋgu buran	'Father saw us.'
11.	ŋana buralŋan^{y}u ŋumangu	. . . 'we all saw father.'
12.	n^{y}urra buralŋan^{y}u yabugu	. . . 'you all saw mother.'
13.	yabu buralŋan^{y}u ŋumangu	. . . 'mother saw father.'
14.	ŋuma buralŋan^{y}u yabugu	. . . 'father saw mother.'

Note: Examples like 11 through 14 are generally used only in conjunction with other clauses, as reflected by the three dots. However, they are fully grammatical on their own.

A.   Describe the system for organizing grammatical relations employed in Dyirbal.

B.   What valence-decreasing construction type or types do you see operating in these data? Give evidence for your claims.

Exercise 9.6: Evenki

From Nedjalkov (1997)

A.   Where is Evenki spoken? How many speakers are there?

B.   In the following examples, several morphemes are glossed with capital letters rather than meaningful glosses. Please provide reasonable glosses for each of these morphemes, and give evidence for your answer.

Morphemes: -me, -pken, -va, -v, -ve and -ki.

C.   What type of valence-adjusting construction is operating in these data? Please be specific (give the conceptual category, and the expression type involved):

1. a. Asatkan   suru-re-n.   'The girl went away.'
                  go.away-past-3SG

   b. Atyrkan   asatkan-me   suru-pken-e-n.
                  -ME   -PKEN-past-3SG
      'The old woman made the girl go away.'

2. a. Beje   emeren.   'The man came.'
   b. Beje   moo-l-va   eme-v-re-n.   'The man brought the trees.'
                  tree-PL-VA   -V

3. a. Tyge   d'alup-ta-n.   'The cup filled.'
                  become.full-past-3SG

   b. Asatkan   tyge-ve   d'alup-ki-ra-n.   'The girl filled the cup.'
                  -VE   -KI-PAST-3SG

Exercise 9.7: Ilokano

Carl Rubino

1. Agsursuratka.   'You are writing.'
2. Agsursurat.   'He is writing.'
3. Agbuybuyaak.   'I am watching.'
4. *Sinurat iti ubing ti surat.   ——
5. Sinurat ti ubing ti surat.   'The child wrote the letter.'
6. Nagsuratak iti simbaan.   'I wrote in church.'
7. Aggatgatangak.   'I am shopping.'
8. Linutok ti saba.   'I cooked the banana.'
9. Iniwana ti saba.   'He sliced the banana.'

10. Nagiwa iti saba.	'He sliced a banana.'
11. Binuyana ti pallot iti minuyongan.	'He watched the cockfight in the garden.'
12. Pinataymo ti nalukmeg a kalding?	'Did you kill the fat goat?'
13. Sursuraten ti nalukmeg ti sarsuela.	'The fat one is writing the opera.'
14. Ginatangmo ti kalding?	'Did you buy the goat?'
15. Nagbuyaka iti pallot iti balay?	'Did you watch a cockfight in the house?'
16. Aglaglagtoka.	'You are jumping.'
17. Nagsuratka iti daniw.	'You wrote a poem.'
18. Sursuratek ti daniw.	'I am writing the poem.'
19. Sinuratko ti daniw.	'I wrote the poem.'
20. ————	'I wrote a poem.'
21. Naglutoka?	'Did you cook?'
22. Ginatangko.	'I bought it.'
23. Naglagto ti kalding.	'The goat jumped.'
24. ————	'The goat is jumping.'
25. Gatangek ti bagas.	'I buy/will buy the rice.'
26. *Gatangek iti bagas.	————
27. Aglutluto ti adipen iti kalding.	'The slave is cooking a goat.'
28. *Aglutluto ti adipen ti kalding.	
29. Ginatang ti adipen ti tulbek.	'The slave bought the key.'
30. Naggatang ti adipen iti bagas.	'The slave bought rice.'

A.   Fill in the probable Ilokano clauses in 20 and 24.
B.   List and gloss all the verb stems that occur in these data.
C.   List and give examples of all the morphological patterns that you see in these data.
D.   What valence-decreasing construction is evident in these data? Give evidence for your claims.

Exercise 9.8: Samoan III

Langacker (1972)

1. E faʻa paʻu e faifeʻau le niu.	'The missionaries fell the coconut palm.'
2. ʻUa puʻe e le fafine le pusi.	'The woman caught the cat.'
3. E faʻa papaʻu e le faifeʻau niu.	'The missionary fells the coconut palms.'
4. E puʻe upega Siaosi.	'The nets catch George.'
5. ʻUa paʻu le pusi.	'The cat fell.'
6. ʻUa papaʻu faifeʻau	'The missionaries fell.'
7. ʻUa puʻe le upega le faifeʻau.	'The net caught the missionary.'
8. E paʻu le upega.	————
9. ʻUa faʻa paʻu e Malia le laʻau.	'Mary felled the tree.'
10. ʻUa puʻe e Siaosi le pusi i le upega.	'George caught the cat with the net.'
11. ʻUa faʻa puʻe e Malia le pusi le upega.	'Mary caught the cat with the net.'
12. E puʻe e le faifeʻau le pusi i upega.	————

A.   Fill in the probable translations for 8 and 12.

B.   What valence-increasing construction or constructions do you see
          operating in these data? Give all the evidence for your claims.

Exercise 9.9: Tanglapui 1

Mark Donohue and Carl Rubino

This problem is based primarily on the Naumang variety of Tanglapui, which is
spoken in the villages of Kobra and Naumang in the eastern highlands of Alor, in
eastern Indonesia. Supplementary data are from the Lantoka dialect.

A.   List and gloss all of the morphemes in the following data.
B.   In Tanglapui transitive clauses, how can you tell who is acting upon
          whom? In other words, how are A and O expressed? Describe how
          the system works and give the evidence.
C.   Is there any evidence as to whether the Tanglapui system for organiz-
          ing grammatical relations is basically nominative/accusative or erga-
          tive/absolutive? If so, what is this evidence?

1.	Yaŋanababa.	'You hit me.'
2.	Toby ŋagadia.	'I saw Toby.'
3.	*Toby ŋaganababa.	'I hit Toby.'
4.	Lena ŋagababa.	'I hit Lena.'
5.	*Yaŋababa.	('You hit me.')
6.	ŋayasɨlale.	'I looked for you.'
7.	Toby Lena gasɨlale.	'Toby looked for Lena.'
8.	Toby gaŋanasɨlale.	'Toby looked for me.'
9.	Kris Toby ganababa.	'Toby hit Kris.'
10.	Gamɨti.	'She sat.'
11.	*Kris gayasɨlale.	('Kris looked for you.')
12.	Gerson gayanababa.	'Gerson hit you.'
13.	Toby yagadia.	'You saw Toby.'
14.	*gaŋababa.	('He hit me.')
15.	Lena Kris gadia.	'Lena saw Kris.'
16.	Fanus Lena ganababa.	'Lena hit Stephanus.'
17.	Toby ŋagababa.	'I hit Toby.'
18.	Fanus suba gadia.	'Stephanus saw the house.'
19.	Yave.	'You left.'
20.	*yaganababa.	('You hit her.')
21.	Kris Lena ganadia.	'Lena saw Kris.'
22.	Kris Toby gababa.	'Kris hit Toby.'
23.	Yanduamɨti.	'Y'all sat.'
24.	ŋamɨti.	'I sat.'
25.	ŋayanduababa.	'I hit y'all.'
26.	*Yanduaŋanababa.	('Y'all hit me.')
27.	*Yanduagababa.	('Y'all hit him.')
28.	Yanduaŋababa.	'Y'all hit me.'
29.	Yanduaganababa.	'Y'all hit him.'

Exercise 9.10: Bàsàa

Madeleine Ngo Ndjeyiha and Tom Payne

Bàsàa is a Bantu language spoken in Central and Littoral Provinces of Cameroon, in Central Africa. The following are several causative constructions in this language.

A.   For each example, indicate which type of causative it is: lexical, mor-
        phological, or analytic.
B.   Draw argument-structure diagrams for examples 1 through 5.

1. Mela   à   bi-nɔ̄l   ǹ-lom.   'Mela killed her husband.'
   M.   she   PAST-kill   CL1-husband

2. M-àŋgɛ   à   ŋ-kî-s   ma-towà.   'The child starts the car.'
   CL1-child she   PR-start-CAUSE   CL6-car

3. M-àlêt   à   bi-kɔ̀ŋl-àhà   6a-udu   bi-kay.
   CL1-teacher she   PAST-peel-CAUSE   CL2-students   CL8-vegetables
   'The teacher got the children to peel vegetables.'

4. M-ùdàa   à   bi-j-àhà   m-an   bi-kay.
   CL1-woman   she   PAST-eat-CAUSE   CL1-baby   CL8-vegetables
   'The woman made the baby eat vegetables.'

5. M-ùdàa   à   bi-jɛ-s   m-an   bi-kay.
   CL1-woman   she   PAST-eat-CAUSE   CL1-baby   CL8-vegetables
   'The woman fed the baby vegetables.'

6. M-àlêt   à   bi-ànɛ   6a-udu   i   sāl   wɔ̄m.
   CL1-teacher she   PAST-require   CL2-students to   clear   field
   'The teacher required the students to clear the field.'

7. M-àlêt   à   bi-ànɛ   6a-udu   le   6a   sāl   wɔ̄m.
   CL1-teacher she   PAST-require   CL2-students that   they   clear   field
   'The teacher asked the students to clear the field.'

Exercise 9.11: Swahili, Safi dialect, part 3

David Perlmutter, Mary Rhodes, and Paul Thomas

(This exercise is a continuation of exercises 8.5 and 8.6. In answering the questions below, be sure to keep the data and your answers to exercises 8.5 and 8.6 in mind.)

The data below contain both active and passive clauses. Part of your task is to determine which of the grammatical, untranslated clauses are passive, and which are active:

31. Mtoto alikivunja kikombe.   'The child broke the cup.'
32. Mtoto alivunja kikombe.   'The child broke a cup.'
33. Kikombe kilivunjwa (na mtoto).

34. *Kikombe alivunjwa (na mtoto).
35. *Kikombe kilivunja (na mtoto).
36. Wageni wanampenda mtoto.
37. Mtoto anapendwa (na wageni).
38. *Mtoto anawapendwa . . .
39. Mtoto alivivunja vikombe.
40. Vikombe vilivunjwa (na mtoto).
41. Watoto waliwaona wageni.
42. Wageni walionwa (na watoto).
43. Alivunja vikombe.
44. Vikombe vilivunjwa.

A. Translate all of the grammatical clauses in these data into English (you will need your answers to exercises 8.5 and 8.6).

B. What kind of passive construction does Swahili employ? State the rule or rules for passive formation.

Exercise 9.12: Samoan IV

Langacker (1972)

This is a continuation of exercise 9.8. You will need to do exercise 9.8 before you attempt this exercise.

13. E sogi e le tama le ufi i le to'i.   'The boy cuts the yam with the axe.'
14. E sogi e le teine le ufi.   'The girl cuts the yam.'
15. E pa'u le to'i.   'The axe falls.'
16. E fa'a pa'u e le tama le to'i.   'The boy drops the axe.'
17. E pa'u le tama.   'The boy falls.'
18. E malamalama le teine.   'The girl knows.'
19. E malamalama e le teine le uiga.   'The girl learns the meaning.'
20. E malamalama le teine i le uiga.   'The girl knows the meaning.'
21. E mana'o e le tama le to'i.   'The boy covets the axe.' (i.e. he wants it badly enough that he might steal it).
22. E mana'o le tama i le to'i.   'The boy wants the axe.' (i.e. he would like to have it, but not very intensely).
23. *E fa'a pa'u le tama i le to'i.

A. What *grammatical relations* and *semantic roles* do each of the following case markers express? e, i and Ø (zero)
B. What valence-increasing construction or constructions do we see functioning in these data? Give the evidence, with example numbers.
C. What valence-decreasing construction or constructions do we see functioning in these data? Give the evidence, with example numbers.
D. Explain why example 11 is ungrammatical.

Exercise 9.13: Archi

Alexandr Kibrik. Adapted by Tom Payne
Archi is one of twenty-five languages spoken in Daghestan, a semi-autonomous
region within the Russian Federation. The following are some Archi sentences
and their English translations:

1. Diya verkurshi vi.	'The father is falling down.'
2. Holn h'oti irkkurshi bi.	'The cow is seeking the grass.'
3. Boshor baba dirkkurshi vi.	'The man is seeking the aunt.'
4. Shusha erkurshi i.	'The bottle is falling down.'
5. Holn borcirshi bi.	'The cow is standing.'
6. Diyamu buva dark'arshi di.	'The mother is left by the father.'
7. Buvamu dogi birkkurshi bi.	'The donkey is sought by the mother.'
8. Dadamu h'oti irkkurshi i.	'The grass is sought by the uncle.'
9. Lo orcirshi i.	'The child is standing.'

A.   Translate the following Archi sentences into English:

    10. Lo holn birkkurshi vi.
    11. Diya boshor vark'arshi vi.

B.   Translate the following English sentences into Archi:

    12. The uncle is sought by the aunt.
    13. The donkey is falling down.
    14. The mother is leaving the father.

C.   List and gloss all the morphemes in these data.
D.   What constituent orders of Archi are evident in these data?

Exercise 9.14: Maa

Doris Payne and Leonard Kotikash
Maa is a language spoken by about 400,000 people in East Africa, mostly in
Kenya and Tanzania.
    Here are some clauses in Maa, followed by the English translations in random
order. Indicate which translation goes with each Maa clause by placing the letter of the correct translation in the space provided. Then answer the questions
below:

    1. éósh ɔlmʊraní ɔlásʊráí   —————
    2. áadɔl ɔlásʊráí   —————
    3. éló ɔlásʊráí   —————
    4. áaósh ɔlmʊraní   —————
    5. ídɔl ɔlmʊránì   —————
    6. íóshokí ɔlmʊránì ɔlásʊráì   —————
    7. ádúŋokí ɔlmʊránì ɔlcɛtá   —————

8. ádúŋ ɔlcɛtá   _____

9. áaduŋokí ɔlmʊraní ɔlcɛtá   _____

10. áadúŋ ɔlmʊraní   _____

11. édúŋ ɔlmʊraní   _____

12. ɛ́ípak ɔlmʊraní   _____

13. éló ɔlmʊraní   _____

14. áípák   _____

15. íló   _____

English translations in random order:

    a. 'The warrior cuts me.'

    b. 'The warrior dances (before war).'

    c. 'The warrior cuts the tree for me.'

    d. 'The warrior cuts it.'

    e. 'You go.'

    f. 'The warrior goes.'

    g. 'The snake goes.'

    h. 'I cut the tree for the warrior.'

    i. 'The warrior hits me.'

    j. 'You see the warrior.'

    k. 'The warrior hits the snake.'

    l. 'The snake sees me.'

    m. 'You hit the snake for the warrior.'

    n. 'I cut the tree.'

    o. 'I dance (before war).'

A.   How are grammatical relations expressed in Maa? Give the evidence for all your claims.

B.   What is a good gloss for the morpheme *-okí*?

Notes

1. Van Valin and LaPolla (1997:392ff.) use the term "lexical reflexive" quite differently than we will be using it in this text. The use of the term here is consistent with the general three-way distinction between lexical, morphological, and syntactic expression types that is a major theme of the present book, as well as much work in descriptive linguistics in general. As all students who go on in linguistics eventually discover, linguistic terminology is constantly changing, and there are many terms and concepts that are used in different ways by different linguists.

2. Some linguists argue that Spanish morphological reflexives are grammatically transitive, partly because the first- and second-person reflexive proclitics are the same as the first- and second-person object proclitics. This makes it seem like these proclitics are referring to a syntactic direct object, in which case these clauses would be grammatically transitive. However, there are also arguments for treating morphological reflexives in Spanish as grammatically intransitive. Briefly: (1) the third-person proclitic, *se*, is not the same as the third-person object proclitics (*lo, la, los, las, le, les*), and it does not vary for number. (2) There are many clearly grammatically intransitive constructions

in Spanish that employ the same set of proclitics as the reflexives do. For example, the verb *caerse* "fall by accident" only occurs in intransitive frames, and takes a harmonic "reflexive" proclitic: *Me cayí* 'I fell (by accident),' *te cayiste* 'you fell (by accident),' and *se cayó* 'he/she/it fell (by accident).' The fact is that morphological reflexives in Spanish have a lot of syntactic commonalities with prototypical intransitive clauses, even though they have some features of transitive clauses as well. This is another illustration of how linguistic categories are not always clear-cut but blend into one another in a continuous scale. For the purposes of this discussion, we will continue to treat Spanish morphological reflexives as intransitives, though students should be aware of other possible analyses.

3. The ergative/absolutive analysis of Philippine languages in general and Cebuano in particular is controversial. However, the controversy does not affect the discussion in this section.

10 Multi-clause constructions

In every language there exist different ways of combining basic clauses to form more complex structures. In this chapter we will discuss several construction types that involve combinations of clauses.

Most of the constructions described in this chapter involve two clauses – one INDEPENDENT clause and one or more DEPENDENT clauses. An independent clause is one that is fully inflected and capable of being used in discourse on its own. A dependent clause is one that depends on some other proposition for at least part of its INFLECTIONAL INFORMATION. For example, in the following construction, clause 1b is dependent on clause a because the subject and tense of clause b are only understood via the subject and tense of clause a:

(1) a. He came in, b. locking the door behind him.

Clause 1b by itself cannot naturally be used in discourse on its own. Sometimes fully inflected verbs are called FINITE verbs, whereas dependent verbs are termed NON-FINITE. However, this distinction must be understood as a continuum, as some verbs may be dependent in one respect, but independent in another. Thus we may talk about one verb being *more* finite or *less* finite than another.

The following discussion will be organized according to six general construction types: (1) SERIAL VERBS, (2) COMPLEMENT CLAUSES, (3) ADVERBIAL CLAUSES, (4) CLAUSE CHAINS, (5) RELATIVE CLAUSES, and (6) COORDINATION. These six construction types are arranged in such a way that the earlier ones represent relatively "tight" GRAMMATICAL INTEGRATION between two verbs or clauses, whereas the later ones represent "looser" grammatical integration. Another way of describing this arrangement is in terms of a continuum in which one end is a single clause, and the other end is two grammatically distinct clauses. A given language may possess any number of construction types that fall somewhere in between these extremes (see figure 10.1).

The continuum illustrated in figure 10.1 also mirrors many pathways of historical change whereby "loose" syntactic structures become more tightly knit over time (see many of the articles in Traugott and Heine 1991).

Serial verbs

A serial verb construction contains two or more verb roots that are neither compounded (see chapter 2) nor members of separate clauses. English marginally employs serial verbs in such constructions as the following:

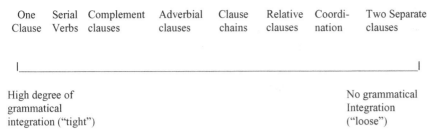

One Clause	Serial Verbs	Complement clauses	Adverbial clauses	Clause chains	Relative clauses	Coordi- nation	Two Separate clauses

High degree of
grammatical
integration ("tight")

No grammatical
Integration
("loose")

Figure 10.1 *A continuum of grammatical integration*

(2)   **Run go get** me a newspaper.

In many other languages, serial verbs are a much more common feature of the grammar. Typically, verbs in a series will express various facets of one complex event. For example, the concept expressed by the English verb *bring* is divisible into at least two components, the picking up or taking of an object and the movement toward a deictic center. In many languages, including Yoruba (a Kwa language spoken primarily in Nigeria), this complex concept is embodied in a serial verb construction (3a) (Yoruba data from Bamgbose 1974):

(3) a.   Mo **mú** ìwé **wá** ilé.
          I   take book come house
          'I brought a book home.'

    b.   Mo **mú** ìwé; mo sì **wá** ilé.
          I   take book I   and come house
          'I took a book and came home.'

Example 3b illustrates a pair of coordinate clauses that employ the same two verb roots as the serial construction in 3a. The formal factors that distinguish 3a as a serial construction are the following:

There is no independent expression of the subject of the second verb.
There is no independent tense/aspect marking of the second verb.
The intonation is characteristic of a single clause.

The following examples illustrate that in the Yoruba serial verb construction, tense/aspect/mode information is carried by the first verb:

(4)   Mò **n**   mú   ìwé bɔ   (*wá).
         I   PROG take book come.PROG   come.PERF
         'I am bringing a book.'

In example 4 the auxiliary that expresses progressive aspect occurs before the first verb. It is not repeated before the second verb. Nevertheless, the form of the verb meaning 'come' must be consistent with progressive aspect, *bɔ*, rather than perfective aspect *wá*.

Example 5a illustrates that the negative particle is associated with the first verb. Nevertheless, negation applies to the entire clause. Example 5b illustrates that the negative cannot be associated with the second verb:

(5) a.   Èmi   kò   mú   ìwé   wá.
           I.NEG   not   take   book   come
           'I did not bring a book.'

     b.   *Èmi mú ìwé kò wá.

In contrast to these serial constructions, in coordinate clauses each clause can have its own tense, aspect, and mode.

Some serial verb constructions are less than prototypical in that some inflectional information may be carried by both verbs. For example, in Akan both verbs in a serial construction must have the same subject, but the subject is redundantly specified on both (Schachter 1974):

(6)   Mede   aburow   migu   msum.
           I.take   corn   I.flow   water.in
           'I pour corn into the water.'

Sùpyìré and Minyanka are closely related Senufo languages of Mali, West Africa. In Sùpyìré both verbs in a serial construction may contain a reference to the subject (7), while in Minyanka the subject reference in the second clause is omitted (8) (all the Sùpyìré examples in this chapter are courtesy of Bob Carlson. The Minyanka examples are courtesy of Dan Brubaker):

Sùpyìré:

(7)   Pi-a   yì   yàha   pí-á   kàrè   fó   Bàmàko   e.
           they-PERF   them   leave   they-PERF   go   till   Bamako   to
           'They let them go to Bamako.'

Minyanka:

(8)   Pá   yì   yáhá   kárì   fó   Bàmàkò   nì.
           they.ASP   them   leave   go   till   Bamako   to
           'They sent them to Bamako.' (lit: 'let them go.')

Semantically, serial verb constructions often mean something slightly different from what the same series of verbs would mean if they were cast in separate clauses. However, if the semantics has changed very much, it is possible that one of the verbs in the series has been re-analyzed as an auxiliary. In fact, serial verbs are one major diachronic source for auxiliaries.

Verbs of motion are very useful in serial constructions. They are often exploited to express tense, aspect, or modal values. As such, they are well on their way to becoming auxiliaries. For example, it is very common for the verb meaning 'go' to become a marker of future tense. This has happened in English (*he's going to get mad*), Spanish, and many other languages. In some languages, such as Sùpyìré, the construction type that gives rise to this use of the verb 'go' is a serial construction:

(9)   Zànhe *sí* dùfugé   kèègè.
        rain   go   maize.DEF   spoil
        'The rain will spoil the maize.'

In Tibetan, motion verbs in a serial-like construction provide directional orientation for the action described by the other verb (DeLancey 1990):

(10)   qʰó   pʰoo   (cɛɛ) čĩ   pəréè
        he.ABS   escape NF   went   PERF.DISJUNCT
        'He escaped away.'

Serial verbs can also become adpositions. For example, in Yoruba, the preposition that marks RECIPIENTS is obviously related to the verb meaning 'give' (Stahlke 1970):

(11)   mo sɔ   *fún* ɔ ...
        I   say give   you
        'I said to you . . . '

In Efik, the verb meaning 'give' has become a benefactive preposition (Welmers 1973):

(12)   Nám útom ɛ.   *nə*   mì.
        do   work this give   me
        'Do this work for me!'

In Sùpyìré, and many other languages, the verb meaning 'use' becomes a marker of the instrumental role. In Sùpyìré it has become a postposition:

(13)   U-a   lì *tàha-a* ŋùŋke   pwɔ́.
        she-PERF it use-NF   head.DEF tie
        'She tied her hair with it.'

Complement clauses

A prototypical **COMPLEMENT CLAUSE** is a clause that functions as an argument (subject or object) of some other clause (Noonan 1985). A **MAIN** (or **MATRIX**) clause is a clause that has another clause (a complement clause) as one of its core arguments.

The kinds of complement clauses that we will discuss and illustrate in this chapter can be either subjects or objects of the matrix clause. For example:

(14)   **SUBJECT COMPLEMENT**:
                          A   V   O
        [[That Lady Aileron trod on his toe] stunned the Duke of Wimple].
        ◄─────── Complement ──────►
        ◄──────────── Main (matrix) clause ────────────►

(15)   **OBJECT COMPLEMENT**:

    A   V   O

[Lady Aileron wants [to tread on the Duke of Wimple's toe]].

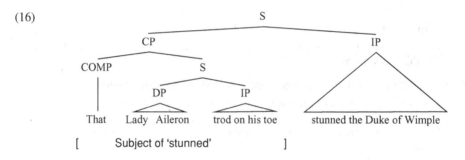

In example 14 what *stunned the Duke of Wimple* is the entire proposition expressed by the clause *that Lady Aileron trod on his toe*. Therefore this clause is the subject of the verb *stunned* and is a subject complement. In 15, what Lady Aileron wants is *to tread on the Duke of Wimple's toe*. Therefore this entire clause is the object of the verb *want* and is an object complement. In both examples, the larger clause that contains the complement is termed the **MATRIX CLAUSE**.

The following tree diagrams illustrate the syntactic position of the complement clauses in these examples. The form *that* is called a **COMPLEMENTIZER**. Since it determines the syntactic behavior of the clause that follows it, it may be considered to be the syntactic head of its phrase. Therefore the phrasal node immediately above the COMP is a CP, or **COMPLEMENT PHRASE**:

(16)

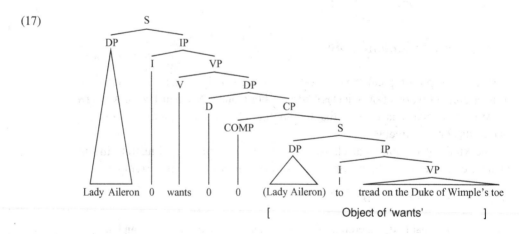

(17)

In example 17, the full object of the verb *wants* is *Lady Aileron to tread on the Duke of Wimple's toe*. However, there is a rule of English that says that the subject of an object complement clause can be omitted if it is the same as the subject of the matrix clause. Notice that if the subjects are different, the subject of the object complement clause is present:

(18)   Lady Aileron wants Buttercup to tread on the Duke of Wimple's toe.

Another notable feature of example 17 is that the complementizer that introduces the clause is zero. English has several types of object complement clauses, and one structural parameter by which they vary is the complementizer that they employ. The following examples illustrate the various possible complementizers of English:

(19) a.   *Zero* complementizer: I know Ø you are left-handed.
     b.   *That* complementizer: I know *that* you are left-handed.
     c.   *If* complementizer: I don't know *if* he is coming.
     d.   *To* complementizer: I know *to* shut up before she gets angry.

In English, subject complement clauses usually come after the verb and the neutral pronoun *it* appears in the preverbal position:

(20)   It stunned the Duke of Wimple that Lady Aileron trod on his toe.

Notice that this clause means the same thing as example 14. In 20, the complement *that Lady Aileron trod on his toe* is still the subject (the event that stuns the Duke), even though it comes at the end of the clause. The pronoun *it* takes the normal place of the subject complement clause. This is called a **POST-POSED** or **EXTRAPOSED** subject complement clause.

A clause can be both a complement *and* a matrix clause, i.e., it can be an argument of one clause and at the same time have a third clause as one of its own core arguments. For example:

(21)   [Aileron wants [to believe [that that oaf is the Duke of Wimple]]].

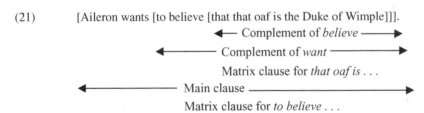

Finite complement clauses

Prototypical **FINITE** complement clauses are like independent clauses, as shown by the following characteristics:

•   They carry their own tense and aspect.
•   They express their subjects directly; subject reference is not restricted to that of the matrix clause.

The following are some examples of finite complement clauses in English:

(22)   Finite object complement clauses:
  a.   I know that *it's raining*.
  b.   I emphasized that *she knows Swahili*.

(23)   Finite subject complement clauses:
  a.   That *it had rained* surprised me.
  b.   It's well known that *she is terribly rude*.

Except for the complementizer *that*, each of the emphasized clauses in 22 and 23 could stand alone as a complete and understandable utterance. Each one is independently marked for tense and subject reference. This is what it means for a clause to be **FINITE**.

As might be expected, in VO languages such as Mandarin, object complement clauses tend to follow the matrix verb (data courtesy of Sandra Thompson):

(24)   wǒ   zhīdào   nèige   *rén*   *chī-le*   *sān*   *wǎn*   *fàn*
         I   know   that   person eat-PERF three   bowl   rice
         'I know that that person ate three bowls of rice.'

The perfective marker in the complement verb shows that the emphasized portion takes its own aspect and is therefore a finite complement clause.

In OV languages, such as Wappo (a nearly extinct language of California, USA; data courtesy of Sandra Thompson, p.c.), object complement clauses tend to precede the matrix verb:

(25)   ʔah   *ce*   *k'ew*   *ew*   *tum-tah*   hatiskhi?
         1SG   that   man   fish   buy-PAST   know
         'I know that man bought fish.'

Again, the complement clause in 25 is finite because it contains all of the inflectional information necessary for independent clauses in Wappo, including past-tense marking.

Non-finite complement clauses

Compared to finite complement clauses, **NON-FINITE** complement clauses are more tightly bound, less independent, and less like a separate clause from the matrix clause. Non-finite complement clauses tend to have the following properties:

- The identity of the subject is highly constrained. It often must be identical to the subject of the matrix verb.
- Tense, aspect, and mode are highly constrained or not specified at all. The complement verb is usually non-finite.

Some examples of non-finite complement clauses in English, Mandarin, and Wappo follow:

English non-finite subject complement clauses:

(26) a.　　*To cook a meal like that* requires a lot of patience.
　　　b.　　It isn't so easy *to do linguistics*.

English non-finite object complement clauses:

(27) a.　　I enjoy *washing my car*.
　　　b.　　She likes *to do linguistics*.

Mandarin non-finite object complement clause:

(28)　　wǒ　　yào　　*nian*　　*(*-le)*　　*shu*
　　　　1SG　　want　　read　　(-PERF)　　book
　　　　'I want to read a book.'

In Mandarin it is ungrammatical to include the perfective aspect particle in clauses that are complements of certain matrix verbs, such as *yào* 'want.'

Wappo non-finite object complement clause:

(29)　　ʔah　　*ce*　　*k'ew*　　*ew*　　*tum-uhk*　　hak'seʔ
　　　　1SG　　that　　man　　fish　　buy-INF　　want
　　　　'I want that man to buy fish.'

In this Wappo clause, the complement verb does not take an independent tense/aspect marker. Instead the infinitive suffix marks it as a non-finite verb.

Direct and indirect speech

We will end the section on complement clauses with a brief description of some of the ways languages treat **DIRECT** and **INDIRECT SPEECH**. Sometimes, direct and indirect speech taken together are referred to as **REPORTED SPEECH**. Direct speech (or direct quotation) is when a speaker reports the exact words of another person. Indirect speech (or indirect quotation) is when a speaker reports the content of what someone said, but not necessarily the exact words. For example, 30a illustrates direct speech while 30b illustrates indirect speech:

(30) a.　　Walter said "I love Taiwan."　　DIRECT SPEECH
　　　b.　　Walter said he loves Taiwan.　　INDIRECT SPEECH

If there is no grammatical distinction between direct and indirect speech in a language, all reported speech is direct – there are no languages documented to date in which all reported speech is indirect. Direct speech complement clauses are always the most independent complement type in any language. This is because the content of what someone says is in no way constrained by someone else's report of what they say. The reported discourse can be distant in time and space from the act of reporting. On the other hand, indirect speech complement clauses are subject to the same kinds of grammatical restrictions that may hold for other types of finite object complement clauses in the language. For example, the tense/aspect/mode of an indirect speech complement may be constrained by the tense/aspect/mode of the matrix clause, as in standard written Spanish:

(31) a. Carlos dijo   que iba   a   venir.
         Carlos say:PERF:3SG   that go:IMPERF:3SG   to   come:INF
         'Carlos said that he was going to come.'

   b.   ?Carlos dijo   que va   a   venir.
          Carlos say:PERF:3SG   that go:PR:3SG   to   come:INF
         'Carlos said that he is going to come.'

   c.   *Carlos dijo   que viene.
          Carlos say:PERF:3SG   that come:PR:3SG
         ('Carlos said that he comes.')

Standard grammars of Spanish will tell you that when you have the perfective aspect ("preterit") in the main clause (*dijo* in these examples), you must have the imperfective aspect in the indirect quote complement, as in 31a. The examples in 31b and c are not standard Spanish, since the tense/aspect in the complement is future in 31b and present in 31c. However, examples similar to these can be heard in ordinary speech.

One interesting feature of verbs of utterance (*say, tell*, etc.) is that their meanings are often extended to include cognition and perception concepts. In Kambera (an Austronesian language of Eastern Indonesia, Klamer 1998), the verb *wà* is a general verb of saying (example 32):

(32)   E,   wà-nggu-nya   na   ama-mu!
         hey say-1SG-3SG.DAT   ART   father-2SG
         'Hey, I was talking to your father!'

This verb also expresses certain cognition concepts (33a, b), and other "extensions" of the concept of utterance (33c, d):

(33) a. Ka   nyimi nggamu-ya na   ana   tau   ba   *wà*-mi?
         CONJ   2PL   who-3SG   ART   child male   COMP   say-2PL
         'And who do you think the boy is?' (*say* extended to mean *think*)

   b.   Na   lei-nggu   amang   nda   *wà*-na.
         ART   husband-1SG   earlier NEG   say-3SG
         'She didn't realize he was her former husband.' (lit: 'She didn't say "he is my former husband."')

   c.   Mbùtu   *wà*-na   tuna . . .
         'thud'   say-3SG   thus
         'It said "thud!"'

   d.   Likir   *wà*-na-bia-ka.
         tilt:head   say-3SG-CONT-PERF
         'He just kept his head tilted.' (lit: 'He just kept saying "tilt:head."')

A second common feature of utterance verbs is that they often evolve into complementizers or **QUOTATIVE PARTICLES**. In Buru (an Austronesian language of Eastern Indonesia) a special complementizer, *fen*, is used with cognition-utterance verbs. This complementizer is transparently related to the verb meaning 'say' that is used as a matrix verb indicating direct speech (examples from Grimes 1991):

(34)   *Fen*,   "Ng-ina,   nang   dah-deduk."
         say   1SG-mother   1SG.POS   bunch-repeat
         'He said, "Mother, the next hand is mine."'

The following examples illustrate this verb functioning as a complementizer
for indirect quotation (35a), cognition (35b), and perception verbs (35c):

(35) a.   Ku   enika   ama-n   dii   *fen*   ma   iko   leuk   fi   doo.
           2SG   ask   father-GEN DIST   COMP   1PL   go   precede   LOC   where
           'Ask father where we should go first.' ("Ask father saying . . .")

     b.   Sira   em-tako   *fen*   sira   dapak   eflali.
           3PL   STAT-fear   COMP   3PL   get   beat
           'They were afraid they would be beaten.'

     c.   Ya   kita   *fen*   da   iko   haik.
           1SG   see   COMP   3SG   go   PERF
           'I saw that he had already left.'

Other complement-taking verbs in Buru take other complementizers. One could
argue that in contemporary American English the verb *go* and quantifier expression *be all* are becoming quotative particles:

(36) a.   I'm just *all*, like, "thanks a lot!" and he *goes* "sure, no prob," and I'm *all*
           "where's this guy coming from?" ya know?
     b.   I'm sitting there at a stoplight, when all of sudden my car just *goes* "thud."

Adverbial clauses

ADVERBIAL CLAUSES are clauses that serve an "adverbial" function (Longacre and Thompson 1985). They modify a verb phrase or a whole
clause. They are not an argument of the clause. Sometimes adverbial clauses are
termed ADJUNCTS (as opposed to arguments). "Adjunct" is a good term since the
term "complement" implies completion, and a phrase or clause does not express a
complete thought until all its complement positions are filled, i.e., completed. On
the other hand, adverbial clauses and phrases attach to already complete clauses.
The adverbial clause simply adds some information to what is expressed in the
other clause.
     Sometimes adverbial clauses have the same form as complement clauses:

(37) a.   He ran *to get help*.   (purpose)
     b.   We're sorry *that you feel that way*.   (reason)
     c.   She went out, *locking the door behind her*. (sequence)

The adverbial clauses in these examples all have the same form as certain complement types of English (non-finite, finite, and participial respectively). Nevertheless, they are not complement clauses because they do not constitute logical
arguments of the main verb. Rather, they simply add "adverbial" information,
namely purpose, reason, and sequence respectively.

The kind of information expressed in adverbial clauses is similar to information expressed by adverbs, e.g., time, place, manner, purpose, reason, etc. The following sections provide a selection of examples of various kinds of adverbial clauses, in several languages. In each case, the adverbial clause is given in italics, and the independent clause in normal type:

Time or temporal adverbial clauses:

(38) a.   *When I was your age*, television was called books. (also *before*, *after*)
     b.   *While (we were) eating*, we heard a noise outside the window.
     c.   He woke up *crying*.

(39)   Barai (Papua New Guinea):
       Bae-mo-gana   e   ije   bu-ne   ke.
       ripe-PAST.SEQ-DS   people   these   3PL-FOC   take
       '*When it was ripe*, these people took it.'

Location or locative adverbial clauses

(40)   I'll meet you *where the statue used to be*.

(41)   Turkish: Sen   *Erol-un*   *otur-dug-u*   *yer-e*   otur.
                you   Erol-GEN   sit-OBJ-POS   place-DAT   sit
       'You sit *where Erol was sitting*.' (requires the word for 'place')

Manner adverbial clauses

(42)   a. She talks *like she has a cold*.   b. Carry this *as I told you*.

(43)   Quechua: Alista-pan   *kuura   ni-shan-naw-qa.*
                 prepare-BEN3   priest   say-REL-MAN-SUB
       'They prepared it for him *like the priest said*.'

Purpose adverbial clauses

(44)   He stood on his tiptoes *in order to see better*.

(45)   Panare: T-yen-che'   e'ñapa   tu'ñen   *i'ya-ta-tópe.*
                 IRR-take-GNO   people   medicine   shaman-INCHO-PURP
       'People take medicine *in order to become a shaman*.'

Reason and cause adverbial clauses

(46) a.   Sleep soundly young Rose *for I have built you a good ship*.
     b.   Languages need to be documented *because they are supreme achievements of a uniquely human collective genius*.

Most languages treat purpose and reason similarly, e.g., Yoruba:

(47)   Vǝru   *gàadà   dà   shi   sǝma.*
       go:out:PERF   PURP   IRR   drink   beer
       'He went out to drink beer.' (purpose)

(48)   A-ta   abən *gàadà aci ngaa.*
        eat-PERF   food REAS   he   well
        'He ate because he was well.' (reason)

The only formal difference between purpose and reason in these Yoruba clauses is that the purpose clause contains the IRREALIS marker *dà*.

Conditional clauses

Conditional clauses express situations that may or may not hold true in the message world. Whether a conditional clause is understood as true or not determines or influences the truth value of the independent clause in the construction:

(49)   Simple conditional clauses:
   a.   *If you haven't got your health*, you haven't got anything.
   b.   *If you make her laugh*, you have a life.
   c.   *If you stare at someone long enough*, you discover their humanity.

(50)   Hypothetical conditional clause:
        If I (were to see) David, I would speak Quechua with him.

(51)   Counterfactual conditional clause:
        If you had been at the concert, you would have seen Ravi Shankar.

(52)   Negative conditional clause:
        Unless it rains, we'll have our picnic. (i.e., If and only if it does not rain, we will have our picnic.)

(53)   Concessive conditional clause:
        Even if it rains, we'll have our picnic.

Most languages use the simple conditional marker (*if* in English) in concessive conditionals, but some languages use a different morpheme (Li and Thompson 1981:636):

(54)   Mandarin: *Jiùshi zhème piányi tā   hái   bu   mǎi   ne.*
                   Even:if this   cheap   3SG still not buy   REX
        'Even if it's this cheap, he/she still won't buy it.'

Many languages use the morphosyntax of conditional clauses in a number of fascinating rhetorical ways. These can informally be termed SPEECH-ACT CONDITIONALS in that they accomplish communicative tasks (speech acts) such as giving permission (Longacre and Thompson 1985) and insulting, rather than classical conditionality as described above. For example:

(55)   *If you're thirsty* there's coke in the refrigerator.

This is not a classic conditional clause in that, even if the hearer is *not* thirsty, presumably the situation expressed in the main clause would still hold. Rather, this complex clause can be paraphrased as 'You may be thirsty, and in order to solve this possible problem, I hereby give you permission to drink some of the coke that is in the refrigerator.' Here's another example of a clause that is in the form of a conditional, but which accomplishes a speech act that has nothing to do with conditionality:

(56)   *If there's a mental health organization that raises money for people like you,* be sure to let me know.

The communicative effect of this kind of clause is to insult the hearer, rather than set up a true condition under which the situation in the independent clause holds true.

Clause chains and switch-reference

In many languages of the world there is a tendency to link clauses together into chains in discourse. Such chains consist of one independent clause, and one or more dependent clauses that are linked to one another by the morphology that they exhibit. One common morphological system in such **CLAUSE-CHAINING LANGUAGES** is called **SWITCH-REFERENCE**.

A prototypical switch-reference system is verbal inflection that indicates whether the subject of the verb is the same as the subject of some other verb. For example in Yuman languages, like Maricopa, the verbal suffix *-k* indicates that the subject of the verb is the same as the subject of the next verb in a sequence. The suffix *-m* indicates that the subject is different from the subject of the next verb. The abbreviations SS and DS in these examples stand for "same-subject" and "different-subject" respectively (examples courtesy of Lynn Gordon):

(57) a.   Nyaa   '-ashvar-*k*   '-iima-k.   'I sang and I danced.'
           I   1-sing-ss   1-dance-PERF

    b.   Bonnie-sh   0-ashvar-*m*   '-iima-k.   'Bonnie sang and I danced.'
           Bonnie-SUBJ   3-sing-DS   1-dance-PERF

In Maricopa, switch-reference markers are distinct from verb agreement, i.e., they are a different inflectional category (note that both verbs "agree" with their subjects by way of prefixes). Hence there is redundancy. Sometimes, however, switch-reference markers are incorporated into the system of verb agreement. In this case the category of "third person" is subdivided into two, one for same reference and another for switch-reference. Various terminology is used to refer to such systems, e.g., reflexive, **FOURTH PERSON, RECURRENT**, etc.

Yup'ik exhibits such a system. In the following examples, the subscripts i and j indicate coreference (i = i) or switch-reference (i ≠ j) between participants:

(58) a.   Dena-q   quya-u-q   Toni-aq   cinga-llra-∅-ku.
              -ABS   happy-INTRNS-3   -ABS   greet-because-3/3-DEP
           'Dena$_i$ is happy because she$_j$ greeted Tony.'

Table 10.1 *Kâte switch-reference markers*

	Overlap ("while")	Succession ("then")
SS	-huk	-ra
DS	-ha	-0

b.   Dena-q quya-u-q Toni-aq cinga-llra-*mi*-ku.

                                                -SS

        'Dena$_i$ is happy because she$_i$ greeted Tony.'

The second clause in example 58a takes the standard verb agreement marking for adverbial clauses. The interpretation of 58a is that the actor of each clause is different. The second clause in 58b, on the other hand, takes a special suffix, *-mi*, that indicates that the actor of this clause is the same as the actor of the previous clause. Sometimes this suffix is called the "fourth person."

More complex systems of switch-reference occur in the languages of highland Papua New Guinea. For example, Kâte has a switch-reference system consisting of four markers (Longacre 1972), as presented in table 10.1.

(59) a.   Fisi-*huk*   na-wek.   'As he$_i$ arrived, he$_i$ was eating.'
            arrive-SS   ate-3SG

     b.   Fisi-*ra*   na-wek.   'He$_i$ arrived, then he$_i$ ate.'
            arrive-SS   ate-3SG

     c.   Mu-*ha*-pie   kio-wek.   'As they spoke, he was weeping.'
            speak-DS-3PL   weep-3SG

     d.   Mu-Ø-pie   kio-wek.   'After they spoke, he wept.'
            speak-DS-3PL   weep-3SG

Some systems are even more complex than this. For example, in Panare, morphemes that indicate same or switch-reference relations between clauses also indicate several temporal or logical relations. Table 10.2 illustrates these suffixes and the various relations they express (T. Payne 1991).

Table 10.2 shows that switch-reference need not be based on the grammatical relation of subject only. Several languages, especially those that organize grammatical relations on an ergative/absolutive basis (see chapter 8), may be sensitive to objects or absolutives. This phenomenon has been documented in Australian languages (Austin 1980) and in Amerindian languages (Jones and Jones 1991 on Barasano).

Relative clauses

A **RELATIVE CLAUSE** is a clause that modifies a noun (Keenan 1985), for example:

(60)   The <u>oaf</u> *that* [Ø trod on Lady Aileron's toe] . . .

Table 10.2 *Panare switch-reference markers*

Morpheme (verb suffix)	Temporal relation	Reference relations	Other relations expressed
-séjpe	Succession	Actor=Actor	purpose
-sé'ñape	Succession	Absolutive=Patient	result
-ñépe	Succession	Actor≠Actor	movement/purpose
-npan	Overlap	Actor=Actor	none
-tááñe	Overlap	Actor≠Actor	none
-jpómën	Anteriority	Actor=Actor	reason

In terms of syntactic structure, a relative clause is a clause that is embedded within a noun phrase. This may be diagrammed as follows:

(61)

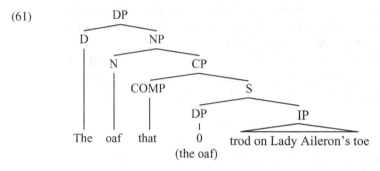

The important parts of a relative clause are the following:

- The **HEAD** is the noun phrase that is modified by the clause. In 60 the head is *oaf*.
- The **RESTRICTING CLAUSE** is the relative clause itself. In 60 the restricting clause is surrounded by brackets.
- The **R-ELEMENT**[1] is the element within the restricting clause that is coreferential with the head noun. In 60 the R-element is represented as Ø (a zero, or "gap").
- The **RELATIVIZER** is the morpheme or particle that sets off the restricting clause as a relative clause.

In English, relativizers are the same as complementizers (see above, p. 00). In 60 the relativizer is the complementizer *that*. If the relativizer reflects some properties of the R-element within the restricting clause (e.g., humanness, grammatical relation in the restricting clause, etc.), then it can be termed a **RELATIVE PRONOUN** (see below).

Notice that in 61, the full embedded clause is *The oaf trod on Lady Aileron's toe*. The subject of this clause is omitted because it is coreferential with the subject of the matrix clause.

There are several parameters by which relative clauses can be typologized. The parameters to be discussed and exemplified in this chapter are (1) the position of the clause with respect to the head noun, (2) the way the R-element is expressed, and (3) which grammatical relations the R-element can refer to.

The position of the head

Relative clauses can be either **PRENOMINAL** (the clause occurs *before* the head), **POST-NOMINAL** (the clause occurs *after* the head), **INTERNALLY HEADED** (the head occurs within the relative clause), or they may be **HEADLESS**. Since relative clauses are noun modifiers, one might expect that they would occur in the same position as other noun modifiers, e.g., adjectives, numerals, etc. Though it is true that the position of the relative clause with respect to the head noun often is the same as the position of other modifiers, there is a distinct tendency for relative clauses to occur after their heads (post-nominal), even in languages for which other modifiers are pre-nominal. This tendency is probably due to a universal pragmatic principle that shifts "heavy," i.e., long, phonologically complex, information late in the clause. This is the same principle that motivates post-posing of subject complement clauses in English (see above, p. 295). The following examples illustrate each of these types from several different languages.

Post-nominal relative clauses are the most common type. Languages which are dominantly VO in main-clause constituent order always have post-nominal relative clauses. English is such a language. The following examples are from Luganda, a Bantu Language of Zaire:

(62) a.   omukazi   ya-kuba   omusajja
           woman   she-hit   man
           'The woman hit the man.'

   b.   omusajja   [omukazi   gwe-ya-kuba]
           man   woman   REL-she-hit
           'The man that the woman hit.'

Example 62a illustrates a plain transitive clause. Example 62b illustrates the same clause functioning as a relative clause to modify the noun *omusajja* 'man.' As is typical of VO languages, the relative clause follows the head noun.

Prenominal relative clauses occur in most OV languages, such as Japanese:

(63) a.   Yamada-san   ga   sa'ru   o   ka't-te   i-ru.
           Yamada-Mr.   NOM   monkey   ACC   keep-PART   be-PR
           'Mr. Yamada is keeping a monkey.'

   b.   [Yamada-san ga ka'tte iru] sa'ru
           'The monkey that Mr. Yamada is keeping'

   c.   [sa'ru o ka'tte iru] Yamada-san
           'the Mr. Yamada who is keeping a monkey'

Examples 63b and c illustrate two relative clauses based on the independent clause in 63a. In both of the relative clauses, the restricting clause (in brackets) comes before the head.

Example 64 illustrates a Turkish clause in which a relative clause modifies one of the nominals:

(64)   Eser   [uyuy-na   ]   kadın-i   tanyor.
        Eser   sleep-PART   woman-ACC   knows
        'Eser knows the woman who is sleeping.'

Turkish is an OV language and, true to its type, it employs prenominal relative clauses. The head of the relative clause in 64 is *kadın* 'woman.' This noun is preceded by the relative clause in brackets. Notice also that the verb within the relative clause is marked as a participle. This is a very common feature of relative clauses, especially in languages that have a lot of verbal morphology (polysynthetic languages). Even English has participial relative clauses:

(65) a.   Eser knows the [sleep-*ing*] woman.
    b.   Eser sat on a [fall-*en*] log.
    c.   Eser ripped up her [reject-*ed*] novel.

All of the highlighted morphemes in these examples are markers of adjectives derived from verbs of one type or another. Though traditional English grammar would not call such verb forms clauses at all, they fulfill our definition of relative clause. For many languages (e.g., Turkish), constructions analogous to these are the only means of modifying a noun phrase using anything like a clause, i.e., they function just like relative clauses even though they may not be very clause-like formally.

Internally headed relative clauses are those for which the head is within the relative clause. Many OV languages, including Bambara, a Niger-Congo language of West Africa, have internally headed relative clauses:

(66) a.   ne   ye   so   ye.
        1SG   PAST   horse   see
        'I saw a horse.'

    b.   ce   ye   [ne   ye   so   min   ye]   san
        man   PAST   1SG   PAST   horse   REL   see   buy
        'The man bought the horse that I saw.'

The relativizer *min* is the only thing that marks the clause in brackets as a relative clause in 66b. The head noun remains *in situ* within the relative clause and is not mentioned outside of the relative clause, as in the other examples above.

Headless relative clauses are those clauses which themselves refer to the noun that they modify. English, and many other languages, can use headless relative clauses when the head noun is non-specific:

(67) a.   You're [why cavemen chiseled on walls].
        (cf. 'the *reason* why . . .')
    b.   [Whoever goes to the store] should get some water balloons.
        (cf. 'any *person* who goes to the store . . .')

English, and many other languages, use headless relative clauses for non-specific referents, as illustrated in 67. Some languages, on the other hand, employ headless relative clauses for both non-specific and specific referents. The following are sentences from Ndjuká (Suriname Creole, examples courtesy of George Huttar):

(68) a.　[Di　o　doo　fosi]　o　wini.　SUBJECT, NON-SPECIFIC
　　　　REL　FUT　arrive　first　FUT　win
　　　　'Whoever arrives first will win.'

b.　A　mainsi　ya　a　[di　e　tan　a　ini　se]　SUBJECT,
　　the　eel　here　COP　REL　CONT　stay　LOC　inside　sea　SPECIFIC
　　'This eel is what (the one that) lives in the sea.'

c.　A　daai　go　anga　[di　a　be　puu]　OBJECT, SPECIFIC
　　3SG　turn　go　with　REL　3SG　ANT　remove
　　'He turned and returned with what (the ones) he had removed.'

How the R-element is expressed

The second major parameter by which relative clauses can vary is how the R-element is expressed. This parameter is sometimes stated as a CASE RECOVERABILITY problem (Keenan 1985). That is, in any relative clause there must be some way of identifying the grammatical relation of the referent of the head noun *within the relative clause*, otherwise ambiguity may result. The head noun itself has a function in the main clause. However, it always has a coreferent within the relative clause (the R-element in our terms). The role of the R-element can be different from the role of the head noun within the main clause. For example, in 69a *the alligator* is the subject of the main-clause verb *eats*. It is also the subject of the relative-clause verb *saw*. In 69b, however, *the alligator* is still the subject of *eats*, but it is now the object of the relative clause verb:

(69) a.　The alligator [that saw me] eats tofu.
　　b.　The alligator [that I saw] eats tofu.

These clauses can be diagrammed as follows:

(70) a.

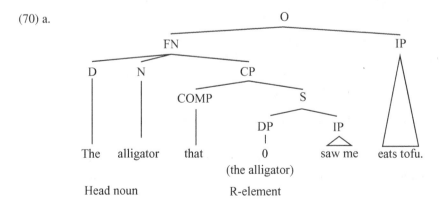

b.

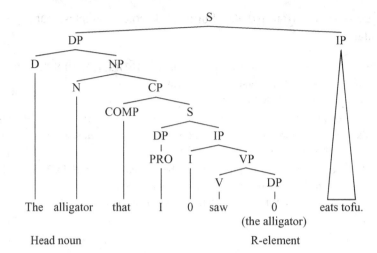

Head noun   R-element

Since the R-element is left out in the surface structure of these clauses (69a, b), a problem arises as to how the hearer is to identify the grammatical relation of this invisible noun phrase within the bracketed clause. English solves this problem by simply leaving a conspicuous gap in the position where the R-element would be if it were overtly expressed. This is called the **GAP STRATEGY**. This strategy works for languages that have a fairly fixed constituent order, i.e., those for which grammatical relations are expressed by the position of the core nominals in a clause. In such languages a missing argument is very obvious. However, if the language allows many constituent orders, and/or if grammatical relations are identified by case marking or verb agreement, the gap strategy may leave the relative clause ambiguous.

If the gap strategy is insufficient, the language is likely to use a more explicit construction type to express the grammatical relation of the R-element. The next construction type we will discuss is termed **PRONOUN RETENTION**. In this strategy a pronoun that explicitly expresses the grammatical relation of the R-element, either by its position, its form, or both, is retained within the relative clause. Pronoun retention is used in many types of relative clauses in spoken English:

(71) That's the guy who [I can never remember *his* name].

In this example, the R-element is expressed by the genitive pronoun *his*. The fact that pronoun is in the genitive form (rather than the subjective *he* or non-subjective *him*), and precedes the noun *name*, make it clear that the grammatical relation of the R-element in this clause is genitive.

(72) We've got sixteen drums here that we don't even know what's in *them*.
    (Heard on a television news interview).

Again, the fact that the retained pronoun, *them*, occurs in the non-subjective form and occurs after the preposition *in* indicates that the grammatical relation of the R-element is oblique.

Here is an example of the pronoun-retention strategy in modern Israeli Hebrew (Keenan 1985:146):

(73)   ha-sarim   she   [ha-nasi   shalax   *otam*   la-mitsraim]
        DEF-ministers   REL   DEF-president   sent   them   to-Egypt
        'The ministers that the President sent to Egypt . . .'

In this relative clause, the pronoun *otam* 'them,' referring to the ministers, is retained within the relative clause in the position and form required of direct objects.

Samoan uses the pronoun retention strategy when the R-element has any semantic role other than AGENT or PATIENT:

(74)   'o   le   mea   sa   nofo   *ai*   le   fafine . . .
        PR   ART   place   PAST   stay   PRO   ART   woman
        'The place where the woman stayed.' (lit: 'The place the woman stayed there.')

In this example the pronoun *ai* refers to the R-element in the position and form a location is normally expressed with respect to the verb *nofo*, which could perhaps be glossed 'to stay at.'

It is rare for pronoun retention to be used to relativize the subject of the relative clause in any language. For example, the following RC is ungrammatical in Hebrew, even though pronoun retention is standard for other relations (see example 73):

(75)   *ha-ish   she   [*hu*   makir   oti   ]
        DEF-man   REL   he   knows   me
        '*The man who he knows me.'

Many languages employ a special form called a **RELATIVIZER** to identify a clause as a relative clause. Often the relativizer is the same form as a complementizer. For example, English can employ the relativizer *that* (normally unstressed):

(76)   The man *that* I saw.
        The man *that* saw me.
        The bed *that* I slept in.
        ?The house *that* I went to.

A prototypical relativizer does not constitute a reference to the R-element and thus cannot itself help recover the role of the R-element in the relative clause. This is evidenced by the fact that the complementizer cannot be preceded by prepositions specifying the role of the R-element:

(77)   *The bed *in that* I slept.
        *The house *to that* I went.

Instead, in such circumstances a different kind of form must be used to introduce the relative clause. This is called a **RELATIVE PRONOUN**:

(78)   The bed *in which* I slept.
              The house *where* I went.

Relative pronouns are typically similar to other pronouns in the language,
either the question words or pronouns used to refer to non-specific, indefinite
items. Relative pronouns can be thought of as combining the functions of a
plain relativizer and a clause-internal pronoun that refers to the relativized NP.
English allows the relative pronoun strategy (Rel Pro), a relativizer plus gap
strategy (Rel + gap), and an unmarked "no relativizer" plus gap strategy (No
Rel). Sometimes all three are allowed in the same environment, and it is difficult to determine what semantic nuances are conveyed, if any, by the various allowable structures. The following illustrate some English possibilities and
impossibilities:

(79) a.   Rel Pro: The man who saw me
     b.   Rel + gap: The man that saw me
     c.   No Rel: *The man [0 saw me]

(80) a.   Rel Pro: The man whom [I saw]
     b.   Rel + gap: The man that [I saw 0]
     c.   No Rel: The man [I saw 0]

(81) a.   Rel pro: The place where I live
     b.   Rel + gap: *The place that I live
     c.   No Rel: The place I live

(82) a.   Rel pro: The reason why I came
     b.   Rel + gap: The reason that I came
     c.   No Rel: The reason I came

(83) a.   Rel pro: ?The way how he did it
     b.   Rel + gap: The way that he did it
     c.   No Rel: The way he did it

(84) a.   Rel pro: The table which he put it on
     b.   Rel + gap: The table that he put it on
     c.   No Rel: The table he put it on

In contrast to the English relativizer *that*, the element that introduces a relative
clause in Chickasaw can be inflected for the role of the R-element in the relative
clause. The following examples show the form *yamma* 'that' takes subject marking, *-at*, when the R-element is the subject of the RC ('the woman saw the dog,'
85a), and takes object marking when the R-element is the object of the RC (85b)
(examples from Munro 1983:230):

(85) a.   Ihoo   *yamm-at*   ofi'   pis-tokat   illi-tok.
            woman   that-SUBJ   dog   see-PAST.DEP.SS   die-PAST
            'The woman that saw the dog died.'

b. Ihoo-at   ofi' *yamma* pi<u>s</u>-toka   illi-tok.
    woman-SUBJ   dog   that   see-PAST.DEP.DS   die-PAST
    'The woman that the dog saw died.'

This is evidence that in Chickasaw *yamma* constitutes a reference to the R-element and thus can be termed a relative pronoun, rather than simply a relativizer.

Coordination

Languages often have morphosyntactic means of linking two clauses of equal grammatical status. Such linkage is termed **COORDINATION**. It is distinct from **SUBORDINATION** in that in subordination one clause is grammatically dependent on the other. All of the dependent clause types discussed in the previous sections (i.e., complement clauses, adverbial clauses, and relative clauses) may be considered to be examples of subordination. However, there is really not much commonality to this broad group of clause types other than grammatical dependency. Therefore, the notion of "subordinate clause" is not very useful as a universal linguistic category (see Haiman and Thompson 1984).

Coordination is sometimes difficult to distinguish from mere juxtaposition of clauses in discourse. In fact, in spoken discourse some kind of morphosyntactic clause linkage, either coordination or subordination, may be evident at nearly all clause junctures. Many readers will be familiar with the English colloquial narrative style that inserts "and . . ." or "and then . . ." after each clause. In general, the fact that two clauses are grammatically coordinated simply asserts that (1) the two clauses have more or less the same function in terms of the event structure of the text (e.g., they both express events, they both express non-events, they both express foregrounded information or they both express background information, etc.) and (2) they are presented as being conceptually linked in some way.

Often some strategies for conjoining clauses are identical to strategies for conjoining noun phrases. For example, English uses the conjunction *and* for both phrasal and clausal conjunction:

(86)   Aidan *and* Aileron   Noun Phrase + Noun Phrase
        Aidan cried *and* Aileron laughed   Clause + Clause

However, it is also common for there to be special strategies for conjoining clauses that are not used for conjoining phrases. For example, the English *but* does not easily function as a noun-phrase conjunction:

(87)   *Aidan *but* Aileron   NP + NP
        Aidan cried *but* Aileron laughed   CL + CL

The simplest means of conjoining two clauses is what J. Payne (1985) describes as the **ZERO STRATEGY**. This is where two phrases or clauses are simply juxtaposed. According to J. Payne, most languages probably allow the zero strategy at least as a stylistic variation. Some languages, however, use it more extensively than do others. Pacoh is a language that uses the zero strategy extensively in both phrasal and clausal coordination (examples from Watson 1966:176):

(88) a.   Nháng tiráp   [tilĕt, callóh, acŏq]   NP + NP
        we   prepare basket spear   knife
        'We prepare baskets, spears, and knives.'

    b.   Do cho   [tŏq cayâq,   tŏq   apây]   PP + PP
        she return to   husband to   grandmother
        'She returns to (her) husband and to (her) grandmother.'

    c.   Do [chŏ tŏq cayâq,   cho   tŏq apây]   VP + VP
        she return to husband return to   grandmother
        'She returns to (her) husband and returns to (her) grandmother.'

The most common means of indicating conjunction is by the use of a **COORDINATING CONJUNCTION** such as *and* in English. For VO languages this conjunction normally occurs in between the two conjoined clauses:

(89)   Robespierre fell out of favor *and* the revolutionaries killed him.

However, sometimes in VO languages the coordinating conjunction follows the first element of the second clause, as in Yoruba:

(90)   Mo mú   ìwé;   mo *sì*   wá   ilé.
           I   take book I   and come house
           'I took a book and I came home.'

For OV languages, the coordinating conjunction comes either between the two conjoined elements, as in Farsi (91a, b, c, from J. Payne 1985:28), or after the last element, as in Walapai (92):

(91) a.   Jân   [xandid *va*   dast tekân dâd]$_{VP}$
        John   smiled and hand sign   gave
        'John smiled and waved.' (V-Phrase coordination)

    b.   Jân   [puldar *va*   mašhur]$_{AP}$ bud
        John   rich   and famous   was
        'John was rich and famous.' (Adj. coordination)

    c.   [Jân raft *va*   meri dast tekân dâd]$_{CL}$
        John left   and Mary hand sign   gave
        'John left and Mary waved.' (Clausal coordination)

The form that conjoins two elements is often the same as the morpheme that expresses the comitative sense of *with*. In Walapai (Yuman), both instrumental and **COMITATIVE** elements are signaled with the enclitic *-m*. Example 92 illustrates this *-m* in its common role as an instrumental case marker (Redden 1966:160–61, as cited in J. Payne 1985:30):

(92)   ža-č   žikwâi- č-a   avon-a-*m*   taθ-k-wíl
         1SG-NOM   clothes-PL-DEF   soap-DEF-with   wash-1SG-CONT
         'I washed the clothes with soap.'

This -*m* suffix also functions as a phrasal and clausal coordinator:

(93)   Wàlpáìkwáùk   háìkùkwáùk-*m*   íče
         Walapai:speech   white:man:speech-with   we:speak
         'We speak Walapai and English.'

Such similarity among the instrumental, comitative, and coordinating morphemes is extremely common in the world's languages.

Many languages employ a different conjunction in coordinate noun phrases
and in clauses. This is very common in Austronesian languages. In Malagasy
(Austronesian, Madagascar) the conjunction *ary* expresses clausal coordination,
while *sy* expresses coordination in noun phrases (examples courtesy of Charles
Randriamasimanana):

(94) a. Lasa   i   Paoly   *ary/*sy*   dia   lasa   koa   i   Jaona.
         gone   ART   Paul   and   SEQ   gone   also   ART   John
         'Paul left and then John also left.'

     b. Lasa   i   Paoly   *sy*   i   Jaona.
         gone   ART   Paul   and   ART   John
         'Paul and John left.'

An interesting twist on the clausal conjunction *ary* is that it can function as a
noun-phrase conjunction when the second conjunct is a reduced clause. Example
95 is a reduced version of 94a:

(95)   Lasa   i   Paoly   *ary*   i   Jaona.
         gone   ART   Paul   and   ART   John
         'Paul and then John left.'

The effect of this extended use of the clausal conjunction is an apparent contrast
between *simultaneous* (94b) and *sequential* (95) noun-phrase conjunction.

Latin possesses a "negative conjunctive" particle *nec*, in addition to the affirmative conjunction *et*. The meaning of the negative conjunctive particle can be
characterized as 'and not' in English (Kühner and Stegmann 1955:48, as cited in
J. Payne 1985:37):

(96)   eques   Romanus   [*nec*   infacetus   *et*   satis   litteratus]AP
         knight   Roman   and:not   dull   and   moderately   literate
         'a not dull and moderately literate Roman knight'

Unlike the English translation 'not . . . and,' the negative conjunctive particle
in Latin does not have scope over the entire conjoined phrase. In other words,
only dullness is negated in the Latin example, whereas the English translation
could be taken as ambiguous as to whether *moderately literate* should be taken
as being negated as well.

Conceptual outline of chapter 10

I.   In this chapter we discuss ways in which languages combine clauses into coherent grammatical constructions. In such clause-combining constructions, there is usually one independent clause and one or more dependent clauses. Dependent clauses can be placed on a continuum according to how "tightly" they are integrated into the independent clause. The following six types of clause-combining constructions are discussed:
- Serial verbs
- Complement clauses
- Adverbial clauses
- Clause chains and switch-reference
- Relative clauses
- Coordination

II.   Dependent clauses can be:
- Non-finite – this means they express no inflectional information (tense, agreement, etc.) whatsoever.
- Semi-finite – they may express some inflectional information.
- Finite – they express all the inflectional information expressed by independent clauses.

III.   Special attention is paid to complement clauses, adverbial clauses, and relative clauses. These can be further typologized as follows:
- Complement clauses:
  - Subject complement clauses (normal and post-posed)
  - Object complement clauses
  - Direct and indirect speech complement clauses
- Adverbial clauses:
  - Time
  - Location
  - Manner
  - Purpose
  - Reason
  - Conditional
    - Simple conditional
    - Hypothetical conditional
    - Counterfactual conditional
    - Negative conditional
    - Concessive conditional
    - "Speech-act" conditional
- Relative clauses
  - Position of the clause relative to the head:
    - Prenominal

- Post-nominal
- Internally headed
- Headless
- Expression of the R-element
  - Gap
  - Pronoun retention
  - Relative pronoun
- Grammatical relations that may be relativized

Exercise 10.1: English dependent clauses

Tom Payne

A.   In each of the following clauses, underline and number the dependent clauses, if any. Some clauses may be dependent on other dependent clauses; such clauses should be underlined twice.

Example: 'I want you   <u>to finish eating your peas</u>'.
                  1   2   2,1

B.   On a separate sheet, for each dependent clause, answer the following questions (lists of possible answers are provided):

a. What functional type of dependent clause is it (complement, adverbial, relative)?

b. For each clause you have labeled "adverbial," indicate its subtype or types (time, location, manner, purpose, conditional, concessive, reason, "speech act").

c. For each clause you have labeled a "complement," indicate its subtype or types (subject or object; post-posed; finite, subjunctive, or infinitive; indirect question).

d. For each clause you have labeled "relative," indicate what the role of the R-element is.

1. He wished she had awakened him.
2. Hugo said I ought to fire the guy that caused this ruckus.
3. It's obvious that we need more equipment.
4. Because the soloist was ill, they canceled the concert.
5. When I last saw you, you lived in Delhi.
6. He didn't start to read until he was ten years old.
7. If I were president, I'd fire the bum.
8. I lent him the money because he needed it to buy groceries.
9. He's still here, because his light's still on.
10. If you had tried to treat her kindly, she would have done anything for you.
11. He leaned forward to see over the rail.

Exercise 10.2: finiteness

Tom Payne

Underline the verb phrases in the following examples, and indicate whether they are finite or non-finite:

Example: <u>Driving like that</u>   <u>must be dangerous.</u>
                non-finite   finite

1. He had started on a ship going out to Canada.
2. He held her hand, and she knew that he was speaking to her.
3. As she mused, the pitiful vision of her mother's life laid its spell on the very quick of her being.
4. It was a life of common sacrifices closing in final craziness.
5. Leaning against the curtain, she inhaled the odour of dusty cretonne.

Exercise 10.3: Konkomba

Ronnie Sim

A.   Where is Konkomba spoken?

1. Uwon   ba   kpo.   'The rabbit died.'
   rabbit   past   die

2. Bi   ba   kan   uwon.   'They saw the rabbit.'
   they   past   see   rabbit

3. Bi   ba   kan   uwon   u   n   ba   kpo   na.
   they   past   saw   rabbit it   past   die
   'They saw the rabbit which had died.'

4. Usapol   ba   fii.   'The mouse got up.'
   mouse   past   get.up

5. Unambuun   ba   gɔən.   'The cat slept.'
   cat   past   slept

6. U   ba   fii.   'He got up.'
   he   past   get.up

7. Unambuun   u   n   ba   gɔən   na   ba   fii.
   cat   it   past   sleep   past   get.up
   'The cat which had slept got up.'

B.   What is the grammatical relation of the R-element in examples 3 and 7?

C.   What is the grammatical relation of the head of the relative clause in examples 3 and 7?

D.   What case-recoverability strategy do we see in examples 3 and 7? Give your evidence

E.   Describe relative-clause formation in this language.

Exercise 10.4: Ponapean

Bob Carlson

1. lii   o   koola   poonpe i
    woman ABS went   Ponape LOC
    'The woman went to Ponape.'

2. i ɔsɔ lii kuutaŋ o
    'I know the big woman.'

3. i ɔsɔ lii mɔ koola poonpe i o
    'I know the woman that went to Ponape.'

4. lii e pɔk ool o
    'The woman hit the man.'

5. lii o ipɔk ool ti
                      LOC
    'The woman hit a/the man.'

6. i kilaŋ ool mɔ lii e pɔk o
    'I saw the man the woman hit.'

7. ool mɔ lii e pɔk e pwain pwɔɔr o
    'The man the woman hit covered the hole.'

8. i kilaŋ lii mɔ ipɔk ool ti o
    'I saw the woman that hit the man.'

9. *i kilaŋ lii mɔ pɔk ool o

10. ɔ   pwain pwɔɔr o   tɔɔn   uut   kii
    he   cover hole   ABS   leaf   banana INST
    'He covered the hole with banana leaves.'

11. ɔ pwainkii tɔɔn uut o pwɔɔr ti
    'He covered banana leaves on a/the hole.' (he used banana leaves to cover a/the hole)

12. i kilaŋ pwɔɔr mɔ ɔ pwain tɔɔn uut kii o

13. i kilaŋ tɔɔn uut mɔ ɔ pwainkii pwɔɔr ti o

14. *i kilaŋ tɔɔn uut mɔ ɔ pwain pwɔɔr o kii

15. *i kilaŋ pwɔɔr mɔ ɔ pwainkii tɔɔn uut o (o)

A.   Where is Ponapean spoken? What language family does it belong to?

B.   What is the order of head noun and restricting clause in Ponapean?

C.   What is *mɔ*?

D.   What strategy does Ponapean employ to recover the semantic role of the R-element in examples 6, 7, and 12?

E.   Why are 9, 14, and 15 ungrammatical?

Extra credit: What is the function of the verb suffix *-kii* in example 11? Give your evidence.

Exercise 10.5: Copainalá Zoque

Adapted from Merrifield et al. 1987, problem #274

A.   Where is Copainalá Zoque spoken? How many speakers are there?

B.   List and gloss all the morphemes in the following data. Specify any morphophonemic rules that are needed to derive the surface forms from your posited underlying forms.

C.   Describe how temporal and locational clauses are formed.

1. minba	'He comes.'
2. ho?pit minu	'He came the next day.'
3. homih nu?kpa jʌj	'He will arrive here tomorrow.'
4. homih cu?kumjahpa	'They will set out tomorrow.'
5. ki?mu?k nu?kjahu ?ʌmʌ	'They arrived there when he went up.'
6. minjahpa?k cu?kumba	'He will set out when they come.'
7. minba?k nu?kjahpa jʌj	'They will arrive here when he comes.'
8. nu?kjahu?k ?ʌmʌ minu	'He came when they arrived there.'
9. minjahu nu?kpamʌj	'They came to where he will arrive.'
10. ki?mjahpa cu?kumbamʌj homih	'They will go to where he will set out tomorrow.'
11. ho?pit nu?ku ki?mumʌj	'Next day he arrived where he went up.'

Exercise 10.6: Tanglapui 2

Mark Donohue and Carl Rubino

This variety of Tanglapui is spoken in the villages of Kobra and Naumang in the eastern highlands of Alor, in eastern Indonesia.

A.   Building on your solution to exercise 9.9, list and gloss the additional morphemes evident in the following data.

B.   Explain how the coreference system in conjoined clauses functions.

30. Yaŋanababa tave	'You hit me and then I left.'
31. Toby ŋagadia gitayi	'I saw Toby and then he went up.'
32. Kris gayanababa gitave	'Kris hit you and then he left.'
33. Lena Toby ganababa tave	'Toby hit Lena and then she left.'
34. Yagasɨlale talula	'You looked for her and then you went home.'
35. ŋayasɨlale gitalula	'I looked for you and then you went home.'
36. Toby Lena gadia talula	'Toby saw Lena and then he went home.'
37. Lena gaŋanasɨlale gitave	'Lena looked for me and then she left.'

C.   Translate the following examples:

    38. Kris ŋagababa talula

    39. I hit Kris and then he went home.

    40. Toby looked for Lena, then she left, and he went home.

Exercise 10.7: Tuvinian

From the Russian Linguistic Olympiad archives, 10th grade

Tuvinian is spoken in the area known as Tuva in Eastern Russia. There are 206,000 speakers of Tuvinian in Russia and another 27,000 in Mongolia. It is an Altaic language, related to Turkish, and possibly even Japanese and Korean. Until 1944 Tuva was an independent country. Now it is a part of Russia. The Tuvinian people hunt, and raise cattle and horses for a living. Here are five English sentences and their free translations in the Tuvinian language:

    1. Oglu avazyn turguzupkash deze-bɛɛr.
       'When the son will wake up the mother, he will run away.'

    2. Avazy oglun turguzuptarga ol yglaj-bɛɛr.
       'When the mother will wake up the son, he will cry.'

    3. Oglu inɛɛn saaptarga ol γne-bergen.
       'When the son milked the cow, it went away.'

    4. Yǝdy oglun yzyrypkash deze-bergen.
       'When the dog bit the son, it ran away.'

    5. Oglu uruun turguzuptarga achazy azhyna-bergen.
       'When the son woke up the daughter, the father got angry.'

Translate the following English sentences into Tuvinian:

    6. When the son woke up the dog, he went away.

    7. When father will milk the cow, he will go away.

    8. When the cow bit the father, the daughter cried.

    9. When the daughter will bite the father, he will get angry.

Exercise 10.8: Alabama

Ivan Derzhanski

1. Aatosik támmìlaakak mikkon hałka.	'The child staggers and kicks the chief.'
2. Boyilkak kootilka.	'We dig and whistle.'
3. Chafalankak maahałkali.	'I wake up and go walking.'
4. Chihalatkalin chahałiska.	'I grab you and you kick me.'
5. Chitámmìlaakan tayyik chitabatka.	'You stagger and the woman catches up with you.'

6. Ittopathan piłkalin halatiskak boyiska.	'I leave the hoe and you grab it and dig.'
7. Mikkok tołłohka.	'The chief coughs.'
8. Naanik potabatkak chahalatka.	'The man catches up with us and grabs me.'
9. Połaatkan chifalanka.	'I snore and you wake up.'
10. Talin hałilkak poháłłapka.	'I kick the stone and stub a toe.'
11. Tayyik maahałkak aatosin piłka.	'The woman goes walking and leaves the child.'

(The sound written as ł is a voiceless lateral.)

A.   Translate the following sentences into English:

12. Tayyik maahałkan aatosik piłka.
13. Chatołłohka.
14. Tołłohkali.

B.   Now translate the following into Alabama:

15. 'The man staggers and the child kicks him.'
16. 'You catch up with the chief and leave us.'

C.   Where is Alabama spoken today? (don't guess – you will be wrong)
D.   What language family does it belong to?

Exercise 10.9: Nigerian Pidgin

N. Faraclas
/ = pause, // = long pause.

1. ìm   gó   báy   fíš   //   ìm   kɔm   tek-am   kíp.   //
   he   go   buy   fish   take-it   keep
   'He went and bought a fish. He then put it away.'

2. às   ìm   kíp-am   dyá   / rát   kɔm   čɔp-am   //
   while   he   keep-it   there   rat   eat-it
   'While he kept it there, a rat came and ate it.' (or 'a rat then ate it.')

3. dì   nɛs   dé   rát   kɔm   dáy   fɔr   háws   //
   the   next   day   rat   die   in   house
   'The next day the rat then died in the house.'

4. ìm   gó   dyá   kíl   dì   rát   fíniš   kɔm   kári-am   rost.
   he   go   there   kill   the   rat   finish   carry-it   roast
   'Having gone there and killed the rat he then took it away and roasted it.'

5. às ìm   rost-am   / ìm   kɔm   sí   dì   fíš-bon   smɔl-smɔl   //
                                see   fish-bone   little:bit
   'While he was roasting it, he saw a little bit of fishbone.'

6. ìm   kɔm   sé   'éhɛ'   //   'He then says "aha!"'
                say   aha!

7. ìm kɔm čɔp dì rát fíniš // 'He then ate the rat all up.'

8. wɛn   yù   sìdɔn   fíniš   /   dát   táym   wɛ   ìm   rɔn   ínsáyd   //
   when   you   sit:down finish   that   time   that   she   run   inside
   'When you have sat down, that's when she runs inside.'

9. mɛbi   dì   màma   ì   gò   dɔn   kɔm   kɔl-am   /   tɔl-am   sé   //
   maybe   the   mother she go   done   call-her   tell-her say
   'Perhaps her mother will have called her and asked her.'

10. hú   bí   dís   pɛsin   naw?
    who   be   this   person   now
    'Who is this person?'

11. ìm róst-am čɔp   'She roast and ate it.'

12. *ìm róst-am čɔp-am

13. *ìm róst čɔp-am

14. ìm róst-am / kɔm čɔp-am   'She roast it and then ate it.'

15. ìm no róst-am čɔp   'She didn't roast and/or eat it.'
                              (i.e., she did neither.)

16. *ìm róst-am no čɔp

17. ìm kɔm (ìm) čɔp-am   'He came, and ate it.'

18. ìm róst-am / (ìm) no čɔp-am 'She roasted it but didn't eat it.'

19. ìm gó kɔm kɔm.   'He will then come.'

A. What kind of multi-verb construction does 11 illustrate?
B. What kind of multi-verb construction does 14 illustrate?

Give evidence for your answers to A and B.

C. What are the functions of the form *kɔm*?
D. How many clauses are there in 1? 4? 9? 7?
E. Why is example 2 ambiguous? Why isn't example 5 ambiguous in the same way?

Glossary

How to use this glossary

Linguistics is a discipline that necessarily involves lots of specialized vocabulary. Unfortunately, not all linguists use terminology in exactly the same way. Terms that mean one thing in one theoretical perspective, may mean something quite different in another. Also, there are often multiple terms used for identical or nearly identical concepts. There are so many unfamiliar terms, and familiar terms used in unfamiliar ways, that beginning linguistics students often feel overwhelmed. This glossary is intended to help reduce the terminological stress level.

Throughout this book, technical terms, or terms used in specialized ways, are highlighted LIKE THIS. All of these words appear in this glossary, in alphabetical order, along with a brief definition.

Although students often ask for such definitions of terms, I would encourage readers not to rely too heavily on the glossary. Knowing the technical definition of all the terms in a chapter will not necessarily guarantee that you will understand the material in that chapter. Even as language learning does not proceed one word at a time, but by immersion in the flow of discourse, so learning a technical field is more than just memorizing definitions. I encourage students to try to learn new terms *in their contexts*, rather than constantly disrupting the flow of reading to check the glossary. Though contextual learning is the ideal, explicit definitions can be useful at times.

A: The most agent-like argument of a multi-argument (transitive) clause.

abilitative: A conceptual category (cf.) that expresses the subject's ability to perform the action described by the clause, e.g., if English had an abilitative inflection (say a prefix *abl-*), *he abl-reads* would mean 'he is able to read.'

absolutive: Any grammatical categorization (e.g., morphological case) that includes O and S but not A (cf.).

accusative: Any grammatical categorization (e.g., morphological case) that includes O but not A or S (cf.).

action-process: An event type in which an actor (AGENT or FORCE) causes a change in an affected participant, e.g., *The king's stinking son fired me*.

actions: An event type controlled by an AGENT or FORCE, but not involving an affected patient, e.g., *Sally danced and danced*.

active voice: A grammatical construction in which a very AGENT-like participant is expressed as a subject (cf.), and a very PATIENT-like participant is expressed as a direct object (cf.).

addressee: In a communicative act, there is usually a communicator and an addressee. These roles can alternate in a conversation. The communicator (sometimes referred to as the "speaker") formulates an utterance and presents it to the addressee. The addressee (sometimes referred to as the "hearer" or "audience") perceives the utterance and interprets it.

ad hoc: Latin "for this." An ad hoc rule, statement or explanation is one that works in only one situation, and not generally. For example, we could make up ad hoc rules to describe how the past tense of the verb *go* becomes *went* rather than **goed*. However, such "rules" would not account for any other past-tense forms in English, and therefore are unlikely to be a part of the internalized grammar of English speakers.

adjective: A grammatically distinct word class that contains mostly words that express "property concepts" (cf.), such as color, size, shape, human propensity, etc.

adposition: A cover term for prepositions and postpositions (cf.). Adpositions are "small" words that express something about the semantic role of a noun phrase. English has mostly prepositions (*to*, *on*, *under*, *of*, *by*, *for*, etc.), but at least one postposition, *ago*, as in *three years ago*.

adverb: A grammatically distinct word class that contains words that add secondary information to phrases or entire clauses. Adverbs typically express such notions as time, manner, purpose, reason, likelihood, etc. Examples include *later*, *earlier*, *surely*, *quickly*, *defiantly*, and *very*.

adverbial clause: A type of dependent clause that fulfills an "adverbial" function within another clause. For example, *locking the door behind her* in *She went out, locking the door behind her*.

adversative (adversative passive): A conceptual category expressing the notion that a described event has an adverse effect, usually with respect to the subject of the clause, e.g., if English had an adversative inflection (say a prefix *adv-*), *he adv-eats* would mean 'he eats to his detriment' (perhaps he is eating something that is bad for his health).

affix: A bound morpheme (cf.) that always attaches to the same class of words. Affix is a cover term for prefix, suffix, infix, and sometimes "suprafix" and "ambifix" (cf.).

affix suppletion: See "suppletion."

AGENT: A semantic role (cf.) defined in terms of a prototype as "the normally conscious, perceived instigator of an event," e.g., the person referred to by the noun *Alice* in a clause like *Alice reached for the key*.

agglutinative: A language in which morphemes can be easily divided, and which tends to express only one meaning per morpheme, is of the agglutinative morphological type.

agreement (sometimes "grammatical agreement"): A conceptual category which reflects some characteristics, usually person, gender and/or number, of one or more elements that are in a syntactic relation with the word that expresses the category. For example, adjectives agree with nouns in gender and number in Spanish.

allomorph: A systematic variant of a morpheme (cf.).

ambiguity: The property possessed by expressions (sentences, words, etc.) that express more than one meaning, e.g., *the right bank*.

ambiguous: When a structure (e.g., a word, a phrase, or a sentence) expresses more than one meaning, it is ambiguous.

analytic causative: A causative (cf.) construction that is expressed by adding a distinct causative verb, e.g., *You make me want to be a better man*.

analytic passive: A passive (cf.) construction that is expressed by adding a distinct auxiliary verb, e.g., *Television was called books*.

analytic pattern: See "syntactic pattern."

analytic reflexive: A reflexive (cf.) construction that is expressed by adding a distinct reflexive pronoun, e.g., *He tied himself to a tree*.

anaphor, anaphoric device: A pronoun or verb-agreement – any grammatical vocabulary item that makes reference to a *thing*. Full nouns do not count, because they are lexical vocabulary.

anticausative: Another term used for a morphological middle construction (cf.).

antipassive: A construction that downplays an O argument by omitting it or assigning it to an oblique role. In a prototypical antipassive, the clause will become formally intransitive, and the most agent-like argument will become the S.

applicative: A construction that increases transitivity by adding an O participant to the scene expressed by a verb. Sometimes applicatives are thought of as "advancing" an oblique argument to direct object status.

apposition: Two units in a syntactic structure are "in apposition" if there is no hierarchical relationship between the two, and they refer to the same message-world entity or situation. For example, in *my son John*, the DPs *my son* and *John* are in apposition.

arbitrariness: One of the properties of the bond between form and function in a symbolic system. Linguistic signs can be arbitrarily related to their meanings. For example, the concept expressed by the noise spelled *tree* in English could as easily be expressed by some randomly different noise, like *blick*, *fulterisk*, or *arbe*.

argument: A noun phrase that has a grammatical relation to something else. For example, subjects and objects are arguments of verbs. Genitives are arguments of nouns.

aspect: A semantic or grammatical notion. Semantically, aspect refers to the internal temporal "shape" of a situation or event, whether it is ongoing, completed, instantaneous, iterative, etc. Grammatically, aspect refers to the verbal inflections that reflect this semantic domain.

assimilation: A phonological or morphophonological pattern (cf.) in which some segment becomes more similar to its environment (cf.).

articles: "Small" words that express pragmatic status, such as identifiability (cf.). English is said to have two articles *the*, "definite," and *a(n)*, "indefinite."

augmentative: A conceptual category associated with nouns that expresses the idea that the noun refers to a large, ugly, or disgusting referent. The prefix *mega-* is almost becoming an augmentative in some standard Englishes: *megamarket*, *megachurch*.

autosegmental variation: A morphological process whereby some feature other than consonant or vowel quality is changed in order to express a conceptual category. Nasalization, tone, stress, and phonation type (breathy or creaky voice) are all possible autosegmental variables.

auxiliary: Auxiliaries or "auxiliary verbs" constitute a closed class of words that occur in verb phrases, and which express tense, aspect, mood, and/or other notions, but do not express the main semantic sense of the verb phrase. In traditional English grammar auxiliaries are sometimes called "helping verbs."

auxiliary stacking: The use of multiple auxiliaries, where each auxiliary is the complement of the previous one, as in *They will have been travelling for three days*.

bare form: A word form that includes no affixation. The term "bare form" is used especially for verb forms when the absence of affixation expresses some conceptual category (cf.). For example, the bare form of a verb in English expresses present-tense, non-third-person singular.

bitransitive: See "ditransitive."

borrowing: When speakers of a language treat a word, morpheme, or construction from another language as a lexical item in their own language. For example, the modern English words *thug*, *pajamas*, *chic*, *canoe*, *tomatoes*, and thousands of others are borrowed.

bounded/boundedness: Having distinct boundaries. Prototypical (cf.) nouns refer to clearly bounded entities, such as rocks, trees, and cars. Unbounded entities include such notions as air, fire, and sincerity. Unbounded concepts are less likely to be expressed with prototypical nouns.

bound morpheme: A morpheme that is not normally pronounced as a separate word, but must be attached phonologically to some other word. Examples in English include the past-tense *-ed* verb suffix, the plural *-s* noun suffix, and the "articles" *a* and *the*.

branch: The lines that connect nodes (cf.) in a syntactic tree.

case: This term has a number of theory-specific meanings in linguistics. As used in this book, case refers to morphosyntactic marking ("case markers") of nouns or noun phrases that expresses something about the relationship of the noun or noun phrase to its syntactic context. Some typical cases include (cf.) genitive, nominative, accusative, ergative, absolutive, dative, instrumental, and locative.

causative, causative construction: A grammatical construction that increases transitivity by adding a controlling participant to the scene embodied by a verb, e.g., *Alice made the cat smile* (analytic causative), or *Bunyan felled the tree* (lexical causative of *the tree fell*).

classifiers: Classifiers are usually morphemes that indicate noun classes (cf.). However, sometimes the term "classifier" can be used for verbal affixes as well.

clause: The grammatical instantiation of a proposition (cf.).

clause chain: A discourse-structuring pattern for expressing sequences of events or situations. Normally one clause in a chain (either the first or the last) takes all or most of the inflectional information for the entire chain, while the other clauses in the chain are dependent (cf.) in some way. Languages that employ clause chains extensively are sometimes called "clause-chaining languages."

clitic: A bound morpheme that functions at a phrase or clause level, rather than attaching only to words of a particular word class.

cognition: Thought, including categorization and conceptualization.

cognitive model: An idealized mental representation that serves as a basis for understanding and storing knowledge. For example, most people have a cognitive model of verticality based on the spatial parameter of "up" versus "down." This model helps English speakers conceptualize many abstract concepts, such as prices (*high* vs. *low*), quantities (*fill it up*) and emotions (*I'm feeling up today*).

collective: A conceptual category that refers to a group of entities in the message world. This is distinct from plural (cf.) in that the emphasis is on the group rather than individual members of the group. The category of collective may be part of the paradigm of number, which may also include singular, dual, paucal, and others (cf.).

comitative: The semantic role played by entities that accompany some other entity, e.g., *I had coffee with my mother*.

complement: If the syntactic head (cf.) of a phrasal category is not also the semantic head, it must have a complement. The complement is the semantic head of the phrasal category. It "completes" the meaning of the category.

complement clause: A type of dependent clause that functions as an argument (usually direct object, but also subject, and other relations) within another clause. For example, *I like to eat beans*.

complementizer: A word that introduces a whole clause when it is embedded within another clause or phrase. Unstressed *that* is a complementizer in English: *the book that I read*.

conceptual category: An element of meaning that is expressed by a systematic variation in form. For example "past tense" is a conceptual category in English because English speakers expect each verb to have a special form to express past tense.

conditional clause: A type of adverbial clause that expresses conditions under which other situations may or may not hold true in the message world. For example, *If I were a carpenter . . .* is a kind of conditional clause in English.

conjugation classes: Grammatically defined subclasses of verbs. For example, there are three conjugation classes of verbs in Spanish: those that end in *-ar*, *-er*, and *-ir*.

conjunction: A word class consisting of "small" words that join two larger constituents. Sometimes there is a distinction made between "coordinating conjunctions" and "subordinating conjunctions." Coordinating conjunctions in English include *and*, *or* and *but*. Subordinating conjunctions include *because*, *so* and *if*.

constituency: Units (cf.) in a syntactic structure exhibit constituency when they "merge" or "clump together" syntactically.

constituent structure: How linguistic structures are "built up" (constituted) in any language.

contrastiveness: A pragmatic (cf.) feature of participants in the message world (cf.), as presented by a speaker. A speaker may treat a participant as contrastive to correct a presumed misconception on the part of a hearer. For example, *SALLY made the salad* (with extra stress on SALLY) is likely to be used when the speaker believes the hearer thinks someone else made the salad.

convention, conventionalize: A pattern of linguistic behavior is conventionalized if it has become regular throughout a speech community. Linguistic forms express meaning "by convention," i.e., because everyone in a speech community tacitly (cf.) "agrees" to use forms in certain predictable ways.

coordination: A grammatical construction in which two syntactic elements are combined with no implication of asymmetry between them. Words, phrases, or clauses can be coordinated, but only elements of the same category may be combined in this way. For example, *N and N*, *DP and DP*, *IP and IP*, *S and S*, etc. are all possible coordinate structures. However, structures like *N and PP*, *IP and S*, etc. are not.

copula: A morpheme, usually a verb but sometimes a particle or pronoun, that "couples" two noun phrases; for example, *My son is a doctor*.

core argument: A nominal clause element that is either subject, object, indirect object, or primary object (cf.). Other clause elements are considered "peripheral," or oblique (cf.).

coreferential: Two anaphoric devices are coreferential if they both refer to the same entity.

coreferential possession: A construction which indicates that the possessor of a noun phrase is coreferential with one of the core arguments of the clause, usually the subject.

count noun: A noun that refers to items that can be easily and usefully counted, e.g., *keys*, *oysters*, or *cabbages*. Count nouns contrast with mass nouns (cf.).

dative (sometimes "indirect object"): A grammatical relation, distinct from subject and direct object, that prototypically expresses the animate RECIPIENT of some action or item, e.g., *Alice* in the clause *He passed the hat to Alice*. "Dative case" is a grammatical inflection on nouns that includes among its functions the expression of the dative grammatical relation.

dative of interest: A construction that upgrades a peripheral participant to a dative role without requiring any other morphological adjustments in the clause.

dative shift: A construction that upgrades a dative (cf.) argument to direct object status without requiring any other morphological adjustments in the clause: *I gave Mildred the book*. In this example, *Mildred* has undergone dative shift.

declension classes: Grammatically defined subclasses of nouns.

definite/definiteness: See "identifiability."

demonstratives: Words that imply "pointing" (demonstrating). Demonstratives may occur within noun phrases, as in *these houses*, or can themselves be heads of noun phrases: *I'll take three of those*. In the former usage they are sometimes referred to as demonstrative adjectives, and in the latter usage as demonstrative pronouns.

demotion: An alternative term for any valence-decreasing construction (cf.). "Demotion" can be considered equivalent to "deperspectivization," or the assignment of a participant to a less prominent grammatical status.

denominalization: A conceptual category whereby a noun is changed into some other word class. For example, the suffix spelled *-ize* in English can be a denominalizer because it turns a noun into a verb: *Finlandize, terrorize, palletize*.

dependent (or subordinate) clause: A clause that cannot normally be integrated into discourse without occurring in construction with some other clause.

derivation: (1) In contrast with inflection (cf.), derivational morphology creates new stems from simpler stems or roots. For example, the suffix often spelled *-able* in English creates adjectives based on verb roots: *questionable, reliable* etc. (2) A morphophonemic derivation is the set of rules posited for the pronunciation of a particular word.

descriptive grammar: The science of understanding and communicating the patterns and correspondences that constitute native speakers' tacit knowledge of their language. Descriptive grammar contrasts with "prescriptive grammar," which consists of rules designed to help individuals write or speak more like members of some culturally determined elite group.

descriptive modifier: Any element that makes the reference of a noun phrase more specific. This would include adjectives, relative clauses, and participial phrases, etc.

determiner: A position in grammatical structure that is filled by various items that specify something about how the audience is to identify the referent of a particular noun. In English, determiners include the articles (*a, the, Ø*), demonstratives (*this, that, these, those*), all possessors, some question words, pronouns, etc.

determiner phrase: A syntactic "clump" headed by a determiner. Abbreviated DP, determiner phrases can also be thought of as "determined noun phrases." The supposition that nominal elements are universally projections of determiners is called the "determiner phrase hypothesis," or the "DP hypothesis."

detransitive (or detransitivizing) constructions: Constructions that downplay (or "deperspectivize") a clausal argument: these include reflexives, reciprocals, middles, passives, antipassives, object demotion, object incorporation, and object omission (cf.).

diminutive: A conceptual category associated with nouns that expresses the idea that the noun refers to a small, cute or beloved referent. For example, the suffix [i] in English sometimes expresses a kind of diminutive idea: *Tommy*, *doggie*, *sweety*.

direct object: See "object."

discourse: The act of communication. Sentences may exist in isolation, divorced from any actual function. Discourse, however, involves actual linguistic acts performed in order to accomplish some social task.

discourse analysis: Discourse analysis involves understanding how communicative acts are accomplished in actual situations. While syntactic analysis can be based on abstract, hypothetical linguistic strings, discourse analysis can only be undertaken by observing, recording, and examining language in use.

discourse manipulability: A pragmatic (cf.) property of prototypical nouns. Entities in the message world (cf.) that can be referred to repeatedly as "the same" are discourse manipulable.

discourse stage: A metaphor often used by linguists to understand how communication occurs. People communicate with one another by setting up mental "scenes" that have "participants," "acts," "scripts," "climaxes," etc.

disjunction: A kind of coordination in which only one member of the coordinated pair is asserted to hold true. For example, *She came in through the window or the door* implies that "she" may have come in through the window, or she may have come in through the door, but not both.

dissimilation: A phonological or morphophonological pattern (cf.) in which some segment becomes more distinct from its environment (cf.).

distribution (also **"distributional properties"**): The distribution of a morphosyntactic unit is how it functions in relation to other units in a grammatical construction.

ditransitive: One term used to describe a situation that involves three obligatory participants, or a clause that has three core arguments, for example: *Alice gave the Mad Hatter a stern look*, or *Rick showed the exit visas to Sam*.

divalent: See "transitive."

DP hypothesis: See "determiner phrase."

dual: A conceptual category that expresses the idea that there are exactly two referents mentioned by a noun, pronoun, or other referential form. Dual can also be a category in agreement paradigms. The category of dual is part of the paradigm of number, which may also include singular, singulative, trial, plural, paucal, and others (cf.).

dynamic: A type of situation that involves motion and/or change. Verbs that describe such situations are sometimes called "dynamic verbs," in opposition to "stative verbs."

ellipsis: The obvious omission of some element of clause structure. For example, answers to questions sometimes contain ellipsis. In answer to the question *Where is she going?* one may reply simply *to the store*, in which case ellipsis replaces *she is going*.

embedded clause: See "embedding."

embedding: Units may be "embedded" within other units in syntactic structure. For example, in the following tree there is a clause (an S node) embedded within a noun phrase, and another clause embedded within the embedded clause (see chapter 10):

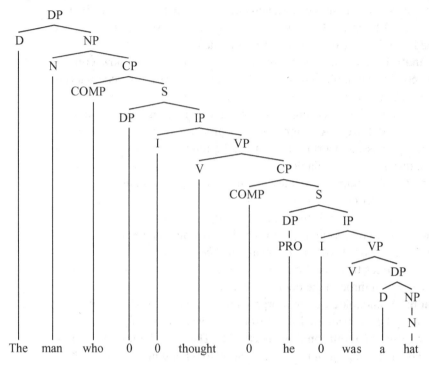

The   man   who   0   0   thought   0   he   0   was   a   hat

environment: The context in which a morphophonemic (cf.) change occurs.

epenthesis (or **"insertion"**): A phonological or morphophonological pattern (cf.) in which a segment is inserted.

epistemic: Conceptual categories that express the speaker's commitment to the truth of an utterance are epistemic. For example, *may*, *might*, and *will* are epistemic modal auxiliaries (cf.) in English.

ergative/absolutive: Any grammatical system that treats O and S as "the same" and A differently, e.g., case marking in Yup'ik regularly marks singular S and O with a -*q* and singular A with an -*m*.

ergative: Any grammatical categorization (e.g., morphological case) that includes A but not O or S.

evidential, evidentiality: Conceptual categories that express the source of the information contained in an utterance. For example, languages sometimes have categories that express whether the information was obtained directly, by hearsay, or by inference.

exclusive: A conceptual subcategory within first-person plural (cf.) that refers to the speaker and someone else, while excluding the hearer: "He/she and I but not you" (cf. "inclusive"). English does not have an exclusive/inclusive distinction. For example, the pronoun *we* can refer to 'you and I only,' 'he/she, you and I' or 'he/she and I but not you.'

existential clause: A clause that expresses the existence of a particular entity, e.g. *There once was a king*, or *There's ants in the syrup!*

experiencer: The semantic role held by participants that receive sensory or emotional impressions, e.g., <u>*Alice*</u> *noticed a small wooden door.*

expression type: Structural ways that languages express conceptual categories (cf.). There are three groups of expression types discussed in this text: lexical expression (cf.), morphological processes (cf.), and syntactic patterns (cf.).

external possession (or "possessor raising"): A construction that upgrades a possessor of a central argument to direct object status: *He hit me on the right front fender*, meaning 'he hit <u>my car</u> on the right front fender.'

extraction: The metaphorical "movement" of a unit out of its normal position in a syntactic structure. For example, *beans* has been extracted in the sentence: <u>*Beans*</u> *I like.*

factives: A type of verb that describes the coming into existence of some entity, e.g., *build, ignite, form, create, make, gather* (as in *a crowd gathered*).

finite: Any verb or auxiliary that has all the inflectional information expressed by verbs in the language is finite.

flat structure: A syntactic structure in which all nodes are at the same hierarchical level. In other words, a structure that does not involve "nesting."

force: The semantic role held by entities that unconsciously initiate events, e.g., *The wind opened the door.*

form: Another term for structure. Any tool, including language, consists of two parts – its form and its function. Form is the part that adapts to its function. In language, the form consists of sounds, morphemes, words, phrases, and sentences, and the function is communicative tasks such as expressing meaning, establishing and maintaining human relationships, etc. (cf. "function").

formalism: A graphic way of representing the implicit patterns that constitute the grammar of a language. Particular formalisms (e.g., phrase structure trees and position-class diagrams) tend to be associated with particular linguistic theories.

free morpheme: Any morpheme that does not have to attach to some other morpheme in order to be understood. Words such as *dog* and *cat* are free morphemes.

full lexical words: Words that have rich semantic content, such as *incredible*, *garden*, and *Wonderland*. These are in opposition to grammatical morphemes (cf.).

full noun: A way of referring to a noun that is a full lexical word, rather than a reduced form, such as a pronoun or zero. The syntactic typology of a language is determined with respect to full nouns.

function: Linguistic functions are "jobs" performed by language structures. Expressing meaning is a major function of language, so meaning features, like semantic roles, tense, participant reference, and many others are among the functions of linguistic structures. Other functions are not so clearly related to meaning but are still part of the functional part of language, for example, getting other people to do something, requesting information, entertaining, invoking supernatural forces, etc. (cf. "form").

functional linguistics: A theoretical approach in which language is conceived as a system of tools that people use to accomplish certain social functions, primarily communication.

fusion: The degree to which a language tends to express one meaning per morpheme.

fusional: A language which tends to express one meaning per morpheme is of the fusional morphological type.

Generative Grammar: A linguistic theory, originating in the 1950s and 1960s, most closely associated with the linguist Noam Chomsky. In Generative Grammar, a language is conceived as an infinitely large, but highly constrained, set of grammatical sentences. Grammar is understood as a "machine" that "generates" all of the grammatical sentences and none of the ungrammatical sentences of a language.

genitive: The grammatical relation that holds between a noun and its argument. Also, the noun that bears the genitive relationship to another noun. Genitive nouns may express any number of semantic roles, but POSSESSOR is usually the prototype. In languages with elaborate case systems (e.g., German, Finnish, Russian), the "genitive case" functions in many other situations as well.

given information: A pragmatic (cf.) feature of participants in the message world (cf.), as presented by a speaker. Information is "given" if the speaker assumes that the addressee is already actively thinking about it.

gloss: A convenient abbreviation for the meaning of a morpheme, used in linguistic examples to help readers understand the structure of the language being described, even if they have no previous knowledge of the language.

govern, government: (1) Syntactic heads (cf.) "govern" their complements (cf.). (2) Certain syntactic elements determine the form of other syntactic elements. Sometimes this relationship is referred to as "government." For example, in Latin, prepositions "govern" the case of their objects, meaning the case of the object of a preposition varies depending on which preposition is used.

grammar: The internalized, unconscious system of conventions and correspondences that allows people to communicate with one another. It consists of everything speakers must know in order to speak their language. Linguistic analysis consists in making this implicit system explicit, usually in the form of written rules and concise statements.

grammatical morphemes: See "full lexical words." Grammatical morphemes express limited "grammatical" meanings (such as "third-person singular," and "past tense") rather than rich "lexical" meanings such as *cacophony*, and *disastrous*.

grammatical relations: Grammatically instantiated relations between words in phrases or clauses. Some typical grammatical relations are genitive (cf.), subject, object, ergative, absolutive, and others (see especially chapter 8).

grammatical rule: A regular pattern in the grammar that determines how a conceptual category (cf.) is expressed structurally (for example "add the suffix -*ed* to form the past tense of a verb").

grounding: Certain conceptual categories "ground" a situation according to time, location, or participants. For example, a notion like *walking* is not grounded until the speaker specifies *where*, *when*, and *who* is walking. *Sylvester is walking to school* is grounded according to all of these parameters.

harmonic reflexive: A reflexive construction that uses different reflexive forms (affixes or pronouns) for each relevant person and number category. Spanish has a harmonic morphological reflexive.

head, semantic: The semantic head of a noun phrase is the noun that refers to the same thing that the whole phrase refers to, for example *man* in *the tall handsome garbage man who lives next door*. Quite often, semantic heads and syntactic heads (cf.) are the same, but not always.

head, syntactic: The element of a phrase that determines (or "projects") the syntactic properties of the whole phrase, e.g., *cat* in *That ridiculous big orange cat that always sits on my porch*. In this case the syntactic head also happens to be the semantic head (cf.). However, in some cases the two can be distinct. For example, prepositions are syntactic heads because they determine the syntactic behavior of their phrases, even though the nominal component expresses most of the meaning.

headless: Some relative clauses are "headless" in that the noun phrase they modify contains no overt semantic head – the clause itself refers to the noun. For example, the noun phrase *whoever goes to the store* contains a headless relative clause.

head-marking: A type of language in which syntactic relations are most often marked on the syntactic head, rather than on the complement (cf., "dependent-marking").

hedging: A conversational technique whereby a speaker "distances" him- or herself from the content of an utterance, so as to avoid social responsibility for its truth. For example, the statement *They sort of took over the department* is a "hedged" way of saying *They took over the department*.

hierarchical structure: The characteristic of syntactic structures whereby units occur "nested" within larger units.

honorifics: A conceptual category or set of categories that express different degrees of politeness, honor, or relative social status, usually between the speaker and hearer.

host: The free morpheme that a bound morpheme (cf.) attaches to.

iconicity: A property of the bond between form and function in a symbolic system. Signs are iconic to the extent that they constitute a "picture" of their meanings.

idealized: A concept in which the details are left vague is idealized. The meanings of words are often stored in memory in terms of idealized images.

identifiability (or "definiteness"): A pragmatic (cf.) feature of participants in the message world (cf.), as presented by a speaker. Participants are identifiable if the speaker assumes that the hearer can uniquely identify the referent. The article *the* is one way of expressing identifiability in English. The phrase *a dog* is probably not identifiable, while *the dog* is being treated by the speaker as identifiable.

idiosyncratic: Unpatterned, random. For example, the plural of *child* in English is idiosyncratic, *children*, in that there are no other nouns in the modern language that form their plurals in precisely this way.

impersonal passive: A passive-like construction in which no specific AGENT is implied, e.g., *She was considered lost*, or *They say there'll be snow tomorrow*.

inclusive: A pronoun or verb agreement marker that refers to the speaker, hearer, and possibly someone else.

incorporation: A kind of compounding (cf.) in which an argument of a verb loses its independent identity and becomes a part of the verb. Incorporation is productive in English in such expressions as *we went fox-hunting*, or *you will be pay-deducted*.

index of fusion: See "fusion."

index of synthesis: See "synthesis."

indirect object: See "dative."

indirect question: A kind of complement clause (cf.) that can arguably be derived from a question, e.g., *I know who came* can be paraphrased as 'I know the answer to the question "Who came?".'

individuated, individuation: The property of being distinct from other entities. Prototypical nouns refer to individuated entities, such as people, cars, and birds. Unindividuated entities include such notions as mud, ants, and marksmanship. These concepts are less likely to be expressed with prototypical nouns.

infinitive: A verb form that expresses no inflectional information (cf., "inflection").

infix: An affix that is inserted inside the root of words. For example, some varieties of English use the infix *-izz-* to express intensification, or emphasis: *I knizzow* 'I really know,' or 'I heartily agree.'

infixation: The morphological process that involves the addition of an infix (cf.).

inflection: See also "derivation," above. Inflectional categories are conceptual categories that do not create new stems. Rather, they add specific "grammatical" information to already existing stems. Inflectional categories tend to occur in "paradigms" (cf.).

inflectional phrase: A syntactic category of English and some other languages that consists of a verb phrase with a (possibly zero) auxiliary. See also "inflection."

inherently reciprocal verb (also "lexical reciprocal"): A verb that describes an event that people often do to each other, e.g., *fight, meet, shake hands, hug,* *embrace, cuddle, kiss*, etc. When these verbs are grammatically intransitive *and the subject is plural* they are automatically understood as reciprocal.

inherently reflexive verb (also "lexical reflexive"): A verb that describes an activity that people usually do to themselves, e.g., *shave, wash hands, dress*, etc. When these verbs are grammatically intransitive they are automatically understood as reflexive.

INSTRUMENT: The semantic role held by entities that are intermediate causes of events, e.g., *Alice opened the door with the key*. The AGENT (*Alice*) acts upon the PATIENT (*the door*) with the INSTRUMENT (*the key*) as a intermediary.

internal head: The heads of some relative clauses are inside the clause itself. For example, if English had internally-headed relative clauses, a noun phrase like *the house that I live in* would be expressed something like *the that I live in house*.

interposition: One of the minor "tests" for constituency. If an adverb or other variable-position element of a syntactic structure may occur between two other elements, chances are there is a syntactic boundary at that point.

intransitive: A clause is intransitive if it does not contain a direct object, either expressed or implied.

inversion: A syntactic construction in which two elements appear in the opposite order from their "normal" position. For example "subject-aux inversion" in English is when the subject and the auxiliary exchange positions in questions and certain negative constructions: *Will he ever learn*?

involuntary process: An event type in which a non-volitional participant undergoes a change of state, e.g., the events expressed by English verbs such as *melt, grow, sweat, explode*, and *die*.

isomorphism: A kind of lexical expression in which a stem expresses a conceptual category by conspicuously failing to undergo any morphological or syntactic change. For example, the past tenses of the verbs *hit, cut, shed*, and others are the same as the non-past tenses for most persons and numbers. Similarly, the plurals of the nouns *fish, sheep, elk*, and *deer* are the same as the singulars.

isolating: A language that tends to express only one meaning per morpheme is of the isolating type.

item and arrangement: A view of morphology in which roots and affixes are considered to be separate morphemes, related in static displays depending on the communicative intention of the speaker. Position-class diagrams (cf.) represent an analytical method based on this view.

item and process: A view of morphology in which roots are considered to be "chunks" of morphology, but affixes and other morphological changes are considered to be "rules" or "processes" that the roots undergo. Process rules (cf.) represent an analytical method based on this view.

labile verbs: See "lexical middle."

language isolate: A language that is not demonstrably related to any other languages.

left-branching: A language in which complements (cf.) tend to precede their syntactic heads (cf.). Other terms for this language type are "complement-head languages" or "head-final" languages.

lexical ambiguity: When a form is ambiguous because it has two inherent meanings. For example, *bank* is lexically ambiguous because it can refer to the edge of a river, or a financial institution. Because of this ambiguity, structures that contain *bank* may also be ambiguous, e.g., *Let's try a different bank*.

lexical category: The lowest (terminal) nodes on a phrase structure tree (cf.) refer to lexical categories. They consist of units that do not have internal syntactic structure themselves.

lexical causative (also "inherently causative verb"): A verb whose lexical entry expresses the meaning of cause and effect. For example, *kill* is an inherently causative verb because it expresses the meaning "cause to die" (cf. "causative construction").

lexical entry: A lexical entry is a specification of all of the structural and functional properties of a linguistic unit (cf. "lexicon").

⊙ **lexical expression**: A way of expressing a conceptual category that requires special knowledge of the lexical entry of the form that expresses the category. Strong stem suppletion, weak stem suppletion, and isomorphism (cf.) are the general subtypes of lexical expression.

lexical middle (also "inherently middle verb" or "labile verb"): A verb that describes a situation that normally involves an AGENT and a PATIENT, but when used intransitively places the PATIENT in the subject relation: *the window broke, the city changed*, etc.

lexical passive (or "inherently passive verb"): A verb that in its basic meaning implies the existence of an AGENT, but for which no reference to the AGENT is made.

lexical reciprocal: See "inherently reciprocal verb."

lexical reflexive: See "inherently reflexive verb."

lexicon: The store of all memorized words, pieces of words and regular patterns of word formation and combination that are available to a language user. In some linguistic theories, e.g., Cognitive Grammar (Langacker 1987), Head-Driven Phrase Structure Grammar (Sag, Wasow, and Bender 2003) and Construction Grammar (Goldberg 1995; Croft 2002), virtually all grammatical patterns would belong in the lexicon. Other theories, e.g., various versions of Generative Grammar (e.g., Radford 1988), distinguish the lexicon from other "components" or "modules" of grammar, such as morphology and syntax.

linear order: The sequential order of elements in the speech stream.

LOCATIVE: A cover term for a variety of semantic roles involving a locational relationship between two things. Objects of the prepositions *at, in, on, under, above*, etc., in English, often play this role.

manipulation: A class of verbs that describe activities in which the actor attempts to manipulate another person. Some manipulative verbs are "stronger" than others. For example, the following English verbs describe manipulative concepts in decreasing order of strength: *force, make, compel, command, urge, ask to, ask that, request.*

manner: An adverbial notion that includes semantic features associated with events or situations (as opposed to participants). Most manner adverbs in English end with a suffix spelled *-ly*; for example: *quickly, disparagingly, freely,* and *surreptitiously.* Some manner adverbs in English do not carry this suffix, e.g., *He fell down hard,* and *She sings well.*

mass noun: A noun that refers to a quantity, and therefore is not normally used in the plural, e.g., *air, sand,* or *water.*

merger: See "syntactic merger."

message world: The shared conceptual scenes cooperatively elaborated in any situation in which people are communicating. This world may correspond more or less to objective reality, but may be entirely fictitious, abstract, or hypothetical. The message world is populated by participants and props whose properties, actions, and relationships form the content of linguistic messages.

metathesis: A phonological or morphophonemic (cf.) pattern whereby segments (consonants or vowels) reverse their positions.

middle, middle construction, middle voice: A grammatical construction that removes an AGENT from the scene evoked by a verb, places the PATIENT in the subject role, and presents the situation as a process undergone by the PATIENT, with no mention or implication of the presence of an AGENT.

minimalism, minimalist criterion: A feature of recent approaches to Generative Grammar that stress the importance of simplicity in syntactic analysis. The "minimalist criterion" is that, given two analyses that adequately account for the same range of data, the simpler analysis is preferred.

minor class: (1) A subclass of words that contains fewer elements than the "major" class. For example, verbs whose past tense involves a stem change from [i] to [æ] in English (*sat, sang, sank, drank,* etc.) constitute a minor class of verbs. Major class verbs in English are those whose past tense ends in the form spelled *-ed.* (2) A "minor word class" is a word class that has fewer members than the "major" word classes. In English, minor word classes include prepositions, articles, and conjunctions.

modal auxiliaries: A class of words in English (and some other languages) consisting of words such as *could, should, would, might, may, can, will, must, ought to,* and *have to.* These words function as auxiliaries (cf.) in English, and express various modes (cf.), or modal conceptual categories.

mode: A set of conceptual categories that express various speaker attitudes or perspectives on an event. Mode is grammaticalized in English mostly via the modal auxiliaries (cf.).

morpheme: A linguistic unit that contributes meaning to an utterance, but cannot itself be divided into smaller meaningful parts. For example, *dog, -ed, -s, the,* and *almanac* are all morphemes of English.

morphological causative: A causative construction (cf.) that is expressed primarily by a morphological process applied to a verb. For example, if English had a morphological causative, say a prefix *caus-*, the clause *she caus-cried him* would mean 'she made him cry.'

morphological passive: A passive construction (cf.) that is expressed primarily by a morphological process applied to a verb. For example, if English had a morphological passive, say, a prefix *pass-*, the clause *she pass-slapped* would mean 'she was slapped.'

morphological process: A way of expressing a conceptual category by altering the shape of a word. There are ten major morphological processes discussed in this book. These are termed the "Big Ten": prefixation, suffixation, infixation, circumfixation, stem change, autosegmental variation, reduplication, subtractive morphology, non-concatenative morphology, and compounding.

morphological reciprocal: A reciprocal construction (cf.) that is expressed by applying a morphological process to a verb. For example, if English had a morphological reciprocal, say a suffix *-rec*, the clause *Wesley and Buttercup kiss-rec-ed* would mean 'Wesley and Buttercup kissed each other.'

morphological reflexive: A reflexive construction (cf.) that is expressed by a morphological process applied to a verb. For example, if English had a morphological reflexive, say reduplication of the first consonant and vowel of a verb, the clause *Wesley bu-burned* would mean 'Wesley burned himself,' and *Alice pi-pinched* would mean 'Alice pinched herself.'

morphology: The study of shapes. In linguistics, morphology is the study of the shapes of words, or, more specifically, how words are constructed out of smaller meaningful pieces (cf., "morpheme") in order to express variations in meaning.

morphophonemic derivation: See "derivation."

morphophonemic rules: Systematic adjustments in pronunciation that require reference to particular morphemes (cf.) or morpheme boundaries in their environments.

morphosyntax: The part of grammatical knowledge that involves how conceptual categories are expressed structurally.

motivation: A reasonable explanation for why a particular pattern occurs. Linguists are always interested in explaining linguistic patterns. However, a few patterns may be unexplainable, or "unmotivated." In most cases this is because the motivation for the pattern is lost in the dark reaches of the history of the language.

nasalization: A phonetic feature that involves air passing through the nose. For example, the vowel in the French word *bon* 'good (masculine)' is nasalized.

nodes: The points on syntactic trees where category labels are found. When trees "branch," they always branch at nodes. However, not every node is a branching node – terminal nodes (cf.) do not branch.

nominalization: Nouns or noun phrases that are built on roots that usually belong to other word classes or syntactic categories, e.g., *the collapse of the empire*. This is a noun phrase that refers to the ACTION of the empire collapsing.

nominalizer: A derivational morpheme that attaches to a non-nominal root and changes it into a noun. For example, one use of the suffix *-er* in English is to change a verb into a noun: *work* → *worker*.

nominative/accusative: Any grammatical system that treats A and S as "the same" and O differently, e.g., basic constituent order in English consistently puts both S and A before the verb and O afterwards.

nominative: Any grammatical categorization (e.g., morphological case) that includes both A and S, but not O.

non-concatenative morphology: A morphological process employed mostly in Semitic languages (Arabic, Hebrew, Amharic, and others) in which roots consist only of consonants (or "consonantal templates"), and conceptual categories are expressed by interposing vowels and other segmental and suprasegmental pieces on these consonantal templates.

non-finite: Any verb or clause that does not carry tense or person inflection; not to be confused with the term "infinitive" from traditional grammar. Many (not all) usages of the bare form, and present and past participles in English are non-finite.

non-harmonic reflexive: A reflexive construction in which the reflexive form (be it an affix or a pronoun) does not change depending on the person and number of the subject of the construction. Russian has non-harmonic reflexives.

noun: The word class that prototypically expresses bounded, individuated entities. Defined in English by ability to function as subject or object of a verb.

noun class system: Any semantically based grammatical categorization of nouns in a language. Grammatical gender (cf.) is one kind of noun class system.

noun phrase: A "clump" in constituent structure that is headed by a noun, and which may or may not contain other elements. Noun phrases derive their grammatical and semantic properties from their head nouns. In other words, nouns project (cf.) their properties onto their phrases.

nuance: A secondary meaning, or shade of meaning – a connotation. For example, the difference in meaning between pairs of words like *spit* and *expectorate* can be said to involve a nuance, rather than a core meaning difference.

number: A paradigm of conceptual categories in the participant reference system of many languages. Categories in this paradigm consist typically of singular, plural, and possibly trial, quadral, paucal, and a few others.

O: The most PATIENT-like argument of a multi-argument clause.

object (also **"direct object"**): A core grammatical relation, defined in English by the following properties: (1) Position immediately following the verb in pragmatically neutral, transitive clauses, (2) when pronominalized, non-subject pronouns are used, and (3) absence of a preceding preposition.

object demotion: A grammatical construction that demotes a participant that is "normally" (i.e., in a scene evoked by the verb) the direct object to an oblique role. The semantic effect of such a construction is to "downplay" the PATIENT, and/or render it less wholly affected by the action of the verb: *Aileron kicked at the Duke*.

object incorporation: A grammatical construction that downplays (or "deperspectivizes") the PATIENT of an event by expressing it as part of the verb, rather than as a distinct noun. For example: *We went fox hunting*.

object omission: A construction that downplays (or "deperspectivizes") an O argument by simply omitting it, without requiring any adjustments in the rest of the clause: *Calvin already ate*.

oblique, oblique argument: A nominal element of a clause that does not bear a core grammatical relation (cf.) to the verb.

paradigm: A related set of conceptual categories. For example, the tense paradigm of a language may consist of past tense, present tense, and future tense. The verb agreement paradigm may consist of first person, second person, and third person, etc.

partial reduplication: Reduplication that involves part of a root, rather than the whole root. For example, if English reduplicated the first two sounds of a noun to express plural, that would be partial reduplication. Then, the forms *dodog* and *cacat* would mean 'dogs' and 'cats' respectively.

participant reference: The job of referring to or mentioning participants in the message world. All languages have a participant reference system, usually consisting of various categories of noun phrases, pronouns, agreement markers, clitics, etc.

participial phrase: A clause in which the main verb is a participle (cf.).

participle: A deverbalized form of a verb. English has present participles, marked with the suffix *-ing*, and past participles marked in various ways, but most commonly with *-ed* or *-en*.

particle: A "small" uninflected word or clitic that normally expresses conceptual categories of tense, aspect, mode, evidentiality, or discourse structure (cf.).

passive, passive voice, passive construction: A grammatical construction that upgrades (or "perspectivizes") a PATIENT to the subject position and either omits or demotes the AGENT to an oblique role: *The baby was named Jane (by her parents)*.

past participle: A kind of deverbalization (cf.) that refers to the resultant state of some event in the past, e.g., in the expression *a fallen log*, the word *fallen* is a past participle.

past tense: A conceptual category in the tense paradigm that expresses the idea that the situation described by a clause occurred before the time the clause is uttered.

patient: The semantic role held prototypically by entities that undergo a visible, concrete change in state, e.g., *the cake* referred to in *Alice ate the cake*.

paucal: A conceptual category that expresses the idea that there is a small number (for count nouns) or a small quantity (mass nouns) of a referent mentioned by a noun, a pronoun, or any other referential form. The category of paucal is part of the paradigm of number, which may also include singular, singulative, dual, trial, plural, and others.

perfect aspect: A conceptual category in the paradigm of aspect (cf.) in many languages that expresses a state in terms of the result of a previous event. The perfect aspect construction in English involves the auxiliary *have*: *I have been there before, They had entered Albanian airspace.*

person: A paradigm of conceptual categories in the participant reference system of a language. Categories in this paradigm consist typically of first person (the speaker), second person (the audience) and third person (other participants not involved in the communicative act).

personal passive: A passive construction (cf.) in which a specific AGENT is clearly implied or present, e.g., *He was attacked by a mad dog.*

perspectivization: The point of view a speaker chooses to take with respect to a message-world situation. For example, one and the same situation can be described from the perspective of an AGENT: *Orna baked these cookies*, or a PATIENT: *These cookies were baked by Orna.*

phonemics: See "phonology."

phonetics: The sub-discipline of linguistics that studies the way linguistic sounds are produced and interpreted.

phonological patterns (or **"rules"**): Systematic patterns of pronunciation that do not require mention of particular morphemes (cf.) or morpheme boundaries.

phonology: The sub-discipline of linguistics that is concerned with the sound *systems* of languages – what makes certain sounds contrast with other sounds in order to express differences in meaning.

phrase: A syntactic constituent (cf.) that is not a terminal node (cf.), and not the highest node in a syntactic structure either.

phrasal categories: Phrasal categories (DP, NP, IP, VP, PP, etc.) are "projections" of their heads, i.e., the phrase is defined by the word class of the head.

phrasal nodes: Points where a phrase structure tree branches such that one branch leads to the "head" of the phrase.

phrase structure (PS) rules: The grammaticalized (i.e., over-learned) patterns that underlie the constituent structure of a language, e.g., the rule S → DP + IP captures the fact that English speakers have a well-oiled habit pattern of constituting clauses, abbreviated S, out of two other elements, a "Determined Noun Phrase" (DP) followed by an "Inflected Verb Phrase."

phrase structure trees (also "tree diagrams," or "phrase markers"): A way of representing the linear order, constituency and hierarchical structure of sentences in a language. Phrase structure trees are "generated" or "sanctioned" by phrase structure rules.

plosive consonant: A consonant in which pressure is built up in the mouth and suddenly released. The plosive consonants (or "plosives") of English are /p, t, k, b, d, and g/.

plural: A conceptual category that expresses the idea that there is more than one referent mentioned by a noun, a pronoun, or any other referential element.

Plural can also be a category in agreement paradigms. The category of plural is part of the paradigm of number, which may also include singular, singulative, dual, trial, paucal, and others (cf.).

polysynthetic: A language in which words tend to have many morphemes is of the polysynthetic type.

position-class diagram: A method for analyzing complex morphological structures.

possessor raising: See "external possession."

postposition: An adposition (cf.) that follows its related noun phrase. For example, if English had postpositions instead of prepositions, the expression *the house to* would mean 'to the house,' and *my mother with* would mean 'with my mother.'

pragmatically marked: A clause is pragmatically marked if it expresses some unusual pragmatic (cf.) function, such as a question, negation, contrastiveness (cf.), etc.

pragmatically neutral: A clause is pragmatically neutral if it has no unusual pragmatic (cf.) function, such as a question, negation, contrastiveness (cf.), etc. The syntactic typology of a language is determined with respect to pragmatically neutral clauses.

pragmatics: The study of how context affects and is affected by linguistic communication.

prefix: A morpheme that attaches to the beginning of a word, e.g., the negative *un-* (*unlovely, unsuccessful, uncola*) or repetitive *re-* (*reconsider, recook, re-engineer*), are prefixes in English.

prefixation: The member of the "big ten" morphological processes that involves the addition of a prefix (cf.).

prenominal: Coming before a noun. For example, articles (cf.) are prenominal in English.

preposition: An adposition (cf.) that precedes its related noun phrase. For example, English employs prepositions in such expressions as *to the house*, and *with my mother*.

prescriptive grammar: Rules of spelling, pronunciation, word and sentence structure designed to help people write or speak more like an educated elite.

present participle: A kind of deverbalization (cf.) that refers to an ongoing action. For example, in the expression *a falling leaf*, the word *falling* is a present participle.

presentative: A construction that functions primarily to bring a new participant onto the discourse stage (cf.).

primary object: The grammatical relation that consistently treats the RECIPIENT of a ditransitive (cf.) clause in the same manner as a PATIENT-like argument of a transitive clause.

primary/secondary object system: A system for organizing grammatical relations in which RECIPIENTS and PATIENTS consistently have the same grammatical relation. This type of system contrasts with the more familiar direct/indirect object system.

process: An event type in which a PATIENT undergoes a change, but not necessarily as a result of any voluntary act on the part of a distinct AGENT. For example, events described by English verbs like *change, hide, roll, fall, break, grow, melt, explode*, etc.

process rule: A kind of morphological representation that treats affixation and other morphological patterns as "processes" that roots undergo. Under this view, roots "start out" as certain idealized forms, and "end up" as others.

proclitic: A clitic (cf.) that attaches to the beginning of its host. These contrast with enclitics, which attach to the ends of their hosts.

pro-form: A linguistic unit that "stands for" another, larger, unit. Pronouns are the major type of pro-form, though pro-verbs (cf.) and perhaps other pro-forms also exist. See "substitution."

pro-verb: A pro-form (cf.) that "stands for" a verb or verb phrase. See "substitution."

projection (or "projection principle"): A phrasal category is the projection of its syntactic head. In other words, the syntactic head of a phrase determines its syntactic properties.

pronoun retention: One strategy for referring to the R-element in a relative clause. For example: *that's the guy who I can never remember his name*.

pronoun: A free grammatical vocabulary item that refers to a thing but is not a full lexical noun, e.g., *he is clearly over-reacting*.

proper names: A subclass of nouns that are automatically determined and identifiable, such as *Winchester Cathedral, Leeds Castle, Mt. Rushmore, Tony Blair*, and *Popeye*.

property concepts: Conceptual notions that describe "properties," such as colors, sizes, shapes, values, human propensity, etc.

proposition: A semantic notion that involves one or more entities (or participants) and a property or relation that involves them. Propositions are the semantic bases for grammatical clauses. For example, any number of clauses may instantiate the proposition MY HEAD ACHES, including *I have a headache, I do have a headache, my head aches, I sure have a headache, me duele la cabeza*, and many others.

prototype: The member of a category that best instantiates the entire category. For example, a sparrow is probably the prototype for the category of "bird" for most English speakers.

quotative: A construction or particle used to describe someone's actual words, e.g., *"Why are we in this handbasket?" asked Alice*.

RECIPIENT: The semantic role held prototypically by entities that receive some item, e.g., the message-world participant referred to by the phrase *the carpenter* in *The walrus gave a sandwich to the carpenter*.

reciprocal construction: A construction that expresses a semantically transitive situation in which the two participants are distinct but their roles as A and O are "combined," i.e., both participants are equally A and O: *Lynn and Cory hugged*, meaning 'Lynn and Cory hugged each other.'

recursion: The property of any system that allows production of an infinite output, given a finite number of basic building blocks. All natural human languages exhibit recursion.

reduplication: A morphological process whereby a root, or part of a root is repeated in order to express some conceptual category. For example, if English used reduplication to express plurality, the forms *dogdog* and *catcat* would mean 'dogs' and 'cats' respectively. Reduplication can be complete, as in these examples, or partial (cf.).

referent: A message-world entity referred to by a noun, a pronoun, or any other referential element. For example, the referent of the phrase *my grandmother* is a person in the message world – the speaker's grandmother, whereas the determined noun phrase *my grandmother* is a referential form that may refer to, or "mention," this referent.

reflexive construction: A valence-decreasing construction that expresses a semantically transitive situation in which the A and O are the same entity, and the situation is presented as an action carried out by an AGENT on him-, her- or itself.

reflexive pronoun: A special pronoun whose main function is to indicate that the subject and object of a transitive clause refer to the same entity.

relative clause: A clause that is a constituent of a noun phrase, and which modifies or characterizes the head of the noun phrase, e.g., *the Duke who tread on Aileron's toe*.

relative pronoun: A special pronoun that introduces a relative clause and simultaneously expresses the relativized element (cf.). In English, as in many other languages, the set of relative pronouns is similar, but not identical, to the set of interrogative pronouns.

relativized element, R-element: The constituent within a relative clause that is coreferential with the head noun. In English the R-element is usually expressed by a zero or a relative pronoun (cf.).

relativizer: A special particle, such as *that* (unstressed) in English, that introduces a relative clause. It contrasts with a relative pronoun (cf.) in that a relativizer does not reflect any features (animacy, case, etc.) of the relativized element (cf.).

right-branching: A language in which complements (cf.) tend to follow their syntactic heads (cf.) is sometimes called a right-branching language. Other terms for this language type are "head-complement languages" or "head-initial" languages.

R-element: See "relativized element" above.

root: A morpheme that expresses the basic meaning of a word and cannot be further divided into smaller morphemes.

S: Unfortunately, the term S is used in three quite distinct ways in this book. This is a reality of the field that all linguistics students need to be aware of.

(1) S is the highest node in a syntactic tree. It is the grammatical category that encompasses an entire clause. (2) In the Greenbergian tradition (chapter (7), S referred informally to the "Subject" of a sentence. Languages could be typologized according to their basic constituent order in clauses as SOV, SVO, etc. (3) In more recent work in morphosyntactic typology, the term S refers to the only argument of a single, argument (intransitive) clause. In this sense it contrasts with A and O (cf.).

scenes: One way in which the human mind stores and categorizes information. Scenes are conventional images involving generalized entities and relationships used as bases on which to build specific messages.

scope: The span of linguistic units over which a particular conceptual category has effect. For example, the following sentence is ambiguous depending on the scope of the adverbial clause: *She doesn't trim her eyebrows because she likes them.* If this sentence is interpreted as meaning she doesn't trim her eyebrows, the adverbial clause has scope over the entire independent clause. However, this sentence can also mean that she does trim her eyebrows, but for some other reason than because she likes them. In this case the adverbial clause has scope only over the verb phrase *trim her eyebrows*.

semantic roles: The roles that participants play in message-world situations, e.g., AGENT, PATIENT, etc. These exist independently of linguistic structure.

semantics: The art of determining whether two things are the same or different.

sensation (or "sensory impression") verbs: A class of verbs that express concepts involving the senses, e.g., *see*, *hear*, *feel*, *taste*, *sense*, *observe*, *smell*, and *perceive*. One of the participants in an event of sensation is an EXPERIENCER, and the other is the SOURCE of the sensation.

sentence: There are two major definitions of the term "sentence" in linguistics. One is equivalent to what we have termed "clause" (cf.) in this book, i.e., the highest node in a syntactic tree. The second definition of "sentence" is a structurally integrated combination of clauses. For example, a string such as *The director came in, closing the door behind her* may be considered one sentence consisting of two clauses.

serial verbs: Verbs that occur together in one verb phrase, e.g., *run go get me a newspaper*.

singular: A conceptual category in the number paradigm of many languages. The singular category specifically expresses the idea that there is one and only one referent of a particular noun, e.g., *dog*, *boy*, and *dragon* are all singular nouns.

singulative: A morphologically marked conceptual category that expresses the idea that there is exactly one referent mentioned by a noun, a pronoun, or any other referential form. The term "singulative," rather than "singular" (cf.), is used for those situations in which plurality is marked by zero.

sound symbolism: When words sound like their meanings, for example *splash*, *thud*, *crash*, *bang*, *pop*, and *bow wow* are all sound symbolic words in English.

specificity: A pragmatic (cf.) feature of participants in the message world (cf.), as presented by a speaker. A referent is specific if the speaker presents it as referring to a particular entity that exists in the message world. Typically languages will have a set of non-specific expressions, such as *whoever, whatever, someone, anyone,* and *no-one* in English.

speech act participants (SAPs): People involved in a communicative situation. Sometimes first- and second-person referents (cf.) are collectively referred to as speech-act participants.

split ergativity: A language that employs a nominative/accusative system (cf.) for organizing grammatical relations in one area of the grammar, but an ergative/absolutive system (cf.) in another part, may be said to exhibit split ergativity.

split intransitivity: A language that expresses S arguments (cf.) of intransitive clauses in two or more morphologically distinct ways. Such systems include those termed "stative/active," "active," "split-S," and "fluid-S."

state: A situation type which involves no action or change, e.g., *to be red, to know, to see, to feel,* etc.

stative verb: A verb that evokes a scene that does not involve action or change.

stem: An inflectible form of a word, often opposed to root (cf.). A stem may be morphologically complex, but need not be.

stress: An autosegmental (cf.) feature that involves extra loudness and/or frequency. For example, the English word *apple* is stressed on the first syllable, whereas the word *announce* is stressed on the second syllable.

strong suppletion: A lexical process whereby a conceptual category is expressed by completely exchanging one root for another, e.g., the past tense of the verb *go* in English is expressed by strong suppletion, because the word *went* is completely distinct from the word *go*.

structural ambiguity: When a structure is ambiguous because it has two possible syntactic analyses. For example, *Lincoln wrote the Gettysburg address on a train* can mean that Lincoln was on a train while he wrote the Gettysburg address, or that he actually used the train as his writing surface. This ambiguity is due to two possible locations in the syntactic tree where the prepositional phrase *on a train* may be attached.

structural change: The output of a process rule (cf.).

structural description: The input of a process rule (cf.).

subject-aux inversion: See "inversion."

subject omission: A construction that downplays an A argument by simply omitting it, without requiring any adjustments in the rest of the clause.

subject: A core grammatical relation, defined in English by the following properties: (1) immediately preverbal position in pragmatically neutral clauses, (2) subject case pronouns, and (3) control of verb agreement.

substitution: One of the major "tests" for constituency. If a sequence of linguistic units can be replaced by a pro-form (cf.), the sequence is probably a constituent at some level.

suffix: A morpheme that attaches to the end of a word, e.g., the past tense -*ed* or plural -*s* morphemes in English.

suffixation: The member of the "big ten" morphological processes that involves the addition of a suffix (cf.).

suppletion: A situation in which one form is exchanged for another that is totally different phonologically. Stem suppletion is when the two forms express different conceptual categories (exemplified by the pair *go/went* in English). Affix suppletion is when two dissimilar affixes express the *same* conceptual category, but for different subclasses of stems (exemplified by -*s*/-*en* as markers of plurality in English). Affix suppletion can also be referred to as "suppletive variants" or "suppletive allomorphs."

switch-reference: A system of clause linkage in which clauses are marked as having the same or different arguments as other clauses in the environment.

syllable: A phonological unit consisting of a vowel or other sonorant segment, plus potentially non-sonorant segments. For example, the English word *strength* consists of one syllable, *any* consists of two syllables, and *syllable* consists of three syllables.

syllable structure: A template for the construction of potential syllables in a language. Syllable-structure preservation is one major motivation for morphophonemic rules (cf.).

synchronic: Occurring at the same time. In linguistics, synchronic grammar refers to patterns that are part of every speaker's linguistic knowledge. Such patterns are distinct from diachronic ("through time") grammar – patterns that are the result of historical changes.

syntactic categories: A cover term for all the types of units that figure into a syntactic structure. Syntactic categories include lexical categories (cf.), phrasal categories (cf.), and in earlier versions of Generative grammar (cf.), the category S, or Sentence.

syntactic pattern: A way of expressing conceptual categories that involves the addition of one or more free morphemes, or an adjustment in the order of free morphemes. These are also called analytic or periphrastic patterns.

syntactic merger: When two elements in a syntactic structure "clump together" to form a constituent (cf.).

syntactic structure: The linear order, constituency, and hierarchical relationships that hold among linguistic units in an utterance.

syntax: The study of how words "clump together" in phrases and clauses.

synthesis: The degree to which a language tends to have many morphemes per word.

tacit: Unconscious knowledge. For example, the grammatical structure of a language is tacit knowledge to speakers of that language (unless they have taken linguistics courses).

tense: A semantic or grammatical notion. Semantically, tense refers to the temporal orientation of an event with respect to a point of reference, usually "now." Events can happen before "now" (past), at the same time as "now" (present), or after "now" (future). Grammatically, tense is a paradigm of verbal inflections that reflect this semantic domain.

terminal node: The lowest nodes on a syntactic tree are the terminal nodes, e.g. D, N, I, and V in the tree for a structure like:

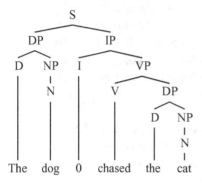

tone: Variation in pitch (sound frequency) to express differences in meaning. English does not employ tone to a great extent, though many other languages, such as Mandarin, Vietnamese, Yoruba (Nigeria) and Chinantec (Mexico) do.

topic: This term has many different uses in linguistics. The general notion that seems to underlie all usages, however, is that a topic is "what someone is talking *about*." This is a pragmatic (cf.) notion that sometimes relates to individual clauses and sometimes to longer spans of discourse.

transitive clause: Traditionally, a clause that has more than one core argument, e.g., *They will never stop hunting you*, *The King's stinking son fired me*, and *You mock my pain!* However, more recent approaches tend to treat transitivity (cf.) as a continuously variable property.

transitivity: A semantic or a grammatical notion. Events and situations are semantically more or less transitive. Clauses are either intransitive, transitive, or ditransitive. Semantic transitivity refers to the degree to which action "carries over" from a prototypical AGENT to a prototypical PATIENT.

translational motion: Motion from one place to another. Verbs that describe translational motion often have grammatical properties that distinguish them from verbs that describe simple motion.

tree diagrams: See "phrase structure trees."

trial: A conceptual category that expresses the idea that there are exactly three referents mentioned by a noun, a pronoun, or any other referential form. Trial can also be a category in verb and other agreement paradigms. The category of trial is part of the paradigm of number, which may also include singular, singulative, dual, paucal, plural and others (cf.).

trivalent: See "ditransitive."

typology: A division of any range of phenomena into types.

typological linguistics: The sub-field of linguistics which is concerned with the ways in which languages can be meaningfully grouped into types, the ways in which all languages are alike, and the range of variation among languages.

ungrammatical: A string of linguistic units is ungrammatical if it is not sanctioned by the grammatical patterns of the language. For example, the following strings are ungrammatical as linguistic units in English: *dog the*, *my you mock pain*, *fleas has dog my*, *turnips like I*.

unit: A piece of syntactic structure that is treated as a whole, rather than in terms of its component parts. For example, the following string is a unit (a determined noun phrase to be exact) that can be deployed in a syntactic structure as any other unit of the same phrasal category: *the big black Rottweiller that always growls at me as I furtively inch my way through the junkyard district and along the waterfront, populated by shadowy characters and fraught with unpleasant prospective circumstances, all of which involve pain, misery or at least the loss of several weeks wages*.

univalent: See "intransitive."

utterance: A linguistic expression used in a context to accomplish an actual communicative act. Utterances are distinct from words, phrases, clauses, and sentences. The latter are possibilities, abstractions sanctioned by the grammatical patterns of a language. Utterances, on the other hand, are those abstractions put to work in communication.

valence: Valence can be thought of as a grammatical notion or a semantic notion; in both cases valence refers to a number. Grammatical valence refers to the number of arguments in a clause, whereas semantic valence refers to the number of core participants in a situation.

valence-decreasing construction: A construction that downplays, or deperspectivizes, a core participant in a message-world situation by expressing it in a less prominent grammatical role.

valence-increasing construction: A construction that upgrades, or perspectivizes, a peripheral participant in a message-world situation by expressing it in a more prominent grammatical role.

verb: The word class that prototypically expresses events. Verbs are defined in English by their ability to take tense marking.

verb phrase: A "clump" in constituent structure that is headed by a verb, and which may or may not contain other elements. Verb phrases may be inflected (cf.), in which case they may be referred to as IPs, or "Inflected Verb Phrases."

voice: Constructions that adjust the relationship between semantic roles (cf.) and grammatical relations (cf.) are sometimes referred to as "voices" (see also "valence").

weak suppletion: A lexical process whereby a conceptual category is expressed by exchanging a root for another similar root. For example, the past tense of the verb *buy* in English is weakly suppletive because the past-tense stem *bought* has some similarity to the present-tense stem *buy*, though there is no regular pattern that relates the two.

word: A linguistic unit in syntactic structure that may be delimited by pauses in discourse.

word class: Word classes are traditionally called "parts of speech." They are grammatically distinct classes of lexical items, such as nouns, verbs, adjectives, adverbs, etc.

zero pronoun: An anaphoric device (cf.) that has no phonetic content. It can be thought of as the "conspicuous absence" of an audible form. For example, there is a zero pronoun between the words *and* and *sat* in the following English sentence: *Calvin came in and sat down*. Also referred to as "zero anaphora."

References

Aberdour, Catherine. 1985. Referential devices in Apurinã discourse. In *Porto Velho workpapers*, ed. David L. Fortune, 43–91. Brasília: Summer Institute of Linguistics.

Aikhenvald, Alexandra Y. 2000. *Classifiers: A typology of noun categorization devices.* Oxford: Oxford University Press.

Aikhenvald, Alexandra Y. 2003. *A grammar of Tariana.* Cambridge: Cambridge University Press.

Allott, Robin. 1995. Sound symbolism. In *Language in the Würm Glaciation*, ed. Udo L. Figge, 15–38. Bochum: Brockmeyer.

Anderson, Steven R. 1992. *A-Morphous morphology.* Cambridge: Cambridge University Press.

Arensen, Jonathan E. 1982. Murle grammar. *Occasional Papers in the Study of Sudanese Languages* 2:1–143.

Austin, Peter. 1980. Switch reference in Australian languages. In *Studies of switch reference* (UCLA Papers in Syntax 8), ed. Pamela Munro, 1–54.

Baart, Joan L. G. 1999. *A sketch of Kalam Kohistani grammar.* Islamabad: National Institute of Pakistan Studies, Quaid-i-Azam University.

Bamgbose, A. 1974. On serial verbs and verbal status. *Journal of West African linguistics* 9:17–48.

Barry, Randall K. (ed.). 1997. *ALA-LC Romanization tables: Transliteration schemes for non-roman scripts.* Washington, DC: Library of Congress.

Bentivoglio, Paola. 1983. Topic continuity and discontinuity in discourse: A study of spoken Latin-American Spanish. In *Topic continuity in discourse: A quantitative cross-language study*, ed. T. Givón (Typological Studies in Language 3), 255–312. Philadelphia/Amsterdam: John Benjamins.

Borgman, D. M. 1990. Sanuma. In *Handbook of Amazonian languages*, vol. II, eds. Desmond C. Derbyshire and Geoffrey Pullum, 15–248. Berlin: Mouton.

Bresnan, Joan. 2001. *Lexical functional syntax.* Malden, Mass.: Blackwell Textbooks.

Brown, Gillian, and George Yule. 1983. *Discourse analysis.* Cambridge: Cambridge University Press.

Burquest, D. A. 2001. *Phonological analysis: a functional approach* (2nd edition). Dallas, Tex.: SIL International.

Bybee, Joan L. 1985. *Morphology: A study of the relation between meaning and form* (Typological Studies in Language, vol. 9). Amsterdam/Philadelphia: John Benjamins Publishing Company.

Carroll, Lewis [pseud.]. 1865. *Alice's adventures in Wonderland.* London: Macmillan and Company.

Carroll, Lewis [pseud.]. 1872. *Through the looking glass, and what Alice found there.* With fifty illustrations by John Tenniel. London: Macmillan and Company.

Chafe, Wallace L. 1970. *Meaning and the structure of language.* Chicago: University of Chicago Press.

Chomsky, Noam. 1965. *Aspects of the theory of syntax.* Cambridge, Mass.: MIT Press.

Chomsky, Noam. 1995. *The minimalist program.* Cambridge, Mass.: MIT Press.

Cipollone, Nick, Steven Keiser, and Shravan Vasishth. 1994. *Language files: materials for an introduction to language* (6th edition), ed. Stefanie Jannedy, Robert Poletto, and Tracey L. Weldon. Columbus, Ohio: Department of Linguistics, Ohio State University.

Coleman, Linda, and Paul Kay. 1981. Prototype semantics: The English word *lie. Language* 57:26–44.

Comrie, Bernard. 1974. *Causatives and universal grammar.* Transactions of the Philological Society. 1–32.

Comrie, Bernard. 1978. Ergativity. In *Syntactic typology: studies in the phenomenology of language*, ed. Winfred P. Lehmann, 329–94. Austin: University of Texas Press.

Comrie, Bernard. 1982. *Grammatical relations in Huichol.* In *Studies in transitivity*, ed. Paul J. Hopper and Sandra A. Thompson (Syntax and Semantics 15), 99–115. New York: Academic Press.

Comrie, Bernard. 1989. *Language universals and linguistic typology* (2nd edition). Chicago: University of Chicago Press.

Corbett, Greville G. 2000. *Number.* Cambridge/New York: Cambridge University Press.

Cowan, William, and Jaromira Rakušan. 1998. *Source book for linguistics.* Philadelphia/Amsterdam: John Benjamins Publishing Company.

Craig, Colette. 1986. *Noun classes and categorization* (Typological Studies in Language, vol. 7). Philadelphia: John Benjamins Publishing Company.

Croft, William. 1990. *Typology and universals.* Cambridge: Cambridge University Press.

Croft, William. 2002. *Radical construction grammar.* Oxford: Oxford University Press.

Cutzal, Martín Chacach. 1990. *Una descripción fonológica y morfológica del Kachiquel.* In England and Elliot, 145–90.

Dahlstrom, Amy. 1991. *Plains Cree morphosyntax.* New York/London: Garland Publishing.

DeLancey, Scott. 1982. Aspect, transitivity and viewpoint. In *Tense-aspect: between semantics and pragmatics*, ed. Paul J. Hopper, 167–84. Amsterdam: John Benjamins Publishing Company.

DeLancey, Scott. 1984. Notes on agentivity and causation. *Studies in Language* 8:181–213.

Delancey, Scott. 1990. Ergativity and the Cognitive model of event structure in Lhasa Tibetan. *Cognitive Linguistics* 1:289–321.

DeLancey, Scott. 1991. Event construal and case role assignment. *Proceedings of the Berkeley Linguistics Society* 17:338–53.

Dickenson, Connie. 2004. Simple and complex predicates in Tsafiki (Colorado). Paper presented at the 30th annual meeting of the Berkeley Linguistics Society, Berkeley, Calif.

Dixon, R. M. W. 1972. *The Dyirbal language of North Queensland.* Cambridge: Cambridge University Press.

Dixon, R. M. W. 1979. Ergativity. *Language* 55:59–138.

Dixon, R. M. W. 1994. *Ergativity*. Cambridge: Cambridge University Press.

Dooley, Robert A., and Stephen H. Levinsohn. 2001. *Analyzing discourse: a manual of basic concepts*. Dallas, Tex.: SIL International.

Dryer, Matthew S. 1986. Primary objects, secondary objects, and antidative. *Language* 62:808–45.

Dryer, Matthew S. 1988. Object-verb order and adjective-noun order: dispelling a myth. *Lingua* 74:185–217.

Dryer, Matthew S. 1992. The Greenbergian word-order correlations. *Language* 68.1:81–138.

Dryer, Matthew. 1996. Grammatical relations in Kutenai (Ktunaxa). The Belcourt Lecture, delivered before the University of Manitoba on 24 February 1995. Winnepeg: Voices of Rupert's Land.

Elson, Benjamin F., and Velma B. Pickett. 1988. *Beginning morphology and syntax*. Dallas, Tex.: Summer Institute of Linguistics.

England, Nora. 1988. *Introducción a la lingüística: idiomas mayas*. Antigua, Guatemala: Proyecto lingüístico Francisco Marroquín.

England, Nora, and Stephen R. Elliott (eds.). 1990. *Lecturas sobre la lingüística Maya*. Guatemala: Centro de Investigaciones Regionales de Mesoamérica (CIRMA).

Farmer, Ann, and Richard A. Demers. 1996. *A linguistics workbook*. Cambridge, Mass.: MIT Press.

Fillmore, Charles J. 1968. The case for case. In *Universals in linguistic theory*, ed. Emond Bach and Robert T. Harms, 1–88. New York: Holt, Rinehart and Winston.

Fillmore, Charles J. 1976. Topics in lexical semantics. In *Current issues in linguistic theory*, ed. Peter Cole, 76–138. Bloomington: Indiana University Press.

Fillmore, Charles J. 1977. The case for case reopened. In *Syntax and Semantics 8: Grammatical Relations*, ed. P. Cole and J. M. Sadock, 59–81. New York: Academic Press.

Finnegan, Edward. 1994. *Language: its structure and use*. Fort Worth: Harcourt Brace College Publishers.

Foley, William, and R. Van Valin. 1984. *Functional syntax and universal grammar*. Cambridge: Cambridge University Press.

Frachtenberg, Leo J. 1913. *Coos texts*. Columbia University contributions to anthropology, vol. 1. New York: Columbia University Press.

Franchetto, Bruna. 1990. Ergativity and nominativity in Kuikuro and other Cariban languages. In *Amazonian linguistics: studies in lowland South American languages*, ed. Doris L. Payne. Austin: University of Texas Press.

Gildea, Spike O. 1994. Semantic and pragmatic inverse: "Inverse alignment" and "inverse voice" in Carib of Surinam. In *Voice and inversion*, ed. Timothy Givón (Typological Studies in Language 28), 186–231. Amsterdam/Philadelphia: John Benjamins Publishing Company.

Goldberg, Adele. 1995. *Constructions: a construction grammar approach to argument structure*. Chicago: University of Chicago Press.

Greenberg, Joseph H. 1963. Some universals of grammar with particular reference to the order of meaningful elements. In *Universals of language*, ed. Joseph H. Greenberg. Cambridge, Mass.: MIT Press.

Greenberg, Joseph H. 1966. Language universals, with special reference to feature hierarchies (*Janua linguarum*, Series minor, 59). The Hague: Mouton.

Grégoire, Claire. 1985. L'expression du passif en maninka. In *African linguistics: essays in memory of M.W.K. Semikenke*, ed. Didier Goyvaerts, 189–208. Amsterdam: John Benjamins Publishing Company.

Grimes, Charles E. 1991. Central Malayo-Polynesian. Paper presented at the 6th international conference on Austronesian linguistics. Honolulu, Hawaii.

Haiman, John, and Sandra A. Thompson. 1984. "Subordination" in universal grammar. *Proceedings of the Berkeley Linguistics Society* 10:510–23.

Harris, Alice C. 1990. Alignment typology and diachronic change. In *Language typology 1987: Systematic balance in language*, ed. Winfred P. Lehmann, 67–90. Amsterdam/Philadelphia: John Benjamins Publishing Company.

Haspelmath, Martin. 1993. *A grammar of Lezgian* (Mouton Grammar Library, 9). Berlin: Mouton de Gruyter.

Haspelmath, Martin. 2002. *Understanding morphology*. London: Arnold Publishers; New York: Oxford University Press.

Hawkins, John A. 1983. *Word order universals*. New York: Academic Press.

Hawkins, John A. 1994. *A performance theory of order and constiuency*. Cambridge: Cambridge University Press.

Hayward, Richard J. 1984. The Arbore language: a first investigation: including a vocabulary (Cushitic Language Studies 2). Hamburg: Buske.

Healey, Phyllis M. 1960. *An Agta grammar*. Manila: Bureau of Printing.

Heath, Jeffrey. 1976. Antipassivization: a functional typology. In *Proceedings of the second annual meeting of the Berkeley Linguistics Society*, 202–11.

Heitzman, Allene. 1982. Some cohesive elements in Pajonal Campa narratives. Ms. 20 pp. Summer Institute of Linguistics: Perú.

Hockett, Charles F. 1958. *A course in modern linguistics*. New York: Macmillan.

Hopper, Paul J., and Sandra A. Thompson. 1980. Transitivity in grammar and discourse. *Language* 56:251–99.

Hopper, Paul J., and Sandra A. Thompson. 1984. The discourse basis for lexical categories in universal grammar. *Language* 60.4:703–52.

Hudson, Grover. 1999. *Essential introductory linguistics*. Oxford: Blackwell Publishers.

Jackendoff, Ray. 1988. Conceptual semantics. In *Meaning and mental representation*, eds. Umberto Eco, Marco Santambrogio, and Patrizia Violi, 81–97. Bloomington: Indiana University Press.

Jones, Wendell, and Paula Jones. 1991. *Barasano syntax: Studies in the Languages of Colombia*, vol. II. Dallas: Summer Institute of Linguistics and University of Texas at Arlington.

Keenan, Edward L. 1985. Relative clauses. In *Language typology and syntactic description*, vol. II: *Complex constructions*, ed. Timothy Shopen, 141–70. Cambridge: Cambridge University Press.

Keenan, Edward L., and Bernard Comrie. 1977. NP accesibility and universal grammar. *Linguistic Inquiry* 8:63–100.

Kimenyi, Alexander. 1980. *A relational grammar of Kinyarwanda*. Berkeley: University of California Press.

Klamer, Marian. 1998. *A grammar of Kambera* (Mouton Grammar Library, no. 18). Berlin: Walter de Gruyter.

Köhler, W. 1929. *Gestalt Psychology*. New York: Liveright.

Kühner, R., and C. Stegmann. 1955. *Ausfürliche Grammatik der lateinischen Sprache: Satzlehre*, vol. II. Leverkusen: Gottschalk.

Lakoff, George. 1977. Linguistic gestalts. *Chicago Linguistics Society* 13:236–87.

Lakoff, George. 1987. *Women, fire and dangerous things: what categories reveal about the mind*. Chicago: University of Chicago Press.

Lakoff, George, and Mark Johnson. 1999. *Philosophy in the flesh: the enbodied mind and its challenge to western thought*. New York: Basic Books.

Langacker, Ronald. 1972. *Fundamentals of linguistic analysis*. New York: Harcourt, Brace, Jovanovich.

Langacker, Ronald. 1990. Settings, participants, and grammatical relations. In *Meanings and prototypes: Studies in Linguistic categorization*, ed. S. L. Tsohatzidis, 213–38. London/New York: Routledge.

Langacker, Ronald. 1987. *Foundations of cognitive grammar*, vol. I: *Theoretical prerequisites*. Stanford: Stanford University Press.

Li, Charles N., and Sandra A. Thompson. 1981. *Mandarin Chinese: a functional reference grammar*. Berkeley and Los Angeles: University of California Press.

Longacre, Robert, and Sandra A. Thompson. 1985. Adverbial clauses. In *Language typology and syntactic description*, vol. II: *Complex constructions*, ed. Timothy Shopen, 171–234. Cambridge: Cambridge University Press.

Longacre, Robert. 1972. *Hierarchy and universality of discourse constituents in New Guinea languages: discussion*. Washington DC: Georgetown University Press.

Martin, Samuel E. 1992. *A reference grammar of Korean: a complete guide to the grammar and history of the Korean language* (Tuttle Language Library). Rutland, Vermont/Tokyo, Japan: Charles E. Tuttle Publishing.

Marusic, Franc. 2002. Aff-stem-ix: on the nature of discontinuous affixes. Paper presented at the CUNY/SUNY/NYU Linguistics Mini-Conference dedicated to the memory of Jerrold J. Katz, 20 April 2002.

Matthew, Sunil, and Maya Susan. 2000. Dungra Bhil phonemic summary. Mumbai: Friends Missionary Prayer Band.

McCawley, James D. 1982. *Thirty million theories of grammar*. Chicago: University of Chicago Press.

McManus, Carolyn, Deborah Stollenwerk, and Zhang-Zheng Sheng. 1987. *Language Files*. Reynoldsburg, Ohio: Advocate Publishing Group.

Merlan, Francesca. 1985. Split intransitivity: functional oppositions in intransitive inflection. In *Grammar inside and outside the clause: some approaches to theory from the field*, ed. Johanna Nichols and Anthony C. Woodbury, 324–62. Cambridge: Cambridge University Press.

Merrifield, William R., Constance M. Naish, Calvin R. Rensch, and Gillian Story. 1987. *Laboratory manual for morphology and syntax*. Dallas, Tex.: Summer Institute of Linguistics.

Minsky, Marvin. 1975. A framework for representing knowledge. In *The psychology of computer vision*, ed. P. Winston, 211–80. New York: McGraw-Hill.

Mithun, Marianne. 1987. Is basic word order universal? In *Coherence and grounding in discourse*, ed. Russel Tomlin (Typological Studies in language 11), 281–328. Philadelphia: John Benjamins Publishing Company.

Mithun, Marianne. 1991. Active/agent case marking and its motivations. *Language* 67.3:510–46.

Mufwene, Salikoko S., John Rickford, Guy Baile, and John Baugh (eds.). 1998. *African-American English: structure, history, and usage*. London/New York: Routledge.

Munro, Pamela. 1983. When "Same" Is Not "Not Different." In *Switch-reference and Universal Grammar*, ed. John Haiman and Pamela Munro, 223–43. Amsterdam: John Benjamins Publishing Company.

Munro, Pamela. 1984. The syntactic status of object possessor raising in Western Muskogean. *Proceedings of the tenth annual meeting of the Berkeley Linguistics Society*, ed. Claudia Brugman and Monica Macauley, 634–49. Berkeley: Berkeley Linguistics Society.

Nedjalkov, 1997. *Resultative constructions*. Philadelphia: John Benjamins Publishing Company.

Nichols, Johanna. 1986. Head-marking and dependent-marking grammar. *Language* 62.1:56–119.

Noonan, Michael. 1985. Complementation. In *Language typology and syntactic description*, vol. II: *Complex constructions*, ed. Timothy Shopen, 42–140. Cambridge: Cambridge University Press.

O'Grady, William, John Archibald, Mark Aronoff, and Janie Rees-Miller. 2001. *Contemporary linguistics: an introduction*. Boston: Bedford/St. Martin's.

Olson, Kenneth S., and Paul H. Schultz. 2002. Can [sonorant] spread? Work Papers of the Summer Institute of Linguistics, University of North Dakota Session 46. Online publication. http://www.und.edu/dept/linguistics/wp/2002.htm.

Pawley, Andrew. 1987. Encoding events in Kalam and English: different logics for reporting experience. In *Coherence and grounding in discourse*, ed. Russell Tomlin, 329–60. Amsterdam: John Benjamins Publishing Company.

Payne, Doris L. 1985. Review of Word order universals, by John Hawkins. *Language* 61:462–66.

Payne, Doris L. 1986. Basic constituent order in Yagua clauses: implications for word order universals. In *Amazon languages handbook*, vol. I, ed. D. Derbyshire and G. Pullum, 440–65. The Hague: Mouton.

Payne, Doris L., and Leonard Kotikash. Ms. 2004. Maa–English dictionary.

Payne, John R. 1985. Complex phrases and complex sentences. In *Language typology and syntactic description*, vol. II: *Complex constructions*, ed. Timothy Shopen, 3–41. Cambridge: Cambridge University Press.

Payne, Judith, and David Payne. 1991. The pragmatics of split intransitivity in Asheninca. Paper read at the Symposium on Arawakan Linguistics, 47th International Congress of Americanists, New Orleans.

Payne, Thomas E. 1991. Medial clauses and interpropositional relations in Panare. *Cognitive linguistics* 2–3:247–81.

Payne, Thomas E. 1992. *The twins stories: participant coding in Yagua narrative*. Berkeley: University of California Press.

Payne, Thomas E. 1997. *Describing morphosyntax*. Cambridge: Cambridge University Press.

Payne, Thomas E. Forthcoming. A grammar as communicative act. *Studies in Language*.

Perlmutter, David M. 1980. Relational Grammar. In *Current approaches to syntax: Syntax and semantics 13*, ed. Edith A. Moravcsik and Jessica R. Wirth, 195–229. New York: Academic Press.

Putnam, Hilary. 1970. Is semantics possible? In *Language, belief, and metaphysics*, ed. H. E. Kiefer and M. K. Munitz, 50–63. New York: State University of New York Press.

Quillian, M. Ross. 1968. Semantic memory. In *Semantic information processing*, ed. M. Minsky, 216–70. Cambridge, Mass.: MIT Press.

Quirk, Randolph, and Sidney Greenbaum. 1973. *A concise grammar of contemporary English*. San Diego (inter alia): Harcourt Brace Jovanovich.

Radford, A. 1988. *Transformational grammar: a first course*. Cambridge: Cambridge University Press.

Radford, A. 1997. *Syntactic theory and the structure of English: a minimalist approach*. Cambridge: Cambridge University Press.

Redden, J. A. 1966. Walapai II: morphology. *International Journal of American Linguistics* 32:141–63.

Reddy, Michael. 1979. The conduit metaphor – a case of frame conflict in our language about language. In *Metaphor and thought*, ed. A. Ortony, 284–324. Cambridge: Cambridge University Press.

Reed, Irene, Osahito Miyaoka, Steven Jacobson, Paschal Afcan, and Michael Krauss. 1977. *Yup'ik Eskimo grammar*. Fairbanks: Alaska Native Language Center and Yup'ik Language Workshop, University of Alaska.

Rosch, Eleanor. 1975. Cognitive representations of semantic categories. *Journal of Experimental Psychology* 104.5:192–233.

Rosch, Eleanor. 1978. Principles of categorization. In *Cognition and categorization*, ed. E. Rosch and B. Lloyd, 27–48. Hillsdale, NJ: Erlbaum.

Saussure, Ferdinand de. 1915. *A course in general linguistics*. Trans. by C. Bally and A. Ferdlinger. New York: Philosophical Library.

Schachter, Paul. 1974. A non-transformational account of serial verbs. *Studies in African Linguistics*, supplement 5:253–70.

Shibatani, Masayoshi. 1985. Passives and related constructions: a prototype analysis. *Language* 61.4:821–48.

Silverstein, Michael. 1976. Hierarchy of features and ergativity. In *Grammatical categories in Australian languages*, ed. R. M. W. Dixon (Linguistic Series 22), 112–71. Canberra: Australian Institute of Aboriginal Studies.

Skorik, Petr J. 1961. *Grammatika chukotskogo jazyka*, vol. I. Leningrad: Nauka.

Stahlke, H. 1970. Serial verbs. *Studies in African linguistics* 1:60–99.

Sweetser, Eve. 1987. The definition of lie. In *Cultural models in language and thought*, ed. D. Holland and N. Quinn, 43–66. Cambridge: Cambridge University Press.

Swetman, James S. J. 1998. *An introduction to the study of New Testament Greek* (2nd edition). Subsidia Biblica 16.1. Roma: Editrice Pontificio Istituto Biblico.

Talmy, Leonard. 1985. Lexicalization patterns: semantic structure in lexical forms. In *Language typology and syntactic description*, vol. III: *Grammatical categories and the lexicon*, ed. Timothy Shopen, 57–149. Cambridge: Cambridge University Press.

Thompson, Sandra A. 1988. A discourse approach to the cross-linguistic category "adjective." In *Explaining language universals*, ed. John A. Hawkins, 167–85. Oxford and New York: Basil Blackwell.

Traugott, Elizabeth Closs, and Bernd Heine (eds). 1991. *Approaches to grammaticalization*, vols. I and II. Amsterdam/Philadelphia: John Benjamins Publishing Company.

Tucker, Archibald N., and John T. Ole Mpaayei. 1955. *A Maasai grammar, with vocabulary* (Publications of the African Institute, Leiden, no. 2). London/New York: Longmans and Green.

van der Merwe, Christo H., Jackie A. Naudé, and Jan H. Kroeze. 1999. *A Biblical Hebrew reference grammar*. Sheffield: Sheffield Academic Press.

van Dijk, Teun. 1972. *Some aspects of text grammars*. The Hague: Mouton.

Van Valin, Robert D., Jr., and Randy J. LaPolla. 1997. *Syntax: structure, meaning and function*. Cambridge: Cambridge University Press.

Vendler, Zeno. 1967. Verbs and times. In *Linguistics in philosophy*, ed. Z. Vendler, 97–121. Ithaca, NY: Cornell University Press.

Watson, R. 1966. Clause to sentence gradations in Pacoh. *Lingua* 16:166–88.

Watters, John. 1979. Focus in Aghem. In *Aghem grammatical structure*, ed. Lawrence Hyman, 137–97. Los Angeles, University of Southern California occasional papers in linguistics 7.

Weber, David John. 1989. *A grammar of Huallaga (Huanuco) Quechua*. Berkeley: University of California Press.

Welmers, William E. 1973. *African language structures*. Berkeley: University of California Press.

Wise, Mary Ruth. 1971. *Identification of participants in discourse: a study of aspects of form and meaning in Nomatsiguenga*. Summer Institute of Linguistics publications in linguistics and related fields no. 28. Dallas, Tex.: Summer Institute of Linguistics.

Wittgenstein, Ludwig. 1958. *Philosophical investigations* (1981 reprint). Oxford: Basil Blackwell.

Yule, George. 1996. *The study of language*. Cambridge: Cambridge University Press.

Subject and language index

abilitative passive 253
absolutive 218
   case 218
   grammatical relation 210
accusative 97, 218
action-processes (situation type) 113
actions (situation type) 113, 248
active systems 224
active voice 237
actor 8
ad hoc solutions 82
addressee 121
adjective phrases 116
adjectives 5, 108, 116–17
adjuncts 297
adpositions 93, 124
advancements 264
adverbs 98, 117–18, 298
adverbial clauses 124, 288, 297–300
adversative passives 250, 253–54
affected participants 240
affix suppletion 138
affixes 15, 17–18
affricates 68
Agbala, exercise 88
AGENT 93, 105, 213
agglutinative languages 190–91
agreement 97, 104
Agta, exercise 57
Akan 290
Alabama, exercise 317
alienable possession 102
alignment (between semantic roles and
      grammatical relations) 237
allomorphs 63
alpha notation 75–78
Altaic languages 259
ambiguity 180–82
   lexical 180
   structural 180–82, exercise 187
Amharic, exercise 86
analytic constructions 11
   causatives 264
   passives 252–53
   reflexives 243–44

anaphoric clitics 119, 120
anaphoric device 120, 238
anticausatives 249
antipassives 255
aorist 248
Apinajé, exercise 127
applicative constructions 264–69,
    274
applied object 264
apposition 95
Apuriná 200
Arabic 43, 51–53
   exercises 59, 186, 229
Arawakan languages 81, 200, 251
arbitrariness 4
Arbore 44–45
Archi, exercise 285
argumentation, exercise 184
argument structures 107–16, 237
   exercises 131, 277
arguments 107, 210–11
   complement clauses as 291–97
articles 97, 101
Asheninka 79, 81–83, 225
aspect 104
assimilation 65, 72, 77, 79
asymmetry 175
augmentative 5, 97
Australian languages 301
Austronesian languages
   causatives 263
   ergativity 219
   Malagasy 311
   possession 102
   prenominal case markers 101
   quotative particles 296–97
   reduplication 43
   reflexives, reciprocals 245
autosegmental variation 43
auxiliaries 18, 122–23, 171
   modal 123
   in serial constructions 290
   stacking 176–77
auxiliary phrase 175
Avar, exercise 230

357